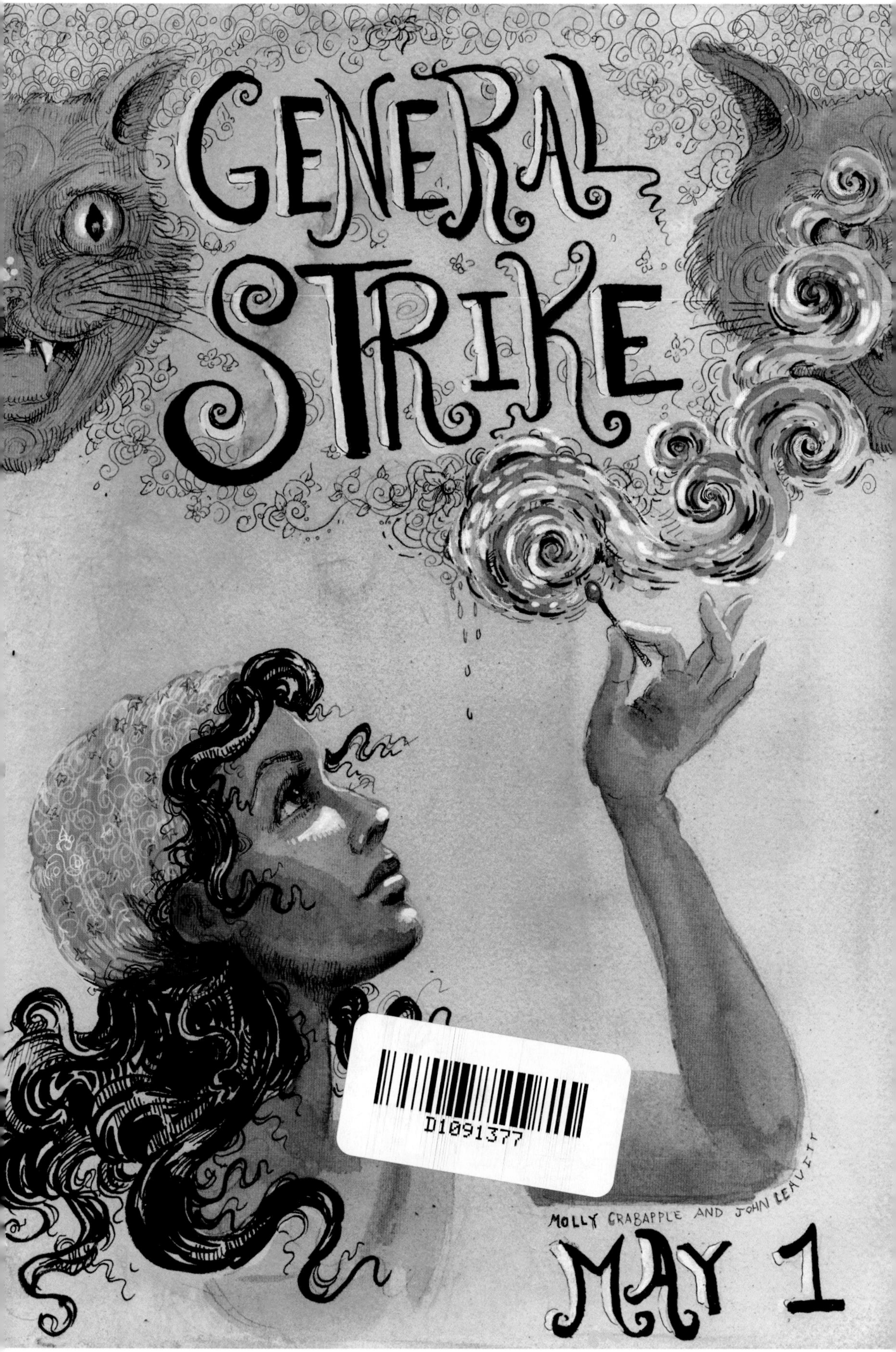
GENERAL STRIKE
MOLLY CRABAPPLE AND JOHN LEAVITT
MAY 1

Table of Contents

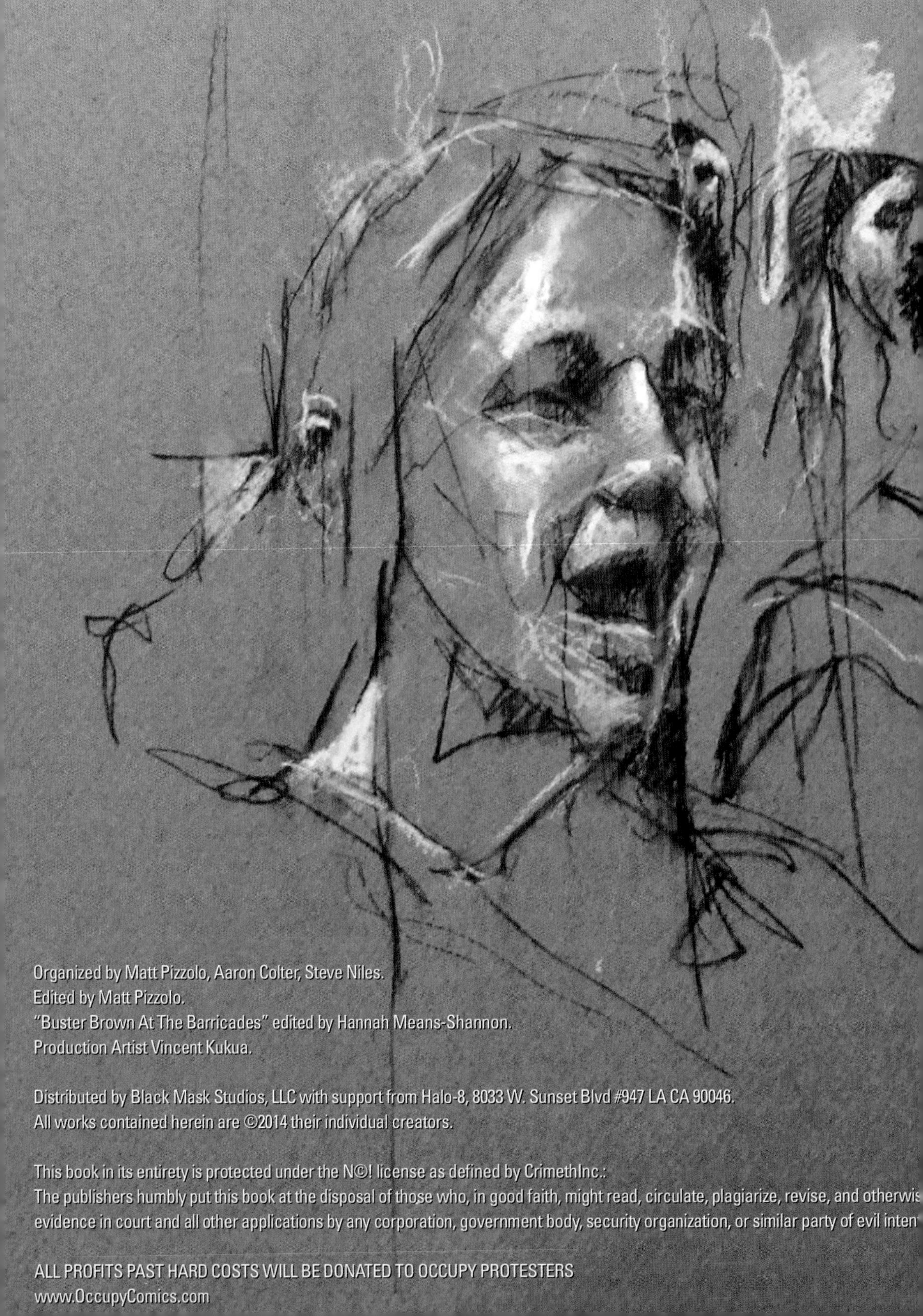

Organized by Matt Pizzolo, Aaron Colter, Steve Niles.
Edited by Matt Pizzolo.
"Buster Brown At The Barricades" edited by Hannah Means-Shannon.
Production Artist Vincent Kukua.

Distributed by Black Mask Studios, LLC with support from Halo-8, 8033 W. Sunset Blvd #947 LA CA 90046.

ALL PROFITS PAST HARD COSTS WILL BE DONATED TO OCCUPY PROTESTERS
www.OccupyComics.com

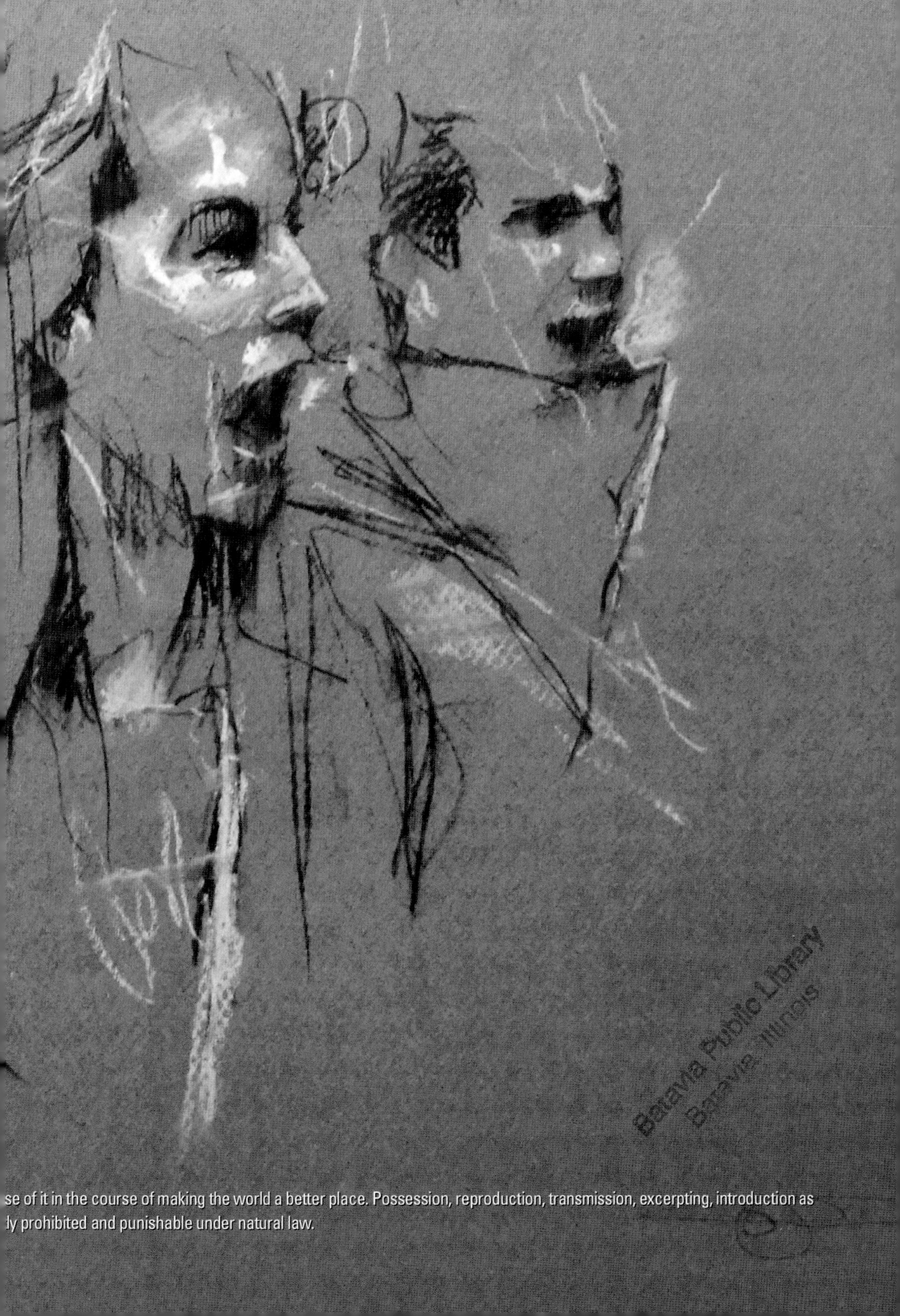

> FOREWORD

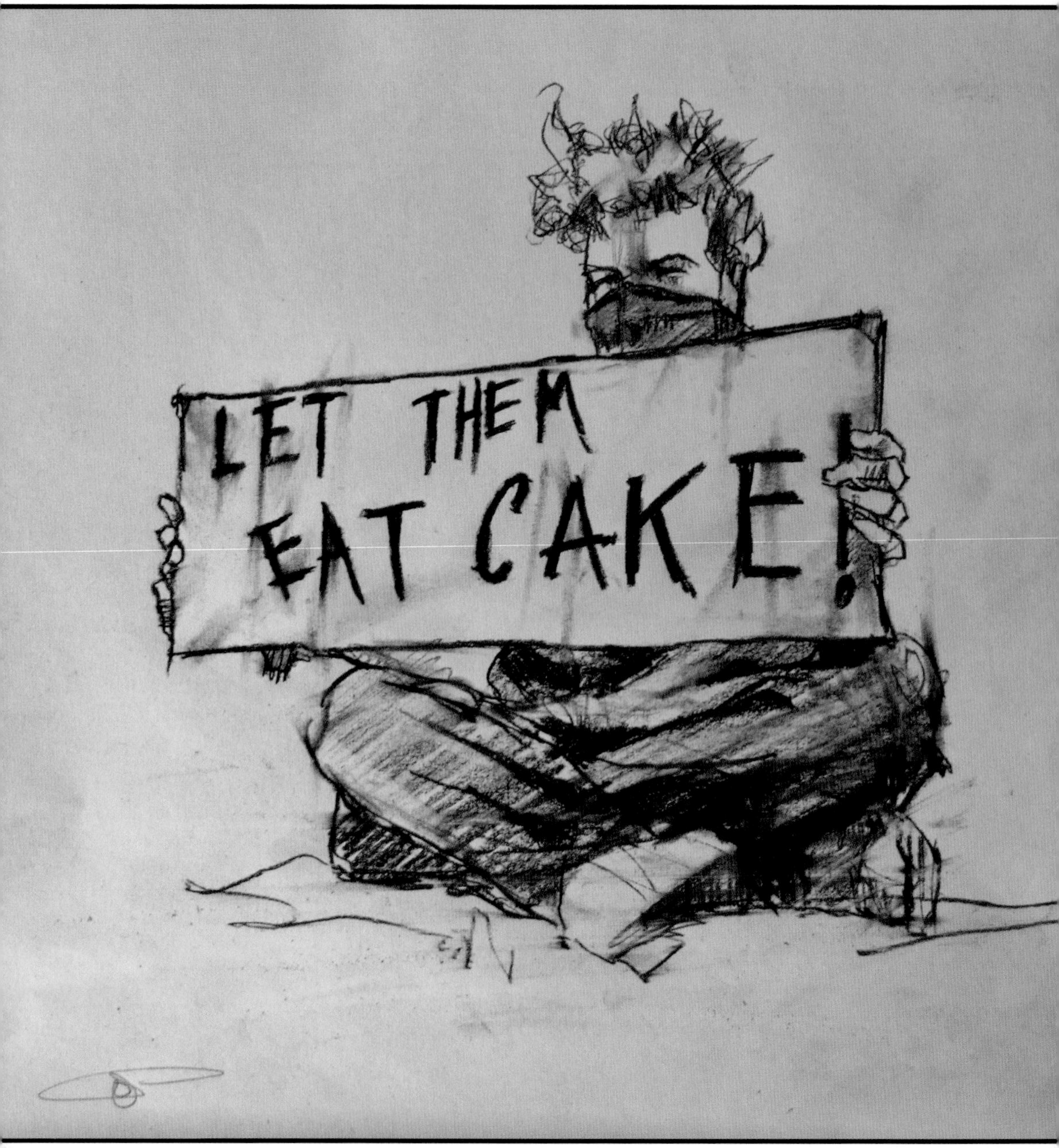
LET THEM
EAT CAKE!

> by Aaron Colter

It's something of a miracle that you're holding this book. Not in the true sense, especially if you lean to the No Gods, No Masters end of the political spectrum. Still, the fact that a group of people worked with little management or capital motivation to put together contributed pieces from some of comics' most celebrated artists solely on the faith of backers through an online donation system is both a testament to the types of new models being built and tried today, and like Occupy itself -- whatever it means -- a cautionary note with flaws for the public to see and hopefully improve upon.

Like The Movement we sought to reflect, we took the best route we thought would benefit the whole at the time. Decisions had to be made; sometimes we found ways around a barricade, sometimes we got kettled. Sometimes we gave up, but we were always encouraged with every new addition.

Years after the tents are gone, after the celebrations, the mistakes, the anger, the joy -- everything that Occupy meant and still means to you as an individual and as a community, even if it's contempt -- understand that Occupy wasn't the end. There is no end for those who wish to create a more just tomorrow. Keep trying. Learn from the past, yet don't wait for a plan to take action.

If you're lucky, you'll end up with something wonderful that can inspire others or at least be a record of the reflections of the time. We hope we've delivered both. Thank you for allowing us to bring this collection together. Don't give up. We need you.

With Love,
-Aaron Colter
December 2013

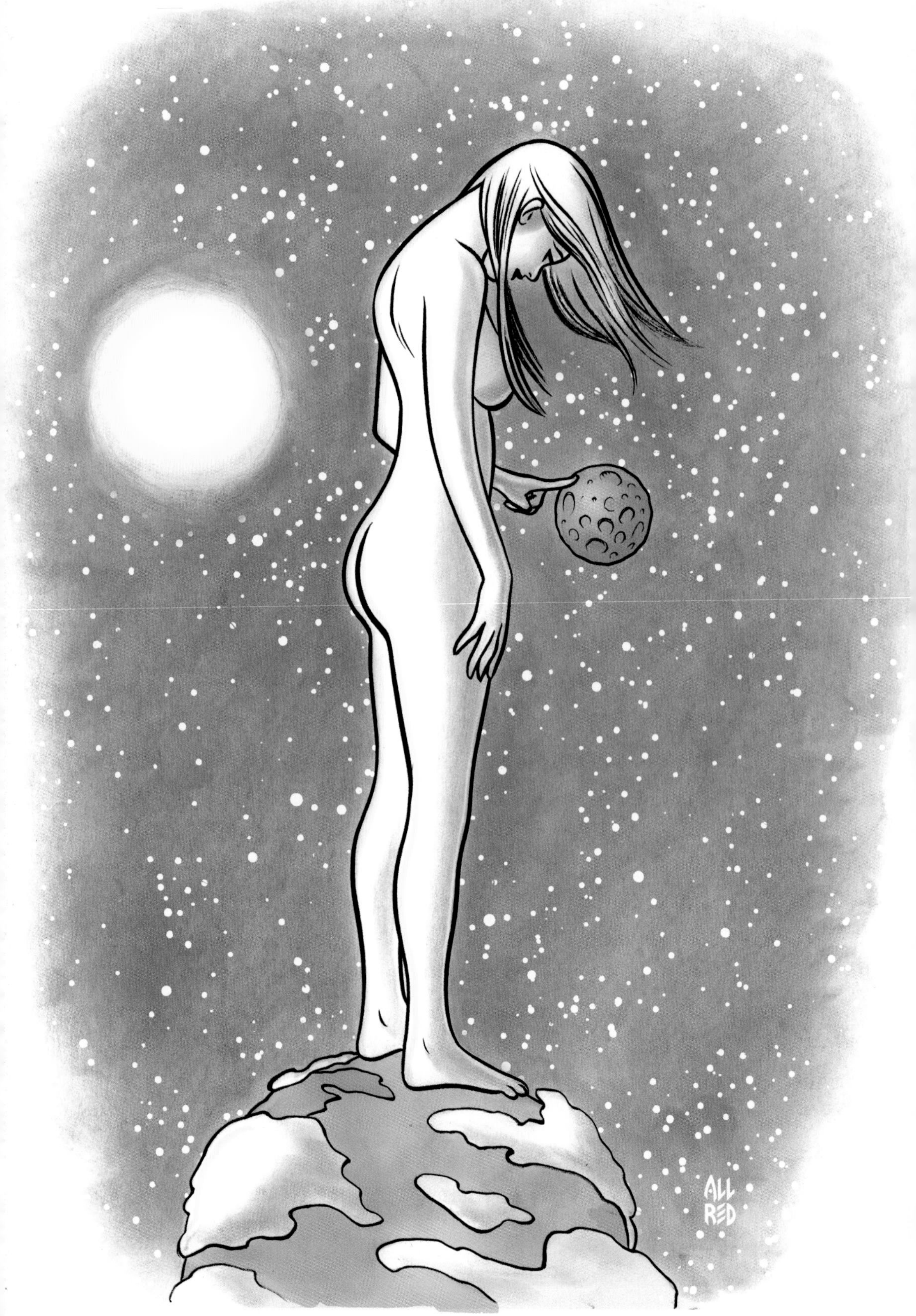
ALL
RED

Thank You!

TO THE WONDERFUL BACKERS WHO SUPPORTED US ON KICKSTARTER

AARON	AR RENDON	BRIAN J. CROWLEY
AARON BAFFUTO	ARCHON COMICS	BRIAN M
AARON BANDLER	ARITY DICKERSON	BRIAN McNAMARA
AARON J SHAY	ARYA PONTO	BRIAN WELLS
AARON LUK	ASHLEY HOWARD	BRIAN WOODS
ADAM J.	ASTE	BRIANNE KIRKPATRICK
MONETTA	AUDREY PENVEN	BRIGETTE CEDILLO
ADAM LAING	AVNER SHILOAH	BROOKE S
ADAM NELSON	BARBARA IVERSON	BRUCE HODSDON
AGENTORANGEFAI	BARTHOLOMEW LAWLESS	BRYAN CHONTO
AHIMSA KERP	BARZAI	BRYAN JANES
ALAN PURDIE	BASTIAN EICHLER	CALDER FERTIG
ALEC BERRY	BECK PASCOE	CALEB OGLESBY
ALEC EMPIRE	BECKY MUSSER	CAMERON BOWEN
ALEX	BEEHIVE DESIGN COLLECTIVE	CAMERON RICE
ALEX FITCH	BELINDA FERNANDEZ	CAN YALCINKAYA
ALEX JOHNSON	BELLOW FELLOW	CAR50N
ALEXANDER PLAUM	BEN ERGA	CARL CUNNINGHAM
ALEXANDRA BEUSCHER	BEN FERRARI	CARL MAGESKI
ALEXIS RASIMOWICZ	BEN HARVEY	CARL RIGNEY
ALICE LIMONCIEL	BEN LE FOE	CARLOS
ALINO	BEN SCHAPIRO	CAROL GUNBY
ALISTAIR KERR	BEN WHITTENBURY	CAROLYN BRAJKOVICH
ALISTER BLAKE	BENJAMIN CHEE	CAROLYN FAACKS
ALLAN NICOLSON	BENJAMIN MAYHEW	CASSIE OATES
ALLIANCE COMICS	BENJAMIN POOLE	CATALYSTPARADOX
ALMA BALDERAS	BENJAMIN RABIN	CATERINA
ALOW	BENS	CATHERINE LAUGHLIN
AMANDA	BETSY ISAACSON	CECE PIZZOLO
AMANDA GHANOONI	BEXXA	CHAD
AMANDA RUDD	BHAVIN SIRITANARATKUL	CHANTELLE BOWEN
AMANDA SHEPHERD	BILL CASH & MONIDOG	CHARIFI WALLY
AMBER NEWTON	BILLY SEGUIRE	CHARLES KANG
AMY ABLES	BLOINK ZIBBIT	CHARLIE SALT
ANDREA SCHAFFERHANS	BOB ANTHONY	CHELSEAP19
ANDREW	BOONE WEST POLLARD	CHLOE
ANDREW DOYLE	BOSCO'S	CHRIS BECKETT
ANDREW DUCKER	BOUKHELIFA	CHRIS CARAN
ANDY AGNEW	BOYBLUE	CHRIS KIRKHAM
ANDY THORINGTON	BRADEN ADAM	CHRIS ORBACH
ANGELA	BRADLEY MARTIN	CHRIS PREEN
ANGELICA AGUILAR	BRANDON CHINN	CHRIS PUGH
ANNA BAUSCH	BRANDON MAHNE	CHRIS RILEY
ANNE	BRANKA TOKIC	CHRIS SCHREIBER
ANSON JEW	BRENDAN TIHANE	CHRIS THOMAS
ANTHONY	BRENDAN WRIGHT	CHRIS McLAREN
ANTHONY WHITE	BRETT DANALAKE	CHRISTIAN SAGER
ANTON WIJS	BRETT GUREWITZ	CHRISTIAN TOMSEY
ANTONELLA VALLELONGA	BRETT SCHENKER	CHRISTINA MULLIN
APRIL BACON	BRIAN BEARDSLEY	CHRISTINE TOBEY

Christine Woomer
Christopher Acevedo
Christopher Beatty
Christopher Butler
Christy Filipich
chrystal
Chunk
cindy dacus
CJ Suzuki
clifford reese
comicspectrum.com
Cornelius Gloria
Cory Balsitis
Craig Hewitt
Curtis Fletcher
Dan Coplan
Dan Gee
Dan Owsen
Dan Pinsk
Dan Ponce
Dana Moss
Daniel
Daniel Grizante de Andrade
Daniel Rodriguez
Daniela
Danielle Rossoni
Danny OBrien
darrell ferguson
Darren Ainsworth
Dartigen
Daryl Davis
Dave Menninger
dave parker
David
David Branson
David Callipygous Smart
David Clarke
David Delbrook
David Frankel
DAVID FREON
David Gregal
David Kebo
David Krolick
David Lawrence
david Loitz
David Macho
David Mangels
David Priestley
David Shipp
David Tai
David Tooley
David Yuguchi
Deb Aoki
Debora Ratliff
Deborah Grech
Denise Thompson
Dennis P. O'Brien
Diane "lo1337a" Gonzalez
Dickon Edwards
Diego Malara
Dimitris John Raptis
Dolores Bilges
dori marshall
Doug blandy
Doug Smith
dougty
Drew L
Dustin Sharpless
Ed Allen
Ed Highfield
Ed Watson
Edward Harris
Elad
eleanor
Eliel Mamousette
Elijah St. Dennis
Elisabeth Flinsch
Elisabeth J. Kilcrease
elitetank
ellen herbert
Emanuel Kluge
Emma Griffith
Emma Marie Young
Eric
Eric Agena
Eric Bisaillon
Eric Larnick
Eric Nieudan
Erik Smith
Erin
Ernesto Bravo Jr.
F.J. DeSanto
Felipe Sobreiro
Fez WS
Fiacre O'Duinn
Flor Gressel
Florent Mathias
FordDent
fourworlds
Francis A DaCosta
Francois Cadieux
Frank Barch
Frank Jaeger
Frank Tang
Freddie Arnold
FredH
friday13fan
frogperson0
Gabriel Michaiels
Gabriel Schubiner
Garnet Faulkner
Gary
Gary Gray
Gary Mendell
Gary Simmons
Gavin Payne
geoffrey miller
George Siosi Samuels
Gethin Lynes
Glen Ivey
greg Geisler
Greg Lee
grischder
Guido Alexander Sanchez
Guilherme Constantino Silva
Guillaume Boutmy
Hanna Tolander
Heidi Bowles Ellis
Helen Dickinson
herebewonder
hiriel
Hollie Allen
Holly Verfall
Howard Gertler
Hugo Mesquita
Iain Triffitt
Ian Struckhoff
Igguk
Illumina
ismael merla
Ivan Gutierrez
J. Mark Leonard
J Scott Knell
J.G. Pozark
JK
Jack W. Lunenfeld
Jacob
Jacob Devaney
Jacque
Jake Wasserman
Jakob Kromann Groth
James G.
James Post
James Venhaus
James Viner
Janine F
Jarod West
Jason A. Quest
Jason Atnip
Jason Bryant
Jason Peter Morris
Jayrose
Jason Sacks
Jason Sutter
Jason VanSlycke
Jasper van Putten
jaymztay
Jazz Dolan
Jeff Hammell
Jeff Kane
Jeff Kleeman
Jeff Schultz
Jeffrey Radcliffe
Jennifer Day
Jennifer & Daniel Hite
Jeremy Brownstein
Jeremiah Clark
Jeremy Cloven
Jeremy Hulette
Jeremy Parker
Jerome Berube
Jesse Fresco
jesse johnson
jesse l mabus
Jesse Sands
Jesse, Evan, and Saul

Jessi
Jessica DeCarlo
Jessica Dreesen, The
Jessica Maslo
Jevon Archie
Jim Burton
Jim Lai
jim rice
Jince Kuruvilla
JoAnne G.
Joe
Joe Stephens
Joel Harper
John Carter
John Mandelker
John Parkin
John Polansky
John Reha
John Wells
Johnathan L Bingham
Jonathan Cable
Jonathan Gelatt
Jonathan Richards
Jonathan Sulkow
jonathon bell
jorge
Jorge Guzman
Jose de Leon
Josh
Josh Bisker
Josh Henaman
Josh Larios
Josh Rainwater
Josh Roby
Joshua Stylman
Joshua Weiner
jPad
Juli black
Julian Orr
Julie Poulos
Julien Masset
Juliette
K. D. Bryan
Karen Eberle-Smith
Karen Green
Kat Orphanides
Kate Ward
katharine krueger
Katherine Donahoe
Katherine Everhart
Kathleen McLeod
Kathryn E. Martin
Kathryn Player
kay chornook
Kees van Putten
Ken Eppstein
Ken Grobe
Ken Hallock
Kerry Lynn Thompson
Kevin Calman
Kevin Harrison
Kevin Hemingway
Kevin J. Maroney
Kevin Kairys
Kevin M. Burke
Kevin McKenzie
Kevin Pointer
Kim Reid
kirk
Kirsten
Kirstin Brueckler
Kris
Kumar Sivasubramanian
Kyla Ryman
Kyle Jacobs
Kyle Robinson
Kyle Royer
Kyle Swinney
Larry
Larry McQuaide
larry yang
Lars Hartmann
Lee Jaszlics
Leef Smith
leif olson
Leonard O'Grady
Libbi Rich
Lincoln Phillips
Lin-Fan Wang
Lisa
Lissa
Liz McGuire
Liz McLellan
Lizzette Walls
LJGhost
Louis Kammerer
LRFeldman
Lucas Magyarics
Lucian Mattison
Lucie Kinchin
Lucy Brown
Luke Thompson
M. C. Matz
MaartenBerns
Madalyn Garrett
Makoche
Marcelo Alves
Margaret Kunz
Mariana Machado de Paula
Albuquerque
Marine
Mario Fischer
Mark
Mark Bain
Mark Barnes
Mark Bowers
Mark James Schryver
Mark Katzoff
Mark Slater
Mark 'vordo' Wlodarkiewicz
Marla Kaya
Martin Gentry
Martin Schonert
Martin Walz
marylyn tippeconnic
Mathew Quitney
Mathieu Doublet
Mathieu Lubrun
Mathilde Sachiko Bouhon
Matt
Matt Caron
Matt DeGennaro
Matt Donaldson
Matt Forbeck
Matt Katch
Matt Mullany-Green
Matt Staggs
Matt Wilson
Matthew
Matthew Frederickson
Matthew Rosenberg
Matthew Suber
Matthew Ward
Maura McHugh
Mauricio Giraldo
maurine stenwick
mburleigh
Megan Thorsfeldt
Meghan
Melanie Branwen
Melissa Gira Grant
Melissa Krause
Melony Chitwood
Menachem Luchins
Mette Podenphant
Micah Baldwin
Michael
Michael Becker
Michael Copeland
Michael Drivas
Michael Farah
Michael Fleming
Michael Hew
Michael Matzat
Michael Moreci
Michael Nimmo
Michael Onken
Michael Perridge
Michael Porcelli
Michael Roman
Michael Wayne DeFore
Michelle
michelle
Miguel Jorge
Mike Bolitho
Mike Caudill
Mike Hurd
Mike Marsalisi
Mike Zwick
Miranda M.
Miriam Merkova
Mitch Ullrich
Monique Simon
moodydoom
morosopher
Myriam

mzflux
Nawid Ahrary
Naylandblake
Neil Gray
Neil Kandalgaonkar
Nicholas Gale
Nick Botto
Nick Fagan
Nick Marshall
Nickalus Phillips
Nicole
niki carlson
Nina Echeverria
Nisha Grayson
Noel Tuazon
notbenh
Oliver Wolken
Olle Jonsson
Ondrej Hrdy
oranparker
Owen Tucker
Petur Yngvi Leosson
Panayiotis Papakyprianou
Pang Peow Yeong
Pat Ludwig
patrick byrne
Patrick Mohlmann
Paul Bonamy
Paul Braidford
Paul Ferguson
Paul Vaughn
Perazza
Peter Climie
Peter Wong
Phil Wrede
PhillUpNorth
pickwick
Pierre Marshall
Poet Mase
POost
Praveen Sinha
rachaar
Rachel Aavang
Rachel Glaves
Rachel Norman
Randi Cardia
Random Person
randy sarbacher
Ravi Ahmad
Raymond Kelly
Rebecca Howie
Rebecca Kennison
Rebecca Sorcini
Remy Vain
Rene Gonzales
Rhett
Ricardo Amaral Filho
Rich
Rich Johnston
Richard Blumberg
Richard Christopher
Richard Law
Richard Nisa
Ricky Reilly
Riju
Rob Miller
Rob Mitchell
Robert Gordon
Robert Hoch
Robert Menegus
Robert Randle
Robert Samples
Roberto Accinelli
Robziel
Rodrigo Ortiz Vinholo
Roger Whitson
roy cowing
Roy Isserlis
Ruben Galle
Rudolf Kremers
Russ Otto
Russell Willis
Rusty Duncan
Ruth Earl
Ryan Burke
Ryan Closs
Ryan Doherty
Ryan Jabba-San Cheshire
Ryan Richards
Ryan Sainio
Ryan Singer
Ryan T. Jenny
Sam Brown
Sandi
sarah
Sarahmarian
Satine Phoenix
Scot Matayoshi
Scott Gaertner
Scott Lewis
Scott Spearman
Sean Harvey
Sean Howren
Sean Kleefeld
Sean Peck-Collier
shane grant
Sharon
Shaun Manning
Shawn Demumbrum
Shawn Van Hecke
Shay Brog
Shiva Wolfe
Sian Harrop
Simon Isenberg
Siobhan Greatorex-Voith
SK
Spencer Hyun
Stacy Flores
Stephanie
Stephanie Barnes
Stephen
Steve Burnett
Steve Flack
Steven Goldman
Steven Honeycutt
Steven Rapacki
Susan Burkhardt
susan rubin
Sven Magotsch
Sweetie314
Tie da Silva
taqholic
Taru
Tay Carpenter
Taylor
Terry Harris
Terry Kinzer
Thadius Krueger
ThatGuy
Thomas O'Donnell
Thwipster
Tim R.
Tiago Stock
Tim DieTwenty Schmolzi
Tim Pilcher
Tim Tjarks
Timm Davison
Todd Gage
Todd Sattersten
Tom Stillwell
Tom Waterman
Tommy Leung
Tonje
Tony
Tony Solomun
Tpadz
Trab Sselwal
Tyler Crook
Tyson
Uta Roghmanns
Ute Friederich
Vanessa Wieland
Vera
Veronika von Volkova
Victor
Vnend
voltagex
Warren Hedges
Warren Pawlowski
Wei Wong
werwolf
Wilhelm Moehlmann
William Ball
William Dunn
William Green
Wim Lewis
Worthy Glover
XJanX
XOMR
Yale Spector
Yogthulhu
Zachary Auron
Zack Guignardi
Zara

> Introduction, from "Occupy Comics #1, Kickstarter Edition"

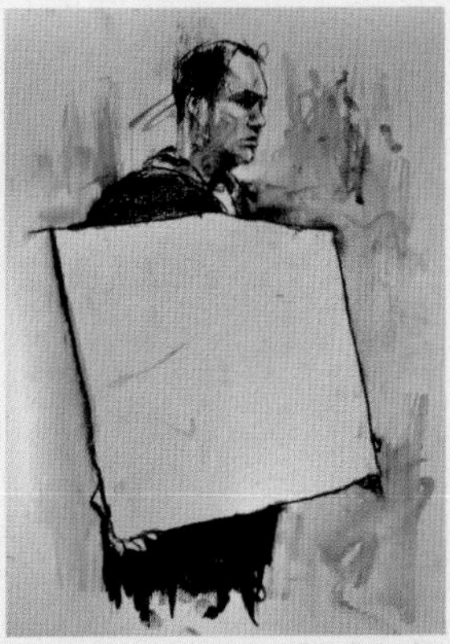

Guy Denning

Do you remember where you were when you first heard people had set up encampments in Zuccotti Park to protest Wall Street? I don't. It's become so ingrained in my mind that it doesn't even seem shocking in retrospect... somehow it seems like the obvious, most logical thing to do. Sure, a bunch of financial elites pump & dumped our economy then our government paid them off, so obviously people should find a park nearby and move in... that'll work. And, strangely, it did--and for a moment it changed the dinner table conversations, water cooler gossip, and social network chatter across the country and around the world. Then Bloomberg finally swept the park, and, once the tents came down and teargas dispersed, everything went back to normal. Or did it? Still hard to say.

Back in the initial days of Occupy Wall Street, before Casual Pepper Spray Cop & 24 hour cable news coverage, I was following Occupy via social networks while preparing for NY Comic Con. It seemed synchronistic that 100,000 or so comics fans obsessed with heroics and justice would be convening a subway ride away from the protesters who, in my humble opinion, were pretty heroically putting themselves at risk to challenge injustice. And, since the Occupy protests were getting hardly any news coverage at the time, I felt we should try and spread the word at NY Comic Con... so I reached out to some of my comics pro friends about making a little self-published comics zine covering the protests to pass around the convention and help spread the word. Before we got very far, Tony Baloney went apeshit with pepper spray and the media blackout turned into a media circus--so exposure was no longer an issue. Well, that's not entirely true. Exposure of the *event* was no longer an issue... but exposure of the *intent* is probably still an issue. After all, watching the news coverage you'd think this was all about police brutality or activists' grooming habits or how safe it is to sleep in a NYC park. There may be no such thing as bad press, but there's certainly such a thing as useless press.

So we took our Occupy Comics idea back into the lab and redesigned it into a two-pronged strategy: (1) a time-capsule anthology comic bringing together dozens of creators articulating the protests from their own unique points of view and, as an eclectic group, reflecting the chorus of diverse perspectives that make up the movement, and (2) a fundraising effort to support the occupiers. It all seems logical and obvious now, but it was a pretty hare-brained scheme at the time. Somehow it all came together.

During the Kickstarter campaign, I was interviewed by Bill Baker at The Morton Report and we had the following Q&A:

Q. I was curious if there's something you'd like to see come about, personally, as a result of all of these efforts [to create Occupy Comics]?

A. Personally, I'd love if the project managed to express the goals of the movement in a unique way that transcends rhetoric or over-intellectualization or lists of demands. I believe this is more a social change movement than a political movement, people are coalescing around an idea, not an ideology... all that makes it poorly suited to discuss in a 24 hour news cycle... I think it's better conveyed through art.

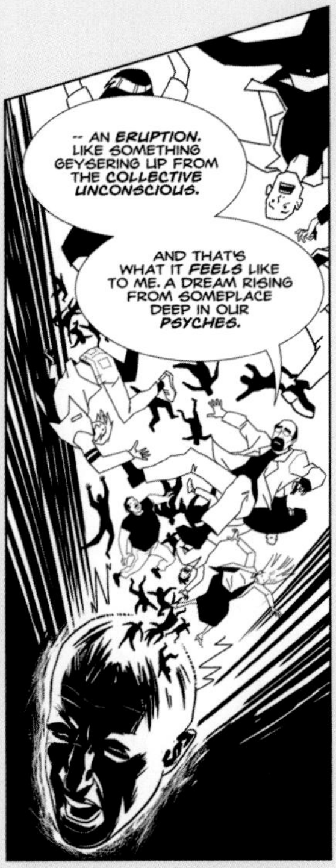
-- AN ERUPTION. LIKE SOMETHING GEYSERING UP FROM THE COLLECTIVE UNCONSCIOUS.
AND THAT'S WHAT IT FEELS LIKE TO ME. A DREAM RISING FROM SOMEPLACE DEEP IN OUR PSYCHES.

J.M. DeMatteis, Mike Cavallaro

Now, months later, looking at this first collection of stories and remembering that initial goal, I couldn't be more pleased.

In my memory, the days of protest are all a mess of activist idealism, media cynicism, belligerent cops, and a general sense of positive but confused solidarity among the broader population of the 99%. After having the events on the ground interpreted by 1%ers in the news media and filtered back to the rest of us, it can be tough to remember the context and the intent of the whole thing and just what a wild idea it really was. I hope these Occupy comics and the ones to come, in their own small way, can help us take a step back and remember what this was and is all about. A bunch of financial elites pump & dumped our economy and then our government paid them off, so people found a park nearby and moved in to force attention on the injustice.

And somehow it worked.

So... what's next?

(-Matt Pizzolo, May 2012)

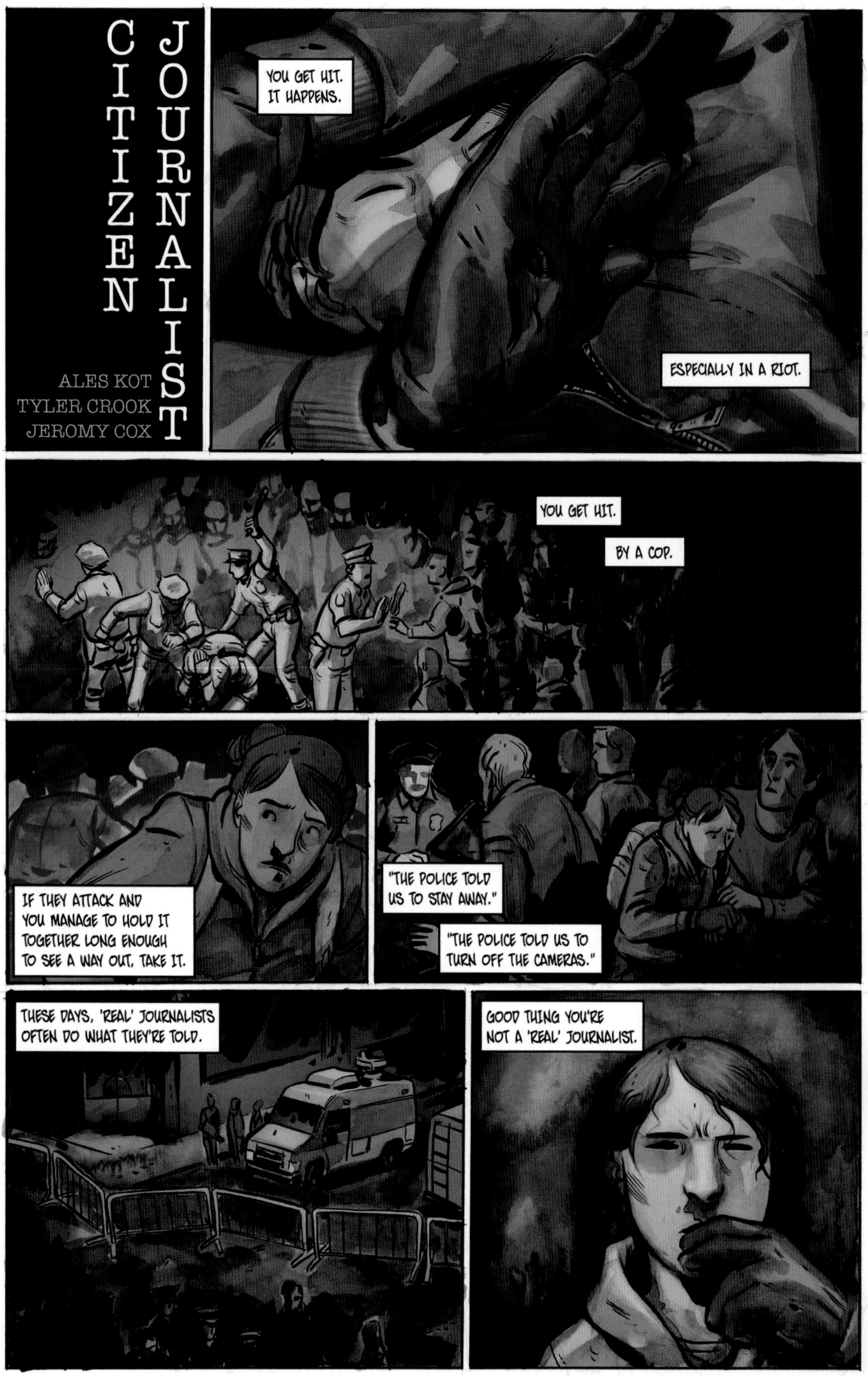
CITIZEN JOURNALIST
ALES KOT
TYLER CROOK
JEROMY COX
YOU GET HIT.
IT HAPPENS.
ESPECIALLY IN A RIOT.
YOU GET HIT.
BY A COP.
IF THEY ATTACK AND YOU MANAGE TO HOLD IT TOGETHER LONG ENOUGH TO SEE A WAY OUT, TAKE IT.
"THE POLICE TOLD US TO STAY AWAY."
"THE POLICE TOLD US TO TURN OFF THE CAMERAS."
THESE DAYS, 'REAL' JOURNALISTS OFTEN DO WHAT THEY'RE TOLD.
GOOD THING YOU'RE NOT A 'REAL' JOURNALIST.

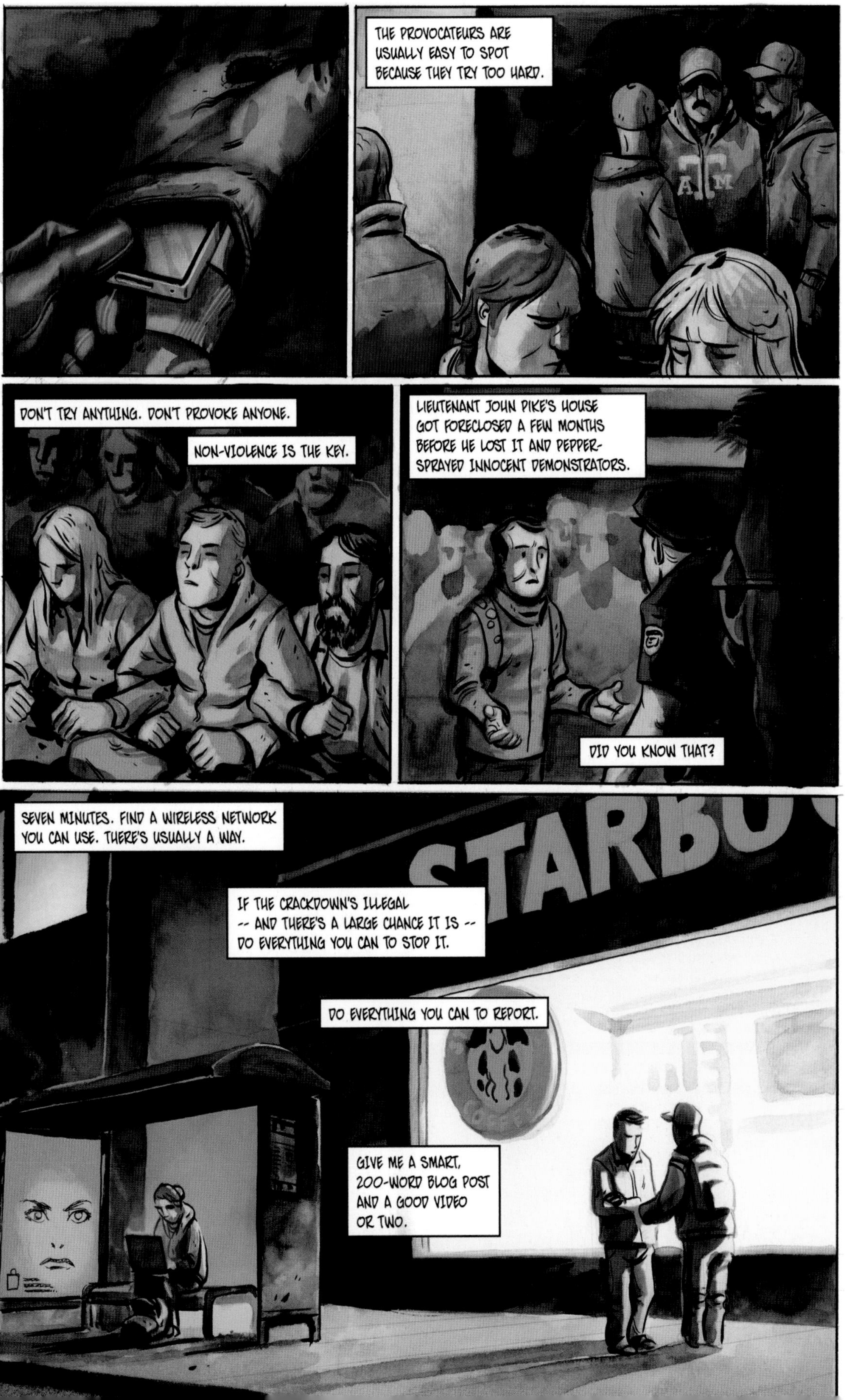

THE PROVOCATEURS ARE USUALLY EASY TO SPOT BECAUSE THEY TRY TOO HARD.
DON'T TRY ANYTHING. DON'T PROVOKE ANYONE.
NON-VIOLENCE IS THE KEY.
LIEUTENANT JOHN PIKE'S HOUSE GOT FORECLOSED A FEW MONTHS BEFORE HE LOST IT AND PEPPER-SPRAYED INNOCENT DEMONSTRATORS.
DID YOU KNOW THAT?
SEVEN MINUTES. FIND A WIRELESS NETWORK YOU CAN USE. THERE'S USUALLY A WAY.
IF THE CRACKDOWN'S ILLEGAL -- AND THERE'S A LARGE CHANCE IT IS -- DO EVERYTHING YOU CAN TO STOP IT.
DO EVERYTHING YOU CAN TO REPORT.
GIVE ME A SMART, 200-WORD BLOG POST AND A GOOD VIDEO OR TWO.

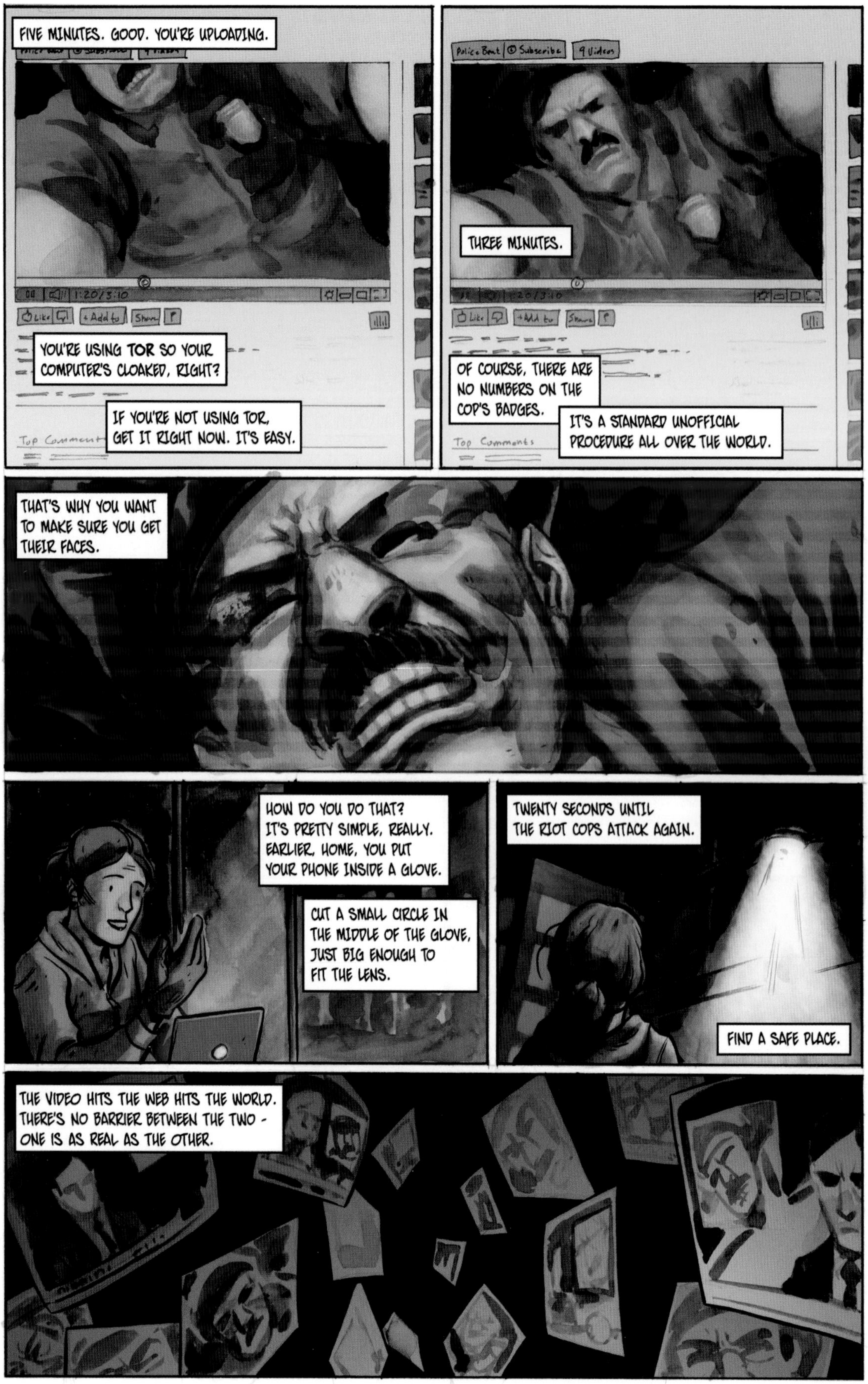
FIVE MINUTES. GOOD. YOU'RE UPLOADING.
YOU'RE USING TOR SO YOUR COMPUTER'S CLOAKED, RIGHT?
IF YOU'RE NOT USING TOR, GET IT RIGHT NOW. IT'S EASY.
THREE MINUTES.
OF COURSE, THERE ARE NO NUMBERS ON THE COP'S BADGES.
IT'S A STANDARD UNOFFICIAL PROCEDURE ALL OVER THE WORLD.
THAT'S WHY YOU WANT TO MAKE SURE YOU GET THEIR FACES.
HOW DO YOU DO THAT? IT'S PRETTY SIMPLE, REALLY. EARLIER, HOME, YOU PUT YOUR PHONE INSIDE A GLOVE.
CUT A SMALL CIRCLE IN THE MIDDLE OF THE GLOVE, JUST BIG ENOUGH TO FIT THE LENS.
TWENTY SECONDS UNTIL THE RIOT COPS ATTACK AGAIN.
FIND A SAFE PLACE.
THE VIDEO HITS THE WEB HITS THE WORLD. THERE'S NO BARRIER BETWEEN THE TWO - ONE IS AS REAL AS THE OTHER.

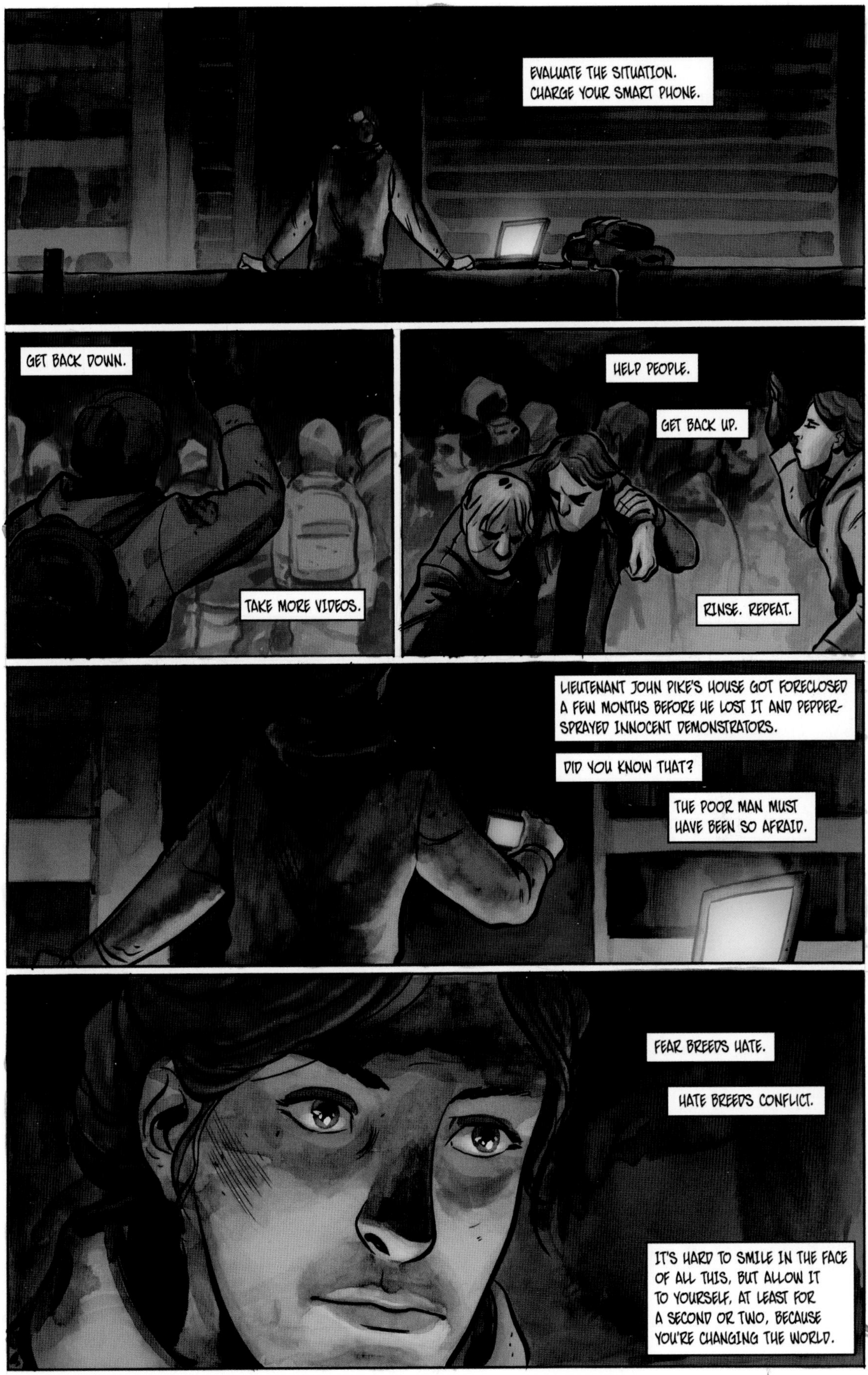
EVALUATE THE SITUATION. CHARGE YOUR SMART PHONE.
GET BACK DOWN.
TAKE MORE VIDEOS.
HELP PEOPLE.
GET BACK UP.
RINSE. REPEAT.
LIEUTENANT JOHN PIKE'S HOUSE GOT FORECLOSED A FEW MONTHS BEFORE HE LOST IT AND PEPPER-SPRAYED INNOCENT DEMONSTRATORS.
DID YOU KNOW THAT?
THE POOR MAN MUST HAVE BEEN SO AFRAID.
FEAR BREEDS HATE.
HATE BREEDS CONFLICT.
IT'S HARD TO SMILE IN THE FACE OF ALL THIS, BUT ALLOW IT TO YOURSELF, AT LEAST FOR A SECOND OR TWO, BECAUSE YOU'RE CHANGING THE WORLD.

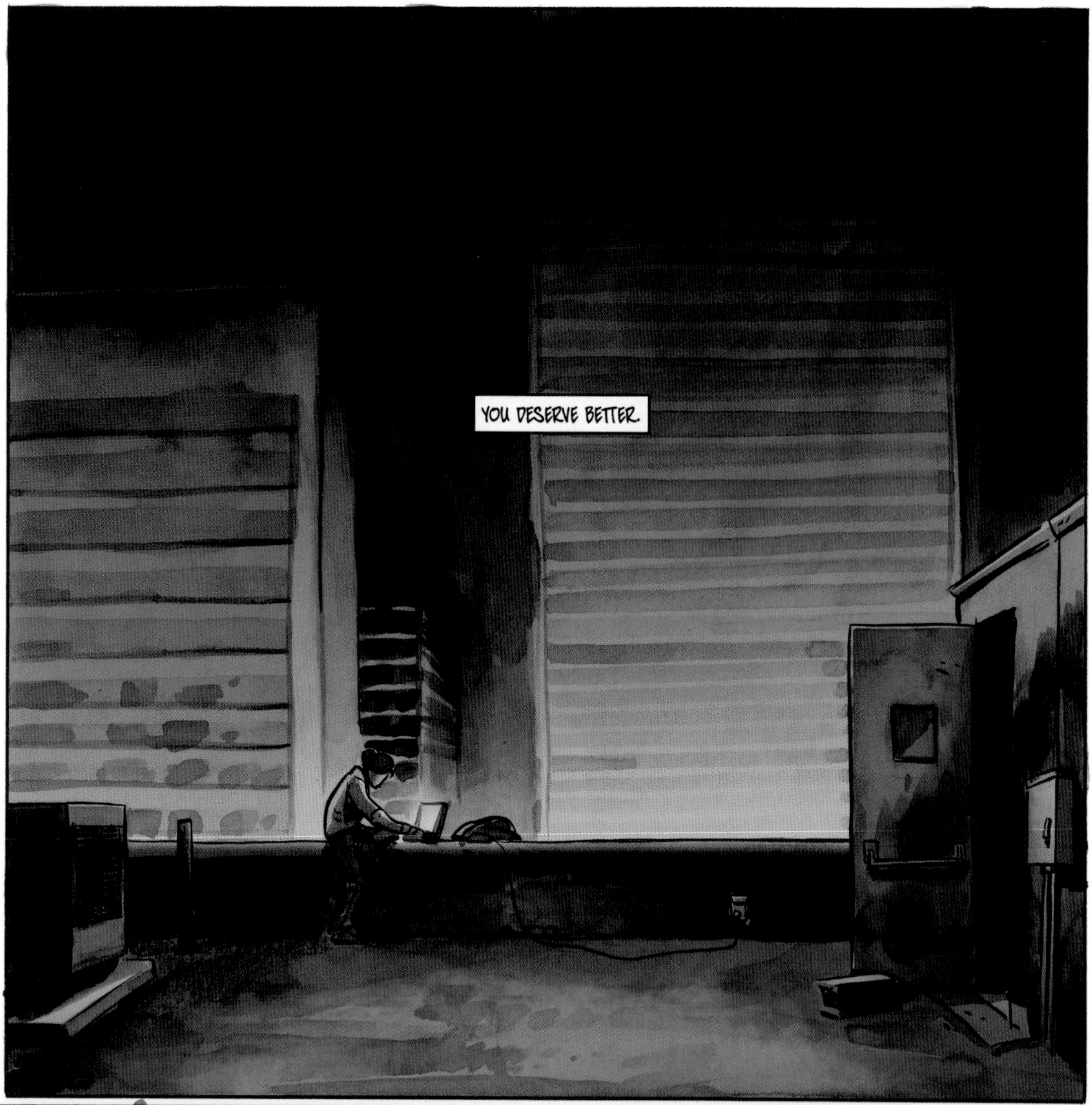
YOU DESERVE BETTER.

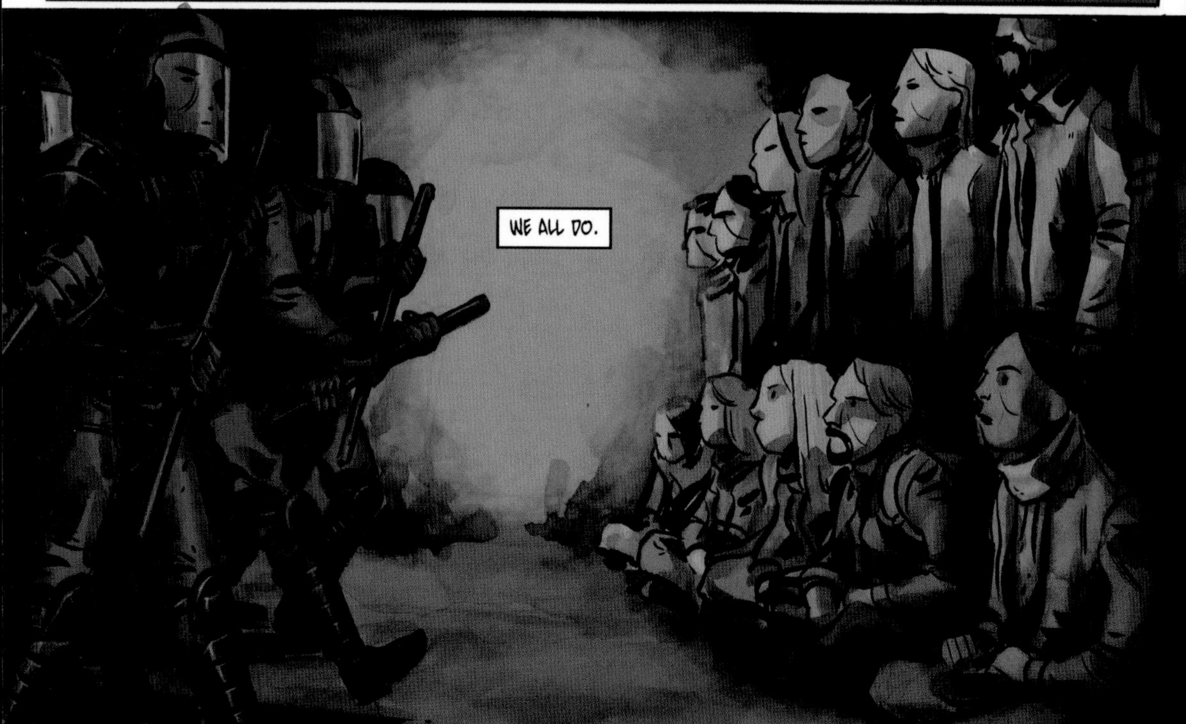
WE ALL DO.

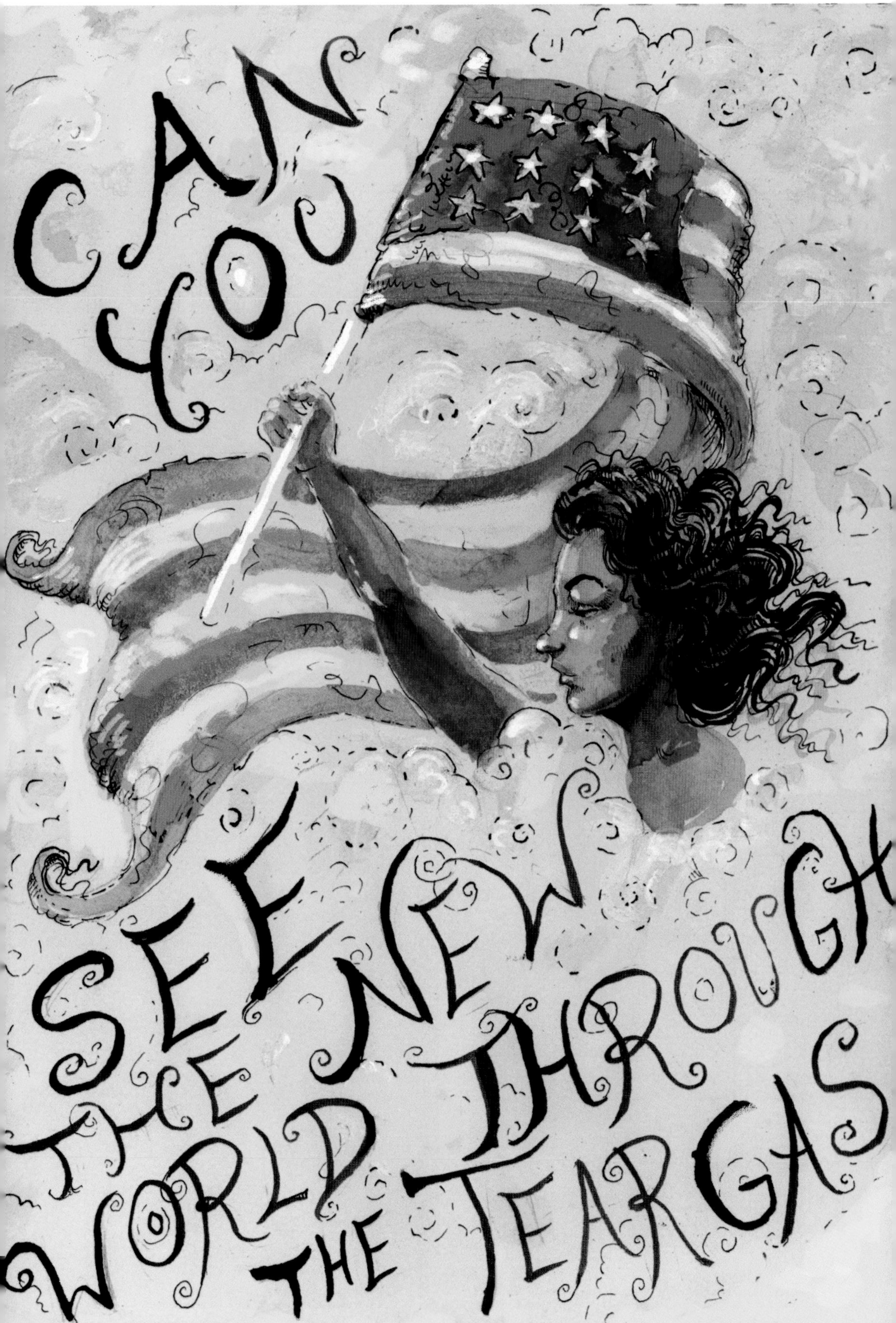
CAN YOU
SEE THE NEW WORLD
THROUGH THE TEARGAS

HOMESTEAD

JOSHUA FIALKOV & JOSEPH INFURNARI

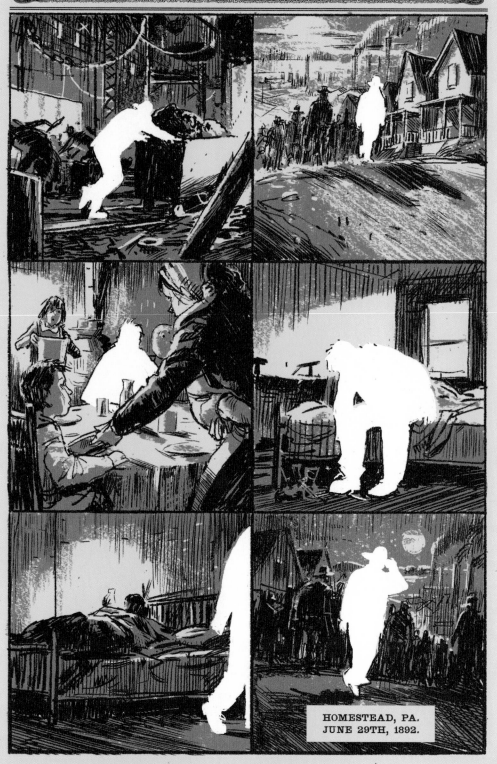

HOMESTEAD, PA.
JUNE 29TH, 1892.

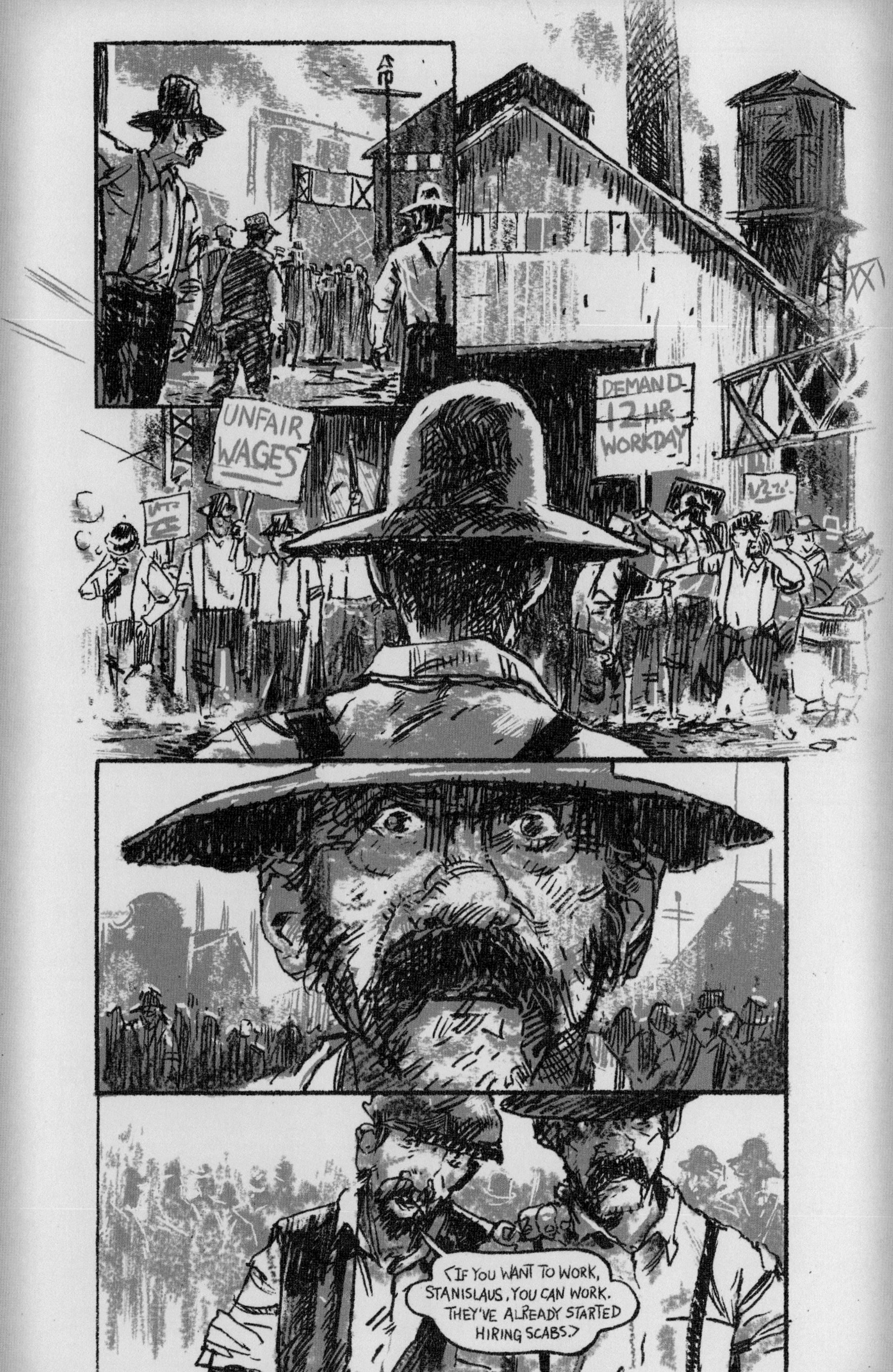
UNFAIR WAGES
DEMAND 12 HR WORKDAY
<IF YOU WANT TO WORK, STANISLAUS, YOU CAN WORK. THEY'VE ALREADY STARTED HIRING SCABS.>

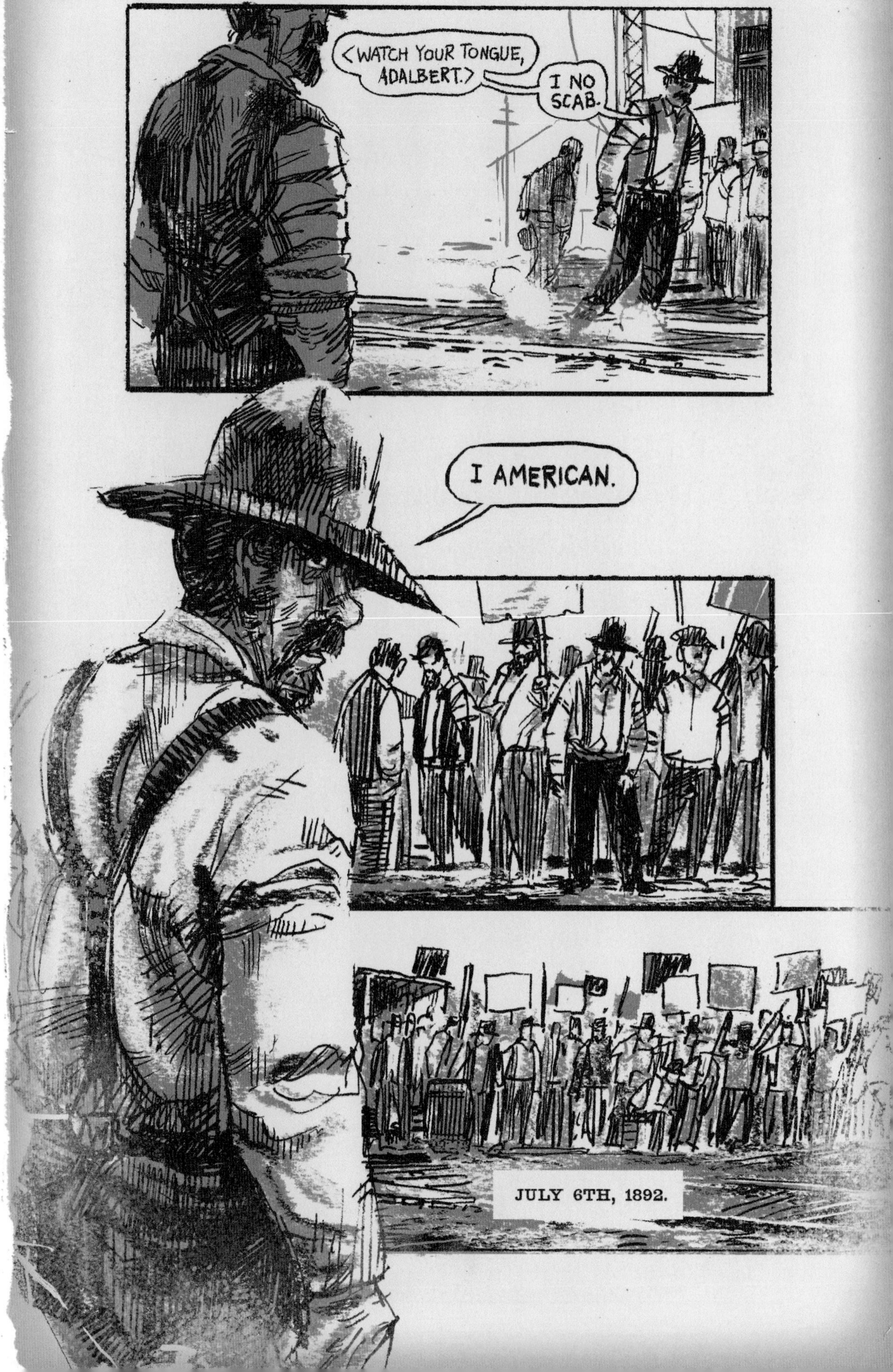
<WATCH YOUR TONGUE, ADALBERT.>
I NO SCAB.
I AMERICAN.
JULY 6TH, 1892.

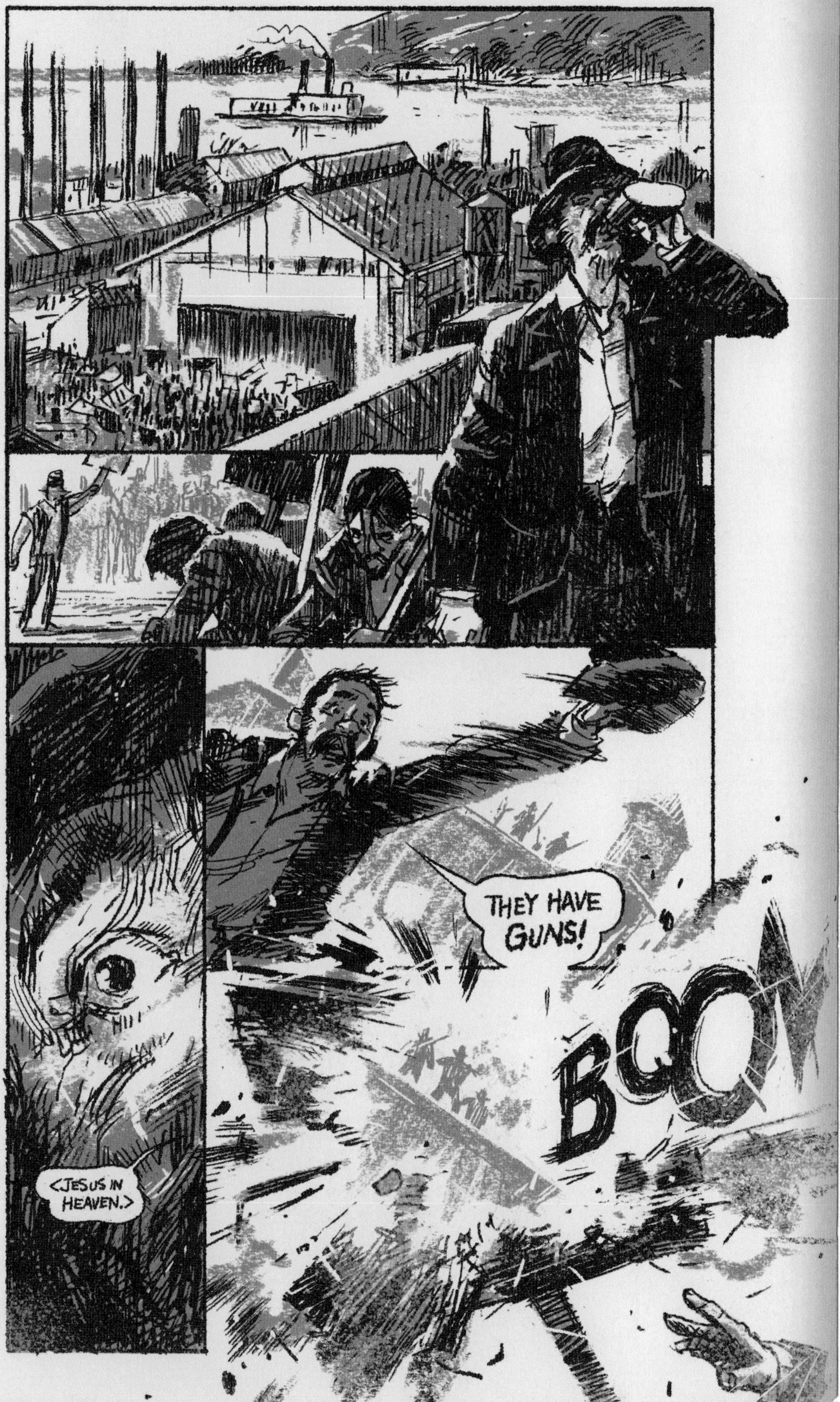
<JESUS IN HEAVEN.>
THEY HAVE GUNS!
BOOM

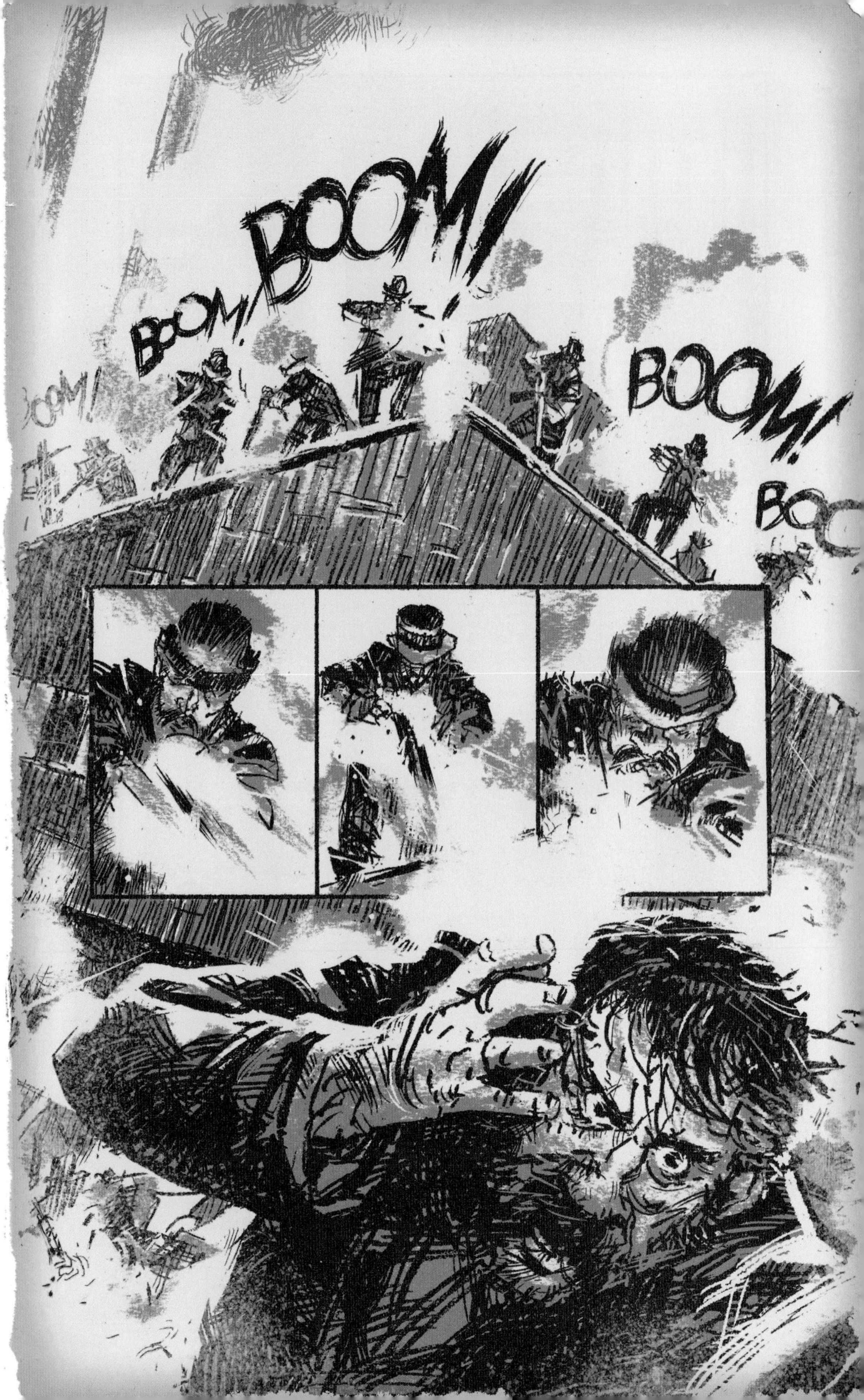
OOM!
BOOM!
BOOM!
BOOM!
BOC

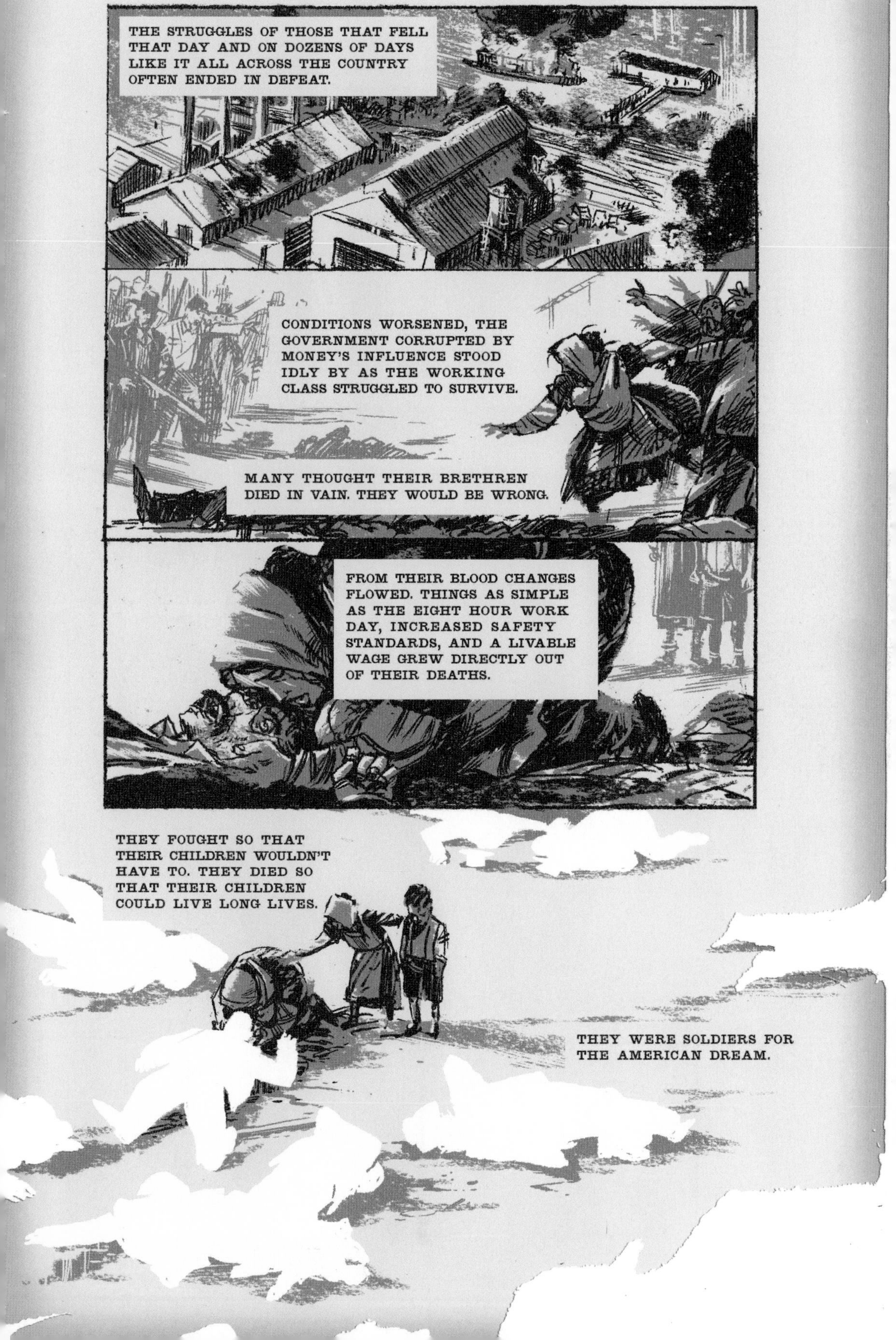
THE STRUGGLES OF THOSE THAT FELL THAT DAY AND ON DOZENS OF DAYS LIKE IT ALL ACROSS THE COUNTRY OFTEN ENDED IN DEFEAT.
CONDITIONS WORSENED, THE GOVERNMENT CORRUPTED BY MONEY'S INFLUENCE STOOD IDLY BY AS THE WORKING CLASS STRUGGLED TO SURVIVE.
MANY THOUGHT THEIR BRETHREN DIED IN VAIN. THEY WOULD BE WRONG.
FROM THEIR BLOOD CHANGES FLOWED. THINGS AS SIMPLE AS THE EIGHT HOUR WORK DAY, INCREASED SAFETY STANDARDS, AND A LIVABLE WAGE GREW DIRECTLY OUT OF THEIR DEATHS.
THEY FOUGHT SO THAT THEIR CHILDREN WOULDN'T HAVE TO. THEY DIED SO THAT THEIR CHILDREN COULD LIVE LONG LIVES.
THEY WERE SOLDIERS FOR THE AMERICAN DREAM.

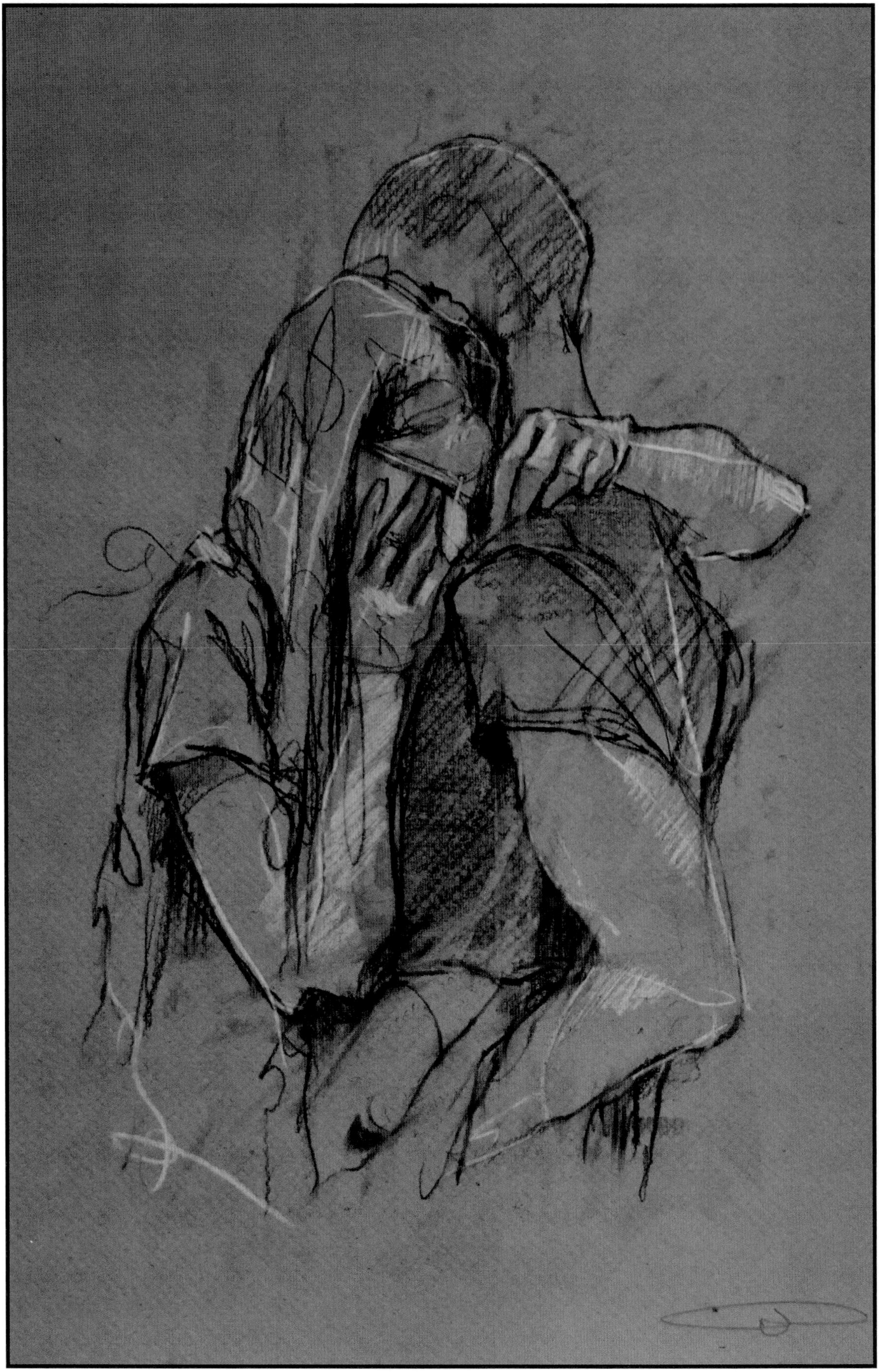

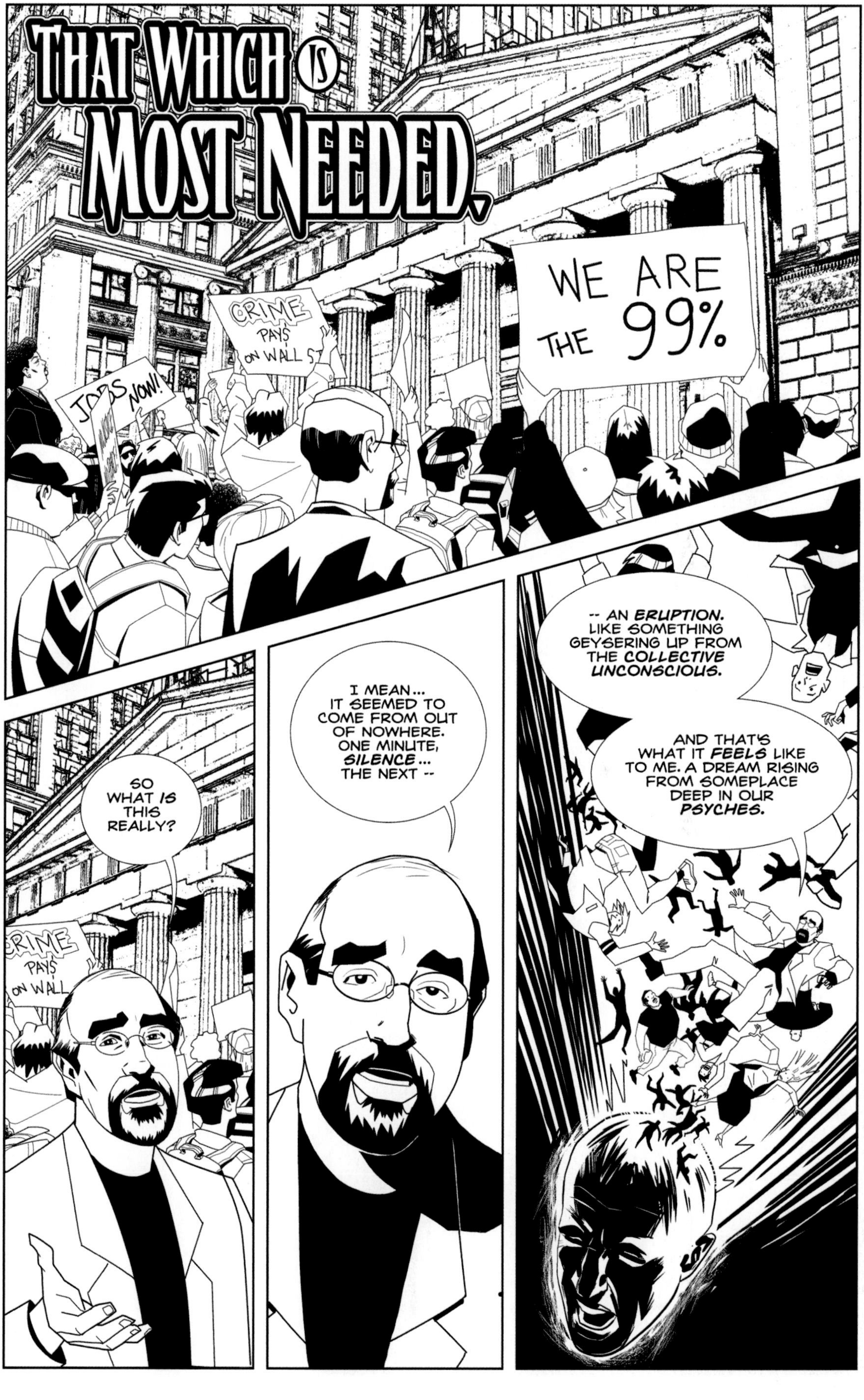
THAT WHICH IS MOST NEEDED,
CRIME PAYS ON WALL ST
JOBS NOW!
WE ARE THE 99%
SO WHAT IS THIS REALLY?
I MEAN... IT SEEMED TO COME FROM OUT OF NOWHERE. ONE MINUTE, SILENCE... THE NEXT --
-- AN ERUPTION. LIKE SOMETHING GEYSERING UP FROM THE COLLECTIVE UNCONSCIOUS.
AND THAT'S WHAT IT FEELS LIKE TO ME. A DREAM RISING FROM SOMEPLACE DEEP IN OUR PSYCHES.

THE REPORTERS KEEP SCRATCHING THEIR WELL-COIFED HEADS. "BUT WHAT'S THE *POINT?*" THEY ASK.

WHAT ARE YOUR *DEMANDS?*

WHAT ARE YOU TRYING TO *DO?*

AND THE ANSWERS -- *SOME* OF THEM ANYWAY -- HAVE BEEN *CONFUSING.*

SO *MANY* VOICES. SO MANY *POINTS OF VIEW.*

BUT TO ME THAT'S THE *BEAUTY* OF THIS THING. ONE MIND. -- BUT A *PARADE* OF THOUGHTS, STREAMING OUT IN AN *INFINITE NUMBER* OF DIRECTIONS.

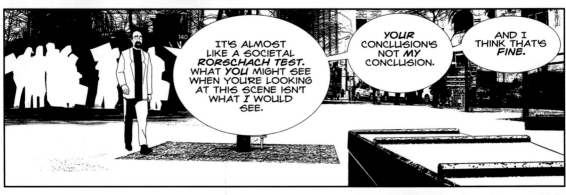

IT'S ALMOST LIKE A SOCIETAL *RORSCHACH TEST.* WHAT *YOU* MIGHT SEE WHEN YOU'RE LOOKING AT THIS SCENE ISN'T WHAT *I* WOULD SEE.

YOUR CONCLUSION'S NOT *MY* CONCLUSION.

AND I THINK THAT'S *FINE.*

SO WHAT *IS* MY CONCLUSION?

WELL, FOR ME -- THIS ISN'T ABOUT *POLITICS.* THIS ISN'T ABOUT *REVOLUTION.* IT'S NOT ABOUT *CLASS WARFARE* OR *DEMONIZING* THE RICH.

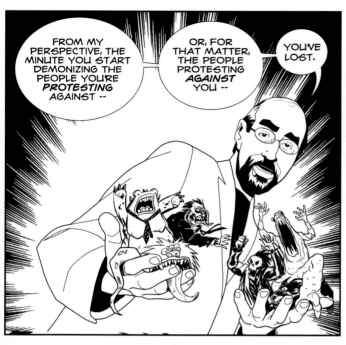

FROM MY PERSPECTIVE, THE MINUTE YOU START DEMONIZING THE PEOPLE YOU'RE *PROTESTING* AGAINST --

OR, FOR THAT MATTER, THE PEOPLE PROTESTING *AGAINST* YOU --

YOU'VE LOST.

YOU CREATE AN "ENEMY" WHO'S SOMEHOW *SUB-HUMAN*. WHO DOESN'T FEEL OR THINK THE WAY YOU DO.

AND THAT MAKES IT EASY TO *TRIVIALIZE* OR *DIMINISH* THEM. WORSE, IT MAKES IT EASY TO *HATE* THEM.

BUT... AS I SAID... I DON'T THINK THAT'S WHAT THIS IS *ABOUT*.

WHAT I FEEL MOST DEEPLY ABOUT THIS MOVEMENT IS THAT IT'S RISEN FROM A DESIRE FOR *FAIRNESS*. MORE THAN THAT: A DESIRE FOR *SIMPLE HUMAN DECENCY*.

BECAUSE IT SEEMS, SOMETIMES, THAT DECENCY HAS BEEN *LOST* IN THIS WORLD.

THAT EVERYWHERE YOU LOOK, THERE'S GREED AND VIOLENCE AND HUMAN UGLINESS AT ITS *ABSOLUTE WORST*.

BUT THAT'S JUST THE *CNN REALITY*. WHAT I CALL *"THE SKIN OF THE WORLD."*

BLAHBLAHBLAH *FEAR*BLAHBLAHBLAH *TERROR*BLAHBLAH BLAH*HORROR*

WHEN YOU PUSH *BENEATH* THAT SKIN, THERE'S *ANOTHER* REALITY. AND I THINK IT'S THE ONE *MOST* OF US LIVE IN.

A REALITY WHERE WE'RE ALL --

REGARDLESS OF OUR POLITICAL OR SPIRITUAL BENT, WHETHER WE'RE LABELED PART OF THE 1% OR 99 --

-- STRIVING TO DO OUR *BEST*, TO TREAT EACH OTHER WITH *RESPECT* AND *COMPASSION*.

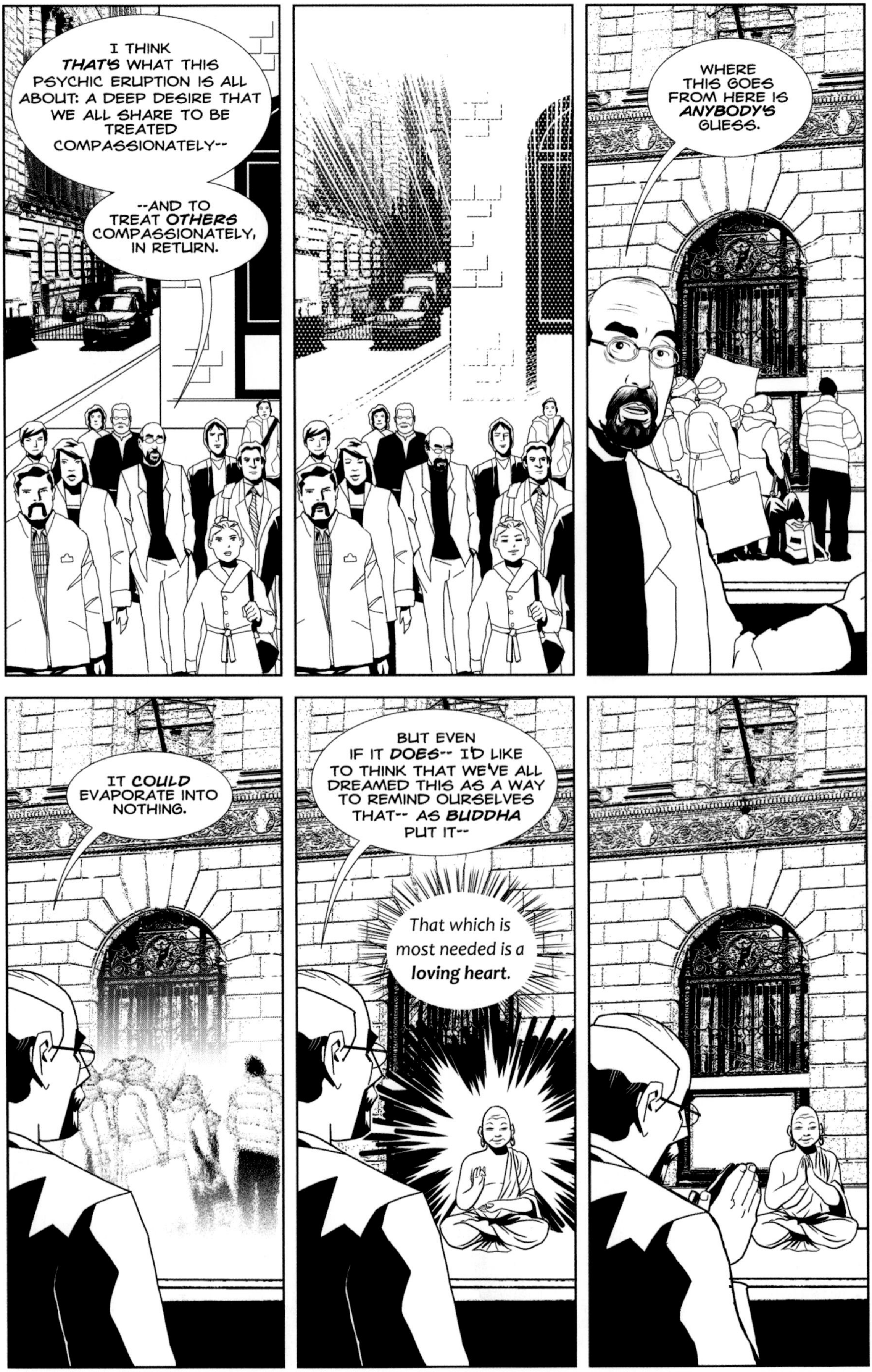
I THINK THAT'S WHAT THIS PSYCHIC ERUPTION IS ALL ABOUT: A DEEP DESIRE THAT WE ALL SHARE TO BE TREATED COMPASSIONATELY--
--AND TO TREAT OTHERS COMPASSIONATELY, IN RETURN.
WHERE THIS GOES FROM HERE IS ANYBODY'S GUESS.
IT COULD EVAPORATE INTO NOTHING.
BUT EVEN IF IT DOES-- I'D LIKE TO THINK THAT WE'VE ALL DREAMED THIS AS A WAY TO REMIND OURSELVES THAT-- AS BUDDHA PUT IT--
That which is most needed is a loving heart.

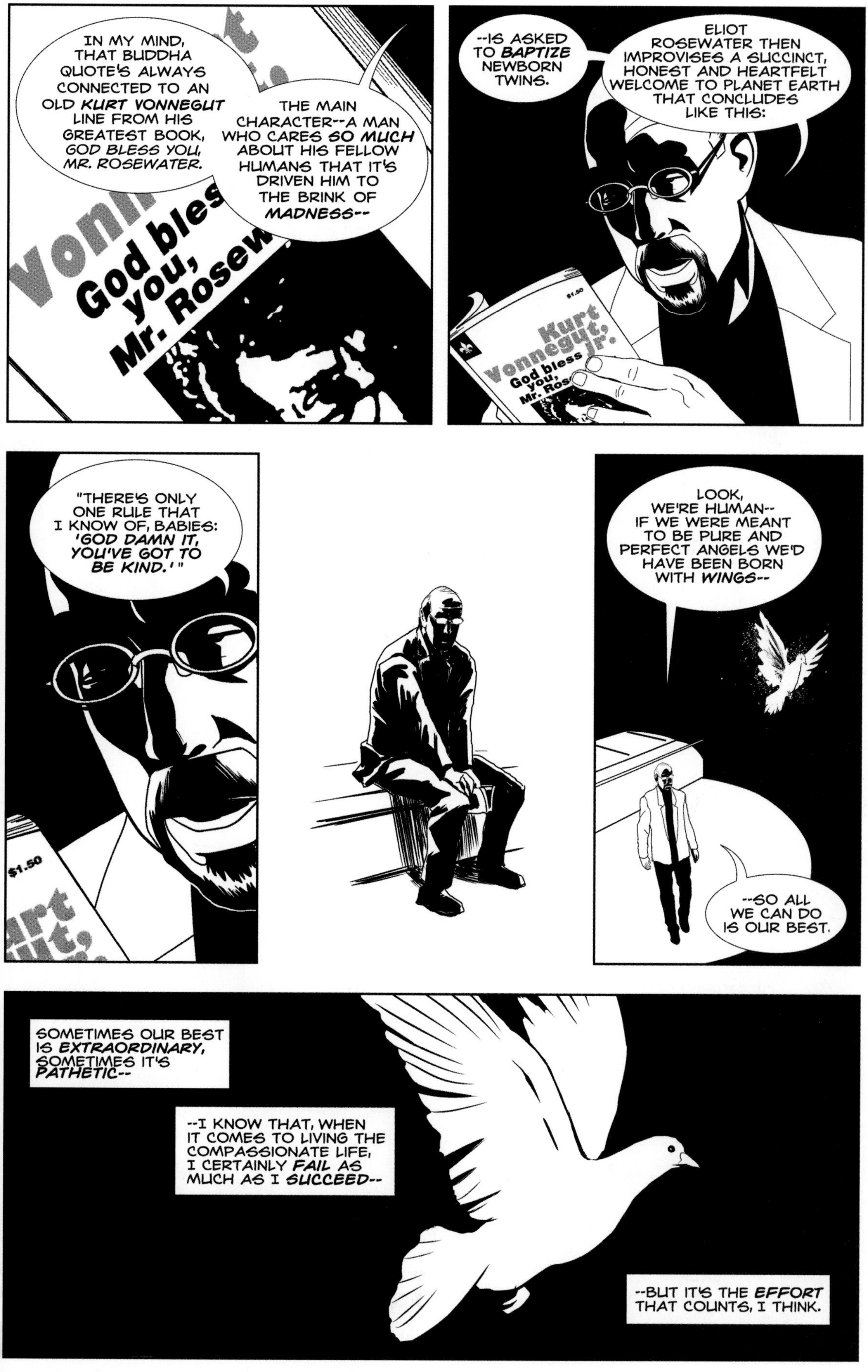

IN MY MIND, THAT BUDDHA QUOTE'S ALWAYS CONNECTED TO AN OLD KURT VONNEGUT LINE FROM HIS GREATEST BOOK, GOD BLESS YOU, MR. ROSEWATER.
THE MAIN CHARACTER--A MAN WHO CARES SO MUCH ABOUT HIS FELLOW HUMANS THAT IT'S DRIVEN HIM TO THE BRINK OF MADNESS--
Vonnegut
God bless you, Mr. Rosew
--IS ASKED TO BAPTIZE NEWBORN TWINS.
ELIOT ROSEWATER THEN IMPROVISES A SUCCINCT, HONEST AND HEARTFELT WELCOME TO PLANET EARTH THAT CONCLUDES LIKE THIS:
$1.50
Kurt Vonnegut, Jr.
God bless you, Mr. Ros
"THERE'S ONLY ONE RULE THAT I KNOW OF, BABIES: 'GOD DAMN IT, YOU'VE GOT TO BE KIND.'"
$1.50
LOOK, WE'RE HUMAN--IF WE WERE MEANT TO BE PURE AND PERFECT ANGELS WE'D HAVE BEEN BORN WITH WINGS--
--SO ALL WE CAN DO IS OUR BEST.
SOMETIMES OUR BEST IS EXTRAORDINARY, SOMETIMES IT'S PATHETIC--
--I KNOW THAT, WHEN IT COMES TO LIVING THE COMPASSIONATE LIFE, I CERTAINLY FAIL AS MUCH AS I SUCCEED--
--BUT IT'S THE EFFORT THAT COUNTS, I THINK.

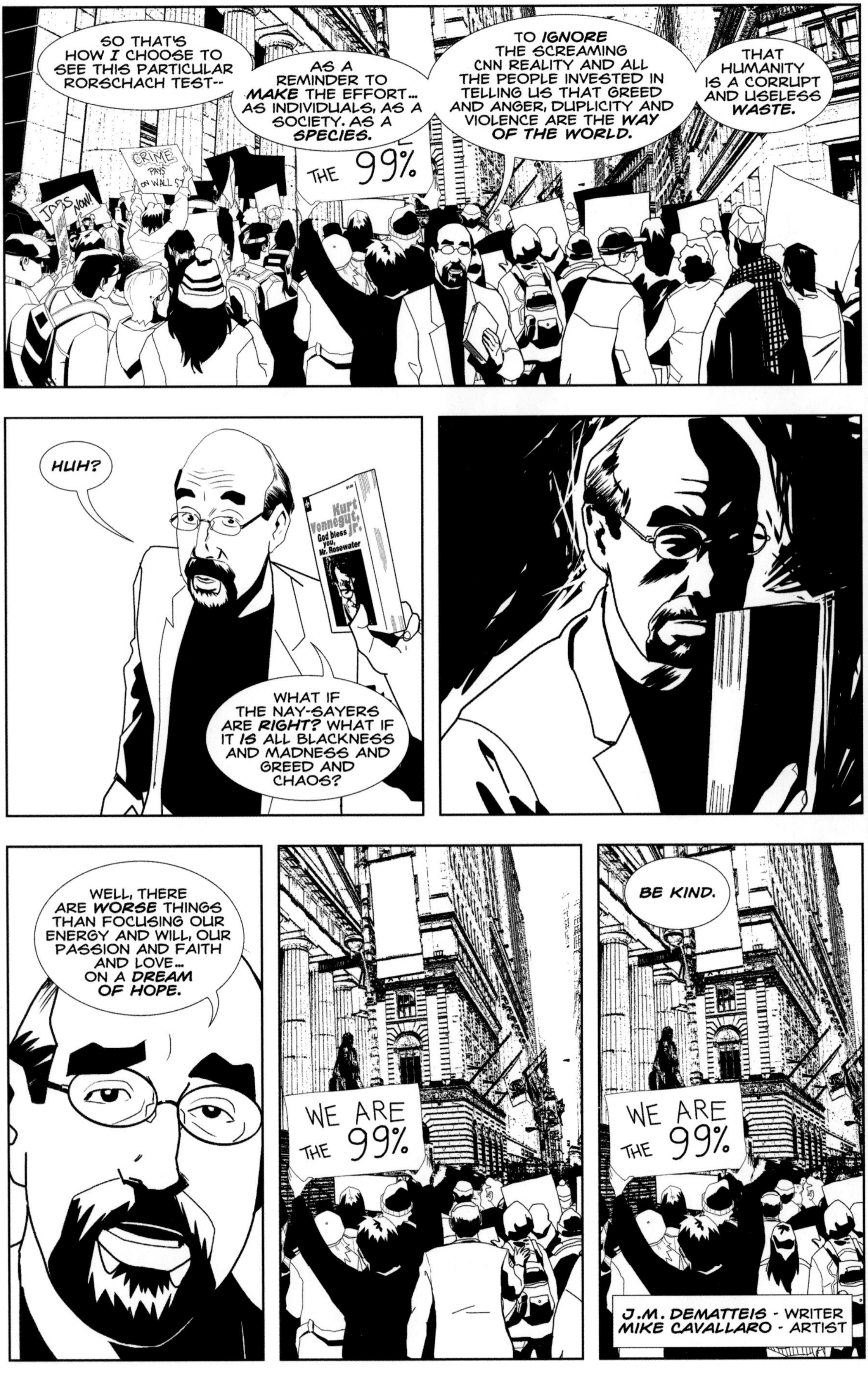

SO THAT'S HOW *I* CHOOSE TO SEE THIS PARTICULAR RORSCHACH TEST--
AS A REMINDER TO *MAKE* THE EFFORT... AS INDIVIDUALS, AS A SOCIETY. AS A *SPECIES.*
TO *IGNORE* THE SCREAMING CNN REALITY AND ALL THE PEOPLE INVESTED IN TELLING US THAT GREED AND ANGER, DUPLICITY AND VIOLENCE ARE THE *WAY OF THE WORLD.*
THAT HUMANITY IS A CORRUPT AND USELESS *WASTE.*
THE 99%
CRIME PAYS ON WALL ST
JOBS NOW!
HUH?
Kurt Vonnegut, Jr.
God bless you, Mr. Rosewater
WHAT IF THE NAY-SAYERS ARE *RIGHT?* WHAT IF IT *IS* ALL BLACKNESS AND MADNESS AND GREED AND CHAOS?
WELL, THERE ARE *WORSE* THINGS THAN FOCUSING OUR ENERGY AND WILL, OUR PASSION AND FAITH AND LOVE... ON A *DREAM OF HOPE.*
WE ARE THE 99%
BE KIND.
WE ARE THE 99%
J.M. DEMATTEIS - WRITER
MIKE CAVALLARO - ARTIST

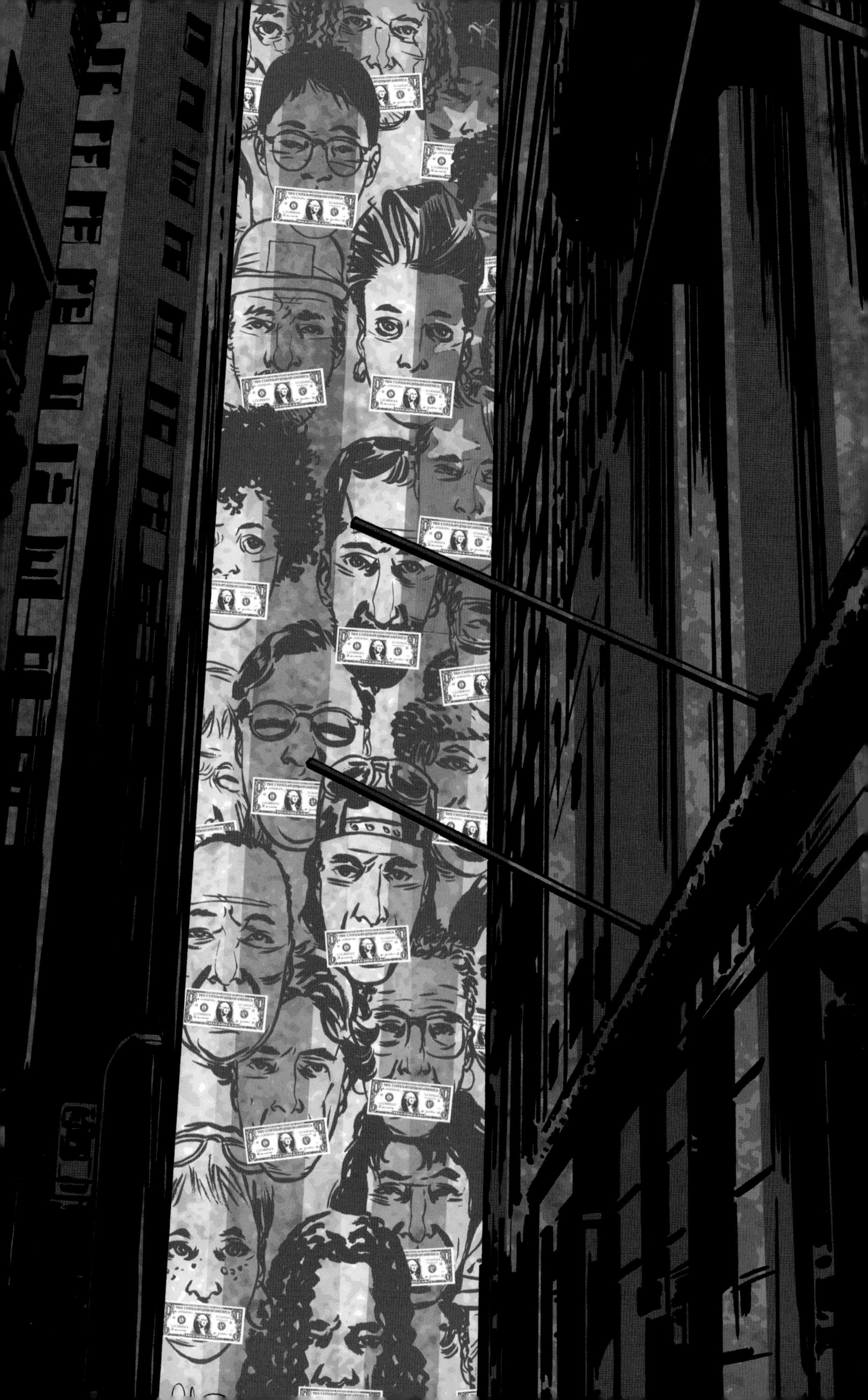

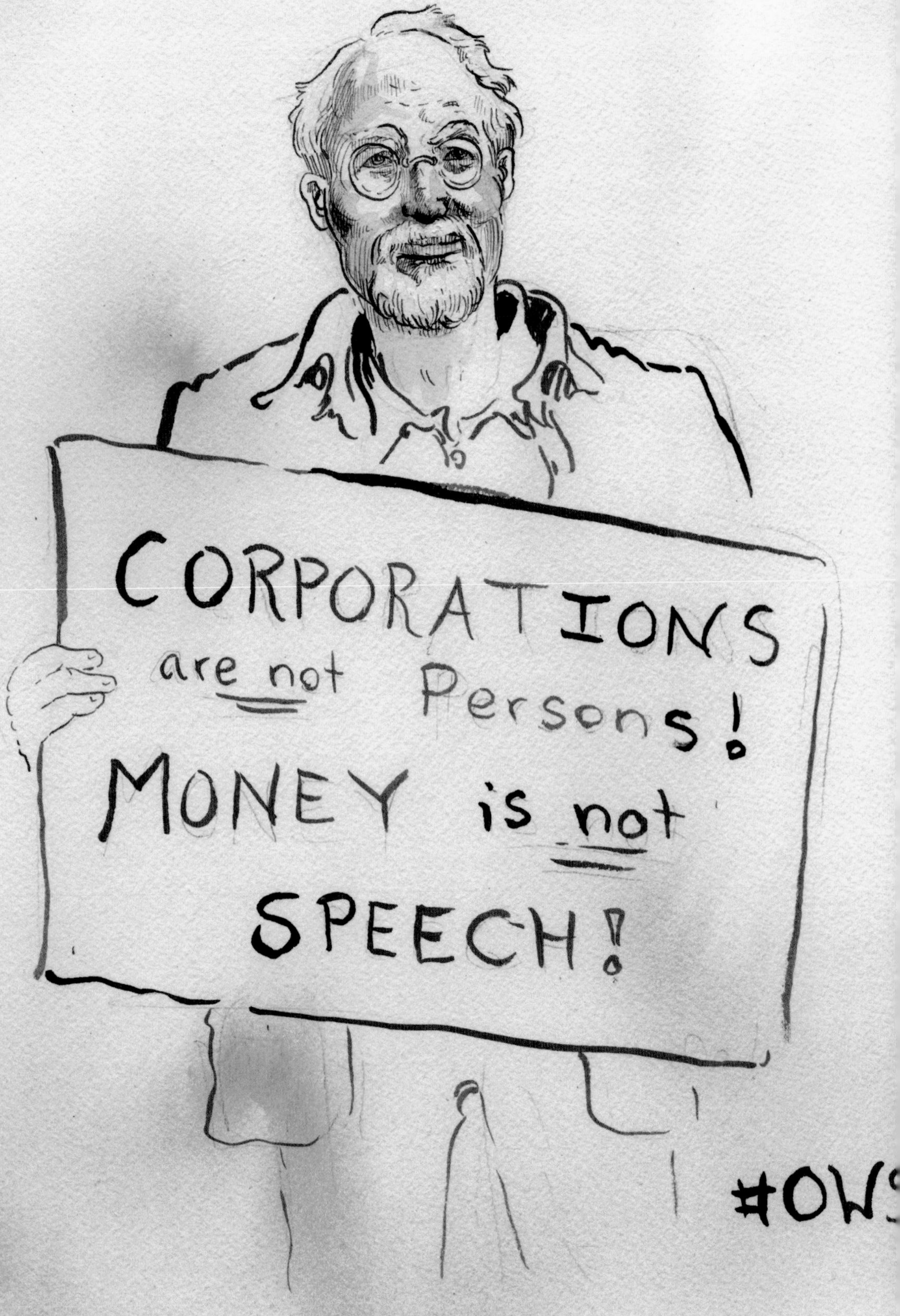

CORPORATIONS
are not Persons!
MONEY is not
SPEECH!
#OWS

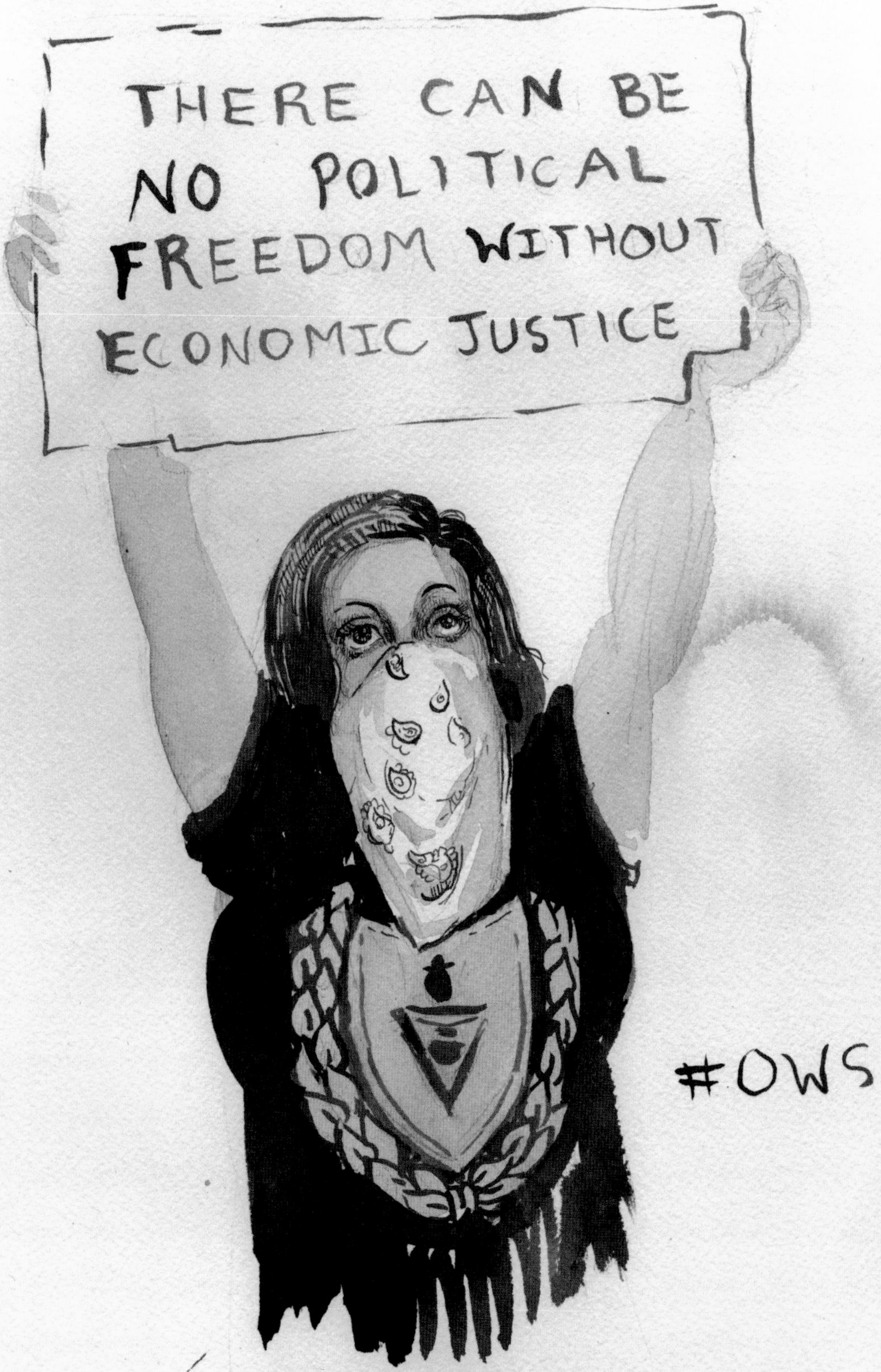
THERE CAN BE NO POLITICAL FREEDOM WITHOUT ECONOMIC JUSTICE
#OWS

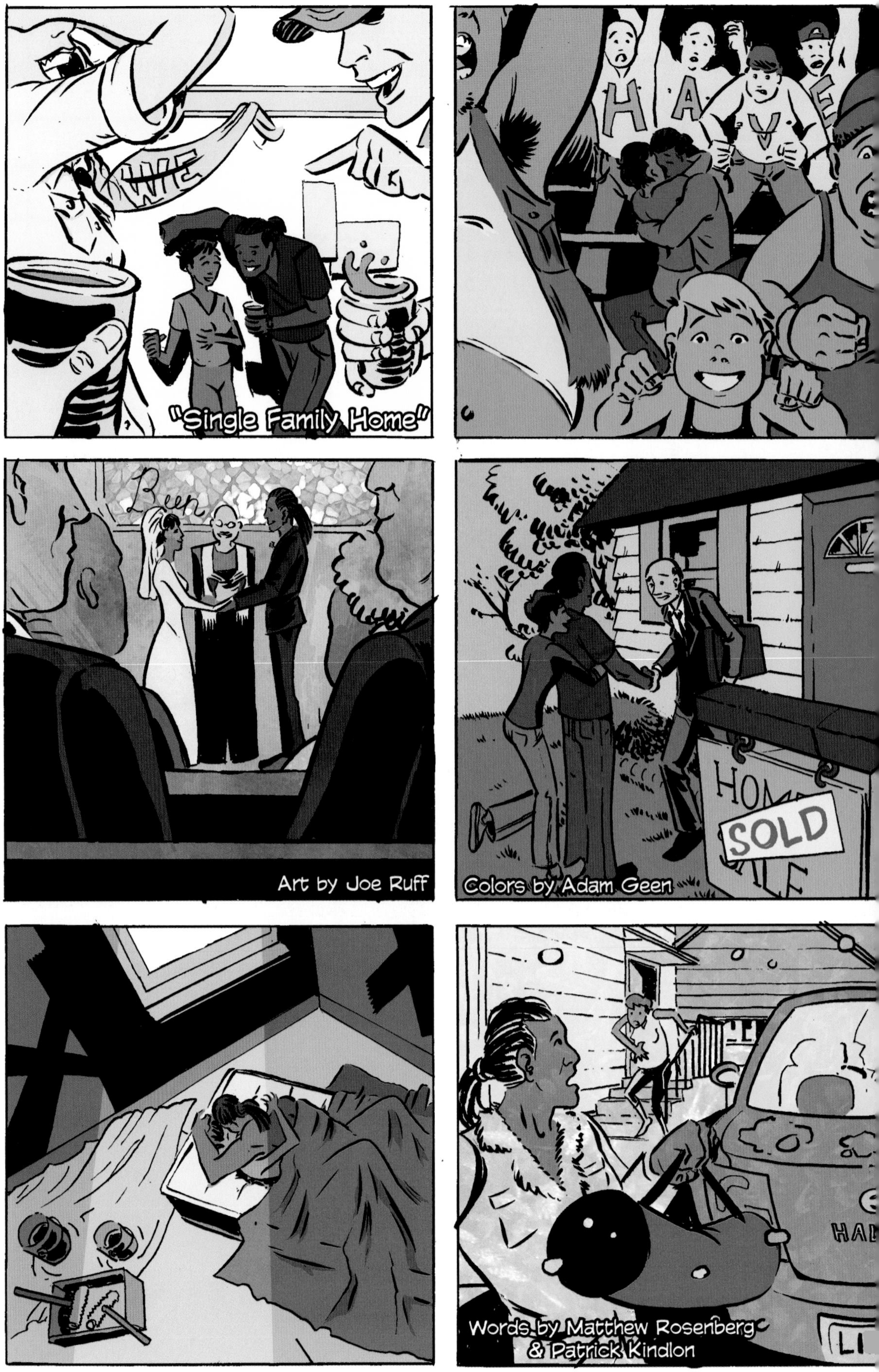
"Single Family Home"
SOLD
Art by Joe Ruff
Colors by Adam Geen
Words by Matthew Rosenberg & Patrick Kindlon

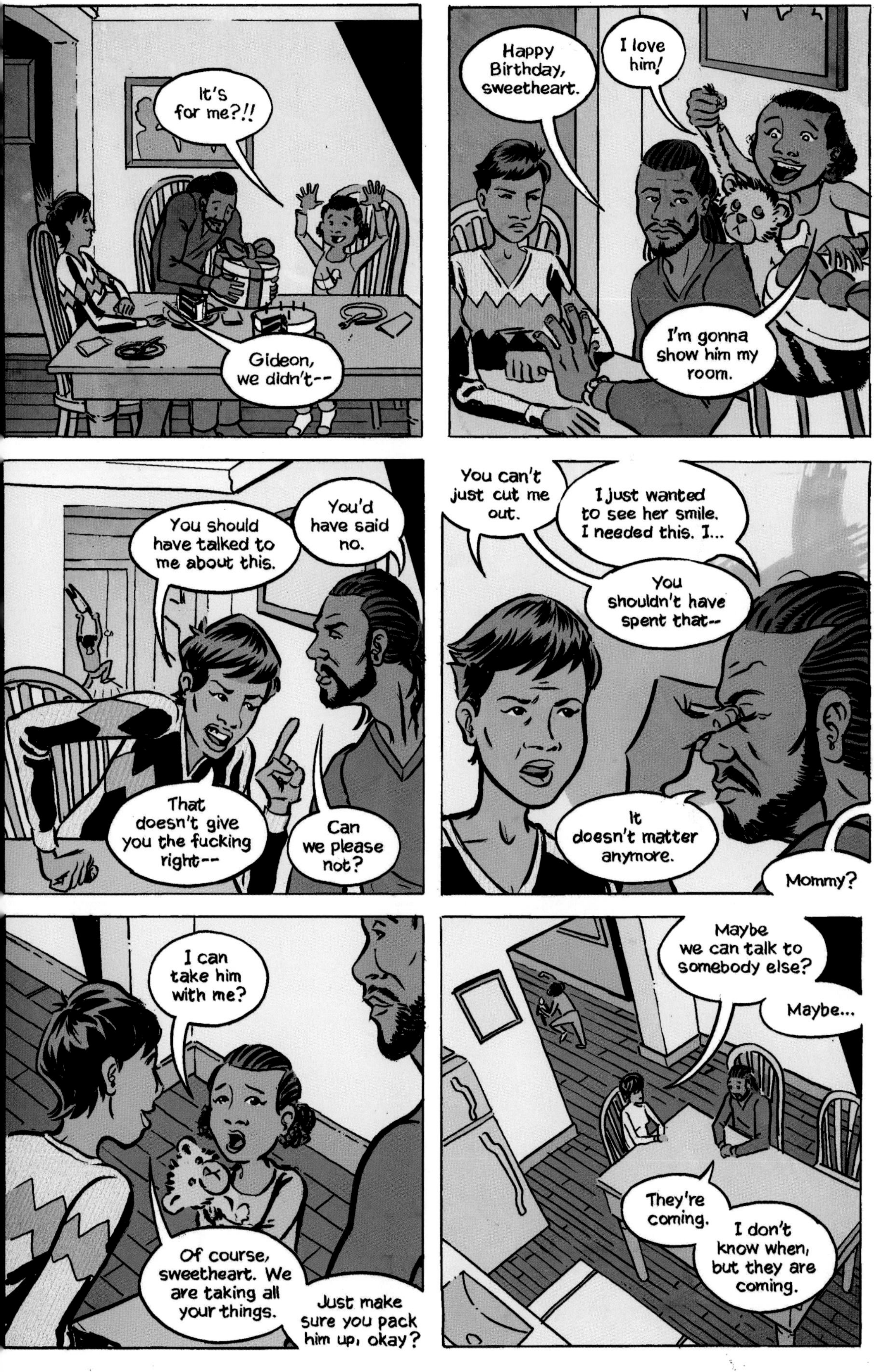
It's for me?!!
Gideon, we didn't--
Happy Birthday, sweetheart.
I love him!
I'm gonna show him my room.
You should have talked to me about this.
You'd have said no.
That doesn't give you the fucking right--
Can we please not?
You can't just cut me out.
I just wanted to see her smile. I needed this. I...
You shouldn't have spent that--
It doesn't matter anymore.
Mommy?
I can take him with me?
Of course, sweetheart. We are taking all your things.
Just make sure you pack him up, okay?
Maybe we can talk to somebody else?
Maybe...
They're coming.
I don't know when, but they are coming.

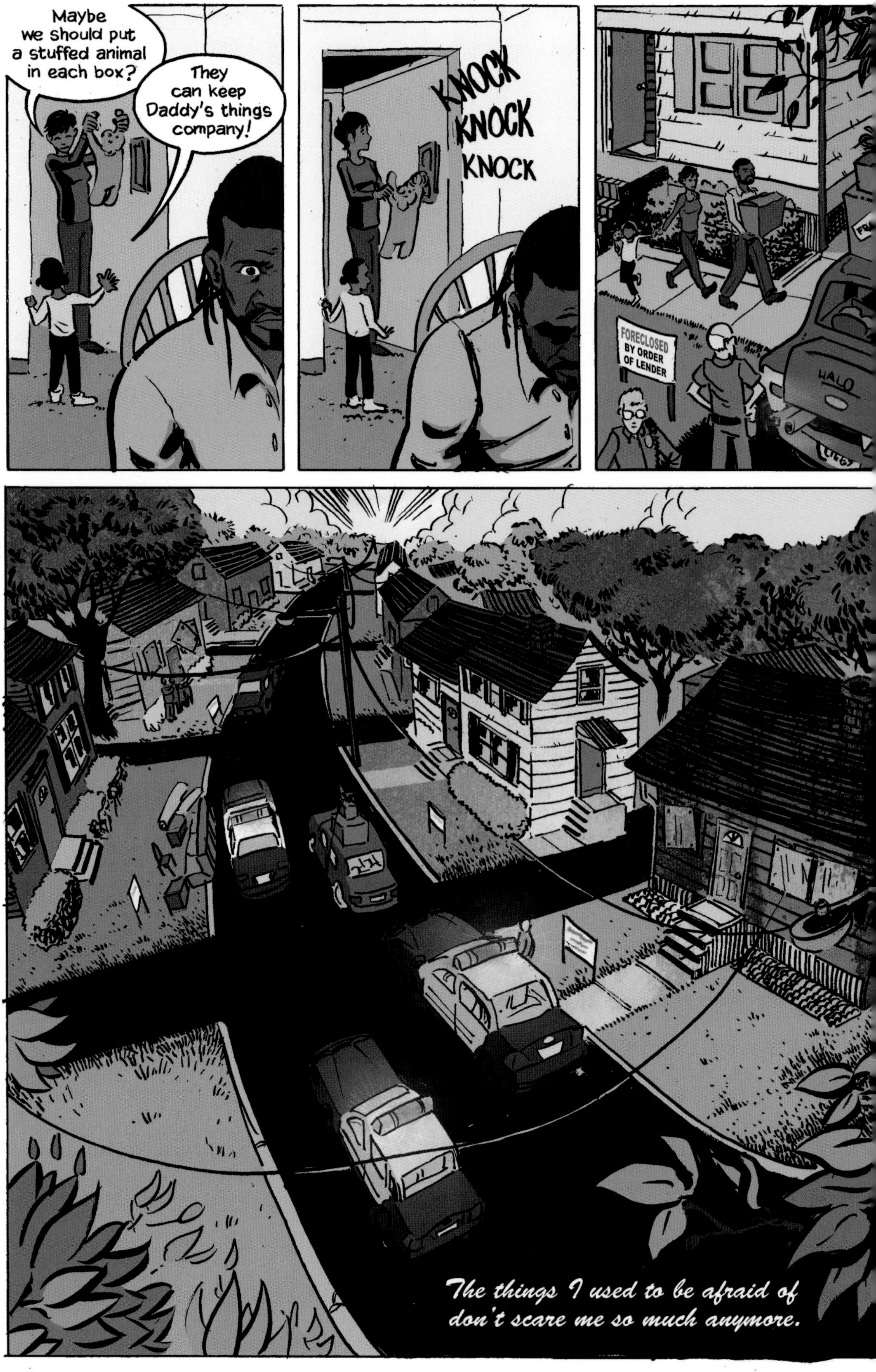
Maybe we should put a stuffed animal in each box?
They can keep Daddy's things company!
KNOCK
KNOCK
KNOCK
FORECLOSED
BY ORDER
OF LENDER
HALO
The things I used to be afraid of don't scare me so much anymore.

EXPLOITATION: OUR NOBLE TRADITION

BY DOUGLAS RUSHKOFF & DEAN HASPIEL

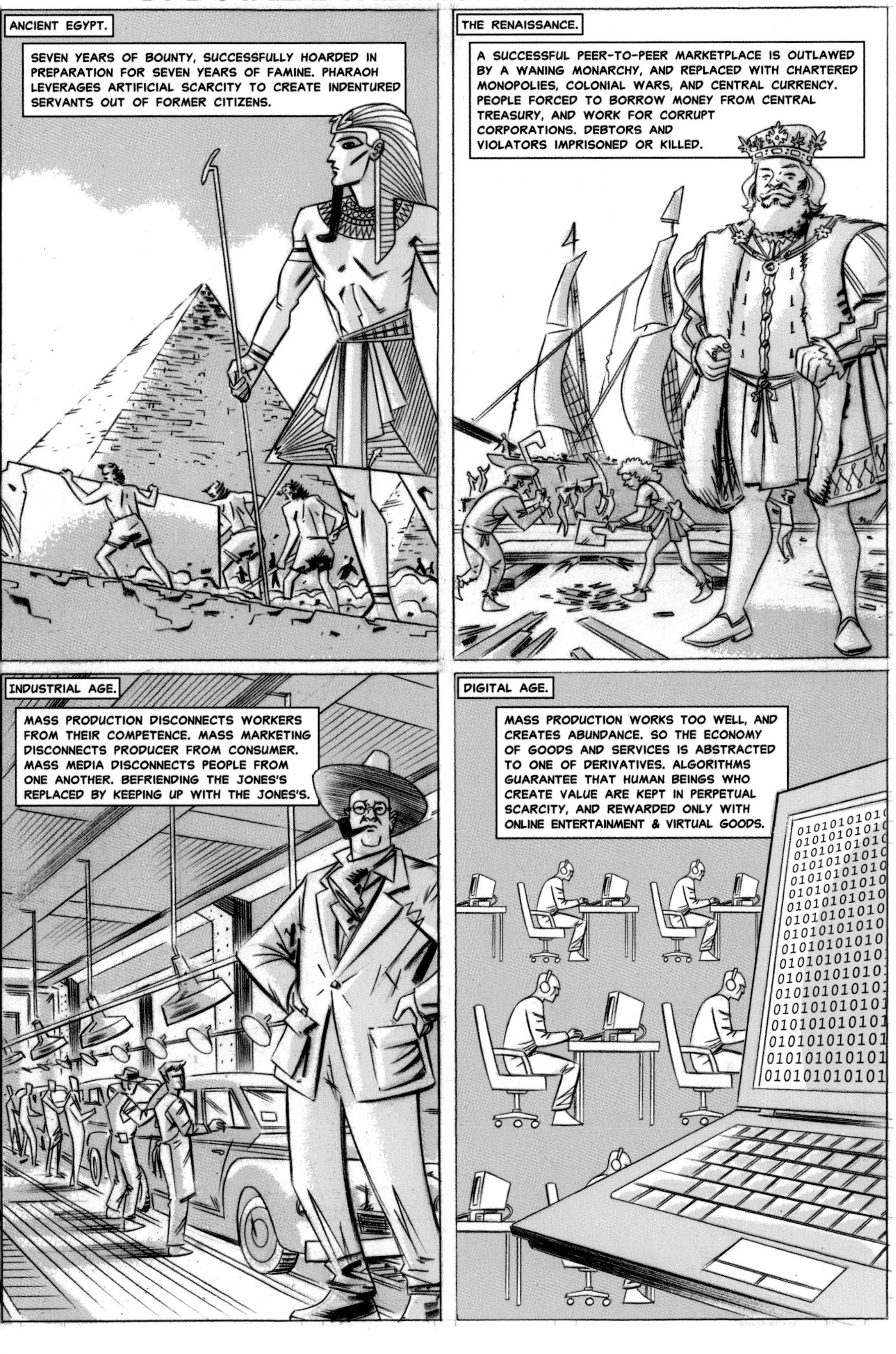
ANCIENT EGYPT.
SEVEN YEARS OF BOUNTY, SUCCESSFULLY HOARDED IN PREPARATION FOR SEVEN YEARS OF FAMINE. PHARAOH LEVERAGES ARTIFICIAL SCARCITY TO CREATE INDENTURED SERVANTS OUT OF FORMER CITIZENS.
THE RENAISSANCE.
A SUCCESSFUL PEER-TO-PEER MARKETPLACE IS OUTLAWED BY A WANING MONARCHY, AND REPLACED WITH CHARTERED MONOPOLIES, COLONIAL WARS, AND CENTRAL CURRENCY. PEOPLE FORCED TO BORROW MONEY FROM CENTRAL TREASURY, AND WORK FOR CORRUPT CORPORATIONS. DEBTORS AND VIOLATORS IMPRISONED OR KILLED.
INDUSTRIAL AGE.
MASS PRODUCTION DISCONNECTS WORKERS FROM THEIR COMPETENCE. MASS MARKETING DISCONNECTS PRODUCER FROM CONSUMER. MASS MEDIA DISCONNECTS PEOPLE FROM ONE ANOTHER. BEFRIENDING THE JONES'S REPLACED BY KEEPING UP WITH THE JONES'S.
DIGITAL AGE.
MASS PRODUCTION WORKS TOO WELL, AND CREATES ABUNDANCE. SO THE ECONOMY OF GOODS AND SERVICES IS ABSTRACTED TO ONE OF DERIVATIVES. ALGORITHMS GUARANTEE THAT HUMAN BEINGS WHO CREATE VALUE ARE KEPT IN PERPETUAL SCARCITY, AND REWARDED ONLY WITH ONLINE ENTERTAINMENT & VIRTUAL GOODS.

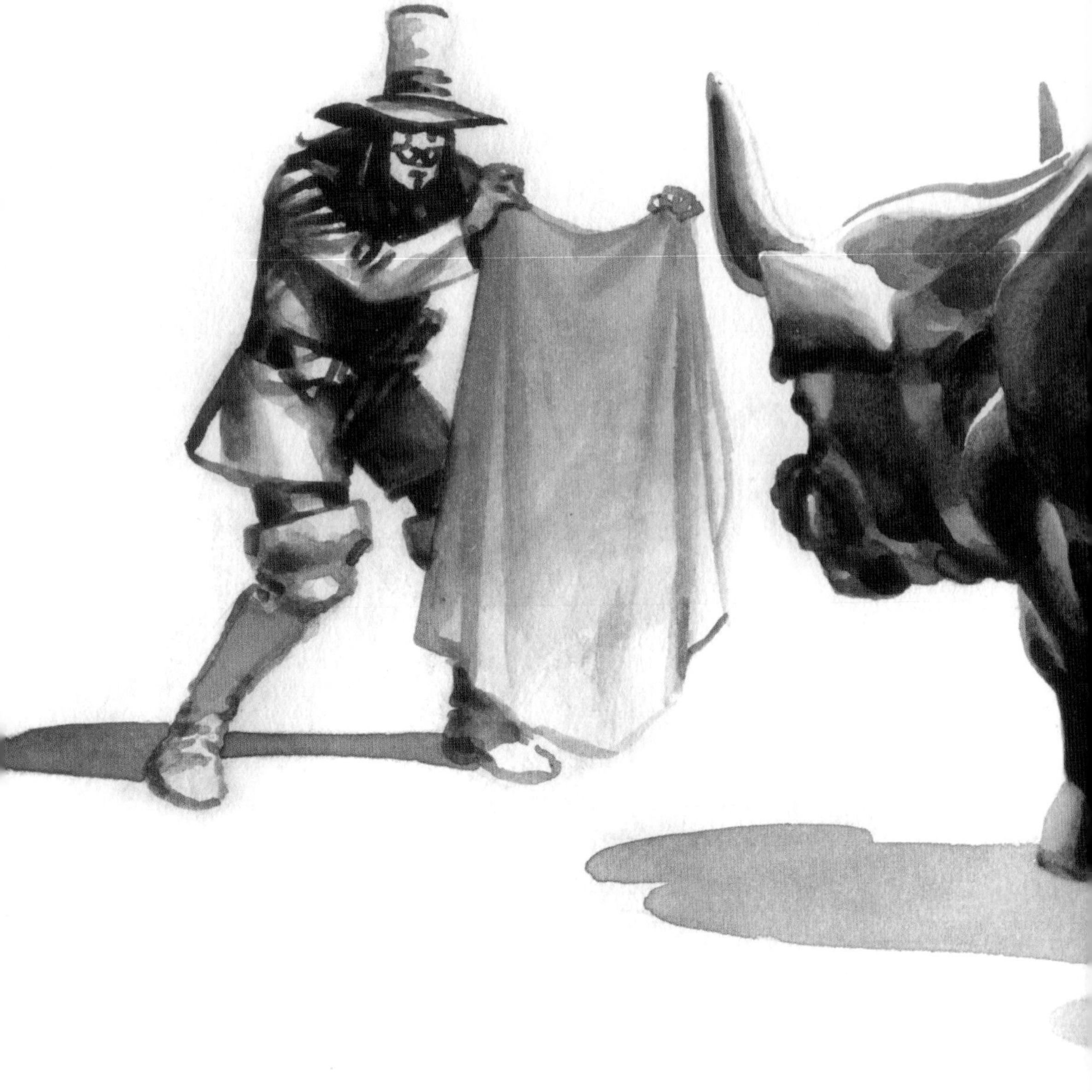

Image originally created in March 2012 to fundraise for the Occupy movement in New York, reprinted here courtesy of David Lloyd.

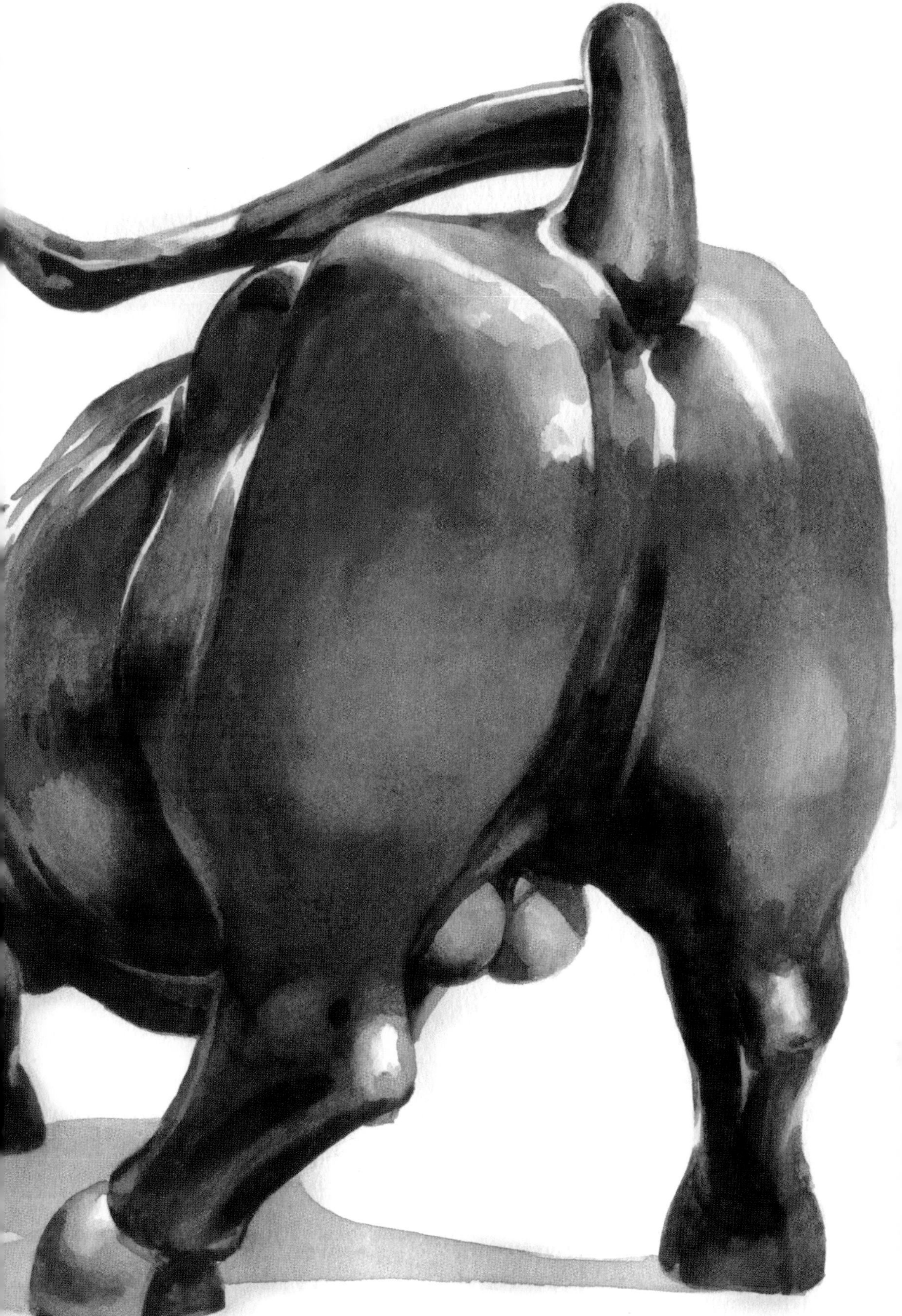

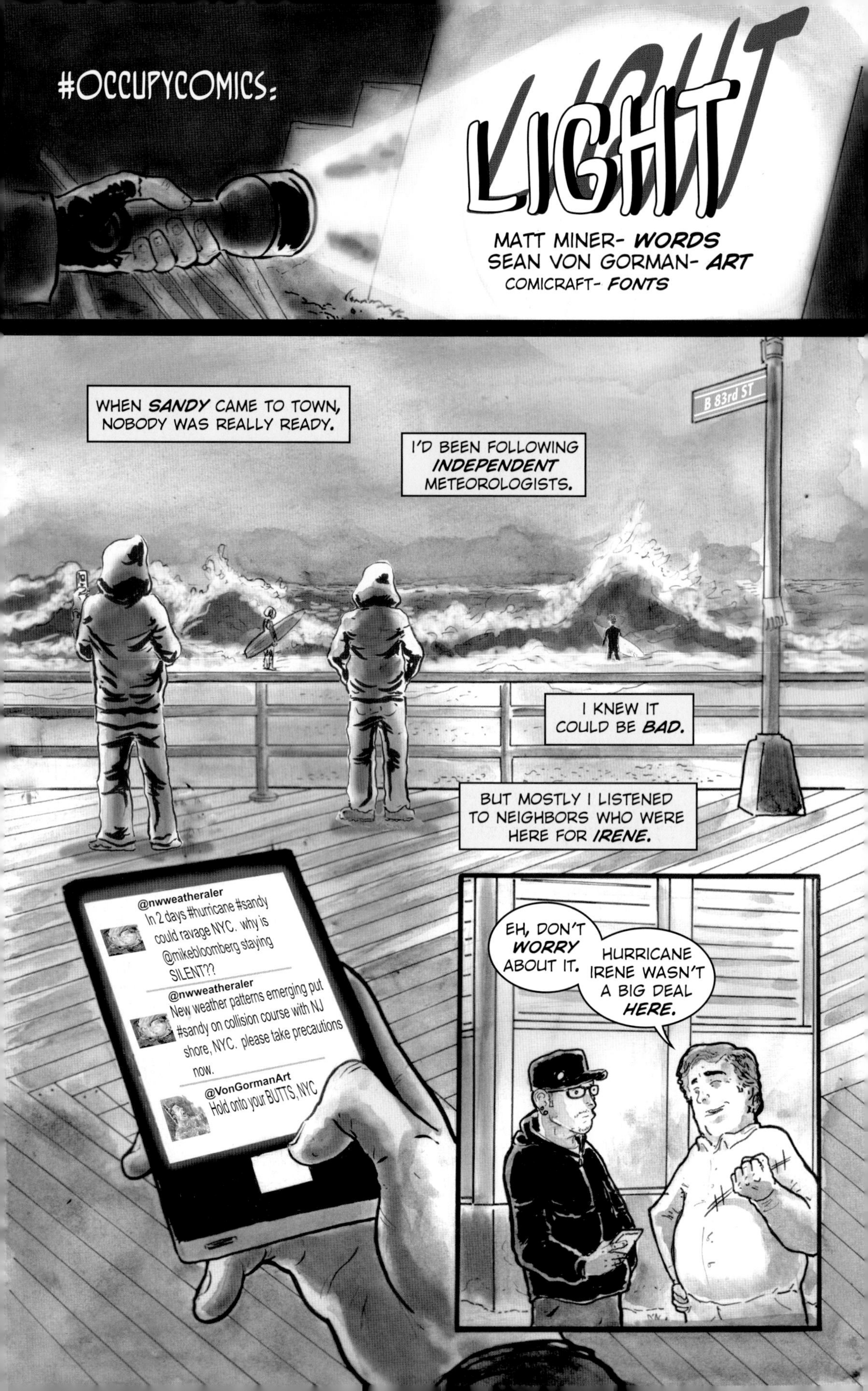
#OCCUPYCOMICS:
LIGHT
MATT MINER- WORDS
SEAN VON GORMAN- ART
COMICRAFT- FONTS
WHEN SANDY CAME TO TOWN, NOBODY WAS REALLY READY.
I'D BEEN FOLLOWING INDEPENDENT METEOROLOGISTS.
B 83rd ST
I KNEW IT COULD BE BAD.
BUT MOSTLY I LISTENED TO NEIGHBORS WHO WERE HERE FOR IRENE.
@nwweatheraler
In 2 days #hurricane #sandy could ravage NYC. why is @mikebloomberg staying SILENT??
@nwweatheraler
New weather patterns emerging put #sandy on collision course with NJ shore, NYC. please take precautions now.
@VonGormanArt
Hold onto your BUTTS, NYC
EH, DON'T WORRY ABOUT IT.
HURRICANE IRENE WASN'T A BIG DEAL HERE.

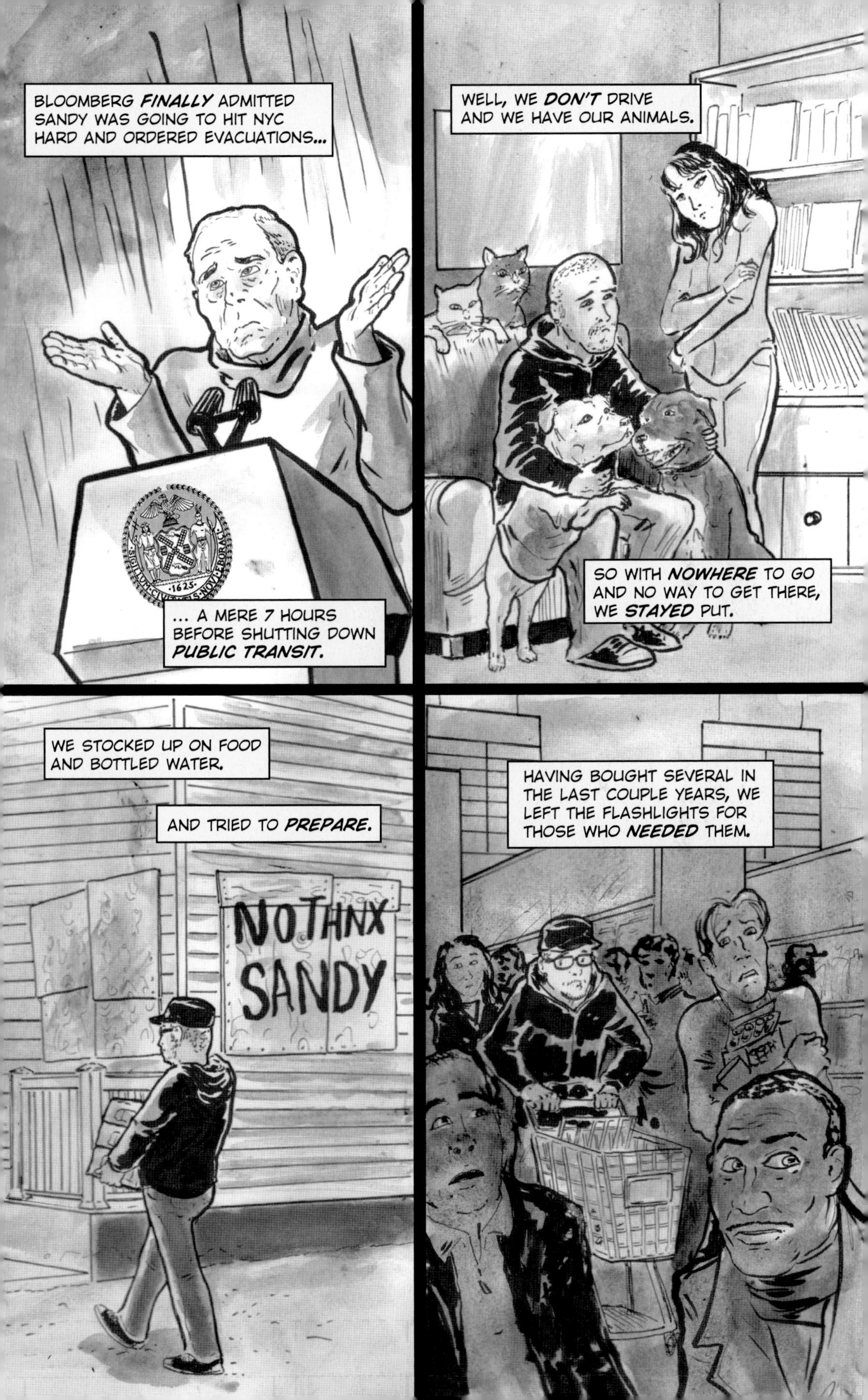
BLOOMBERG *FINALLY* ADMITTED SANDY WAS GOING TO HIT NYC HARD AND ORDERED EVACUATIONS...
... A MERE 7 HOURS BEFORE SHUTTING DOWN *PUBLIC TRANSIT*.
WELL, WE *DON'T* DRIVE AND WE HAVE OUR ANIMALS.
SO WITH *NOWHERE* TO GO AND NO WAY TO GET THERE, WE *STAYED* PUT.
WE STOCKED UP ON FOOD AND BOTTLED WATER.
AND TRIED TO *PREPARE*.
NO THNX SANDY
HAVING BOUGHT SEVERAL IN THE LAST COUPLE YEARS, WE LEFT THE FLASHLIGHTS FOR THOSE WHO *NEEDED* THEM.

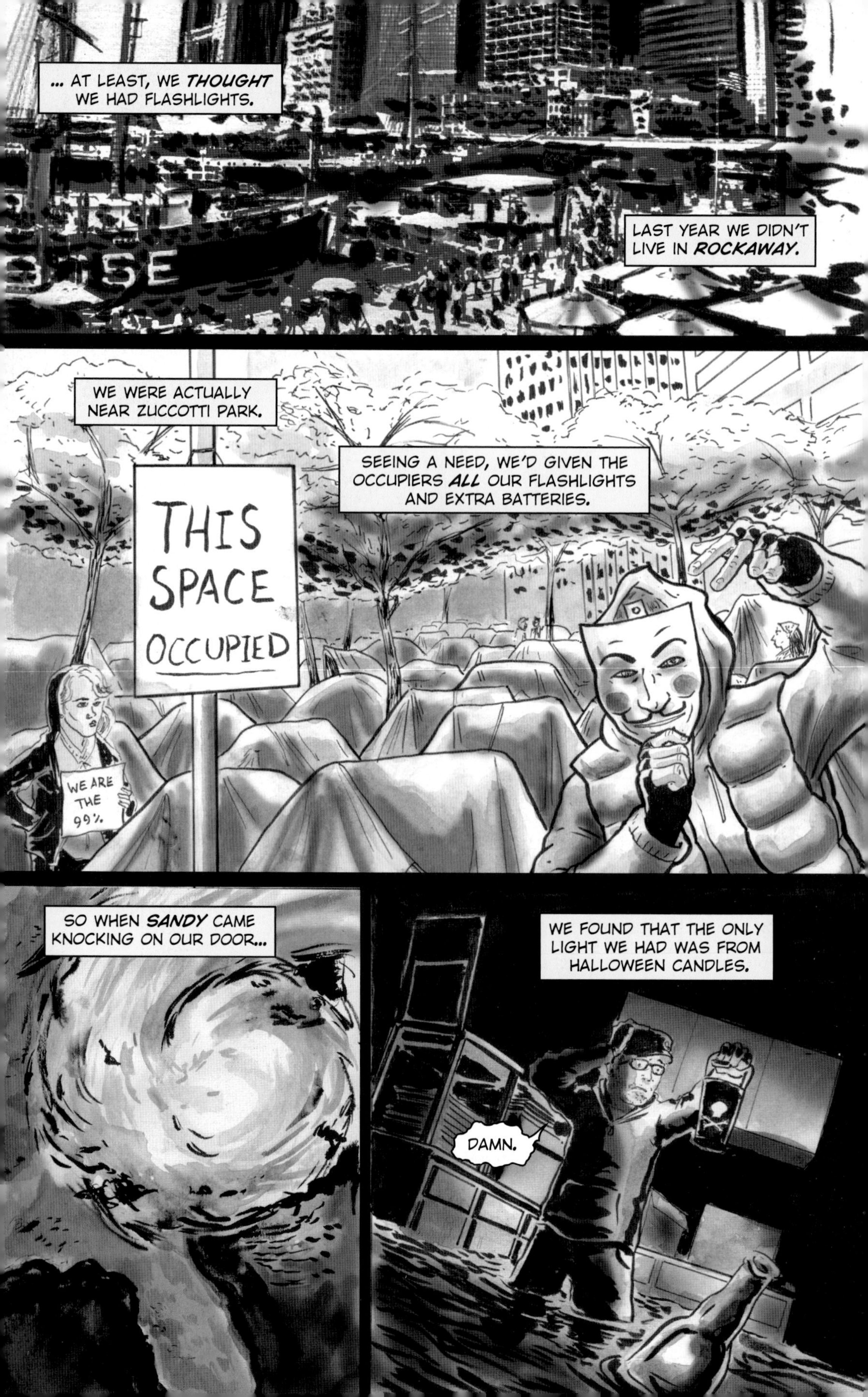
... AT LEAST, WE *THOUGHT* WE HAD FLASHLIGHTS.
LAST YEAR WE DIDN'T LIVE IN *ROCKAWAY.*
WE WERE ACTUALLY NEAR ZUCCOTTI PARK.
SEEING A NEED, WE'D GIVEN THE OCCUPIERS *ALL* OUR FLASHLIGHTS AND EXTRA BATTERIES.
THIS SPACE OCCUPIED
WE ARE THE 99%
SO WHEN *SANDY* CAME KNOCKING ON OUR DOOR...
WE FOUND THAT THE ONLY LIGHT WE HAD WAS FROM HALLOWEEN CANDLES.
DAMN.

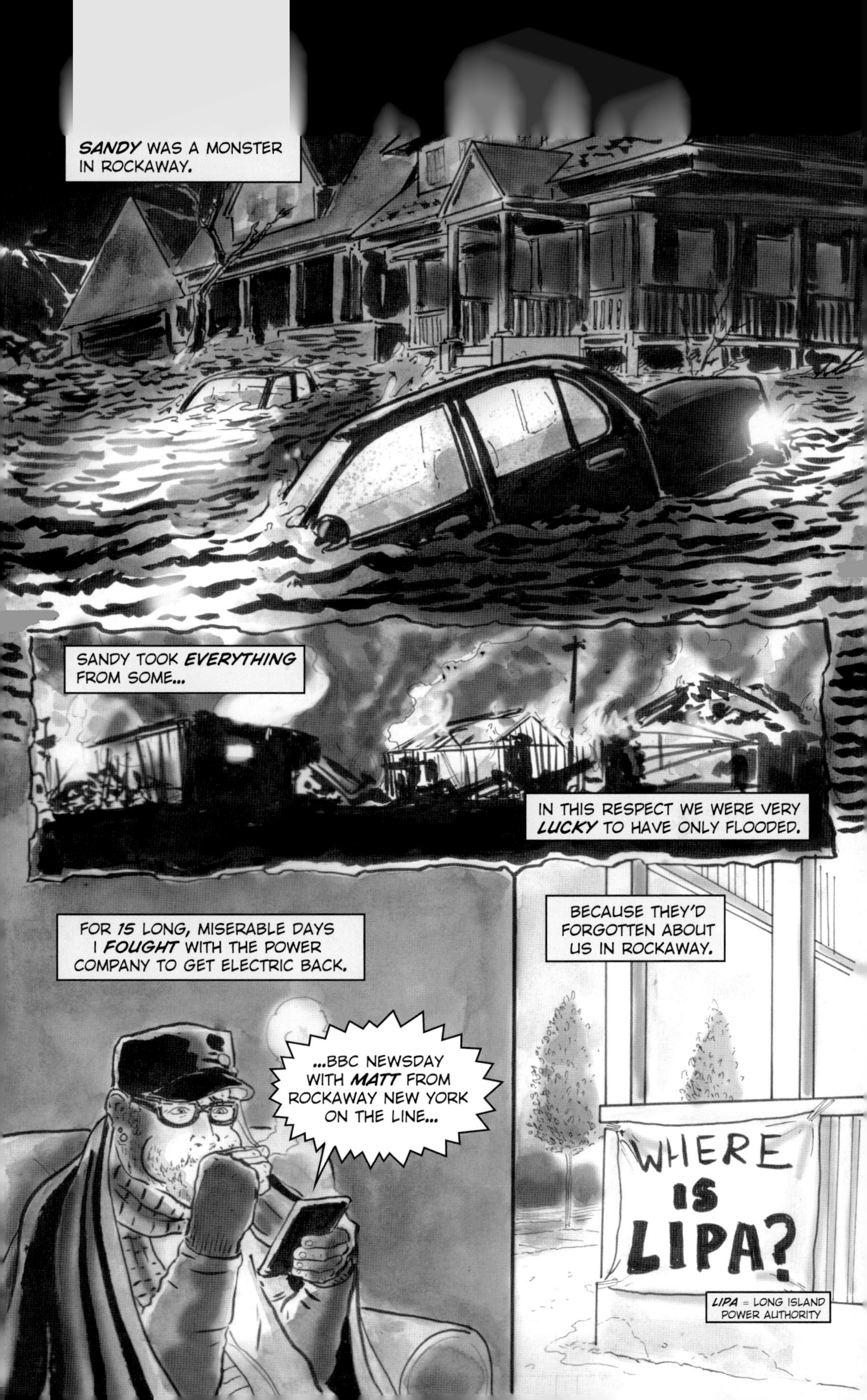
SANDY WAS A MONSTER IN ROCKAWAY.
SANDY TOOK EVERYTHING FROM SOME...
IN THIS RESPECT WE WERE VERY LUCKY TO HAVE ONLY FLOODED.
FOR 15 LONG, MISERABLE DAYS I FOUGHT WITH THE POWER COMPANY TO GET ELECTRIC BACK.
...BBC NEWSDAY WITH MATT FROM ROCKAWAY NEW YORK ON THE LINE...
BECAUSE THEY'D FORGOTTEN ABOUT US IN ROCKAWAY.
WHERE IS LIPA?
LIPA = LONG ISLAND POWER AUTHORITY

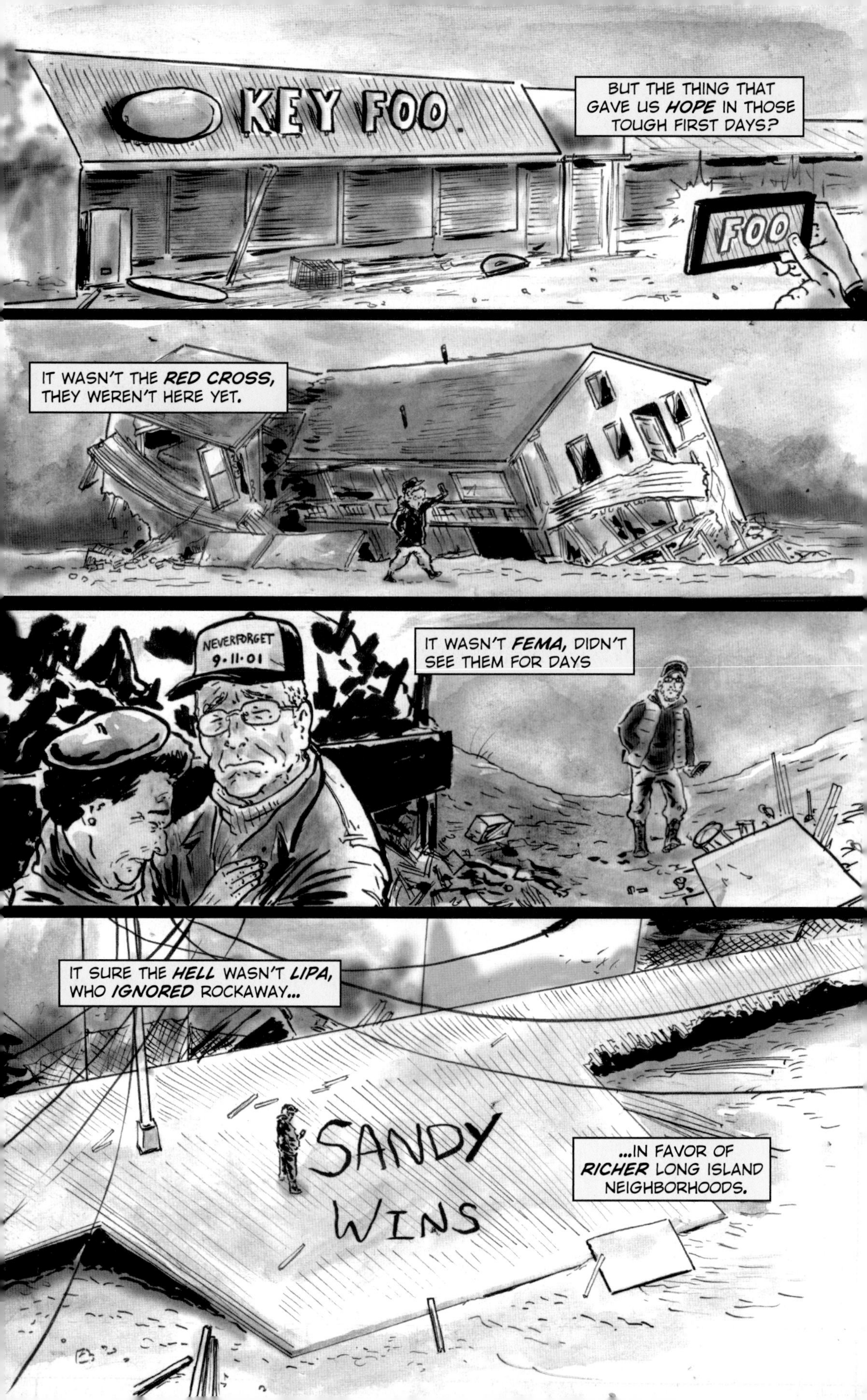
KEY FOO
BUT THE THING THAT GAVE US HOPE IN THOSE TOUGH FIRST DAYS?
FOO
IT WASN'T THE RED CROSS, THEY WEREN'T HERE YET.
NEVERFORGET 9·11·01
IT WASN'T FEMA, DIDN'T SEE THEM FOR DAYS
IT SURE THE HELL WASN'T LIPA, WHO IGNORED ROCKAWAY...
SANDY WINS
...IN FAVOR OF RICHER LONG ISLAND NEIGHBORHOODS.

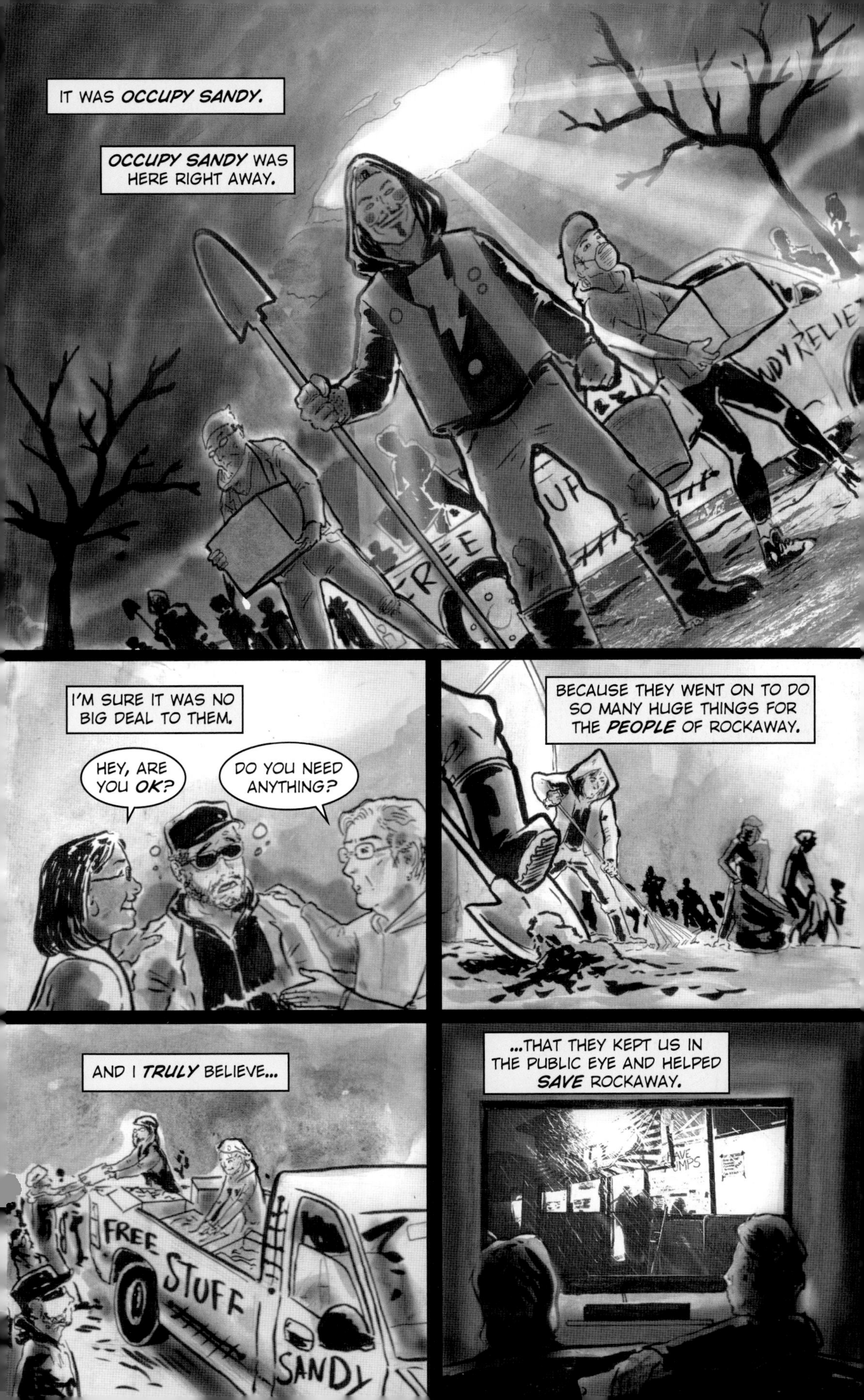
IT WAS *OCCUPY SANDY.*
OCCUPY SANDY WAS HERE RIGHT AWAY.
I'M SURE IT WAS NO BIG DEAL TO THEM.
HEY, ARE YOU *OK?*
DO YOU NEED ANYTHING?
BECAUSE THEY WENT ON TO DO SO MANY HUGE THINGS FOR THE *PEOPLE* OF ROCKAWAY.
AND I *TRULY* BELIEVE...
FREE
STUFF
SANDY
...THAT THEY KEPT US IN THE PUBLIC EYE AND HELPED *SAVE* ROCKAWAY.

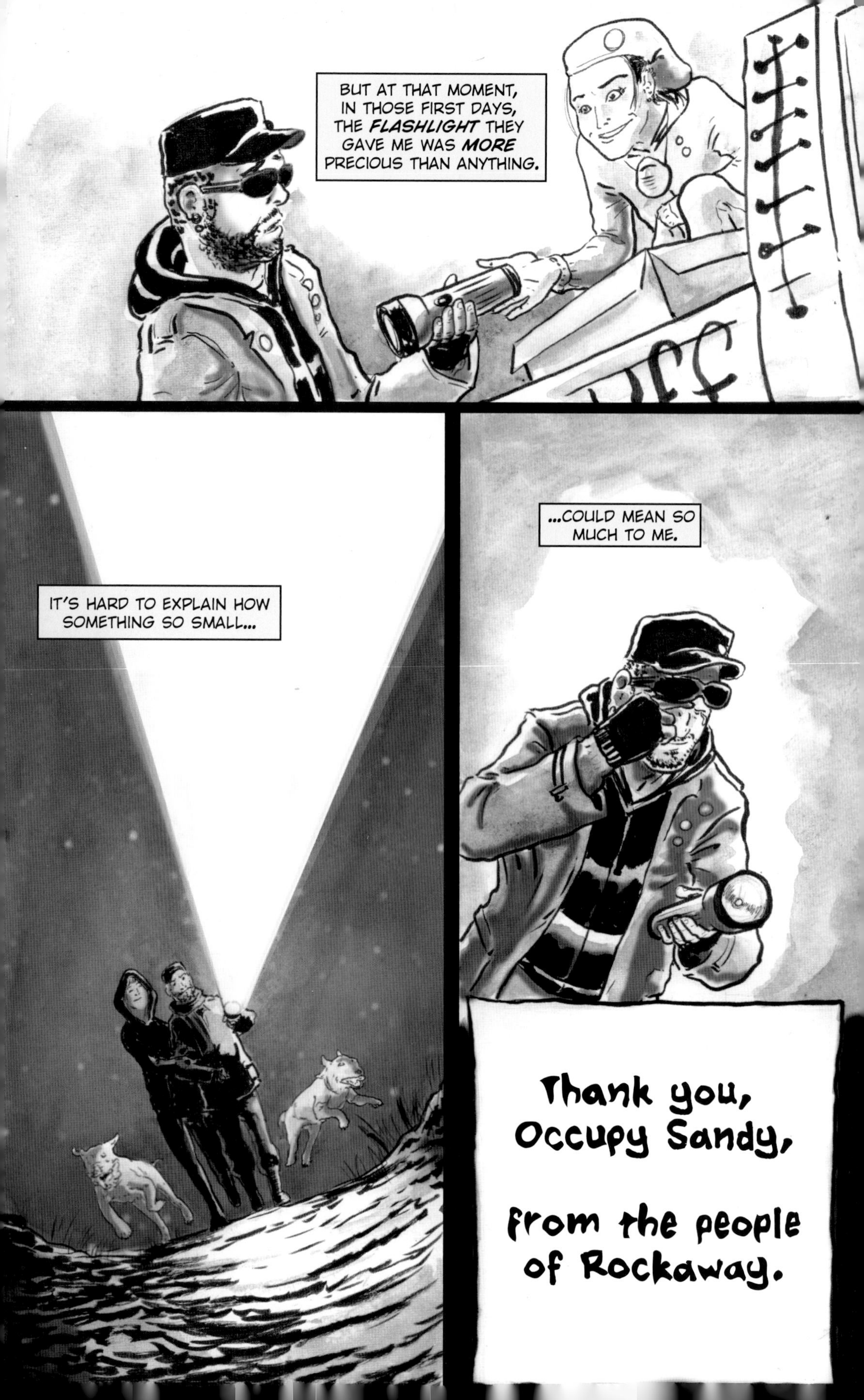
BUT AT THAT MOMENT, IN THOSE FIRST DAYS, THE FLASHLIGHT THEY GAVE ME WAS MORE PRECIOUS THAN ANYTHING.
IT'S HARD TO EXPLAIN HOW SOMETHING SO SMALL...
...COULD MEAN SO MUCH TO ME.
Thank you, Occupy Sandy,
from the people of Rockaway.

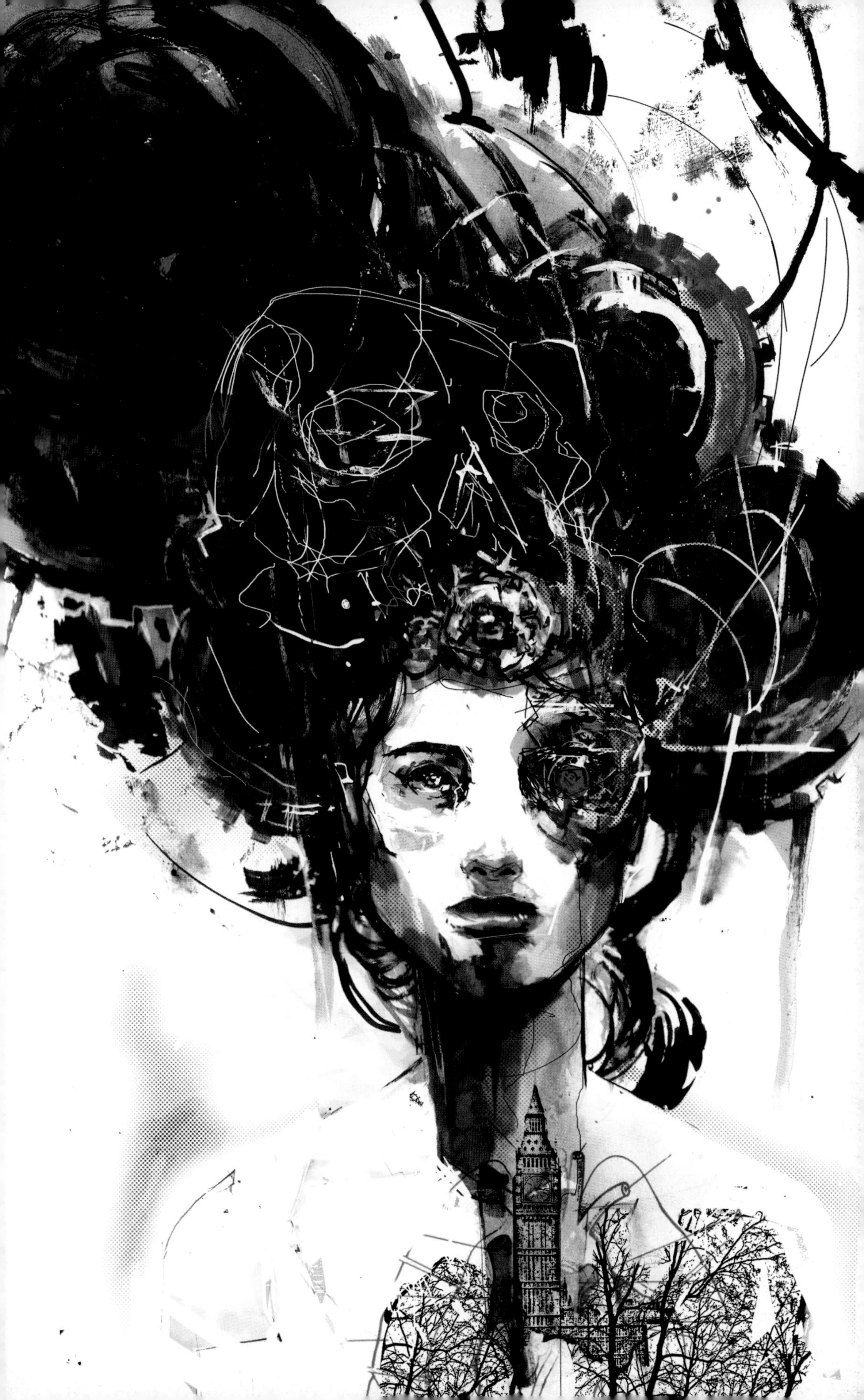

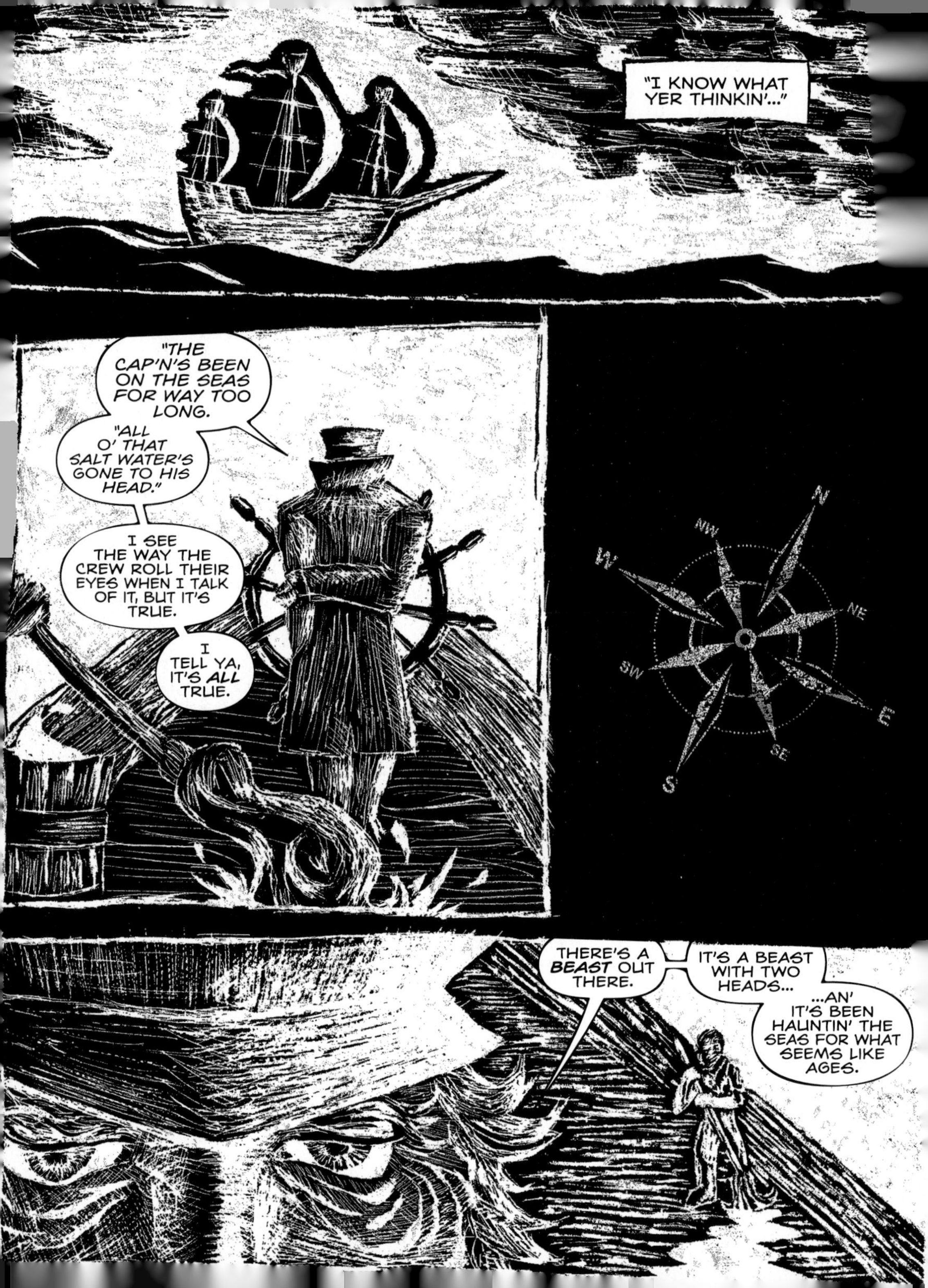
"I KNOW WHAT YER THINKIN'..."
"THE CAP'N'S BEEN ON THE SEAS FOR WAY TOO LONG.
"ALL O' THAT SALT WATER'S GONE TO HIS HEAD."
I SEE THE WAY THE CREW ROLL THEIR EYES WHEN I TALK OF IT, BUT IT'S TRUE.
I TELL YA, IT'S *ALL* TRUE.
N
NW
W
NE
SW
E
SE
S
THERE'S A *BEAST* OUT THERE.
IT'S A BEAST WITH TWO HEADS...
...AN' IT'S BEEN HAUNTIN' THE SEAS FOR WHAT SEEMS LIKE AGES.

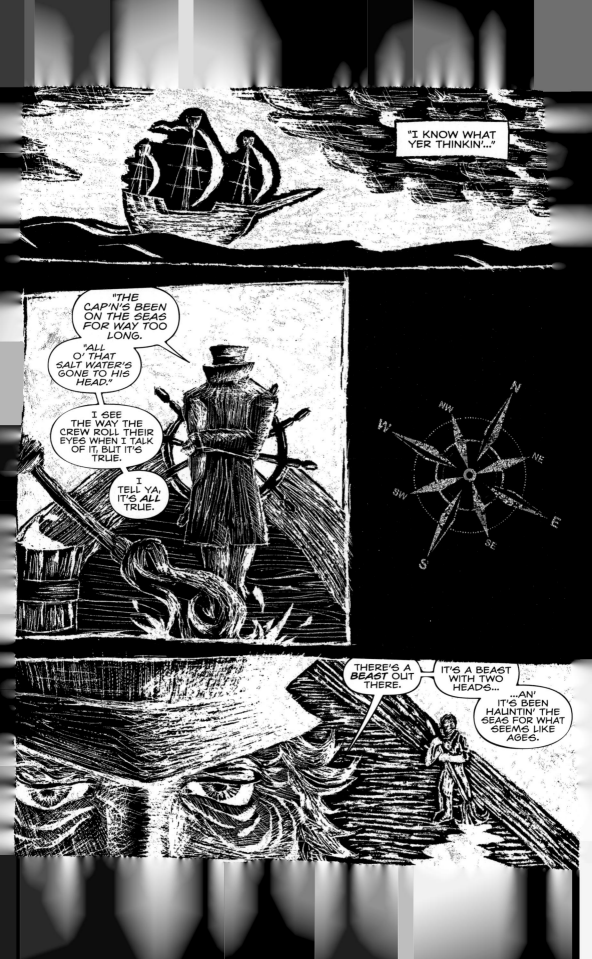

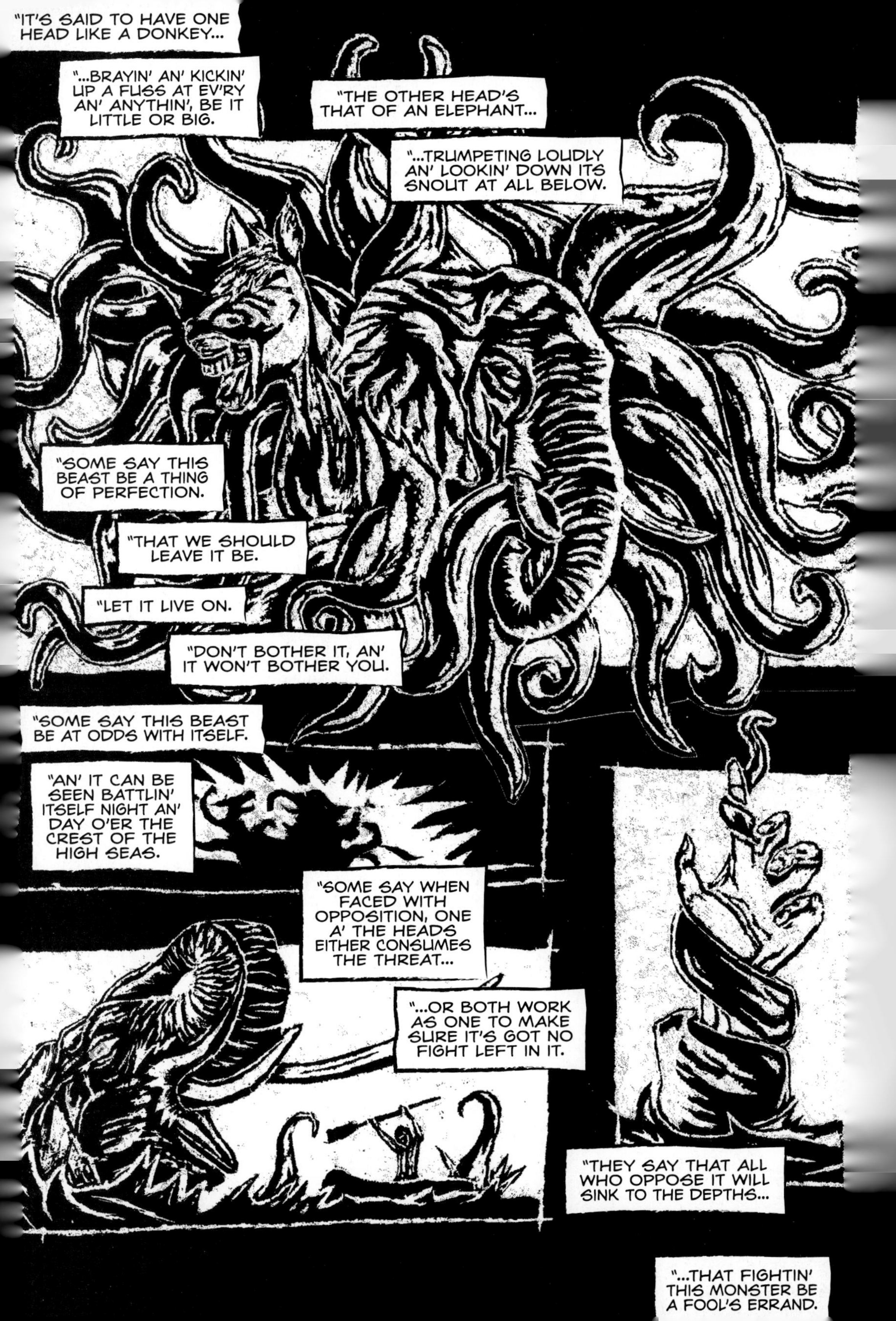

"IT'S SAID TO HAVE ONE HEAD LIKE A DONKEY...
"...BRAYIN' AN' KICKIN' UP A FUSS AT EV'RY AN' ANYTHIN', BE IT LITTLE OR BIG.
"THE OTHER HEAD'S THAT OF AN ELEPHANT...
"...TRUMPETING LOUDLY AN' LOOKIN' DOWN ITS SNOUT AT ALL BELOW.
"SOME SAY THIS BEAST BE A THING OF PERFECTION.
"THAT WE SHOULD LEAVE IT BE.
"LET IT LIVE ON.
"DON'T BOTHER IT, AN' IT WON'T BOTHER YOU.
"SOME SAY THIS BEAST BE AT ODDS WITH ITSELF.
"AN' IT CAN BE SEEN BATTLIN' ITSELF NIGHT AN' DAY O'ER THE CREST OF THE HIGH SEAS.
"SOME SAY WHEN FACED WITH OPPOSITION, ONE A' THE HEADS EITHER CONSUMES THE THREAT...
"...OR BOTH WORK AS ONE TO MAKE SURE IT'S GOT NO FIGHT LEFT IN IT.
"THEY SAY THAT ALL WHO OPPOSE IT WILL SINK TO THE DEPTHS...
"...THAT FIGHTIN' THIS MONSTER BE A FOOL'S ERRAND.

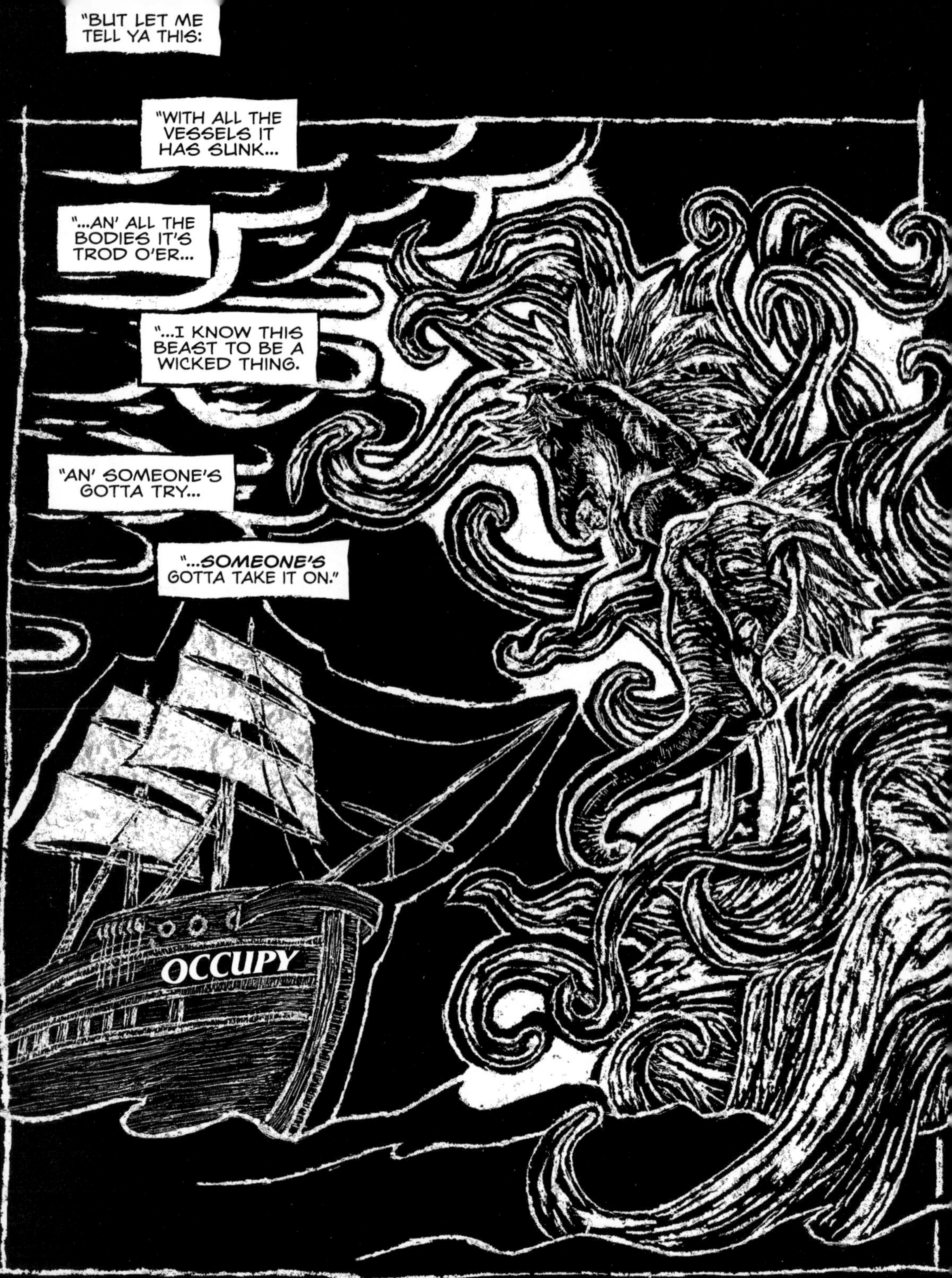
"BUT LET ME TELL YA THIS:
"WITH ALL THE VESSELS IT HAS SUNK...
"...AN' ALL THE BODIES IT'S TROD O'ER...
"...I KNOW THIS BEAST TO BE A WICKED THING.
"AN' SOMEONE'S GOTTA TRY...
"...*SOMEONE'S* GOTTA TAKE IT ON."
OCCUPY

OCCUPY

WORDS & ART BY
MARK L. MILLER

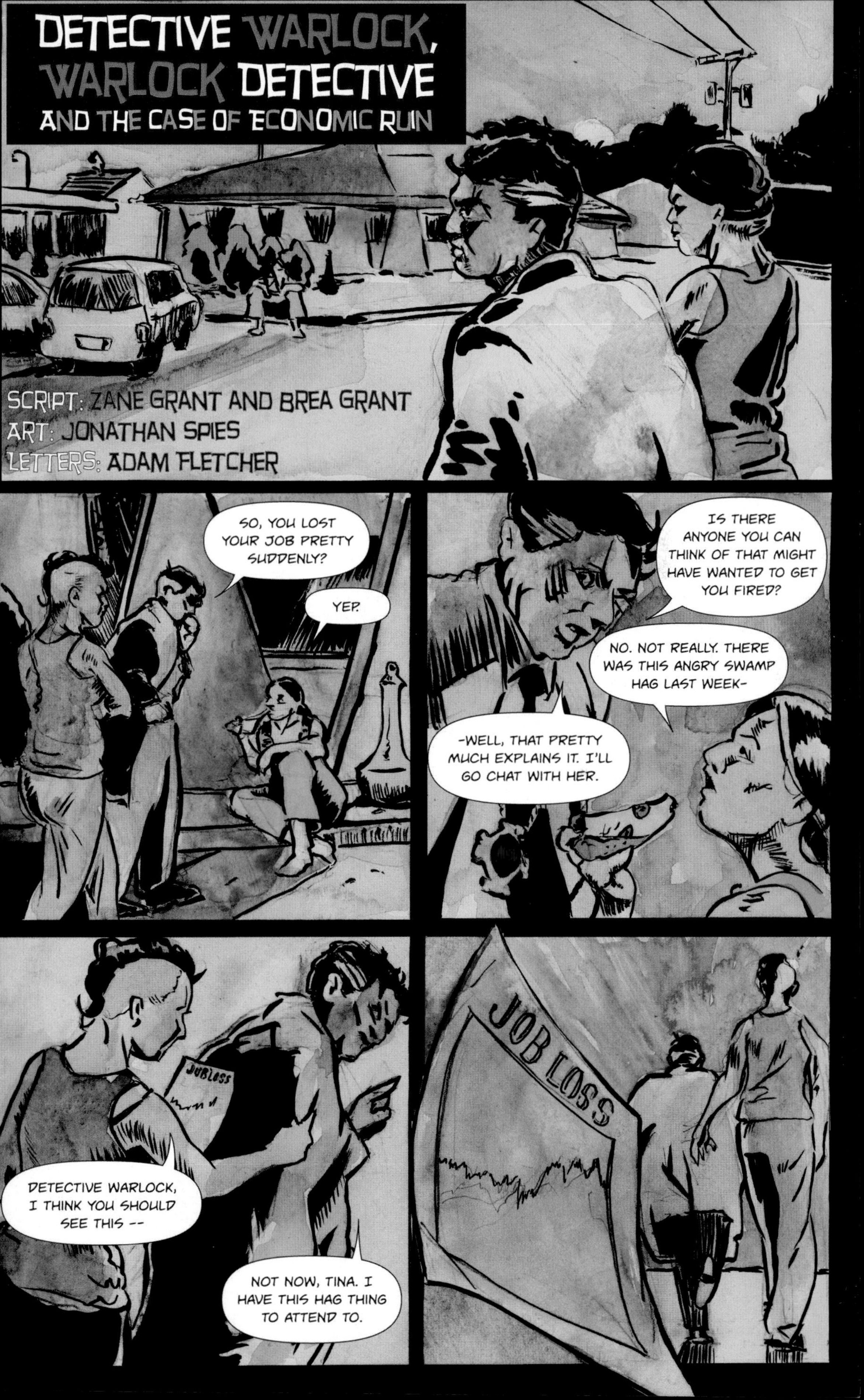
DETECTIVE WARLOCK, WARLOCK DETECTIVE
AND THE CASE OF ECONOMIC RUIN
SCRIPT: ZANE GRANT AND BREA GRANT
ART: JONATHAN SPIES
LETTERS: ADAM FLETCHER
SO, YOU LOST YOUR JOB PRETTY SUDDENLY?
YEP.
IS THERE ANYONE YOU CAN THINK OF THAT MIGHT HAVE WANTED TO GET YOU FIRED?
NO. NOT REALLY. THERE WAS THIS ANGRY SWAMP HAG LAST WEEK-
-WELL, THAT PRETTY MUCH EXPLAINS IT. I'LL GO CHAT WITH HER.
DETECTIVE WARLOCK, I THINK YOU SHOULD SEE THIS --
NOT NOW, TINA. I HAVE THIS HAG THING TO ATTEND TO.
JOB LOSS

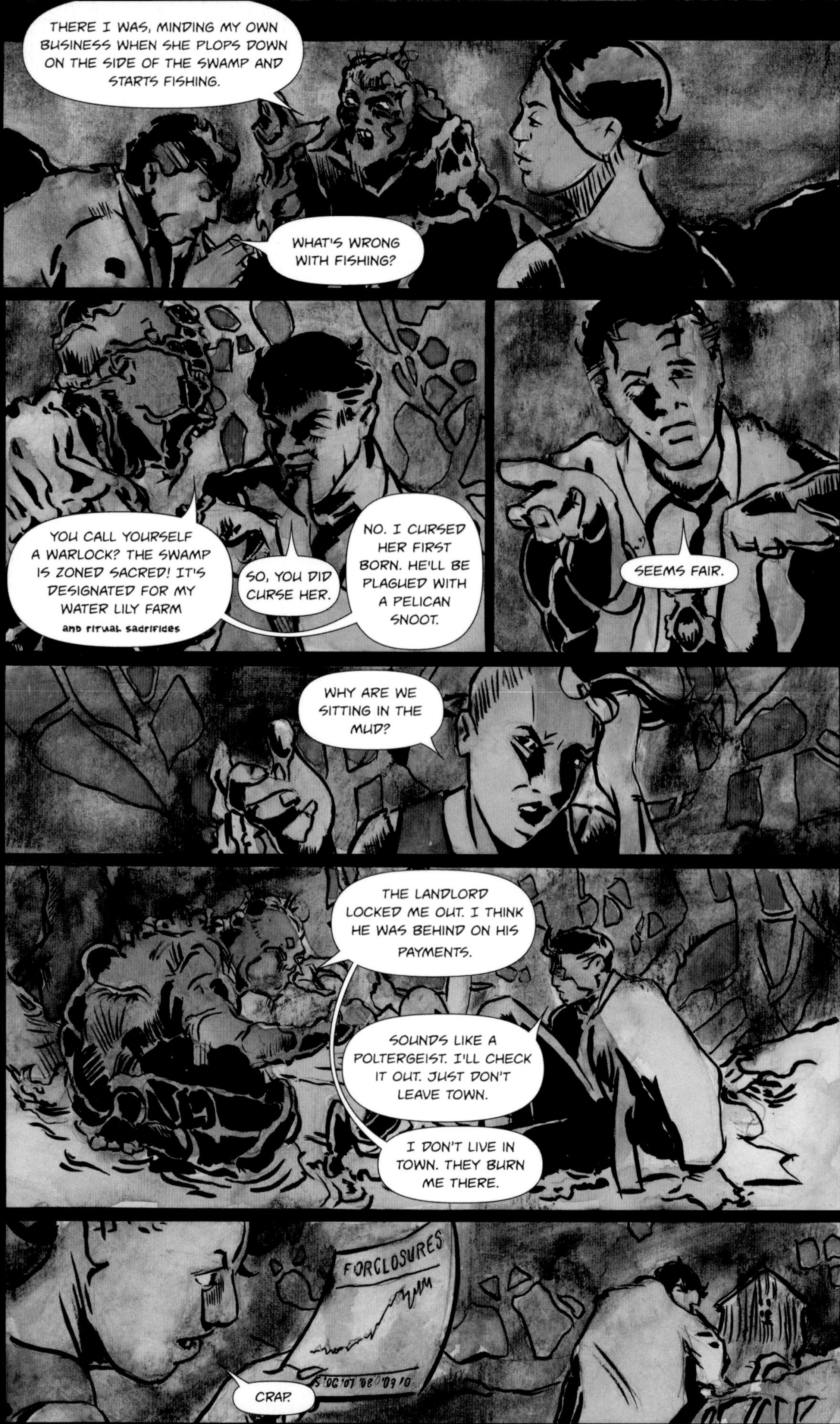
THERE I WAS, MINDING MY OWN BUSINESS WHEN SHE PLOPS DOWN ON THE SIDE OF THE SWAMP AND STARTS FISHING.
WHAT'S WRONG WITH FISHING?
YOU CALL YOURSELF A WARLOCK? THE SWAMP IS ZONED SACRED! IT'S DESIGNATED FOR MY WATER LILY FARM
and ritual sacrifices
SO, YOU DID CURSE HER.
NO. I CURSED HER FIRST BORN. HE'LL BE PLAGUED WITH A PELICAN SNOOT.
SEEMS FAIR.
WHY ARE WE SITTING IN THE MUD?
THE LANDLORD LOCKED ME OUT. I THINK HE WAS BEHIND ON HIS PAYMENTS.
SOUNDS LIKE A POLTERGEIST. I'LL CHECK IT OUT. JUST DON'T LEAVE TOWN.
I DON'T LIVE IN TOWN. THEY BURN ME THERE.
FORCLOSURES
CRAP.

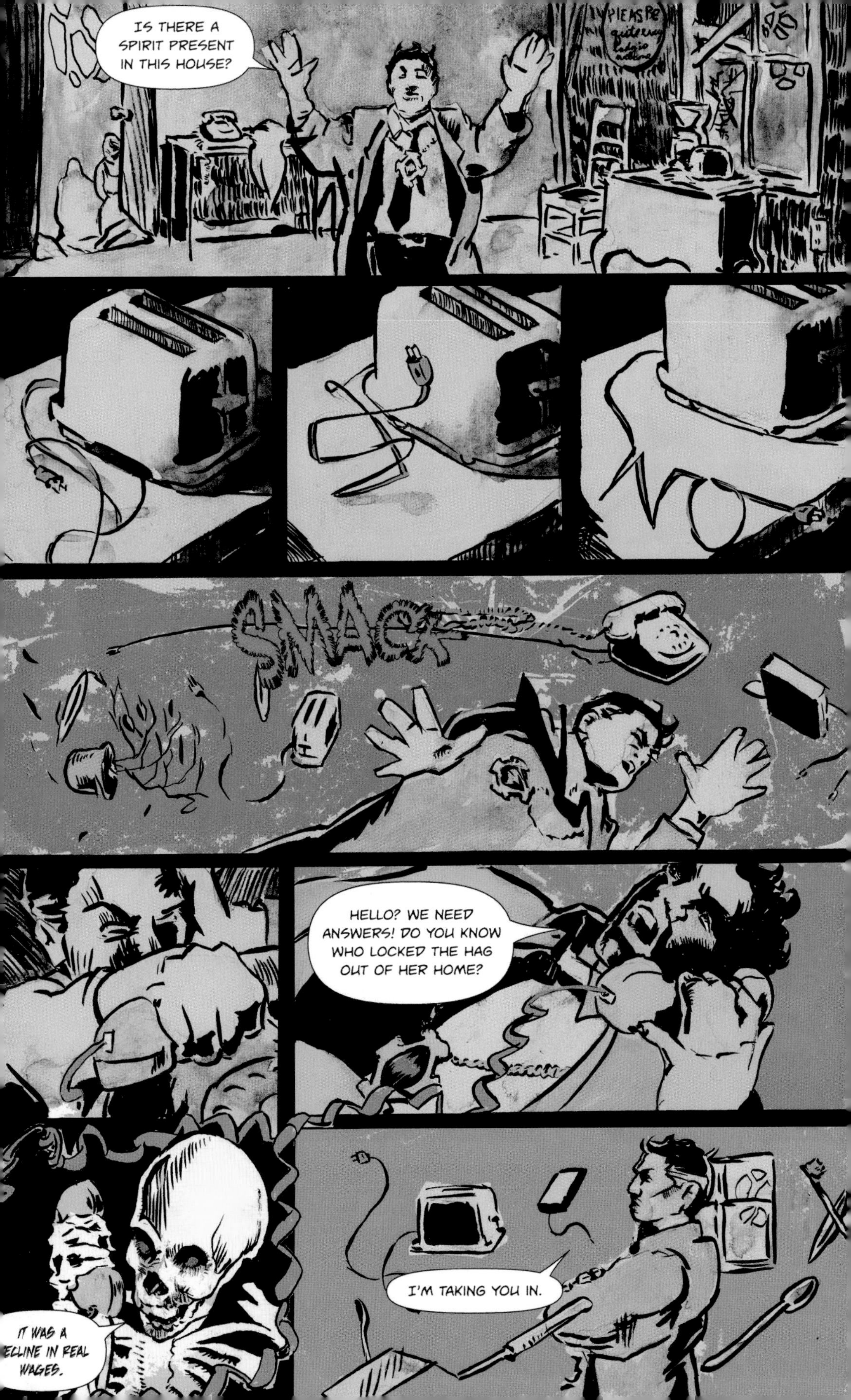
IS THERE A SPIRIT PRESENT IN THIS HOUSE?
SMACK
HELLO? WE NEED ANSWERS! DO YOU KNOW WHO LOCKED THE HAG OUT OF HER HOME?
IT WAS A ECLINE IN REAL WAGES.
I'M TAKING YOU IN.

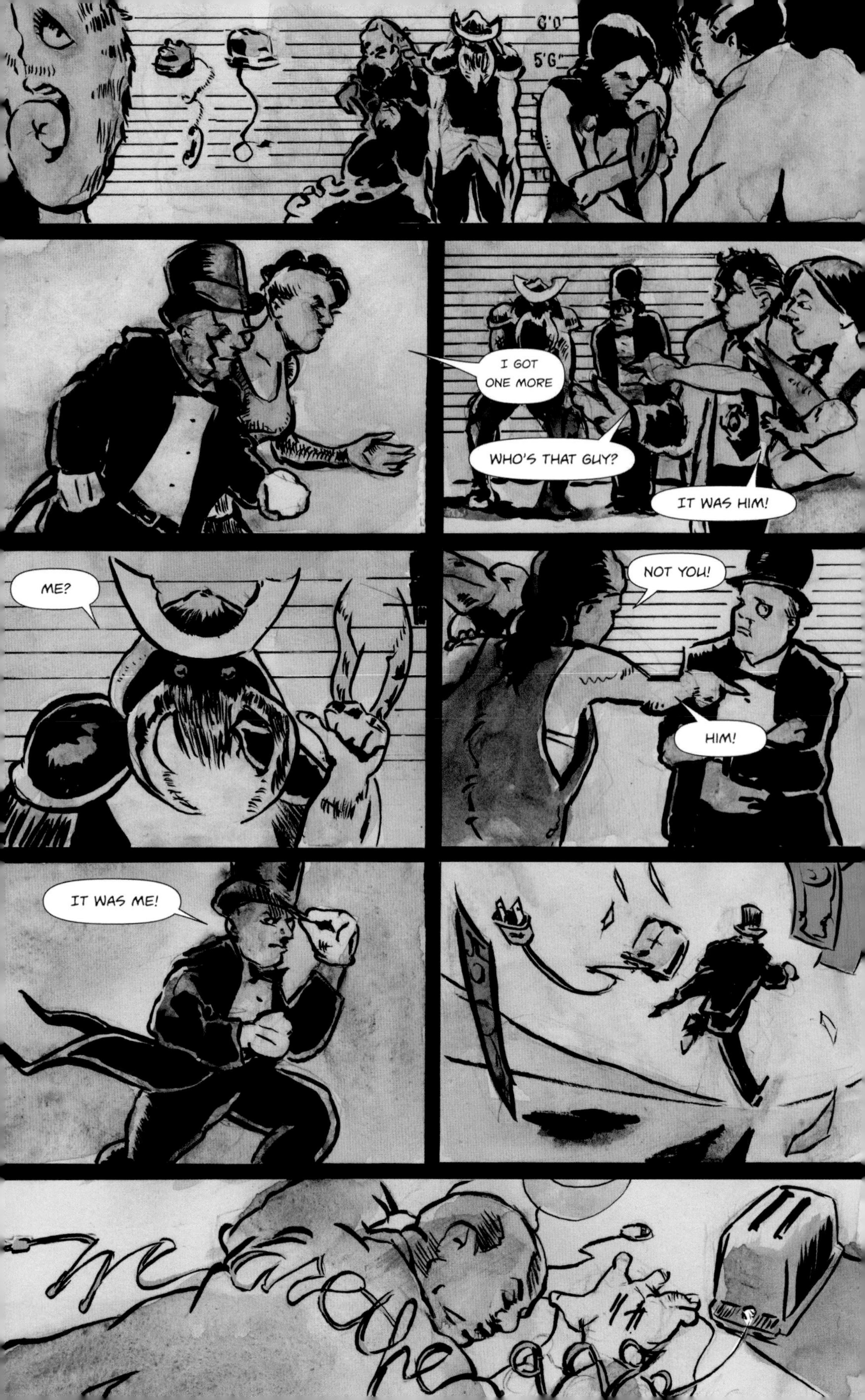
I GOT ONE MORE
WHO'S THAT GUY?
IT WAS HIM!
ME?
NOT YOU!
HIM!
IT WAS ME!

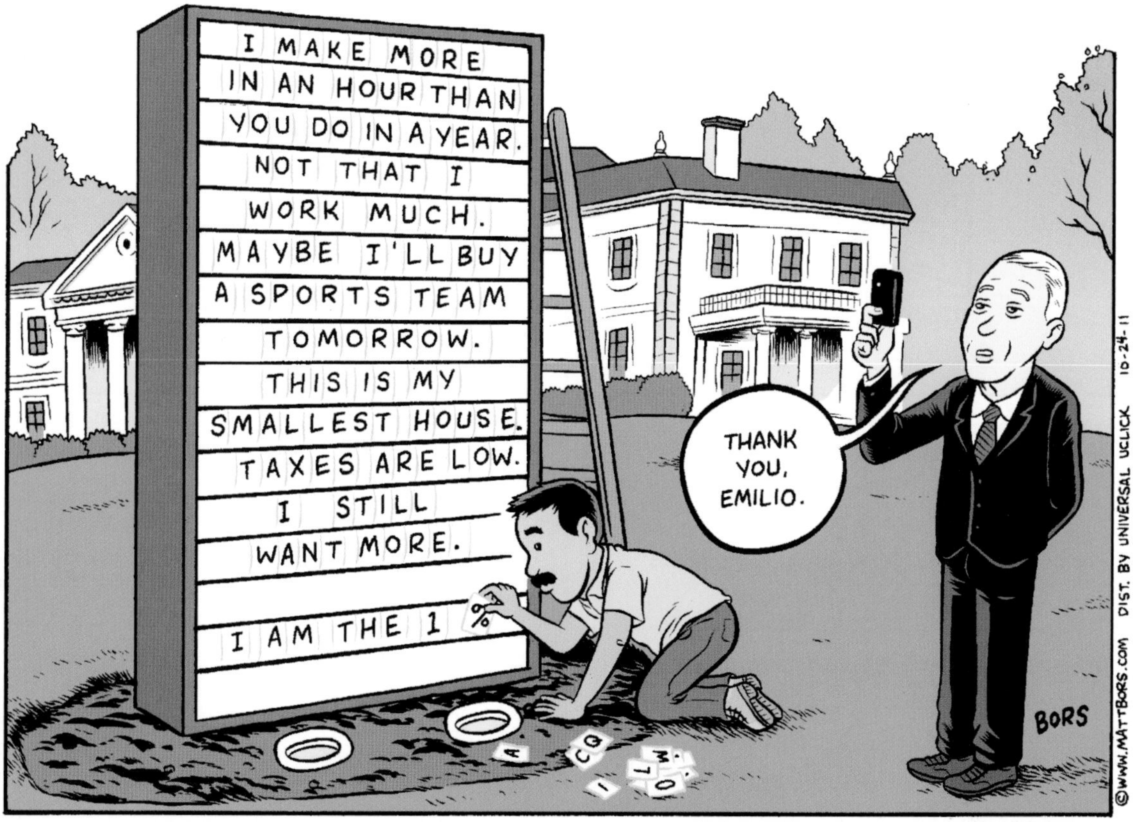
I MAKE MORE
IN AN HOUR THAN
YOU DO IN A YEAR.
NOT THAT I
WORK MUCH.
MAYBE I'LL BUY
A SPORTS TEAM
TOMORROW.
THIS IS MY
SMALLEST HOUSE.
TAXES ARE LOW.
I STILL
WANT MORE.
I AM THE 1 %
THANK YOU, EMILIO.
BORS
©WWW.MATTBORS.COM DIST. BY UNIVERSAL UCLICK 10-24-11

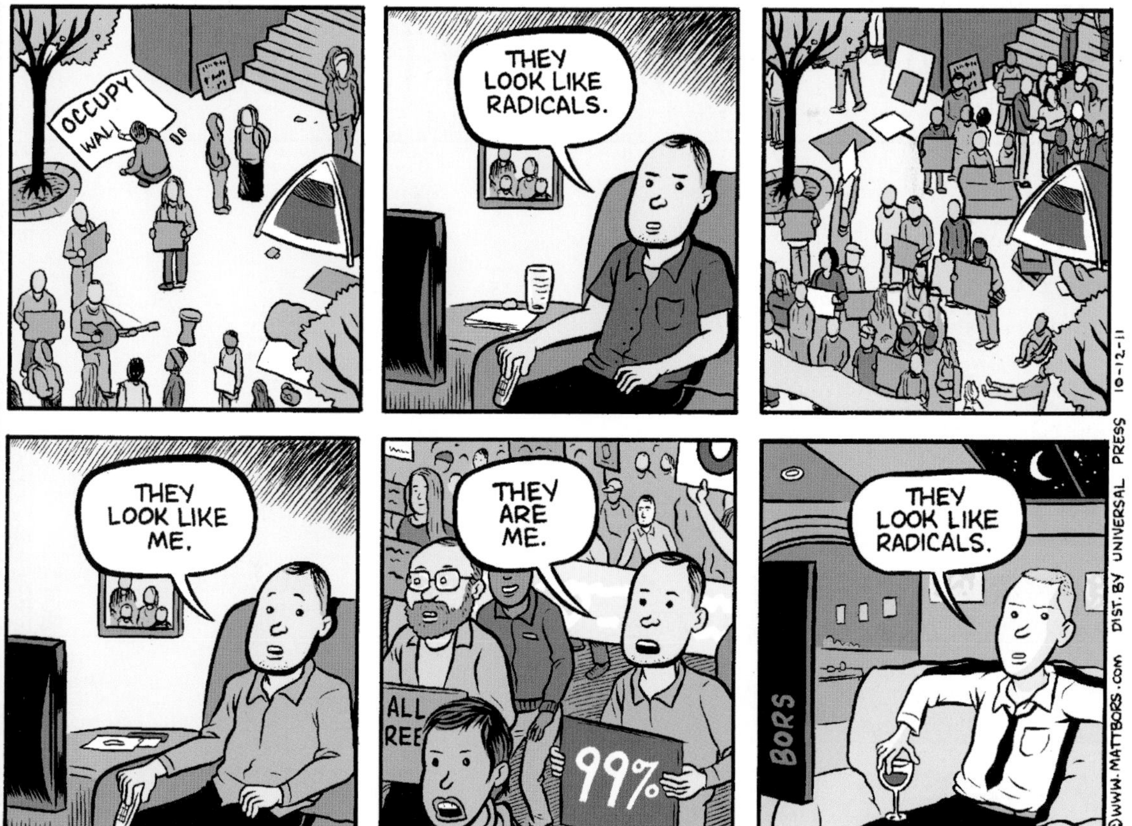
OCCUPY WALL
THEY LOOK LIKE RADICALS.
THEY LOOK LIKE ME.
THEY ARE ME.
99%
THEY LOOK LIKE RADICALS.
BORS
©WWW.MATTBORS.COM DIST. BY UNIVERSAL PRESS 10-12-11

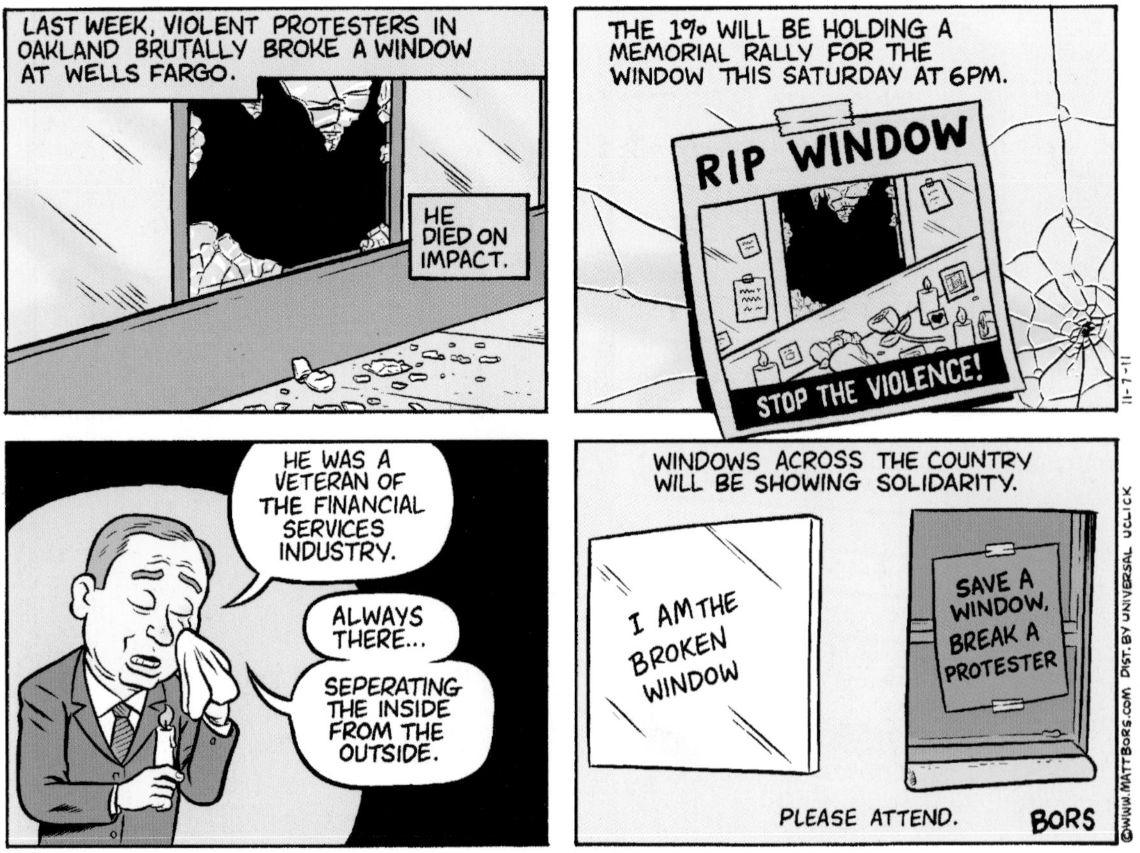
LAST WEEK, VIOLENT PROTESTERS IN OAKLAND BRUTALLY BROKE A WINDOW AT WELLS FARGO.
HE DIED ON IMPACT.
THE 1% WILL BE HOLDING A MEMORIAL RALLY FOR THE WINDOW THIS SATURDAY AT 6PM.
RIP WINDOW
STOP THE VIOLENCE!
11-7-11
HE WAS A VETERAN OF THE FINANCIAL SERVICES INDUSTRY.
ALWAYS THERE...
SEPERATING THE INSIDE FROM THE OUTSIDE.
WINDOWS ACROSS THE COUNTRY WILL BE SHOWING SOLIDARITY.
I AM THE BROKEN WINDOW
SAVE A WINDOW, BREAK A PROTESTER
PLEASE ATTEND.
BORS
©WWW.MATTBORS.COM DIST. BY UNIVERSAL UCLICK

APPROVAL RATINGS

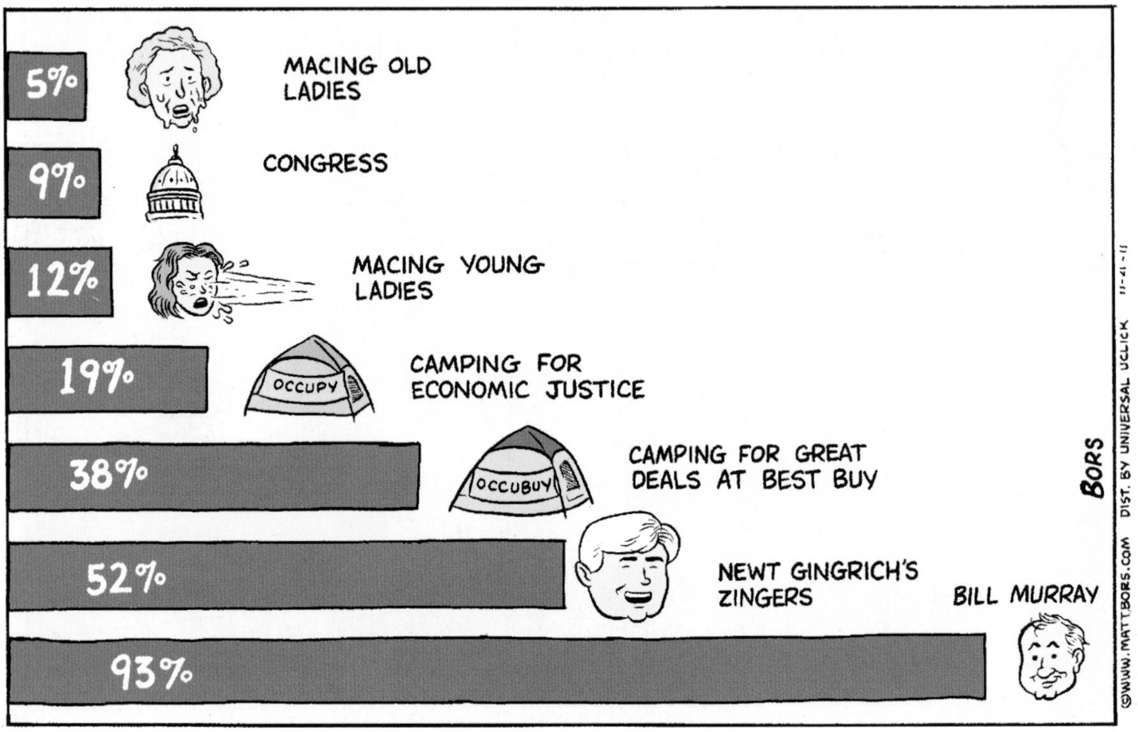
5%
MACING OLD LADIES
9%
CONGRESS
12%
MACING YOUNG LADIES
19%
OCCUPY
CAMPING FOR ECONOMIC JUSTICE
38%
OCCUBUY
CAMPING FOR GREAT DEALS AT BEST BUY
52%
NEWT GINGRICH'S ZINGERS
93%
BILL MURRAY
BORS
©WWW.MATTBORS.COM DIST. BY UNIVERSAL UCLICK

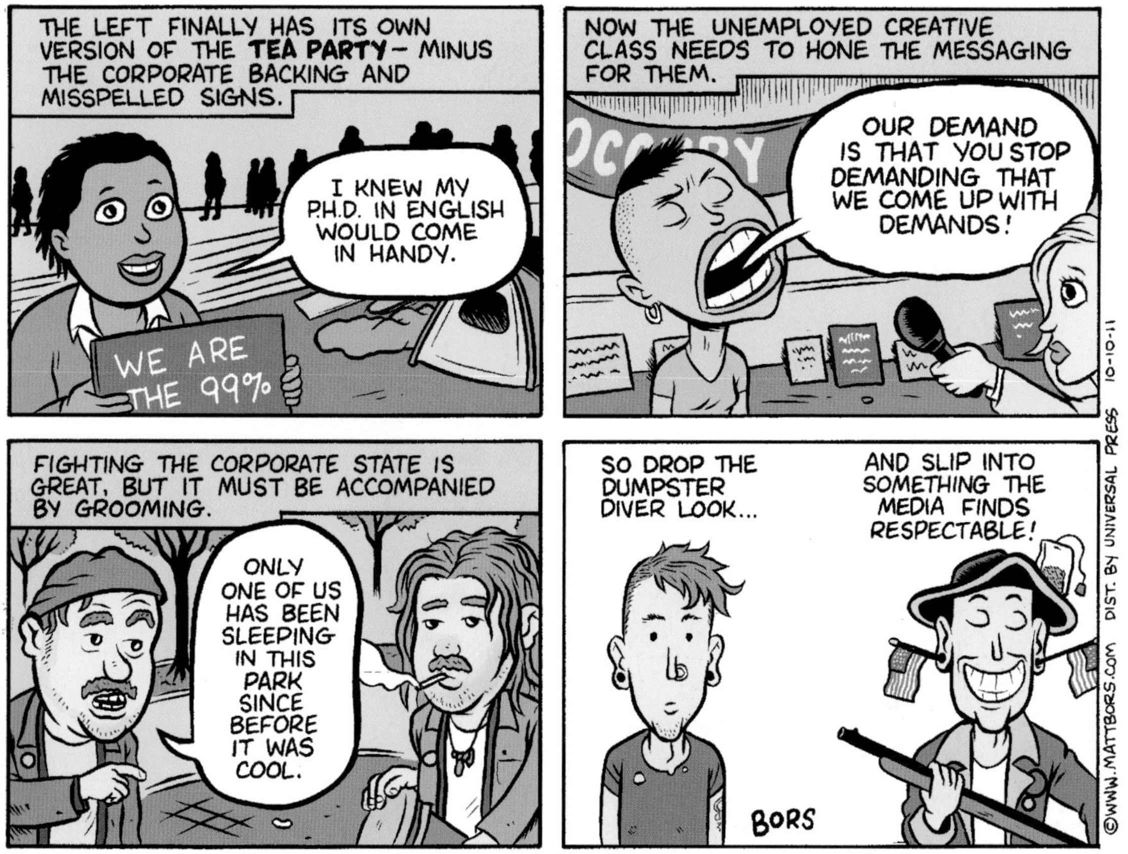
THE LEFT FINALLY HAS ITS OWN VERSION OF THE TEA PARTY – MINUS THE CORPORATE BACKING AND MISSPELLED SIGNS.
I KNEW MY P.H.D. IN ENGLISH WOULD COME IN HANDY.
WE ARE THE 99%
NOW THE UNEMPLOYED CREATIVE CLASS NEEDS TO HONE THE MESSAGING FOR THEM.
OCCUPY
OUR DEMAND IS THAT YOU STOP DEMANDING THAT WE COME UP WITH DEMANDS!
FIGHTING THE CORPORATE STATE IS GREAT, BUT IT MUST BE ACCOMPANIED BY GROOMING.
ONLY ONE OF US HAS BEEN SLEEPING IN THIS PARK SINCE BEFORE IT WAS COOL.
SO DROP THE DUMPSTER DIVER LOOK...
AND SLIP INTO SOMETHING THE MEDIA FINDS RESPECTABLE!
BORS
©WWW.MATTBORS.COM DIST. BY UNIVERSAL PRESS 10-10-11

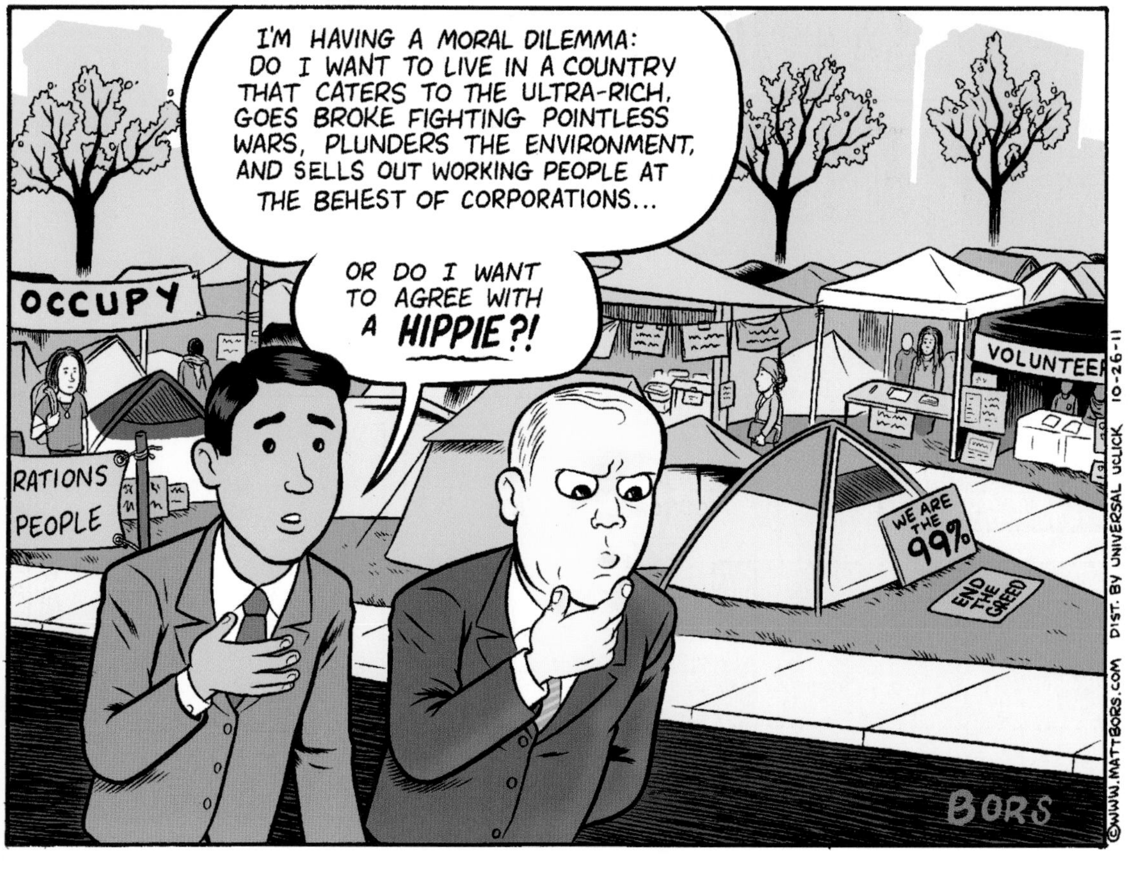
I'M HAVING A MORAL DILEMMA: DO I WANT TO LIVE IN A COUNTRY THAT CATERS TO THE ULTRA-RICH, GOES BROKE FIGHTING POINTLESS WARS, PLUNDERS THE ENVIRONMENT, AND SELLS OUT WORKING PEOPLE AT THE BEHEST OF CORPORATIONS...
OR DO I WANT TO AGREE WITH A HIPPIE?!
OCCUPY
RATIONS
PEOPLE
VOLUNTEE
WE ARE THE 99%
END THE GREED
BORS
©WWW.MATTBORS.COM DIST. BY UNIVERSAL UCLICK 10-26-11

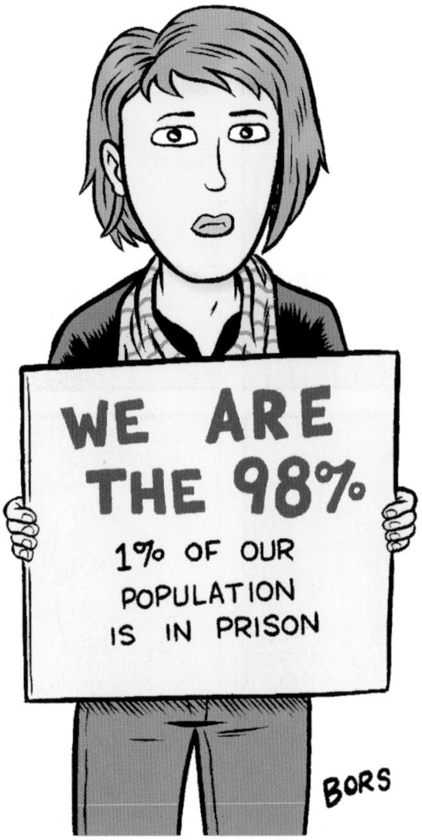
WE ARE THE 98%
1% OF OUR POPULATION IS IN PRISON
BORS

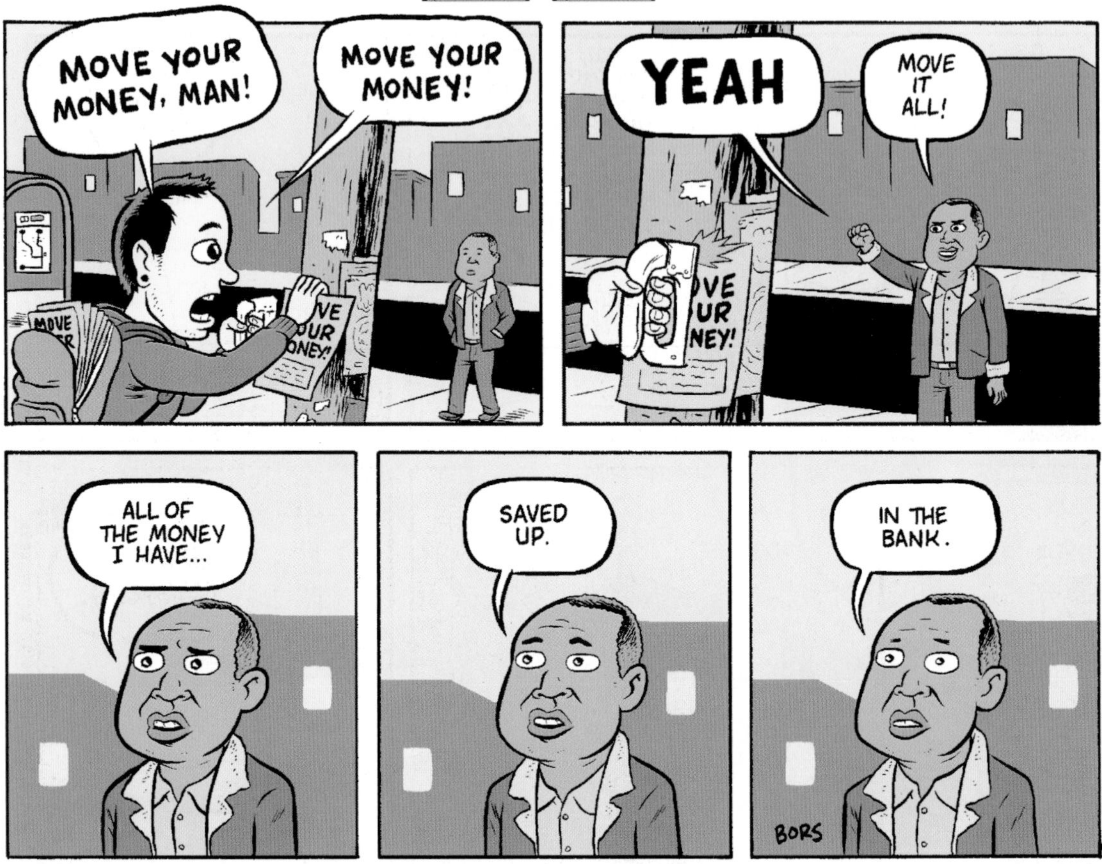
MOVE YOUR MONEY, MAN!
MOVE YOUR MONEY!
YEAH
MOVE IT ALL!
ALL OF THE MONEY I HAVE...
SAVED UP.
IN THE BANK.
BORS

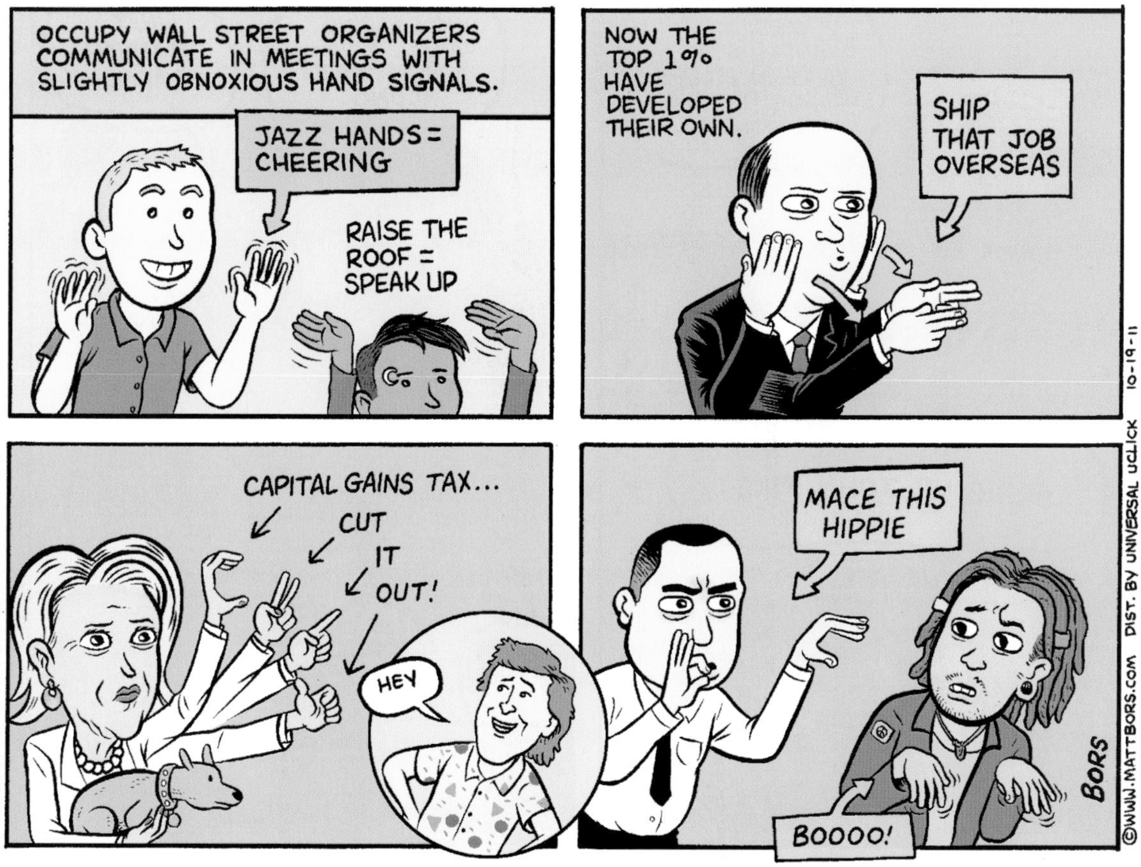
OCCUPY WALL STREET ORGANIZERS COMMUNICATE IN MEETINGS WITH SLIGHTLY OBNOXIOUS HAND SIGNALS.
JAZZ HANDS = CHEERING
RAISE THE ROOF = SPEAK UP
NOW THE TOP 1% HAVE DEVELOPED THEIR OWN.
SHIP THAT JOB OVERSEAS
CAPITAL GAINS TAX... CUT IT OUT!
HEY
MACE THIS HIPPIE
BOOOO!
BORS
10-19-11
©WWW.MATTBORS.COM DIST. BY UNIVERSAL UCLICK

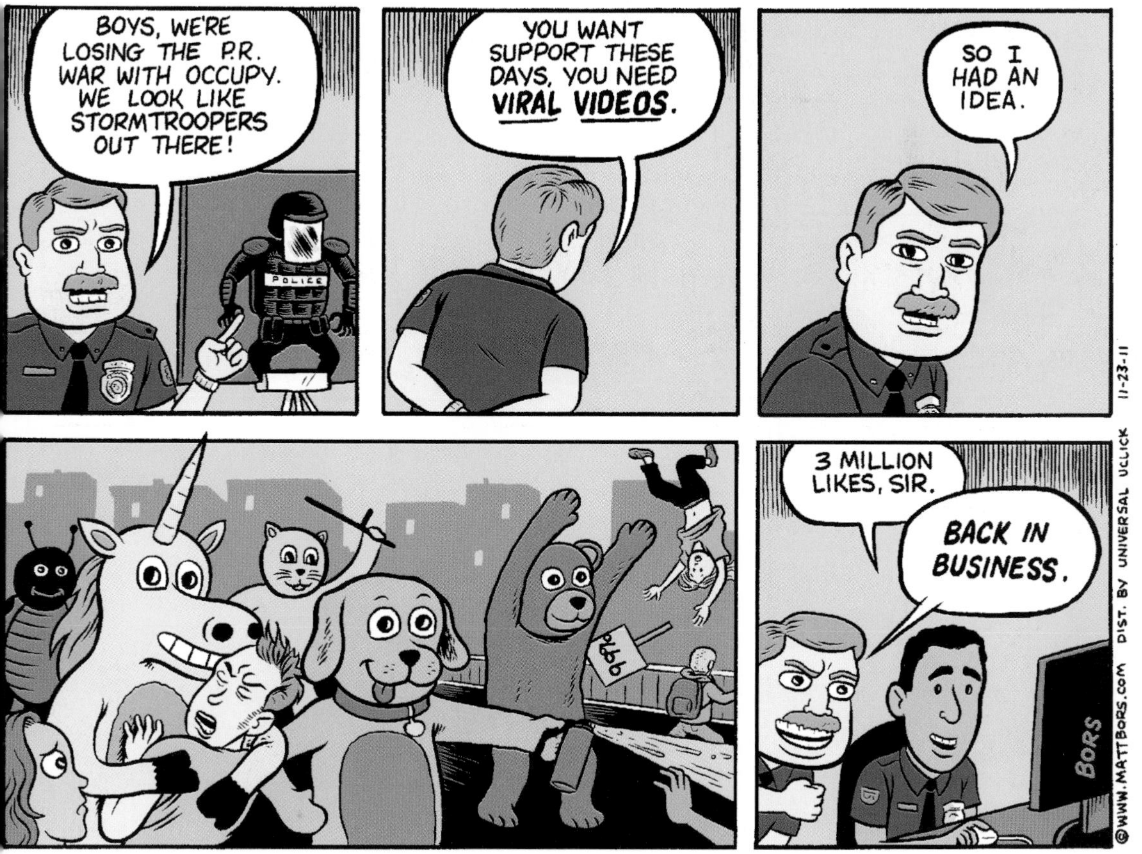
BOYS, WE'RE LOSING THE P.R. WAR WITH OCCUPY. WE LOOK LIKE STORMTROOPERS OUT THERE!
POLICE
YOU WANT SUPPORT THESE DAYS, YOU NEED VIRAL VIDEOS.
SO I HAD AN IDEA.
99%
3 MILLION LIKES, SIR.
BACK IN BUSINESS.
BORS
11-23-11
©WWW.MATTBORS.COM DIST. BY UNIVERSAL UCLICK

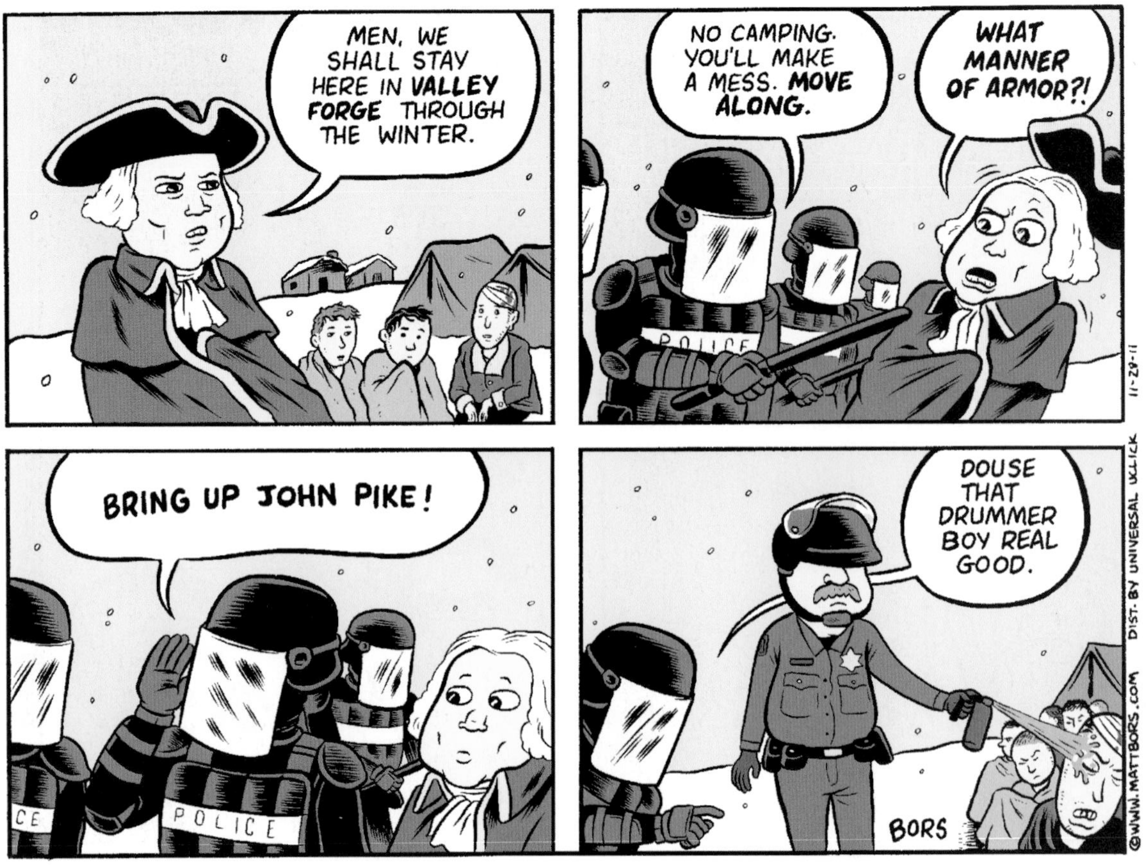
MEN, WE SHALL STAY HERE IN VALLEY FORGE THROUGH THE WINTER.
NO CAMPING. YOU'LL MAKE A MESS. MOVE ALONG.
WHAT MANNER OF ARMOR?!
POLICE
BRING UP JOHN PIKE!
POLICE
CE
DOUSE THAT DRUMMER BOY REAL GOOD.
BORS
11-29-11
©WWW.MATTBORS.COM DIST. BY UNIVERSAL UCLICK

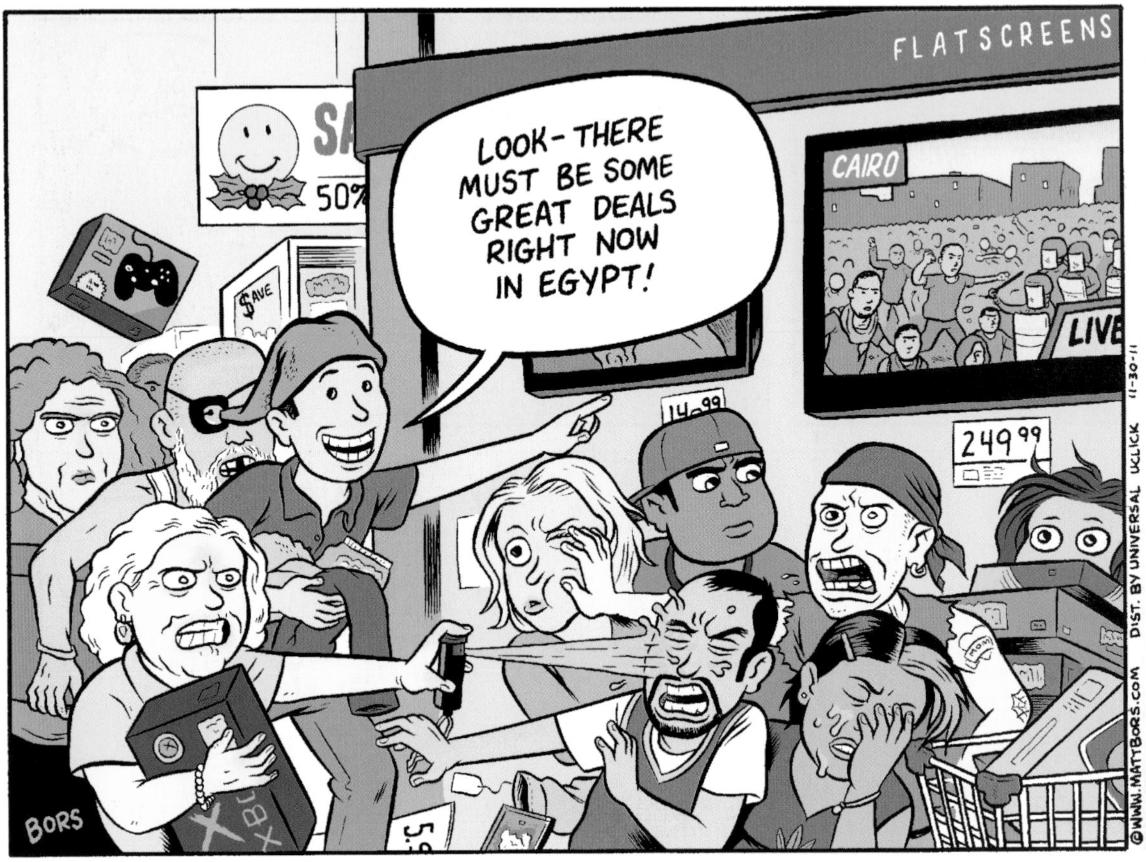
FLATSCREENS
50%
SAVE
CAIRO
LIVE
LOOK- THERE MUST BE SOME GREAT DEALS RIGHT NOW IN EGYPT!
249.99
BORS
11-30-11
©WWW.MATTBORS.COM DIST. BY UNIVERSAL UCLICK

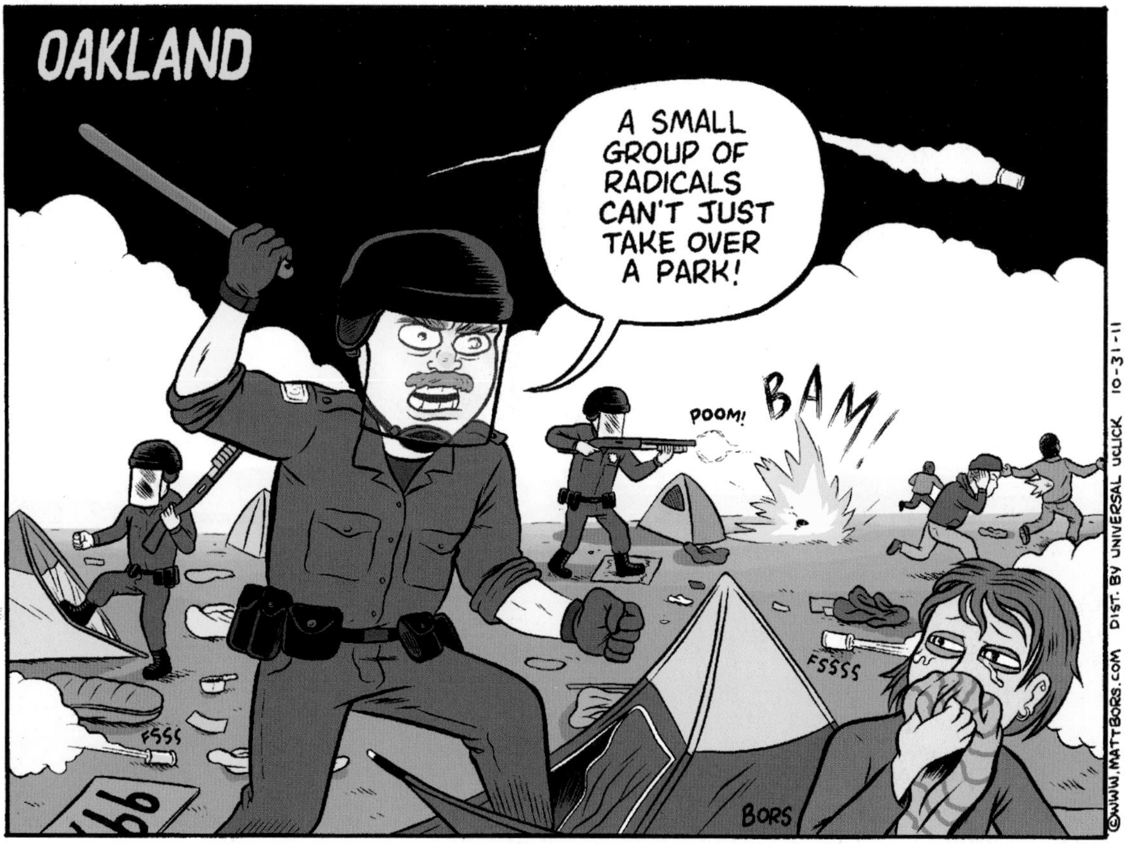
OAKLAND
A SMALL GROUP OF RADICALS CAN'T JUST TAKE OVER A PARK!
POOM!
BAM!
FSSSS
FSSS
BORS
©WWW.MATTBORS.COM DIST. BY UNIVERSAL UCLICK 10-31-11

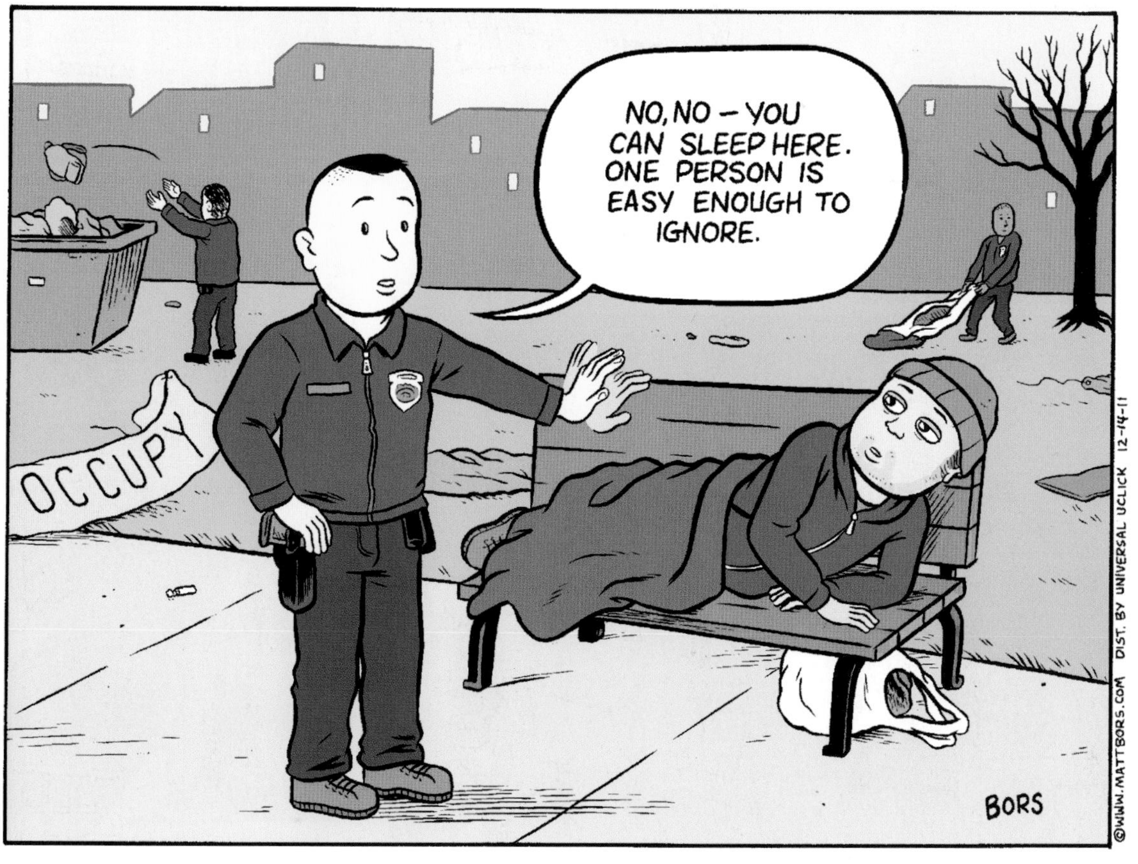
NO, NO – YOU CAN SLEEP HERE. ONE PERSON IS EASY ENOUGH TO IGNORE.
OCCUPY
BORS
©WWW.MATTBORS.COM DIST. BY UNIVERSAL UCLICK 12-14-11

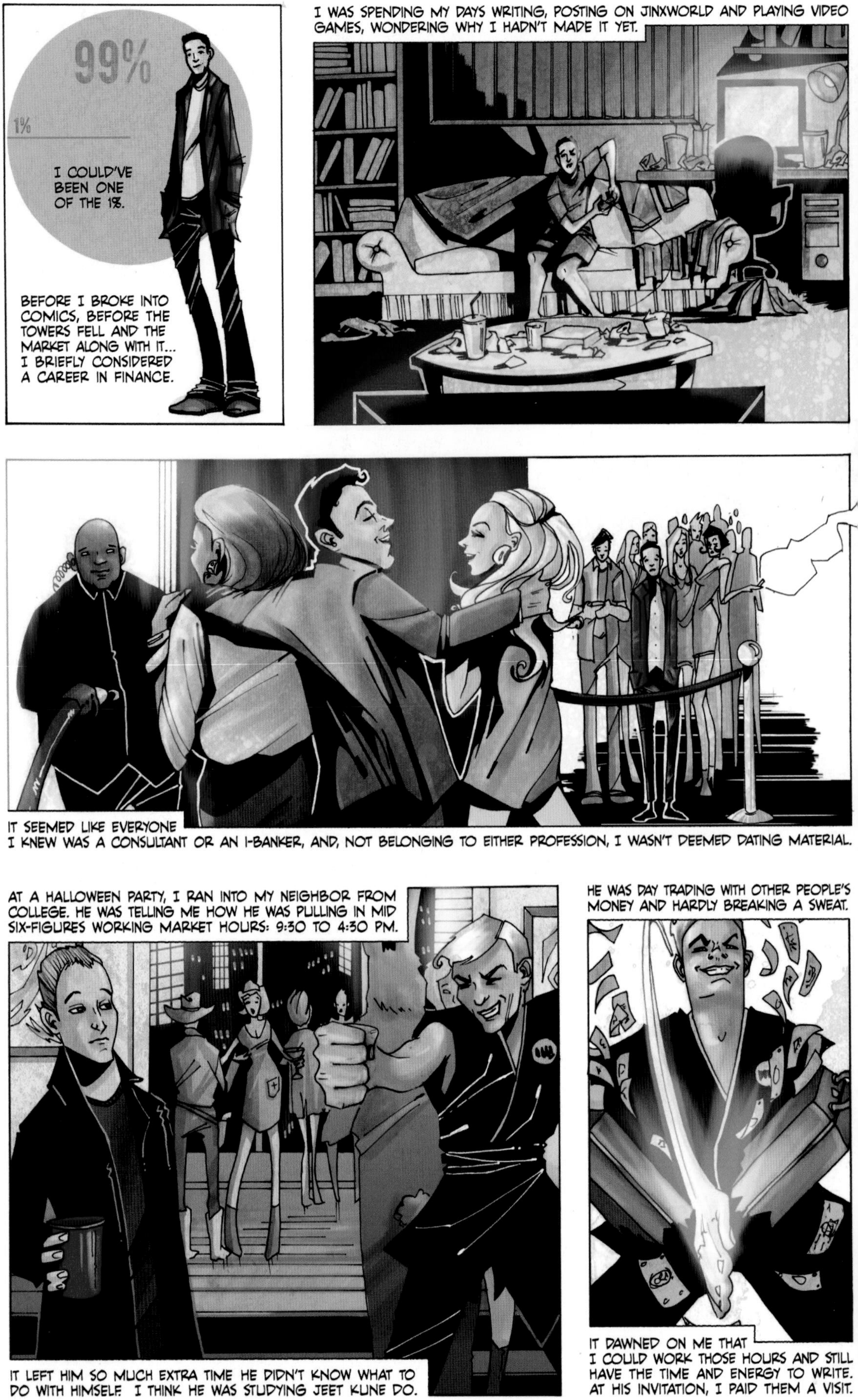
99%
1%
I COULD'VE BEEN ONE OF THE 1%.
BEFORE I BROKE INTO COMICS, BEFORE THE TOWERS FELL AND THE MARKET ALONG WITH IT... I BRIEFLY CONSIDERED A CAREER IN FINANCE.
I WAS SPENDING MY DAYS WRITING, POSTING ON JINXWORLD AND PLAYING VIDEO GAMES, WONDERING WHY I HADN'T MADE IT YET.
IT SEEMED LIKE EVERYONE I KNEW WAS A CONSULTANT OR AN I-BANKER, AND, NOT BELONGING TO EITHER PROFESSION, I WASN'T DEEMED DATING MATERIAL.
AT A HALLOWEEN PARTY, I RAN INTO MY NEIGHBOR FROM COLLEGE. HE WAS TELLING ME HOW HE WAS PULLING IN MID SIX-FIGURES WORKING MARKET HOURS: 9:30 TO 4:30 PM.
IT LEFT HIM SO MUCH EXTRA TIME HE DIDN'T KNOW WHAT TO DO WITH HIMSELF. I THINK HE WAS STUDYING JEET KUNE DO.
HE WAS DAY TRADING WITH OTHER PEOPLE'S MONEY AND HARDLY BREAKING A SWEAT.
IT DAWNED ON ME THAT I COULD WORK THOSE HOURS AND STILL HAVE THE TIME AND ENERGY TO WRITE. AT HIS INVITATION, I PAID THEM A VISIT.

THE COMPANY WAS LITERALLY IN THE SHADOW OF THE TOWERS. I DON'T WANT TO NAME THE FIRM, BUT IT RHYMED WITH ***TRADE RAPE.***

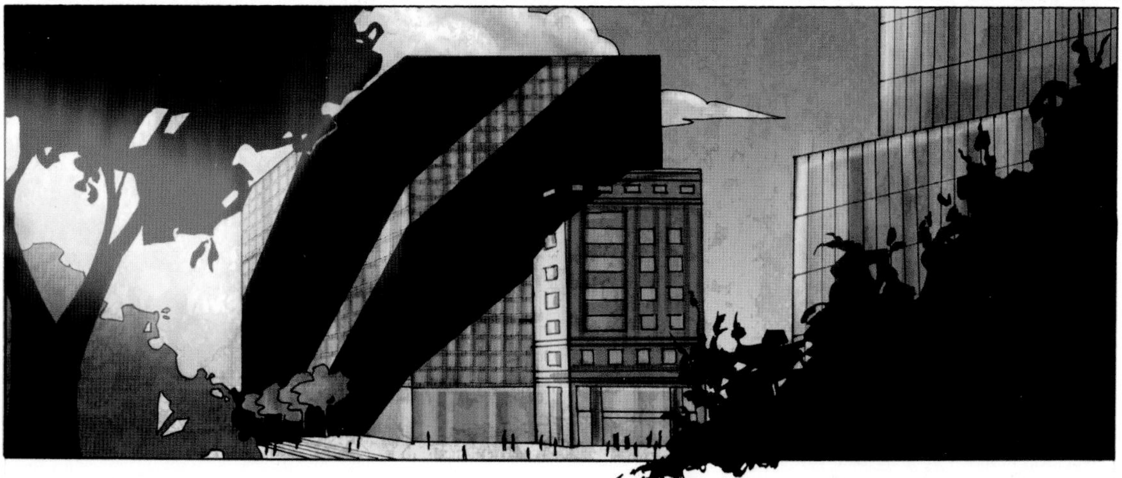

THEY WERE EXECUTING TRADES WITH LIGHTNING SPEED. INTIMIDATED, I FEARED THEY WERE SAVANTS AND I COULDN'T DO THEIR WORK. I KNEW NEXT TO NOTHING ABOUT THE MARKET. MY FRIEND REASSURED ME BY TELLING ME THAT NEITHER DID THEY.

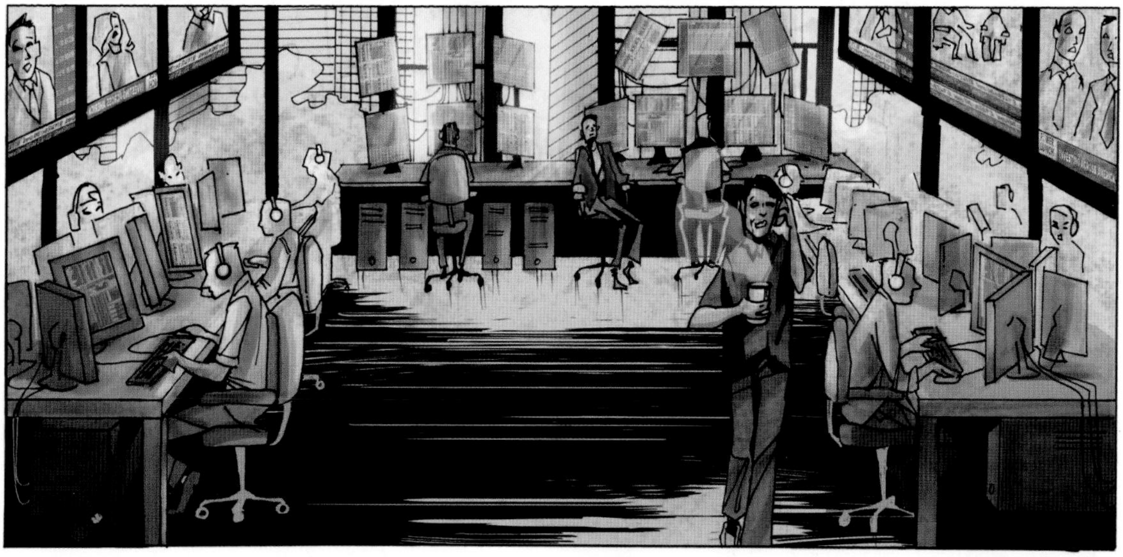

I ASKED ONE IF THEY KNEW WHAT THE COMPANIES WHOSE STOCKS THEY WERE MOVING BOUGHT, SOLD OR PROCESSED.

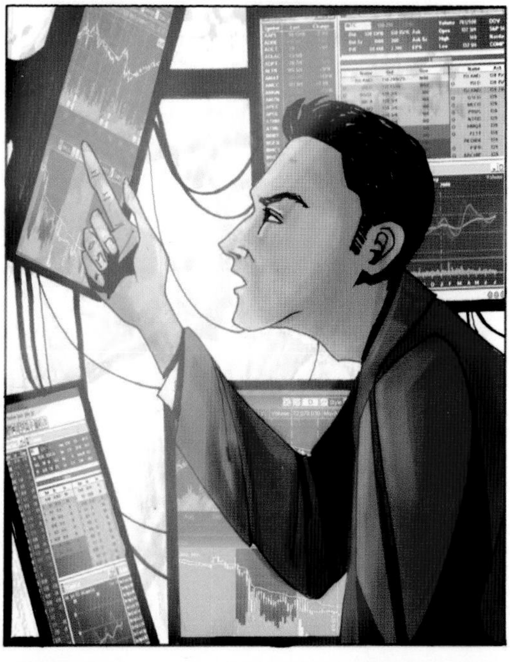

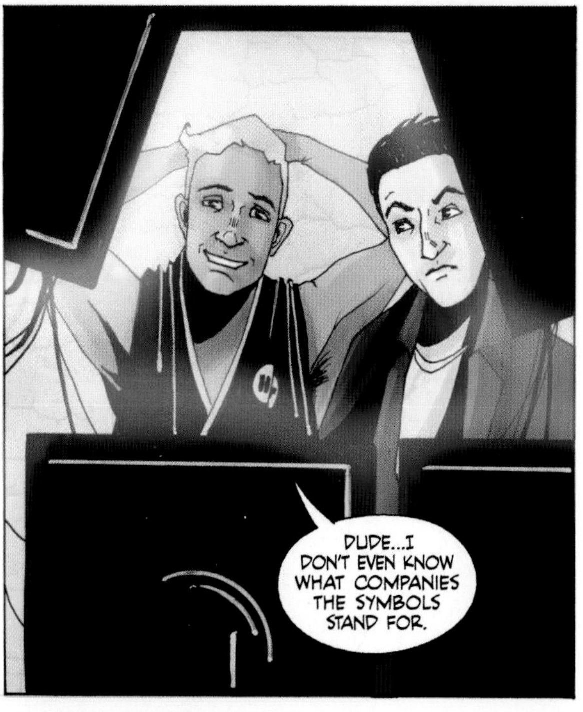
DUDE...I DON'T EVEN KNOW WHAT COMPANIES THE SYMBOLS STAND FOR.

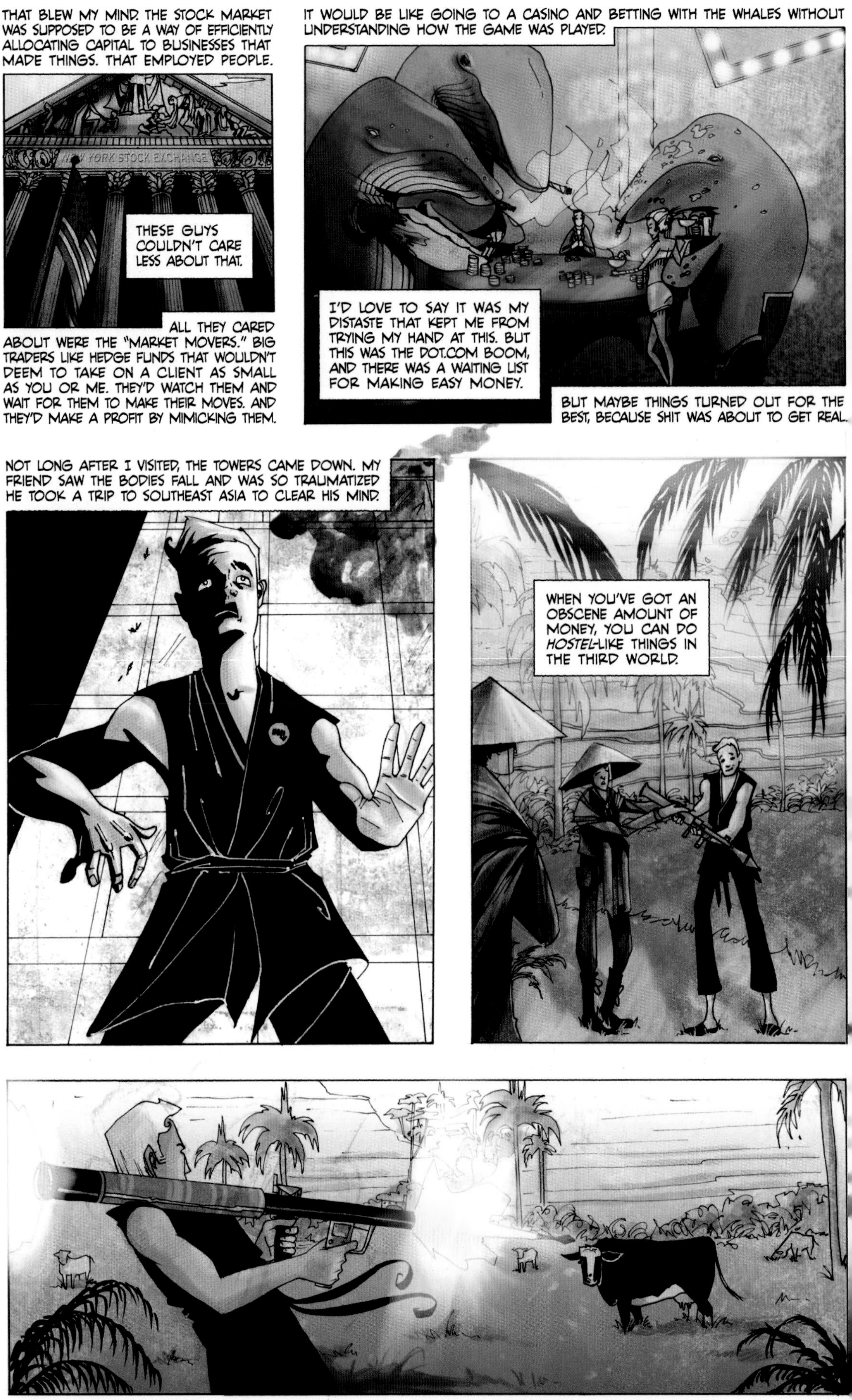
THAT BLEW MY MIND. THE STOCK MARKET WAS SUPPOSED TO BE A WAY OF EFFICIENTLY ALLOCATING CAPITAL TO BUSINESSES THAT MADE THINGS. THAT EMPLOYED PEOPLE.
NEW YORK STOCK EXCHANGE
THESE GUYS COULDN'T CARE LESS ABOUT THAT.
ALL THEY CARED ABOUT WERE THE "MARKET MOVERS." BIG TRADERS LIKE HEDGE FUNDS THAT WOULDN'T DEEM TO TAKE ON A CLIENT AS SMALL AS YOU OR ME. THEY'D WATCH THEM AND WAIT FOR THEM TO MAKE THEIR MOVES. AND THEY'D MAKE A PROFIT BY MIMICKING THEM.
IT WOULD BE LIKE GOING TO A CASINO AND BETTING WITH THE WHALES WITHOUT UNDERSTANDING HOW THE GAME WAS PLAYED.
I'D LOVE TO SAY IT WAS MY DISTASTE THAT KEPT ME FROM TRYING MY HAND AT THIS. BUT THIS WAS THE DOT.COM BOOM, AND THERE WAS A WAITING LIST FOR MAKING EASY MONEY.
BUT MAYBE THINGS TURNED OUT FOR THE BEST, BECAUSE SHIT WAS ABOUT TO GET REAL.
NOT LONG AFTER I VISITED, THE TOWERS CAME DOWN. MY FRIEND SAW THE BODIES FALL AND WAS SO TRAUMATIZED HE TOOK A TRIP TO SOUTHEAST ASIA TO CLEAR HIS MIND.
WHEN YOU'VE GOT AN OBSCENE AMOUNT OF MONEY, YOU CAN DO *HOSTEL*-LIKE THINGS IN THE THIRD WORLD.

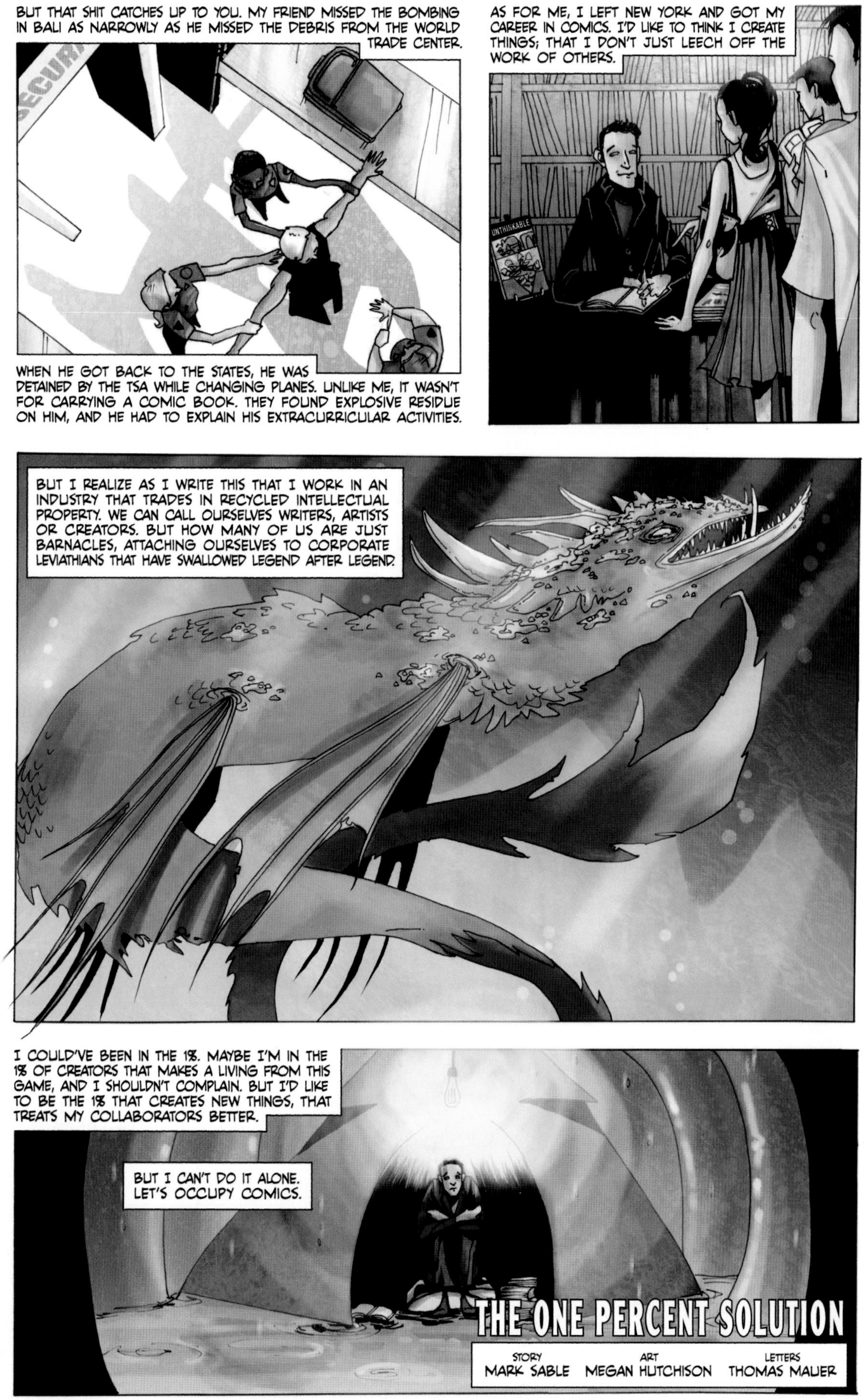
BUT THAT SHIT CATCHES UP TO YOU. MY FRIEND MISSED THE BOMBING IN BALI AS NARROWLY AS HE MISSED THE DEBRIS FROM THE WORLD TRADE CENTER.
SECURI
WHEN HE GOT BACK TO THE STATES, HE WAS DETAINED BY THE TSA WHILE CHANGING PLANES. UNLIKE ME, IT WASN'T FOR CARRYING A COMIC BOOK. THEY FOUND EXPLOSIVE RESIDUE ON HIM, AND HE HAD TO EXPLAIN HIS EXTRACURRICULAR ACTIVITIES.
AS FOR ME, I LEFT NEW YORK AND GOT MY CAREER IN COMICS. I'D LIKE TO THINK I CREATE THINGS; THAT I DON'T JUST LEECH OFF THE WORK OF OTHERS.
UNTHINKABLE
BUT I REALIZE AS I WRITE THIS THAT I WORK IN AN INDUSTRY THAT TRADES IN RECYCLED INTELLECTUAL PROPERTY. WE CAN CALL OURSELVES WRITERS, ARTISTS OR CREATORS. BUT HOW MANY OF US ARE JUST BARNACLES, ATTACHING OURSELVES TO CORPORATE LEVIATHIANS THAT HAVE SWALLOWED LEGEND AFTER LEGEND.
I COULD'VE BEEN IN THE 1%. MAYBE I'M IN THE 1% OF CREATORS THAT MAKES A LIVING FROM THIS GAME, AND I SHOULDN'T COMPLAIN. BUT I'D LIKE TO BE THE 1% THAT CREATES NEW THINGS, THAT TREATS MY COLLABORATORS BETTER.
BUT I CAN'T DO IT ALONE. LET'S OCCUPY COMICS.
THE ONE PERCENT SOLUTION
STORY MARK SABLE
ART MEGAN HUTCHISON
LETTERS THOMAS MAUER

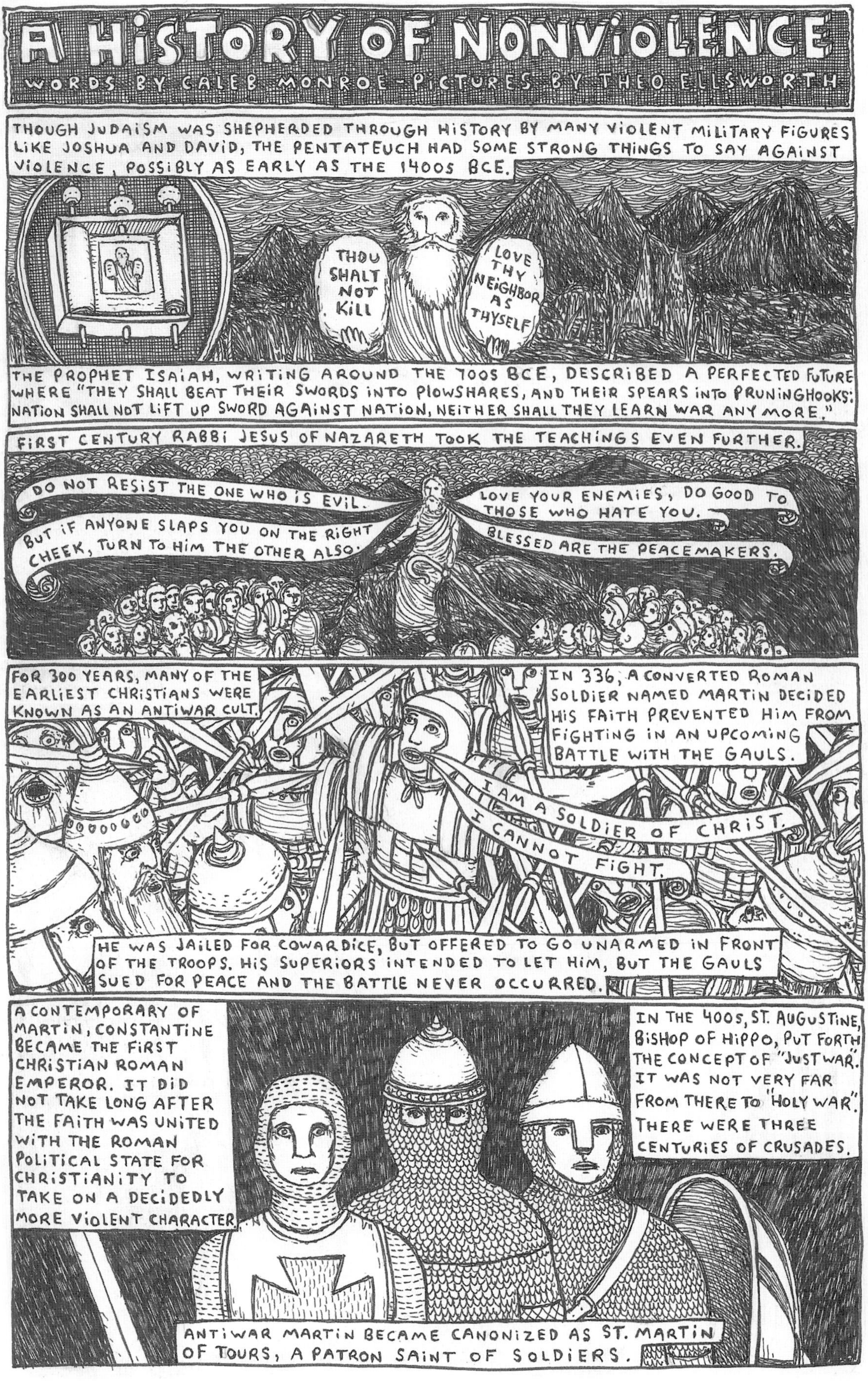
A HISTORY OF NONVIOLENCE
WORDS BY CALEB MONROE - PICTURES BY THEO ELLSWORTH
THOUGH JUDAISM WAS SHEPHERDED THROUGH HISTORY BY MANY VIOLENT MILITARY FIGURES LIKE JOSHUA AND DAVID, THE PENTATEUCH HAD SOME STRONG THINGS TO SAY AGAINST VIOLENCE, POSSIBLY AS EARLY AS THE 1400S BCE.
THOU SHALT NOT KILL
LOVE THY NEIGHBOR AS THYSELF
THE PROPHET ISAIAH, WRITING AROUND THE 700S BCE, DESCRIBED A PERFECTED FUTURE WHERE "THEY SHALL BEAT THEIR SWORDS INTO PLOWSHARES, AND THEIR SPEARS INTO PRUNINGHOOKS: NATION SHALL NOT LIFT UP SWORD AGAINST NATION, NEITHER SHALL THEY LEARN WAR ANY MORE."
FIRST CENTURY RABBI JESUS OF NAZARETH TOOK THE TEACHINGS EVEN FURTHER.
DO NOT RESIST THE ONE WHO IS EVIL.
BUT IF ANYONE SLAPS YOU ON THE RIGHT CHEEK, TURN TO HIM THE OTHER ALSO.
LOVE YOUR ENEMIES, DO GOOD TO THOSE WHO HATE YOU.
BLESSED ARE THE PEACEMAKERS.
FOR 300 YEARS, MANY OF THE EARLIEST CHRISTIANS WERE KNOWN AS AN ANTIWAR CULT.
IN 336, A CONVERTED ROMAN SOLDIER NAMED MARTIN DECIDED HIS FAITH PREVENTED HIM FROM FIGHTING IN AN UPCOMING BATTLE WITH THE GAULS.
I AM A SOLDIER OF CHRIST. I CANNOT FIGHT.
HE WAS JAILED FOR COWARDICE, BUT OFFERED TO GO UNARMED IN FRONT OF THE TROOPS. HIS SUPERIORS INTENDED TO LET HIM, BUT THE GAULS SUED FOR PEACE AND THE BATTLE NEVER OCCURRED.
A CONTEMPORARY OF MARTIN, CONSTANTINE BECAME THE FIRST CHRISTIAN ROMAN EMPEROR. IT DID NOT TAKE LONG AFTER THE FAITH WAS UNITED WITH THE ROMAN POLITICAL STATE FOR CHRISTIANITY TO TAKE ON A DECIDEDLY MORE VIOLENT CHARACTER.
IN THE 400S, ST. AUGUSTINE, BISHOP OF HIPPO, PUT FORTH THE CONCEPT OF "JUST WAR". IT WAS NOT VERY FAR FROM THERE TO "HOLY WAR". THERE WERE THREE CENTURIES OF CRUSADES.
ANTIWAR MARTIN BECAME CANONIZED AS ST. MARTIN OF TOURS, A PATRON SAINT OF SOLDIERS.

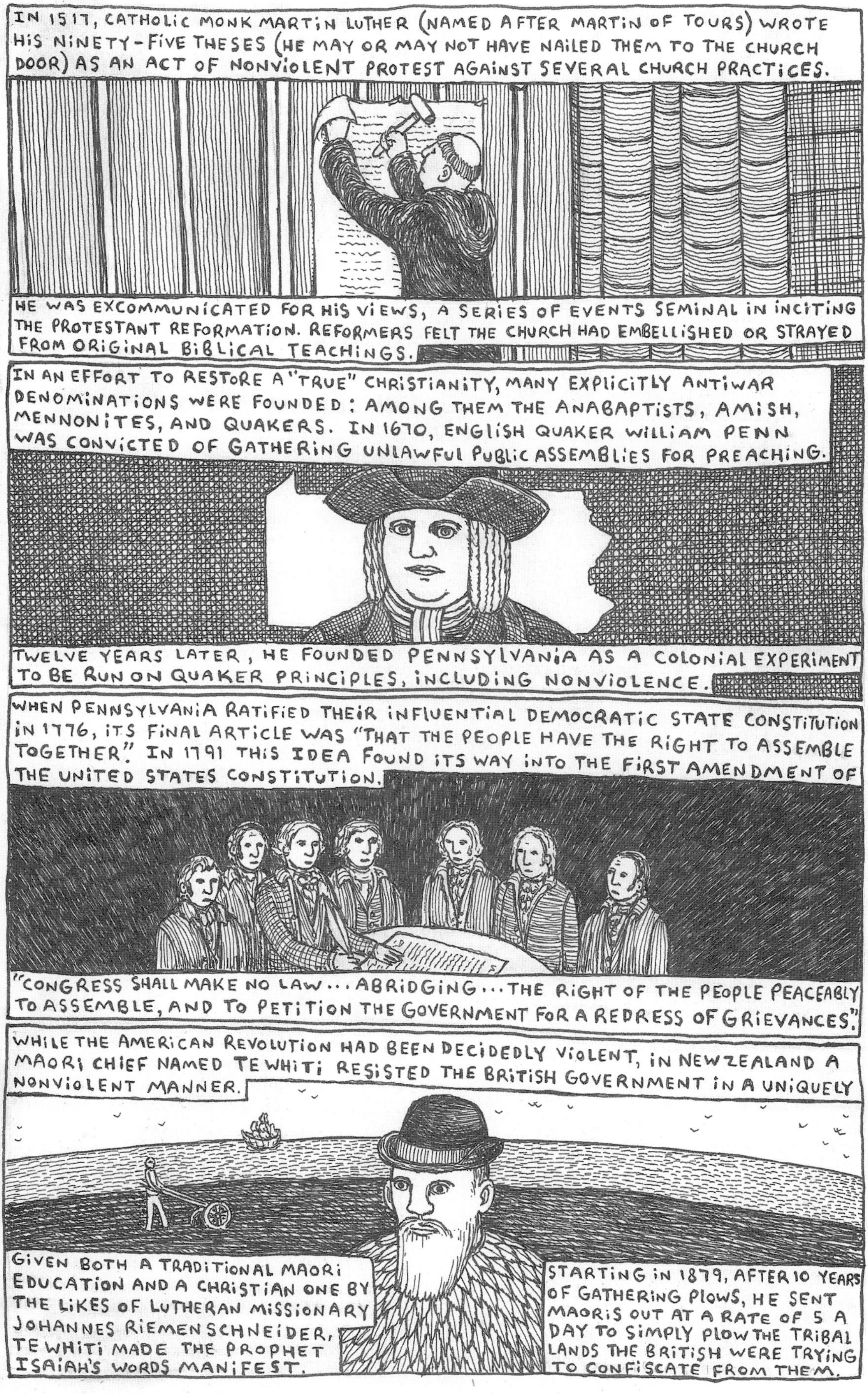
IN 1517, CATHOLIC MONK MARTIN LUTHER (NAMED AFTER MARTIN OF TOURS) WROTE HIS NINETY-FIVE THESES (HE MAY OR MAY NOT HAVE NAILED THEM TO THE CHURCH DOOR) AS AN ACT OF NONVIOLENT PROTEST AGAINST SEVERAL CHURCH PRACTICES.
HE WAS EXCOMMUNICATED FOR HIS VIEWS, A SERIES OF EVENTS SEMINAL IN INCITING THE PROTESTANT REFORMATION. REFORMERS FELT THE CHURCH HAD EMBELLISHED OR STRAYED FROM ORIGINAL BIBLICAL TEACHINGS.
IN AN EFFORT TO RESTORE A "TRUE" CHRISTIANITY, MANY EXPLICITLY ANTIWAR DENOMINATIONS WERE FOUNDED: AMONG THEM THE ANABAPTISTS, AMISH, MENNONITES, AND QUAKERS. IN 1670, ENGLISH QUAKER WILLIAM PENN WAS CONVICTED OF GATHERING UNLAWFUL PUBLIC ASSEMBLIES FOR PREACHING.
TWELVE YEARS LATER, HE FOUNDED PENNSYLVANIA AS A COLONIAL EXPERIMENT TO BE RUN ON QUAKER PRINCIPLES, INCLUDING NONVIOLENCE.
WHEN PENNSYLVANIA RATIFIED THEIR INFLUENTIAL DEMOCRATIC STATE CONSTITUTION IN 1776, ITS FINAL ARTICLE WAS "THAT THE PEOPLE HAVE THE RIGHT TO ASSEMBLE TOGETHER". IN 1791 THIS IDEA FOUND ITS WAY INTO THE FIRST AMENDMENT OF THE UNITED STATES CONSTITUTION.
"CONGRESS SHALL MAKE NO LAW... ABRIDGING... THE RIGHT OF THE PEOPLE PEACEABLY TO ASSEMBLE, AND TO PETITION THE GOVERNMENT FOR A REDRESS OF GRIEVANCES".
WHILE THE AMERICAN REVOLUTION HAD BEEN DECIDEDLY VIOLENT, IN NEW ZEALAND A MAORI CHIEF NAMED TE WHITI RESISTED THE BRITISH GOVERNMENT IN A UNIQUELY NONVIOLENT MANNER.
GIVEN BOTH A TRADITIONAL MAORI EDUCATION AND A CHRISTIAN ONE BY THE LIKES OF LUTHERAN MISSIONARY JOHANNES RIEMENSCHNEIDER, TE WHITI MADE THE PROPHET ISAIAH'S WORDS MANIFEST.
STARTING IN 1879, AFTER 10 YEARS OF GATHERING PLOWS, HE SENT MAORIS OUT AT A RATE OF 5 A DAY TO SIMPLY PLOW THE TRIBAL LANDS THE BRITISH WERE TRYING TO CONFISCATE FROM THEM.

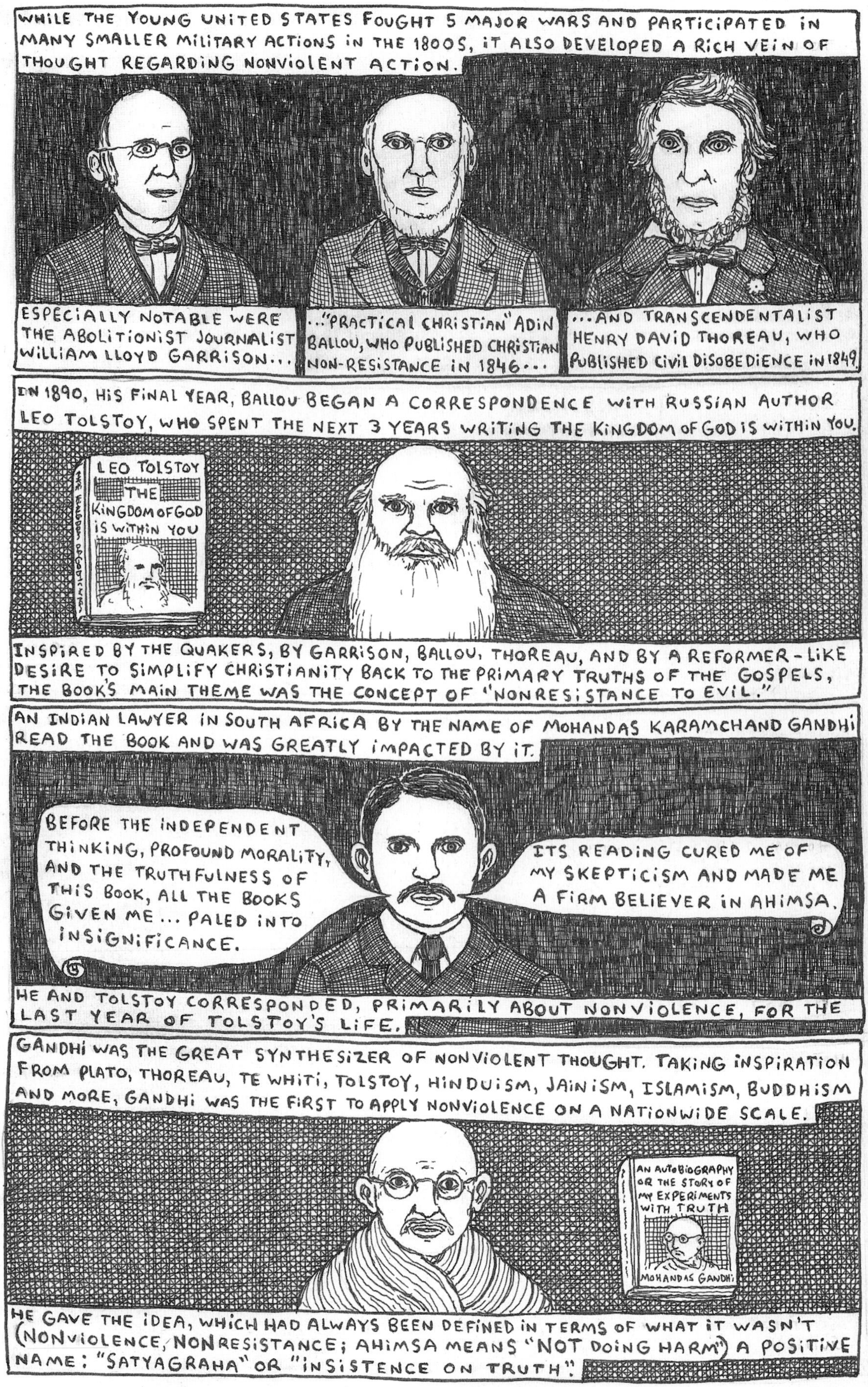
WHILE THE YOUNG UNITED STATES FOUGHT 5 MAJOR WARS AND PARTICIPATED IN MANY SMALLER MILITARY ACTIONS IN THE 1800S, IT ALSO DEVELOPED A RICH VEIN OF THOUGHT REGARDING NONVIOLENT ACTION.
ESPECIALLY NOTABLE WERE THE ABOLITIONIST JOURNALIST WILLIAM LLOYD GARRISON...
..."PRACTICAL CHRISTIAN" ADIN BALLOU, WHO PUBLISHED CHRISTIAN NON-RESISTANCE IN 1846...
...AND TRANSCENDENTALIST HENRY DAVID THOREAU, WHO PUBLISHED CIVIL DISOBEDIENCE IN 1849.
IN 1890, HIS FINAL YEAR, BALLOU BEGAN A CORRESPONDENCE WITH RUSSIAN AUTHOR LEO TOLSTOY, WHO SPENT THE NEXT 3 YEARS WRITING THE KINGDOM OF GOD IS WITHIN YOU.
LEO TOLSTOY
THE KINGDOM OF GOD IS WITHIN YOU
INSPIRED BY THE QUAKERS, BY GARRISON, BALLOU, THOREAU, AND BY A REFORMER-LIKE DESIRE TO SIMPLIFY CHRISTIANITY BACK TO THE PRIMARY TRUTHS OF THE GOSPELS, THE BOOK'S MAIN THEME WAS THE CONCEPT OF "NONRESISTANCE TO EVIL."
AN INDIAN LAWYER IN SOUTH AFRICA BY THE NAME OF MOHANDAS KARAMCHAND GANDHI READ THE BOOK AND WAS GREATLY IMPACTED BY IT.
BEFORE THE INDEPENDENT THINKING, PROFOUND MORALITY, AND THE TRUTHFULNESS OF THIS BOOK, ALL THE BOOKS GIVEN ME... PALED INTO INSIGNIFICANCE.
ITS READING CURED ME OF MY SKEPTICISM AND MADE ME A FIRM BELIEVER IN AHIMSA.
HE AND TOLSTOY CORRESPONDED, PRIMARILY ABOUT NONVIOLENCE, FOR THE LAST YEAR OF TOLSTOY'S LIFE.
GANDHI WAS THE GREAT SYNTHESIZER OF NONVIOLENT THOUGHT. TAKING INSPIRATION FROM PLATO, THOREAU, TE WHITI, TOLSTOY, HINDUISM, JAINISM, ISLAMISM, BUDDHISM AND MORE, GANDHI WAS THE FIRST TO APPLY NONVIOLENCE ON A NATIONWIDE SCALE.
AN AUTOBIOGRAPHY OR THE STORY OF MY EXPERIMENTS WITH TRUTH
MOHANDAS GANDHI
HE GAVE THE IDEA, WHICH HAD ALWAYS BEEN DEFINED IN TERMS OF WHAT IT WASN'T (NONVIOLENCE, NONRESISTANCE; AHIMSA MEANS "NOT DOING HARM") A POSITIVE NAME: "SATYAGRAHA" OR "INSISTENCE ON TRUTH".

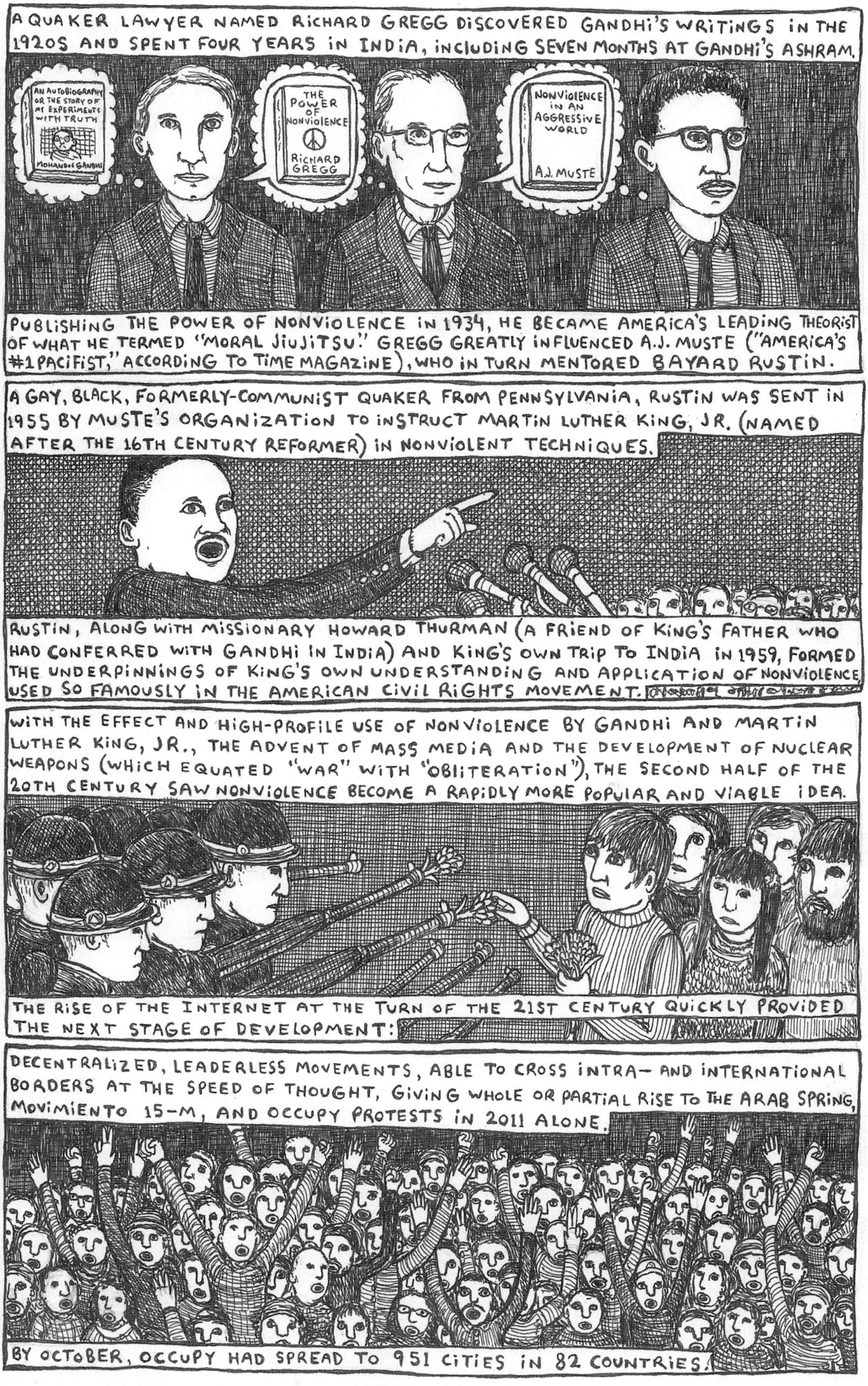
A QUAKER LAWYER NAMED RICHARD GREGG DISCOVERED GANDHI'S WRITINGS IN THE 1920S AND SPENT FOUR YEARS IN INDIA, INCLUDING SEVEN MONTHS AT GANDHI'S ASHRAM.
AN AUTOBIOGRAPHY OR THE STORY OF MY EXPERIMENTS WITH TRUTH
MOHANDAS GANDHI
THE POWER OF NONVIOLENCE
RICHARD GREGG
NONVIOLENCE IN AN AGGRESSIVE WORLD
A.J. MUSTE
PUBLISHING THE POWER OF NONVIOLENCE IN 1934, HE BECAME AMERICA'S LEADING THEORIST OF WHAT HE TERMED "MORAL JIUJITSU." GREGG GREATLY INFLUENCED A.J. MUSTE ("AMERICA'S #1 PACIFIST," ACCORDING TO TIME MAGAZINE), WHO IN TURN MENTORED BAYARD RUSTIN.
A GAY, BLACK, FORMERLY-COMMUNIST QUAKER FROM PENNSYLVANIA, RUSTIN WAS SENT IN 1955 BY MUSTE'S ORGANIZATION TO INSTRUCT MARTIN LUTHER KING, JR. (NAMED AFTER THE 16TH CENTURY REFORMER) IN NONVIOLENT TECHNIQUES.
RUSTIN, ALONG WITH MISSIONARY HOWARD THURMAN (A FRIEND OF KING'S FATHER WHO HAD CONFERRED WITH GANDHI IN INDIA) AND KING'S OWN TRIP TO INDIA IN 1959, FORMED THE UNDERPINNINGS OF KING'S OWN UNDERSTANDING AND APPLICATION OF NONVIOLENCE, USED SO FAMOUSLY IN THE AMERICAN CIVIL RIGHTS MOVEMENT.
WITH THE EFFECT AND HIGH-PROFILE USE OF NONVIOLENCE BY GANDHI AND MARTIN LUTHER KING, JR., THE ADVENT OF MASS MEDIA AND THE DEVELOPMENT OF NUCLEAR WEAPONS (WHICH EQUATED "WAR" WITH "OBLITERATION"), THE SECOND HALF OF THE 20TH CENTURY SAW NONVIOLENCE BECOME A RAPIDLY MORE POPULAR AND VIABLE IDEA.
THE RISE OF THE INTERNET AT THE TURN OF THE 21ST CENTURY QUICKLY PROVIDED THE NEXT STAGE OF DEVELOPMENT:
DECENTRALIZED, LEADERLESS MOVEMENTS, ABLE TO CROSS INTRA- AND INTERNATIONAL BORDERS AT THE SPEED OF THOUGHT, GIVING WHOLE OR PARTIAL RISE TO THE ARAB SPRING, MOVIMIENTO 15-M, AND OCCUPY PROTESTS IN 2011 ALONE.
BY OCTOBER, OCCUPY HAD SPREAD TO 951 CITIES IN 82 COUNTRIES.

AS FOR THE FUTURE HISTORY OF NONVIOLENCE ... WELL, THAT'S UP TO YOU ....

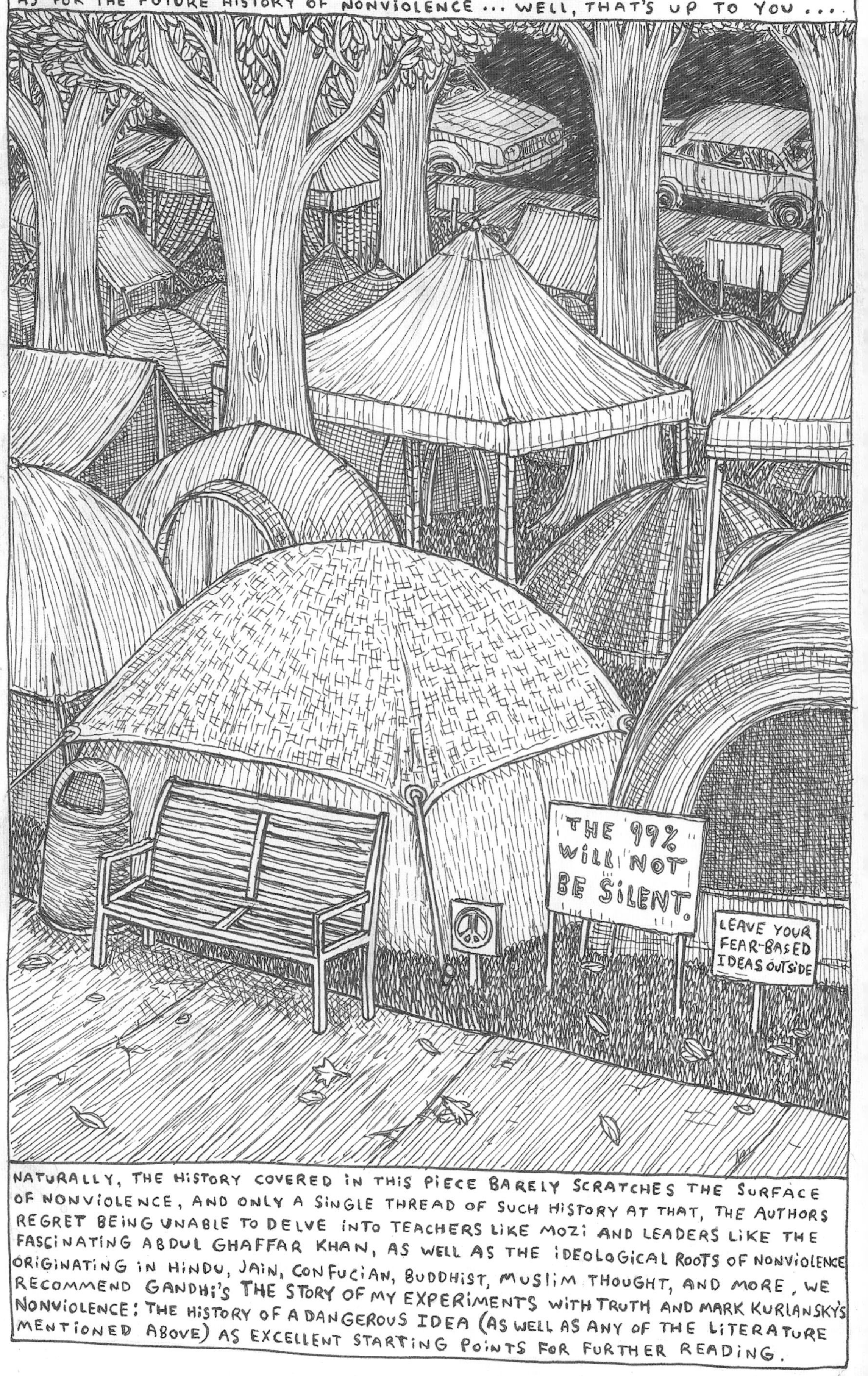
THE 99% WILL NOT BE SILENT.
LEAVE YOUR FEAR-BASED IDEAS OUTSIDE

NATURALLY, THE HISTORY COVERED IN THIS PIECE BARELY SCRATCHES THE SURFACE OF NONVIOLENCE, AND ONLY A SINGLE THREAD OF SUCH HISTORY AT THAT, THE AUTHORS REGRET BEING UNABLE TO DELVE INTO TEACHERS LIKE MOZI AND LEADERS LIKE THE FASCINATING ABDUL GHAFFAR KHAN, AS WELL AS THE IDEOLOGICAL ROOTS OF NONVIOLENCE ORIGINATING IN HINDU, JAIN, CONFUCIAN, BUDDHIST, MUSLIM THOUGHT, AND MORE, WE RECOMMEND GANDHI'S THE STORY OF MY EXPERIMENTS WITH TRUTH AND MARK KURLANSKY'S NONVIOLENCE: THE HISTORY OF A DANGEROUS IDEA (AS WELL AS ANY OF THE LITERATURE MENTIONED ABOVE) AS EXCELLENT STARTING POINTS FOR FURTHER READING.

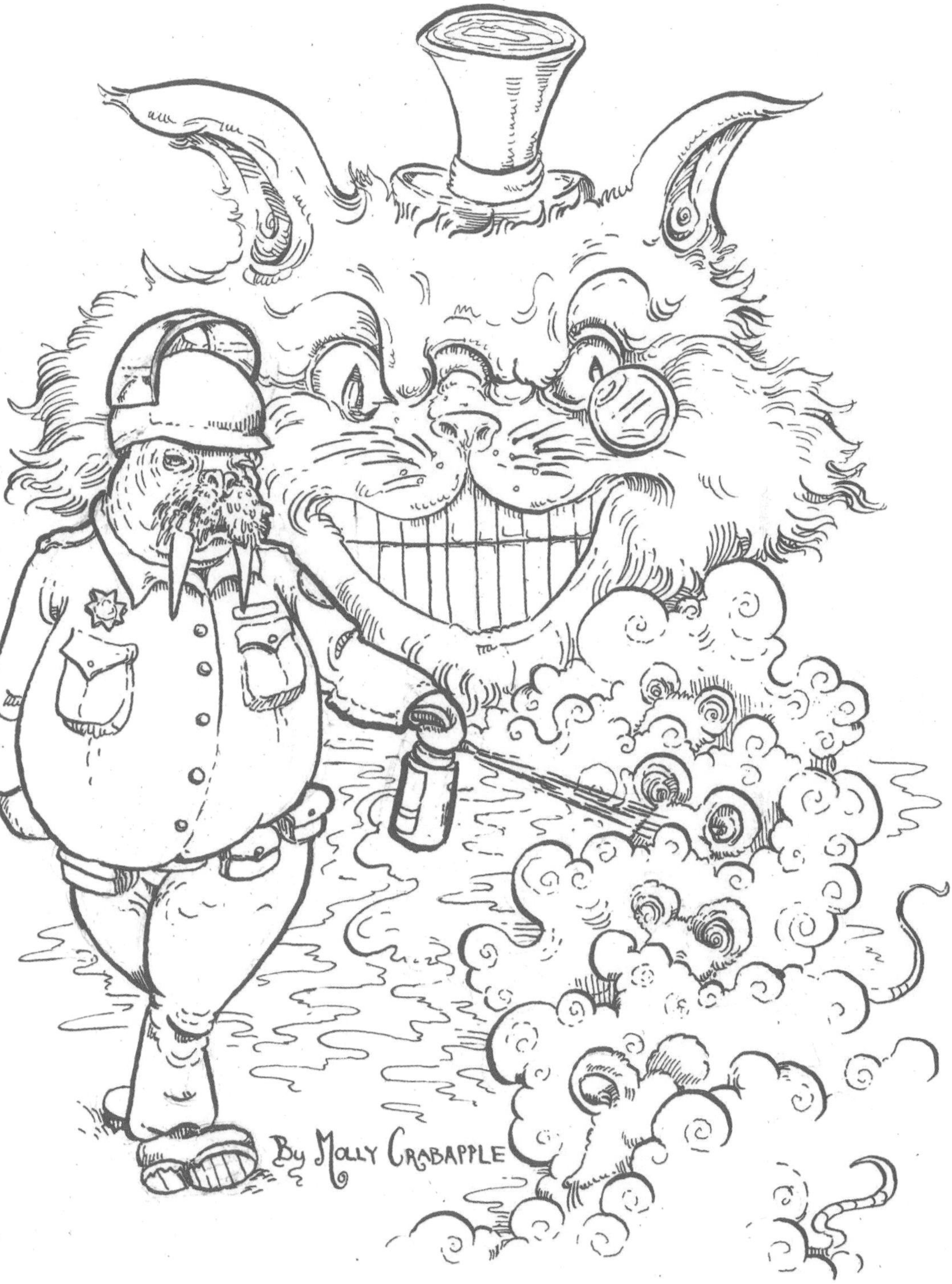
By Molly Crabapple

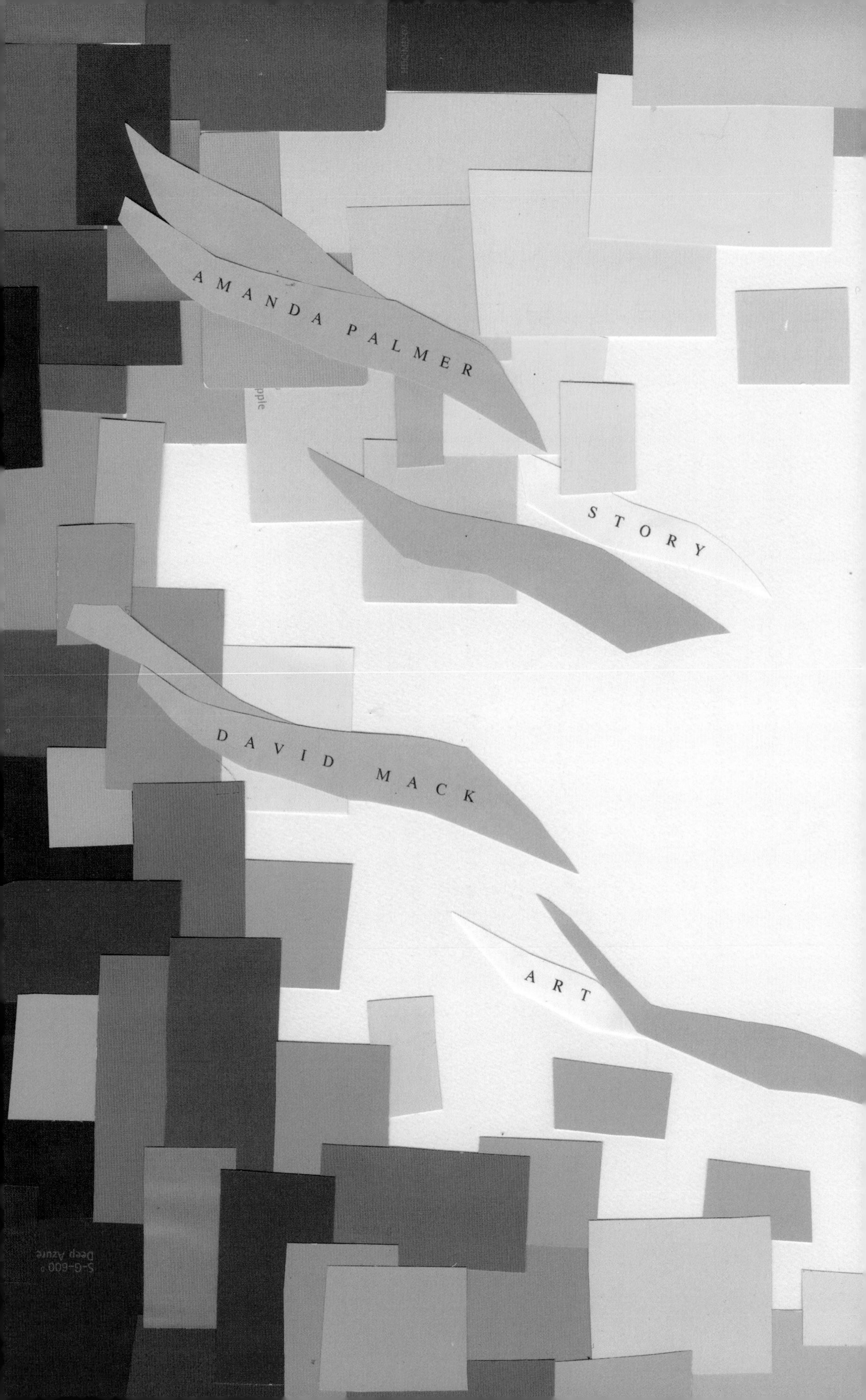
AMANDA PALMER
STORY
DAVID MACK
ART

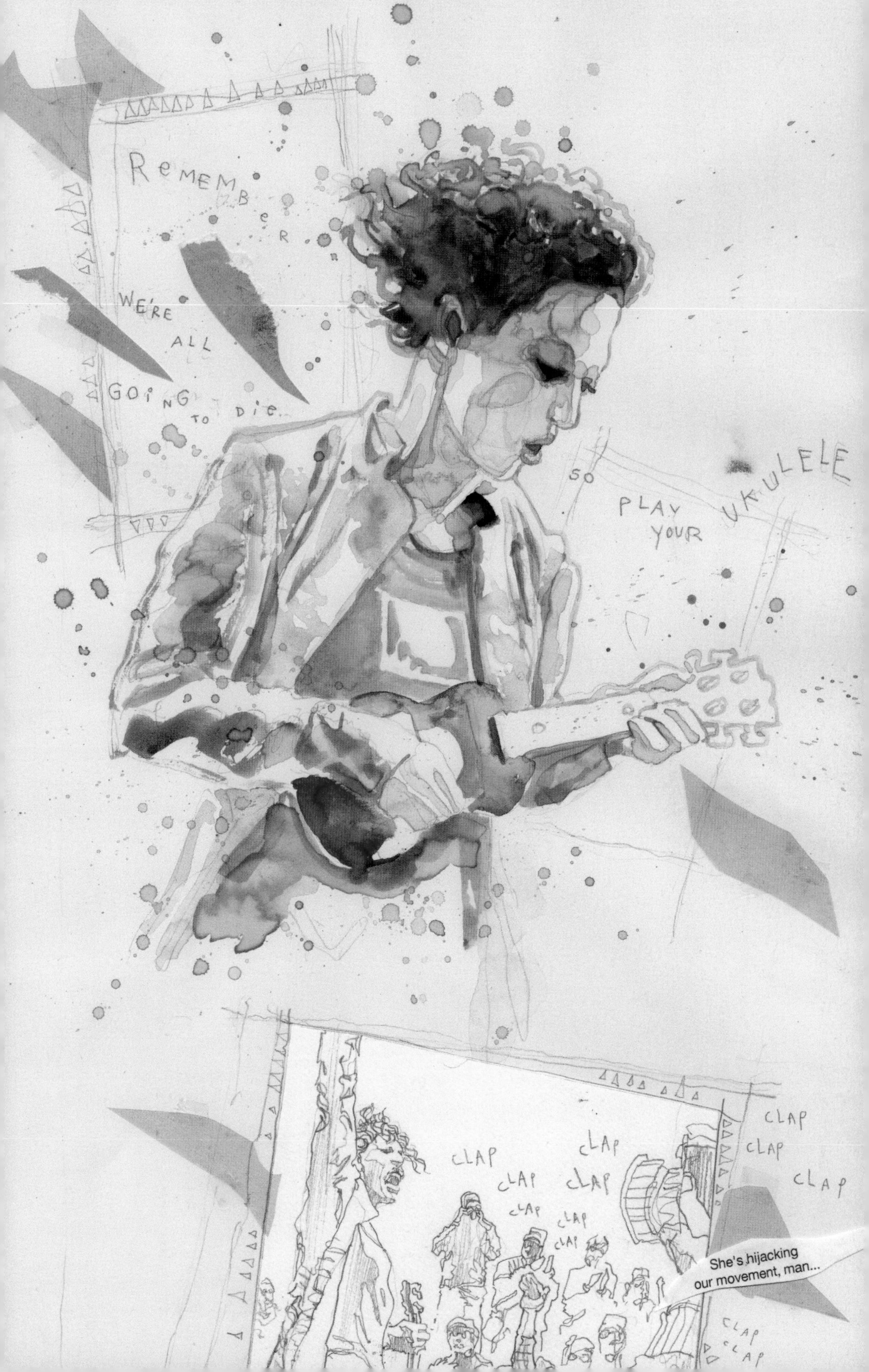

REMEMBER
WE'RE ALL GOING TO DIE
SO PLAY YOUR UKULELE
CLAP CLAP CLAP CLAP CLAP CLAP CLAP CLAP CLAP
She's hijacking our movement, man...
CLAP CLAP

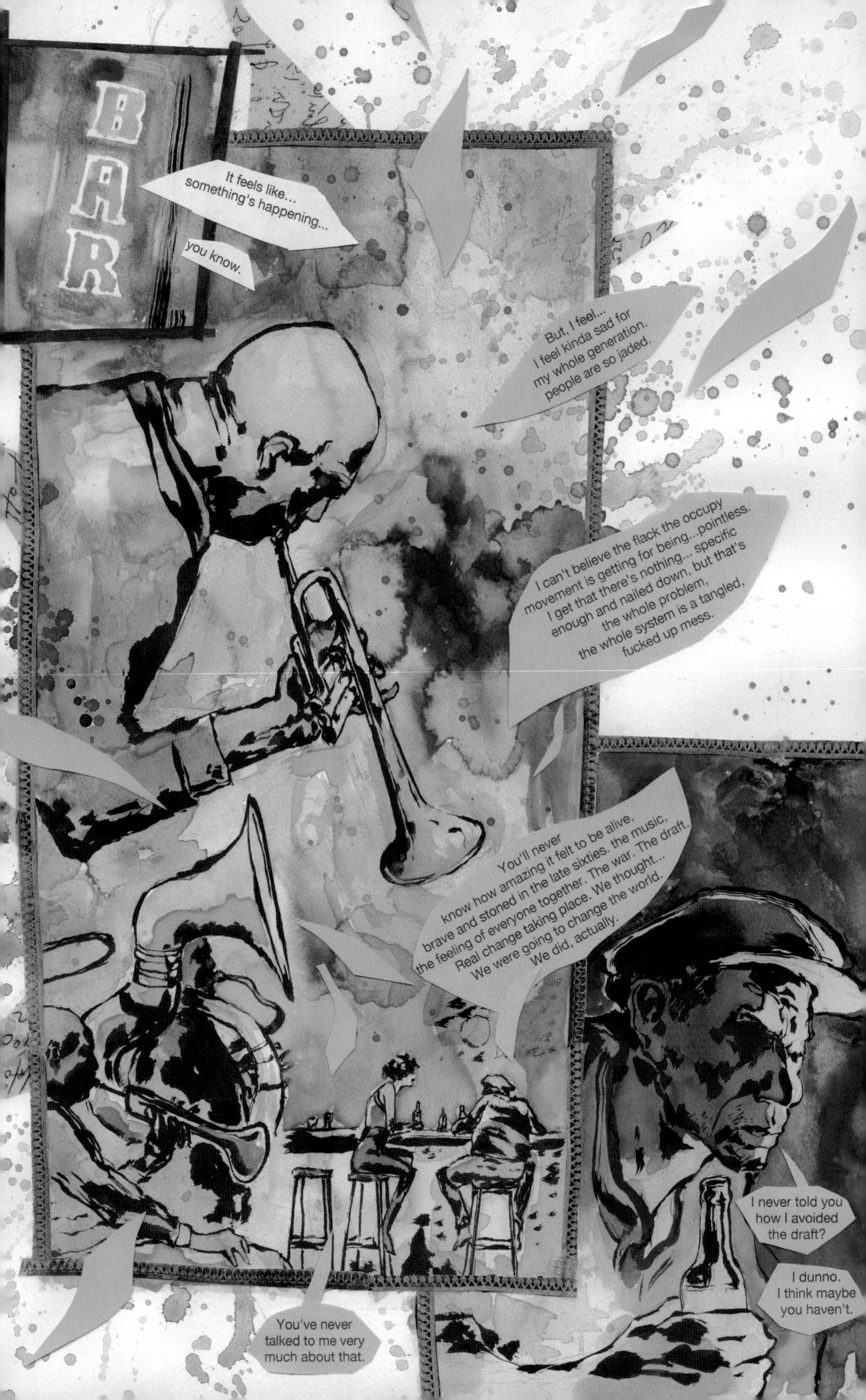
BAR
It feels like... something's happening...
you know.
But, I feel... I feel kinda sad for my whole generation. people are so jaded.
I can't believe the flack the occupy movement is getting for being...pointless. I get that there's nothing... specific enough and nailed down, but that's the whole problem, the whole system is a tangled, fucked up mess.
You'll never know how amazing it felt to be alive, brave and stoned in the late sixties. the music, the feeling of everyone together. The war. The draft. Real change taking place. We thought... We were going to change the world. We did, actually.
You've never talked to me very much about that.
I never told you how I avoided the draft?
I dunno. I think maybe you haven't.

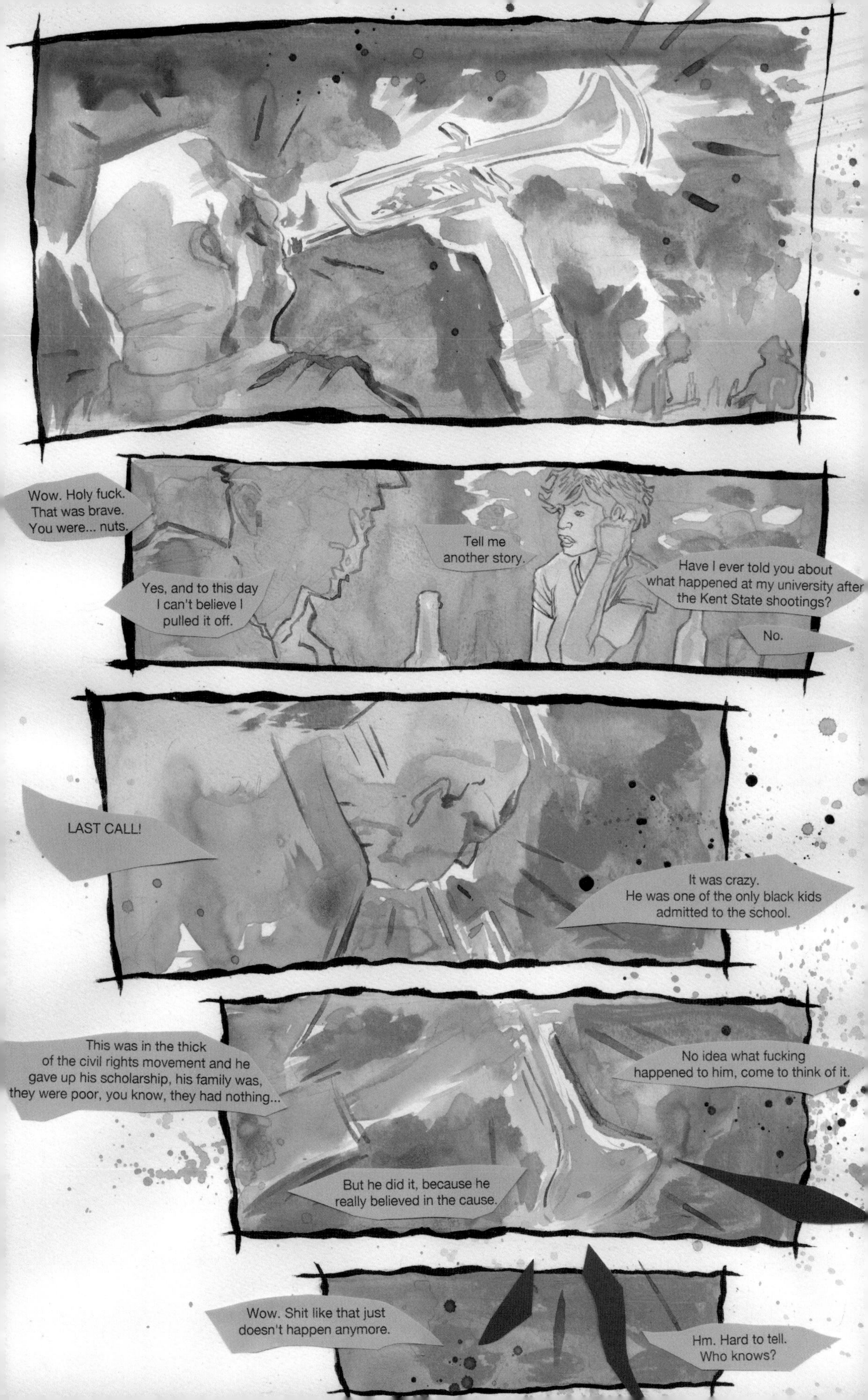

Wow. Holy fuck. That was brave. You were... nuts.
Yes, and to this day I can't believe I pulled it off.
Tell me another story.
Have I ever told you about what happened at my university after the Kent State shootings?
No.
LAST CALL!
It was crazy. He was one of the only black kids admitted to the school.
This was in the thick of the civil rights movement and he gave up his scholarship, his family was, they were poor, you know, they had nothing...
No idea what fucking happened to him, come to think of it.
But he did it, because he really believed in the cause.
Wow. Shit like that just doesn't happen anymore.
Hm. Hard to tell. Who knows?

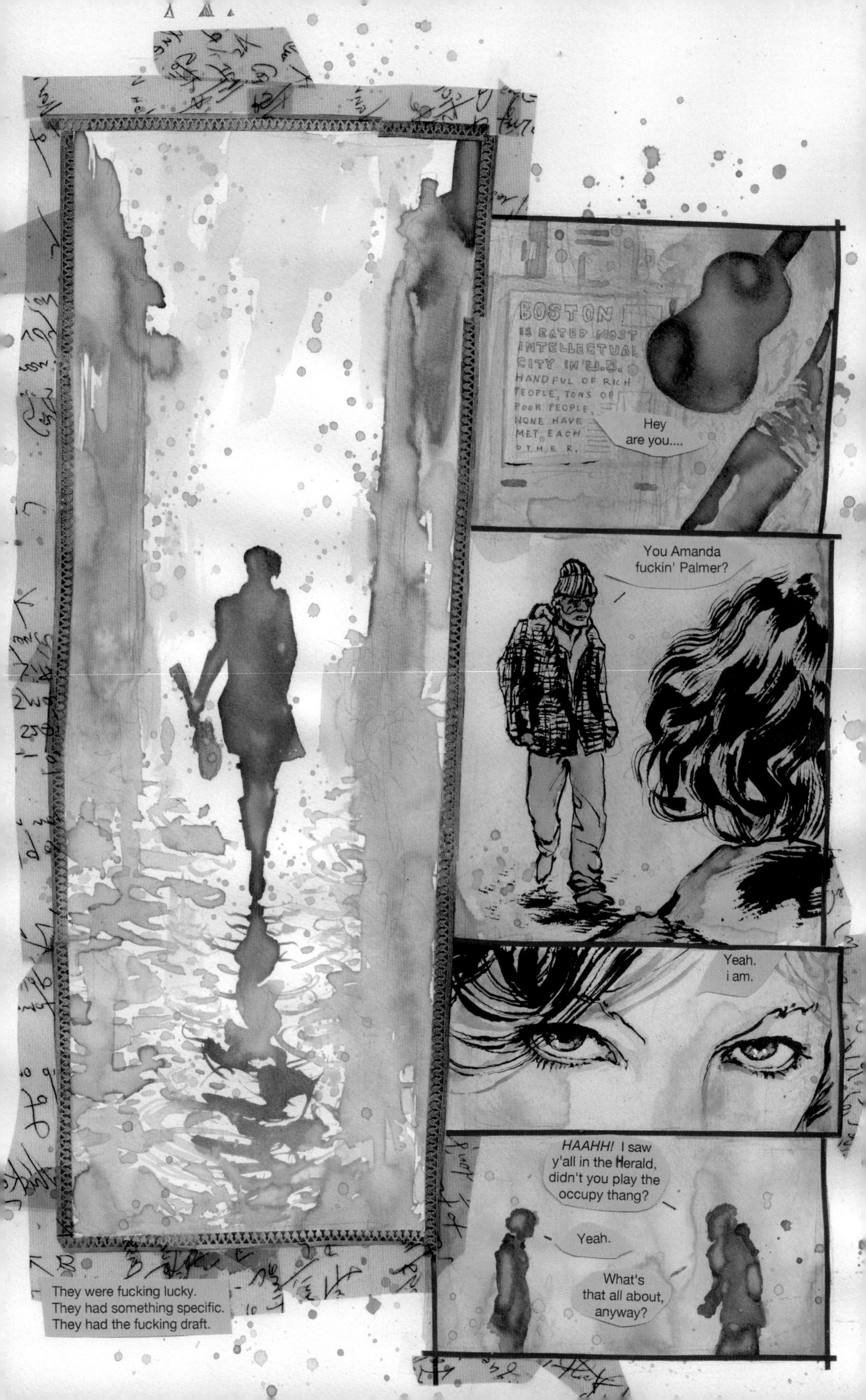
They were fucking lucky.
They had something specific.
They had the fucking draft.
BOSTON IS RATED MOST INTELLECTUAL CITY IN U.S.
HANDFUL OF RICH PEOPLE, TONS OF POOR PEOPLE, NONE HAVE MET EACH OTHER.
Hey are you....
You Amanda fuckin' Palmer?
Yeah. i am.
HAAHH! I saw y'all in the Herald, didn't you play the occupy thang?
Yeah.
What's that all about, anyway?

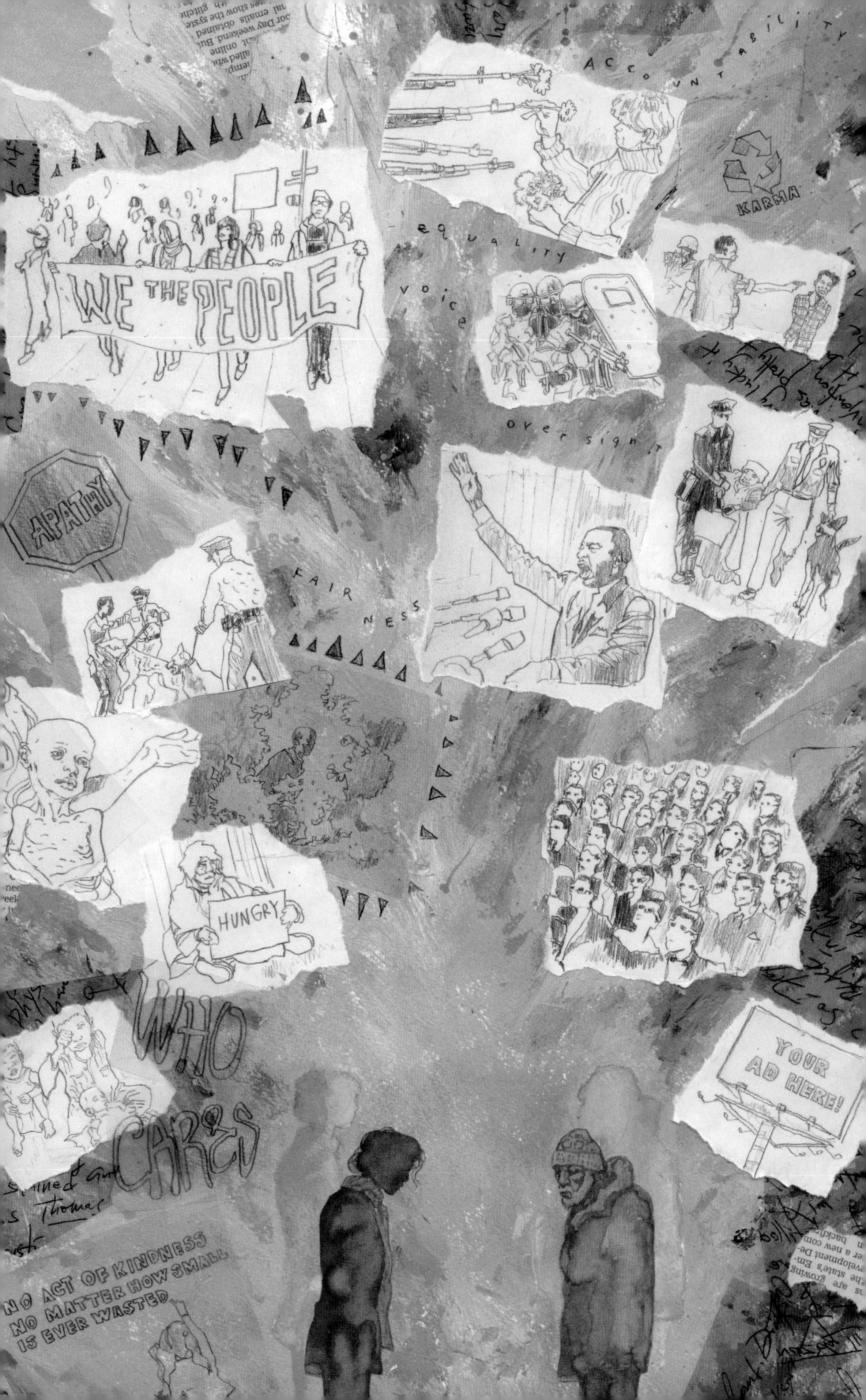
ACCOUNTABILITY
WE THE PEOPLE
KARMA
equality
voice
over sight
APATHY
FAIRNESS
HUNGRY
WHO CARES
YOUR AD HERE!
NO ACT OF KINDNESS
NO MATTER HOW SMALL
IS EVER WASTED

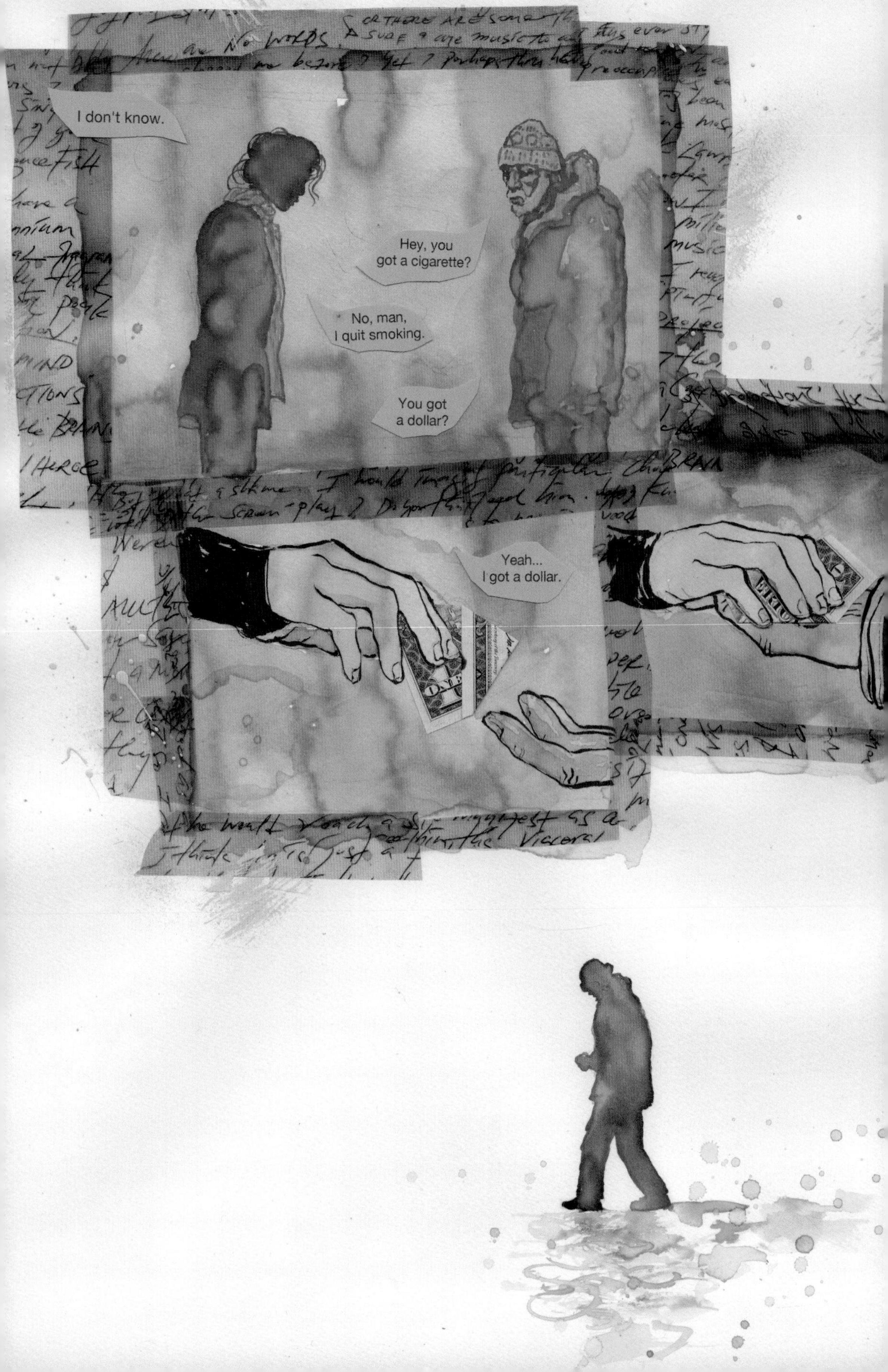
I don't know.
Hey, you got a cigarette?
No, man, I quit smoking.
You got a dollar?
Yeah... I got a dollar.

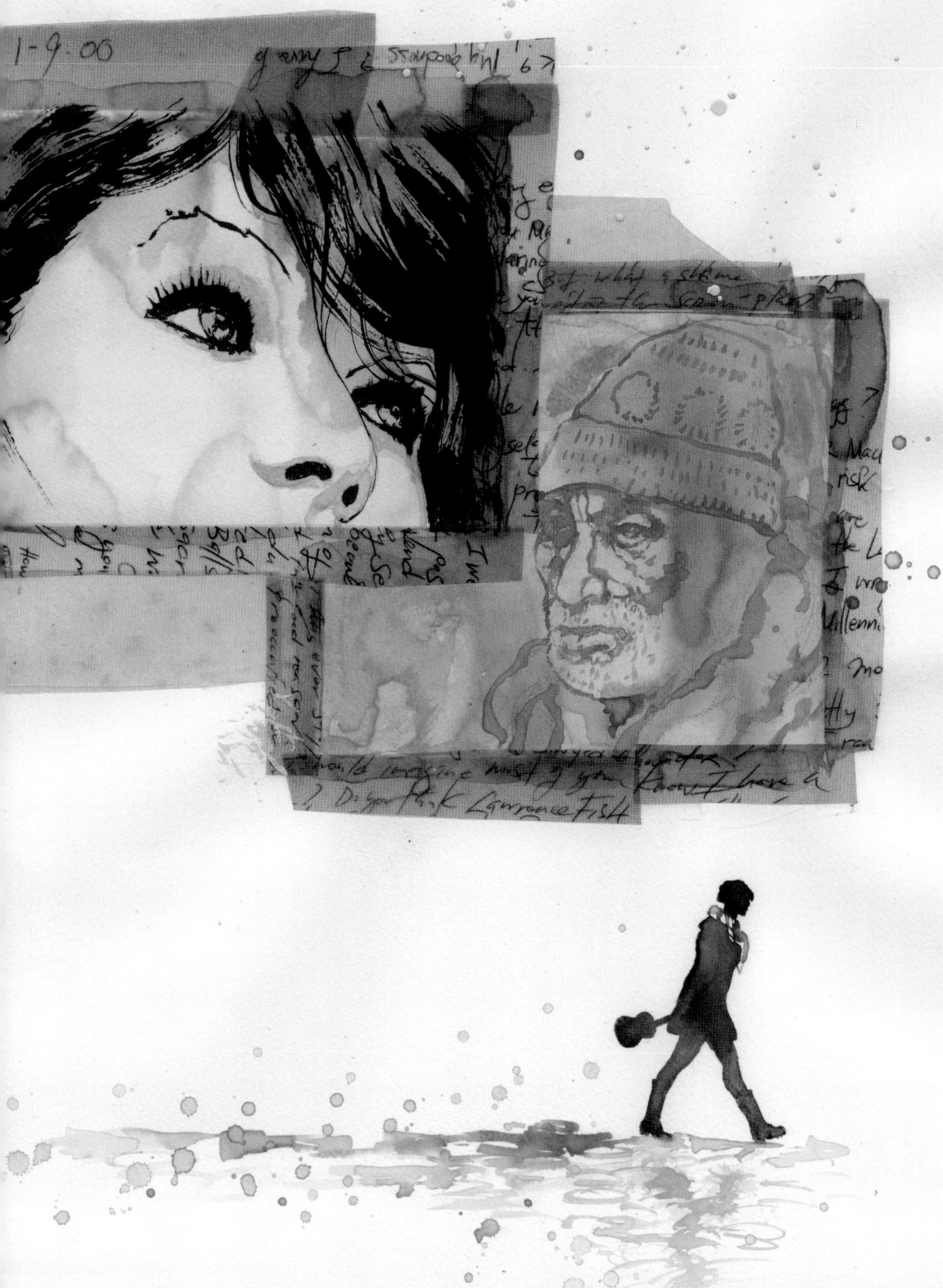
1-9.00

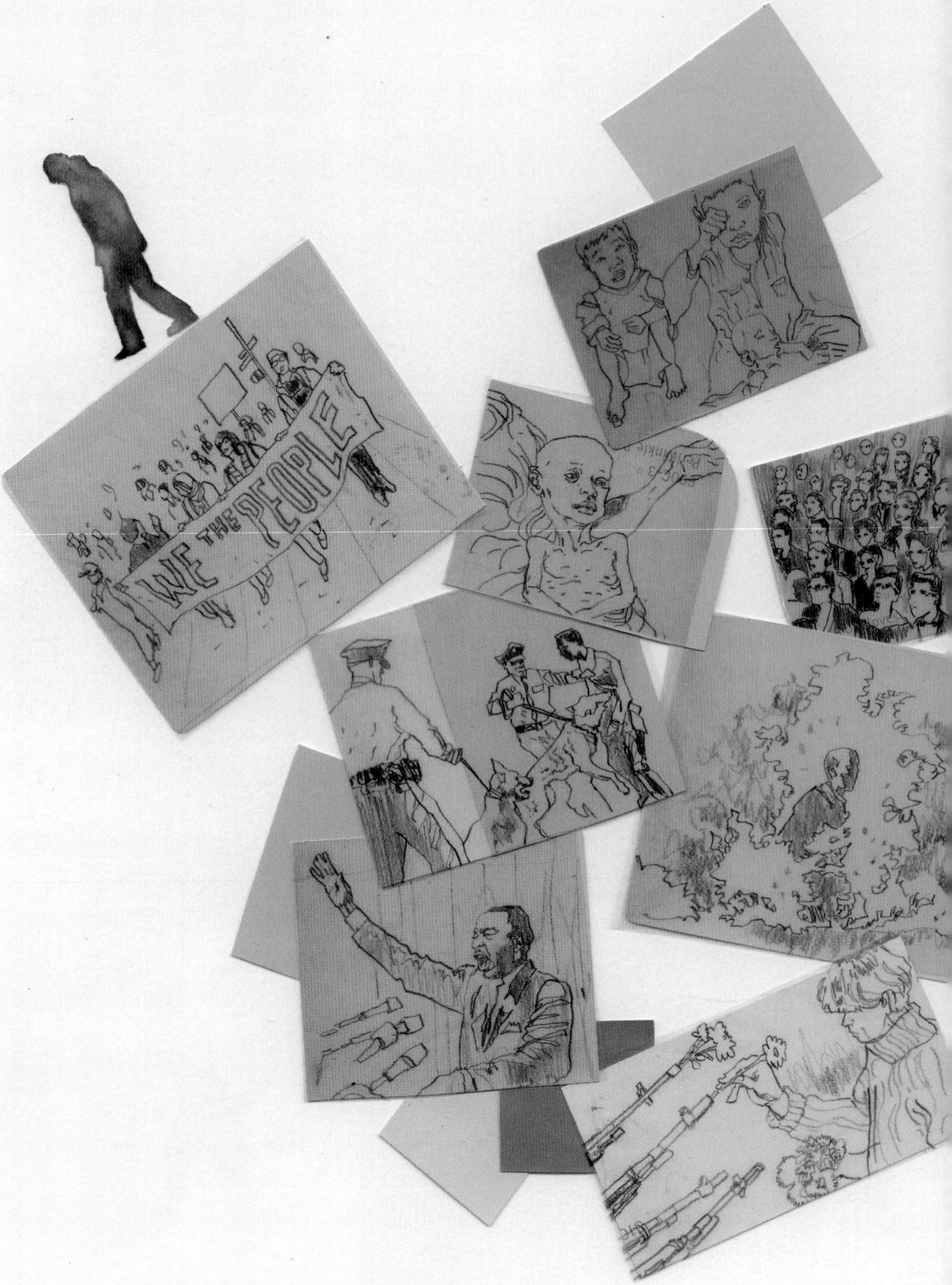
WE THE PEOPLE

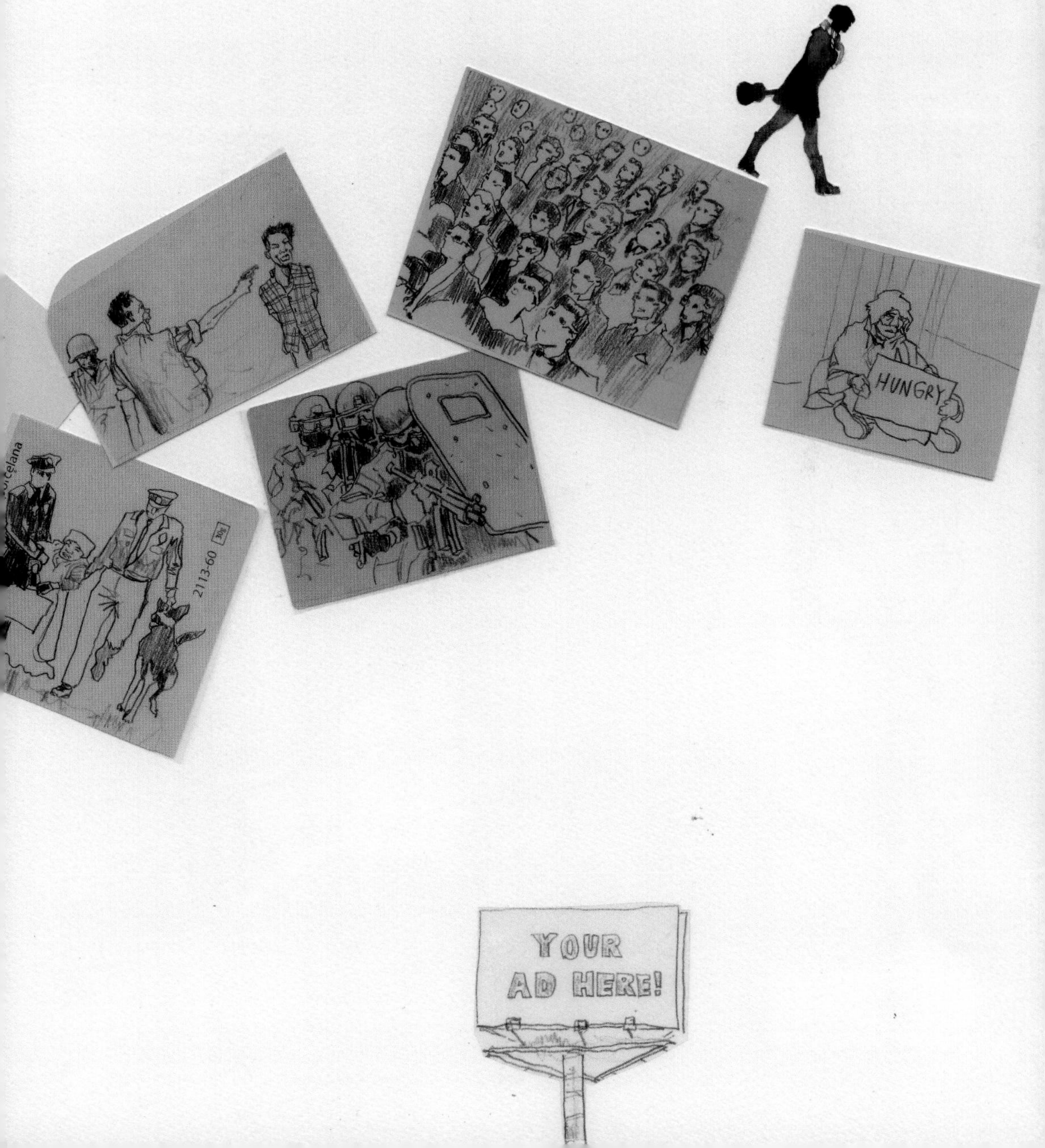
HUNGRY
2113-60
YOUR AD HERE!

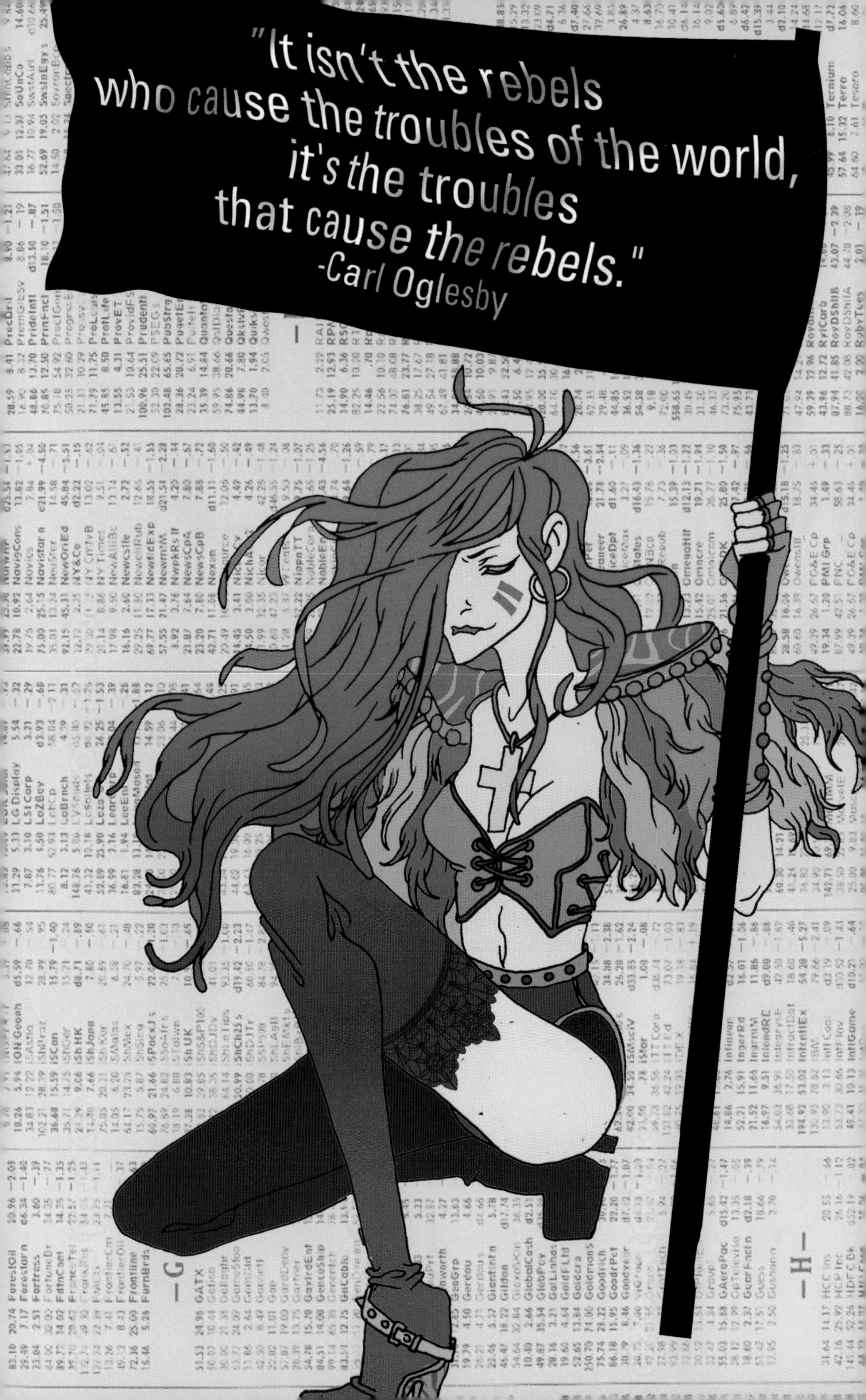
"It isn't the rebels
who cause the troubles of the world,
it's the troubles
that cause the rebels."
-Carl Oglesby

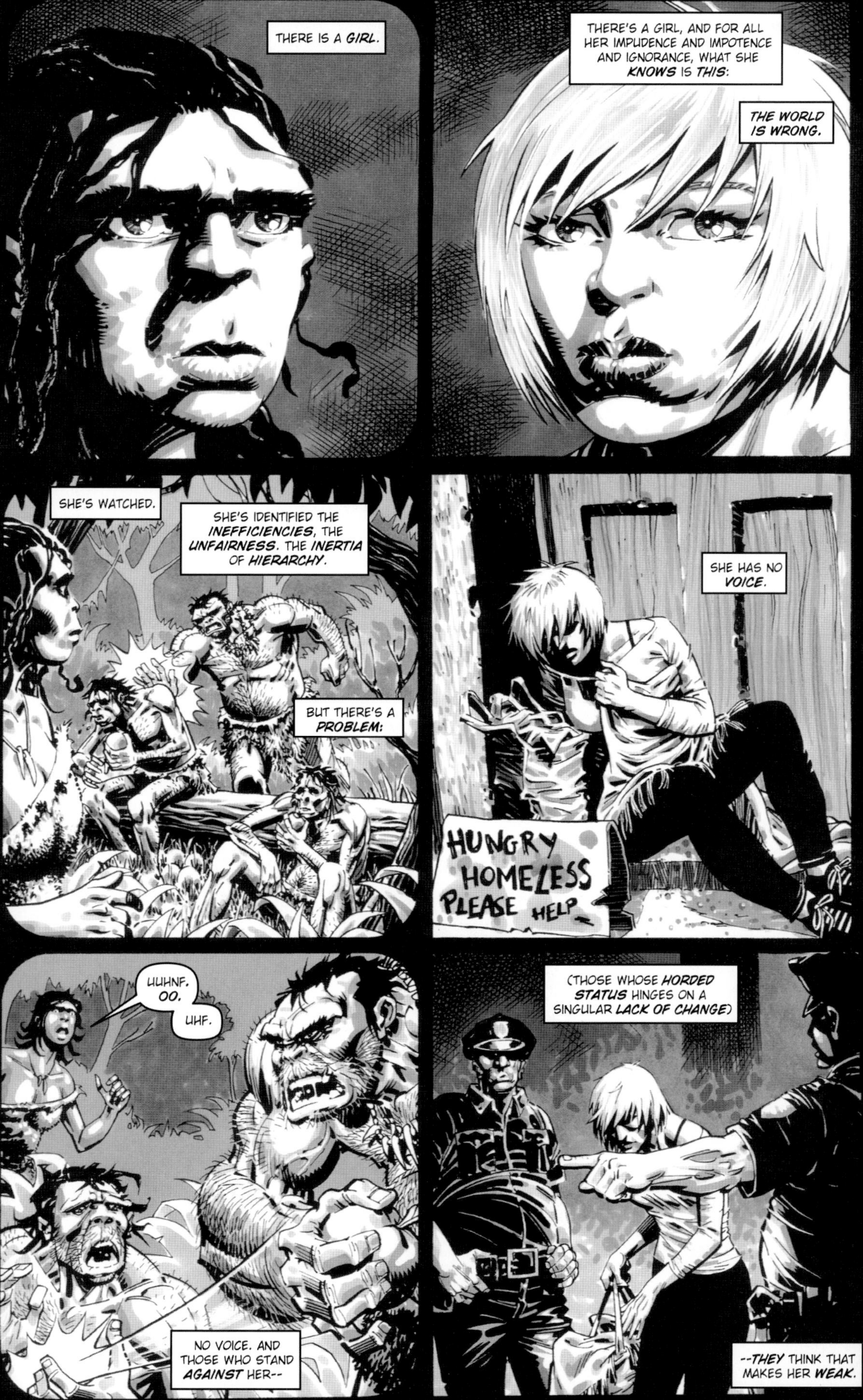
THERE IS A *GIRL.*
THERE'S A GIRL, AND FOR ALL HER IMPUDENCE AND IMPOTENCE AND IGNORANCE, WHAT SHE *KNOWS* IS *THIS:*
THE WORLD IS WRONG.
SHE'S WATCHED.
SHE'S IDENTIFIED THE *INEFFICIENCIES*, THE *UNFAIRNESS*. THE *INERTIA* OF *HIERARCHY*.
BUT THERE'S A *PROBLEM:*
SHE HAS NO *VOICE*.
HUNGRY HOMELESS PLEASE HELP
UUHNF. OO.
UHF.
NO VOICE. AND THOSE WHO STAND *AGAINST* HER--
(THOSE WHOSE *HORDED STATUS* HINGES ON A SINGULAR *LACK OF CHANGE*)
--*THEY* THINK THAT MAKES HER *WEAK*.

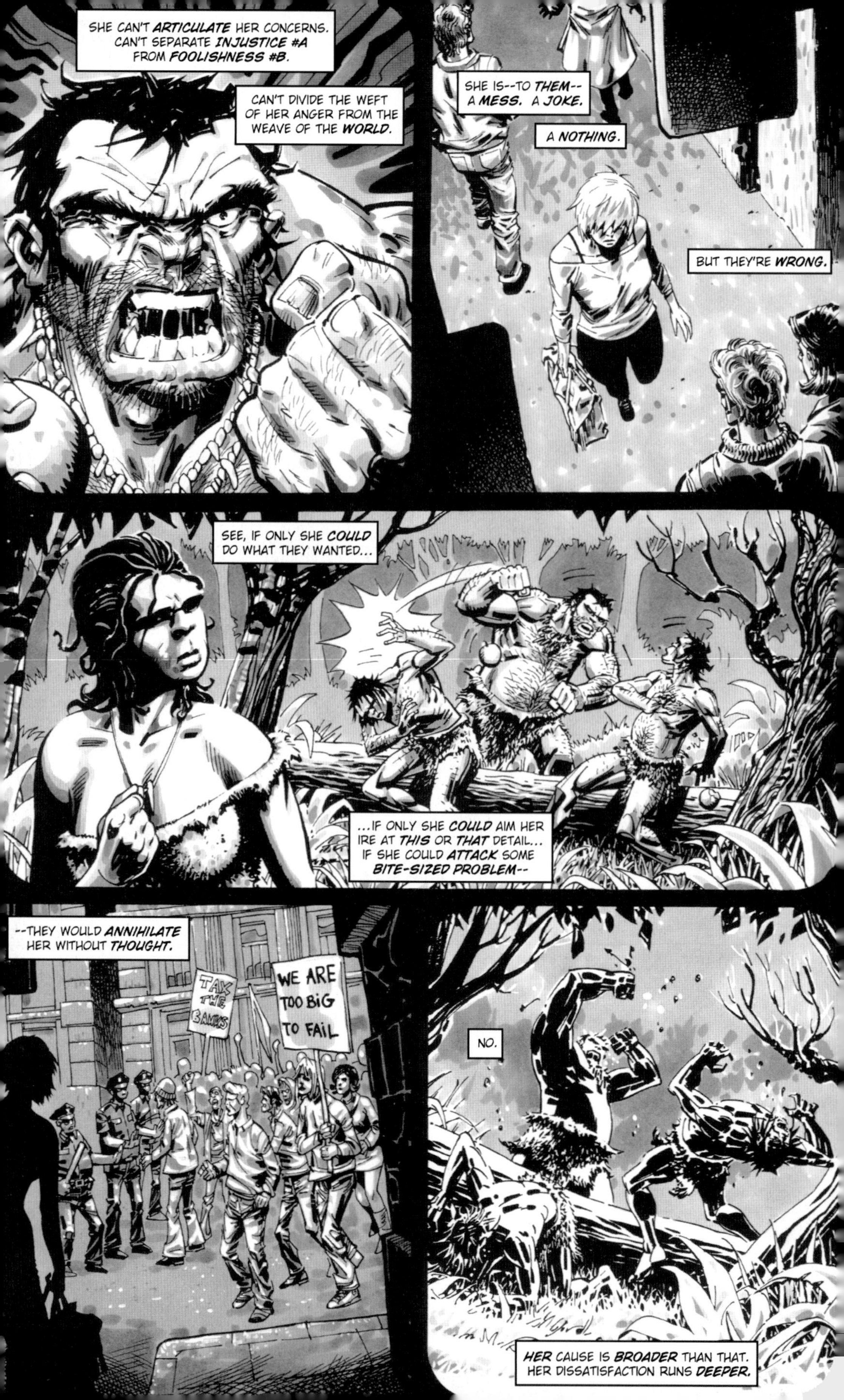
SHE CAN'T ARTICULATE HER CONCERNS. CAN'T SEPARATE INJUSTICE #A FROM FOOLISHNESS #B.
CAN'T DIVIDE THE WEFT OF HER ANGER FROM THE WEAVE OF THE WORLD.
SHE IS--TO THEM--A MESS. A JOKE.
A NOTHING.
BUT THEY'RE WRONG.
SEE, IF ONLY SHE COULD DO WHAT THEY WANTED...
...IF ONLY SHE COULD AIM HER IRE AT THIS OR THAT DETAIL... IF SHE COULD ATTACK SOME BITE-SIZED PROBLEM--
--THEY WOULD ANNIHILATE HER WITHOUT THOUGHT.
TAX THE BANKS
WE ARE TOO BIG TO FAIL
NO.
HER CAUSE IS BROADER THAN THAT. HER DISSATISFACTION RUNS DEEPER.

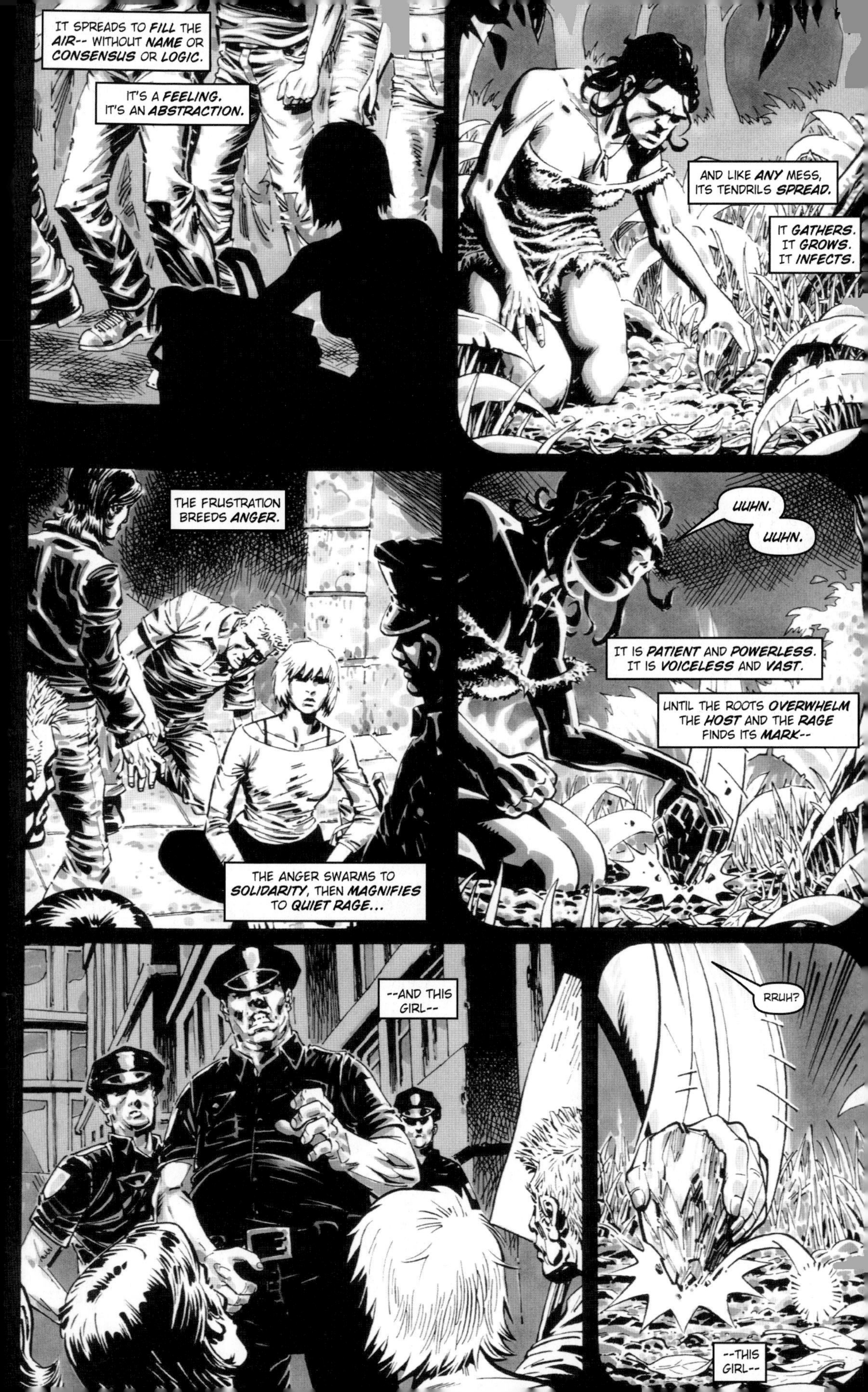
IT SPREADS TO FILL THE AIR-- WITHOUT NAME OR CONSENSUS OR LOGIC.
IT'S A FEELING. IT'S AN ABSTRACTION.
AND LIKE ANY MESS, ITS TENDRILS SPREAD.
IT GATHERS. IT GROWS. IT INFECTS.
THE FRUSTRATION BREEDS ANGER.
THE ANGER SWARMS TO SOLIDARITY, THEN MAGNIFIES TO QUIET RAGE...
UUHN.
UUHN.
IT IS PATIENT AND POWERLESS. IT IS VOICELESS AND VAST.
UNTIL THE ROOTS OVERWHELM THE HOST AND THE RAGE FINDS ITS MARK--
--AND THIS GIRL--
RRUH?
--THIS GIRL--

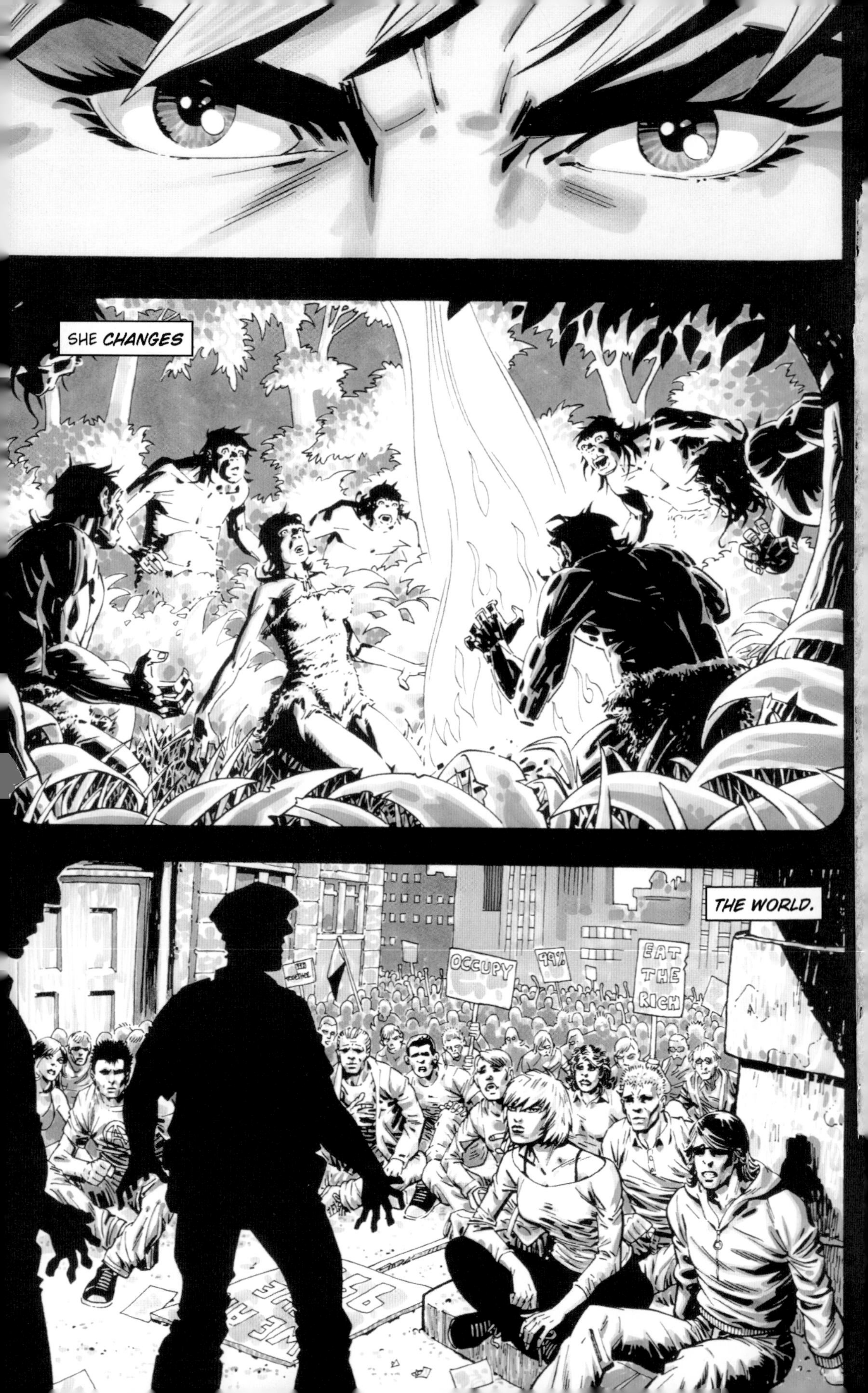
SHE CHANGES
THE WORLD.
OCCUPY
99%
EAT THE RICH

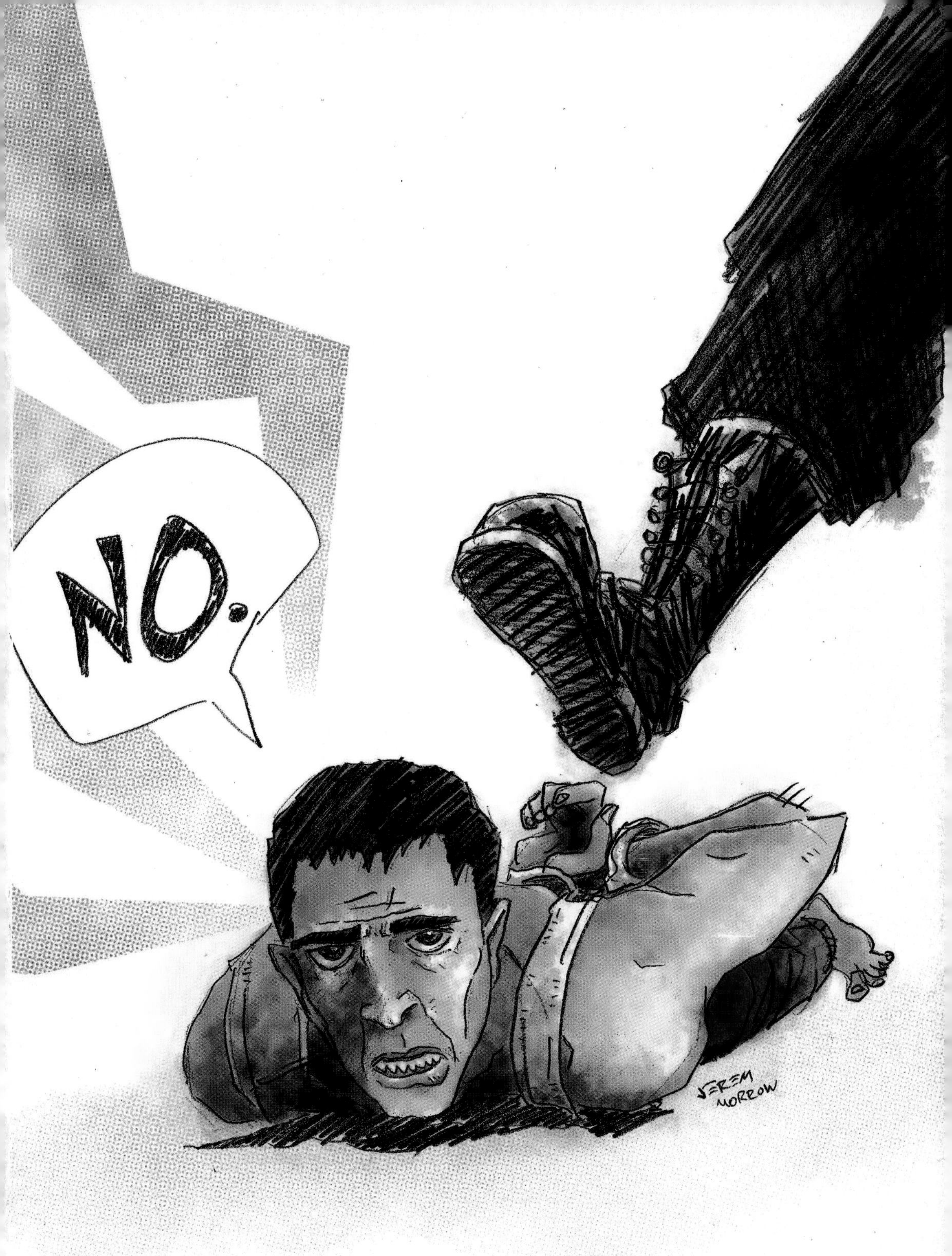
NO.
JEREM MORROW

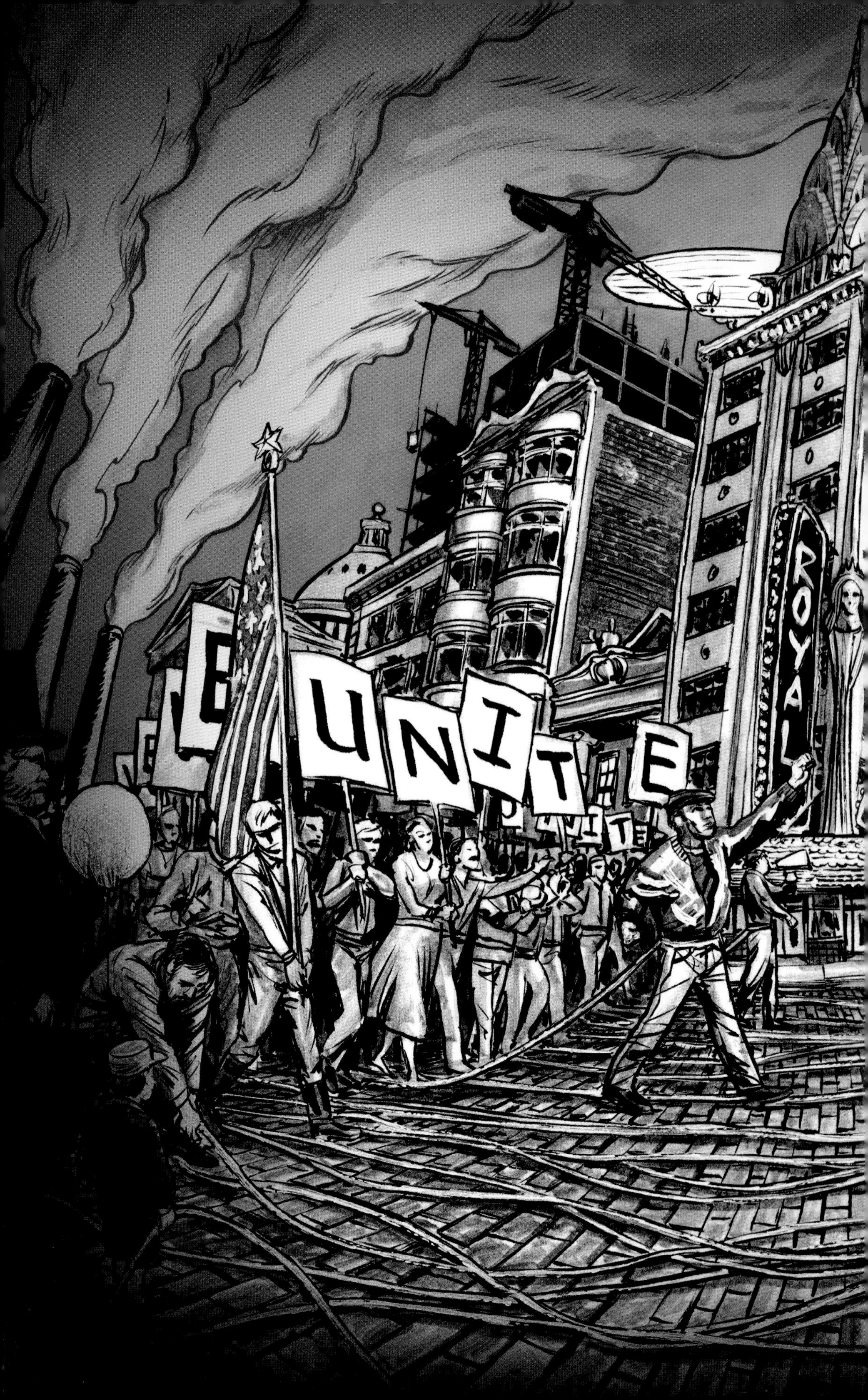
UNITE
ROYAL

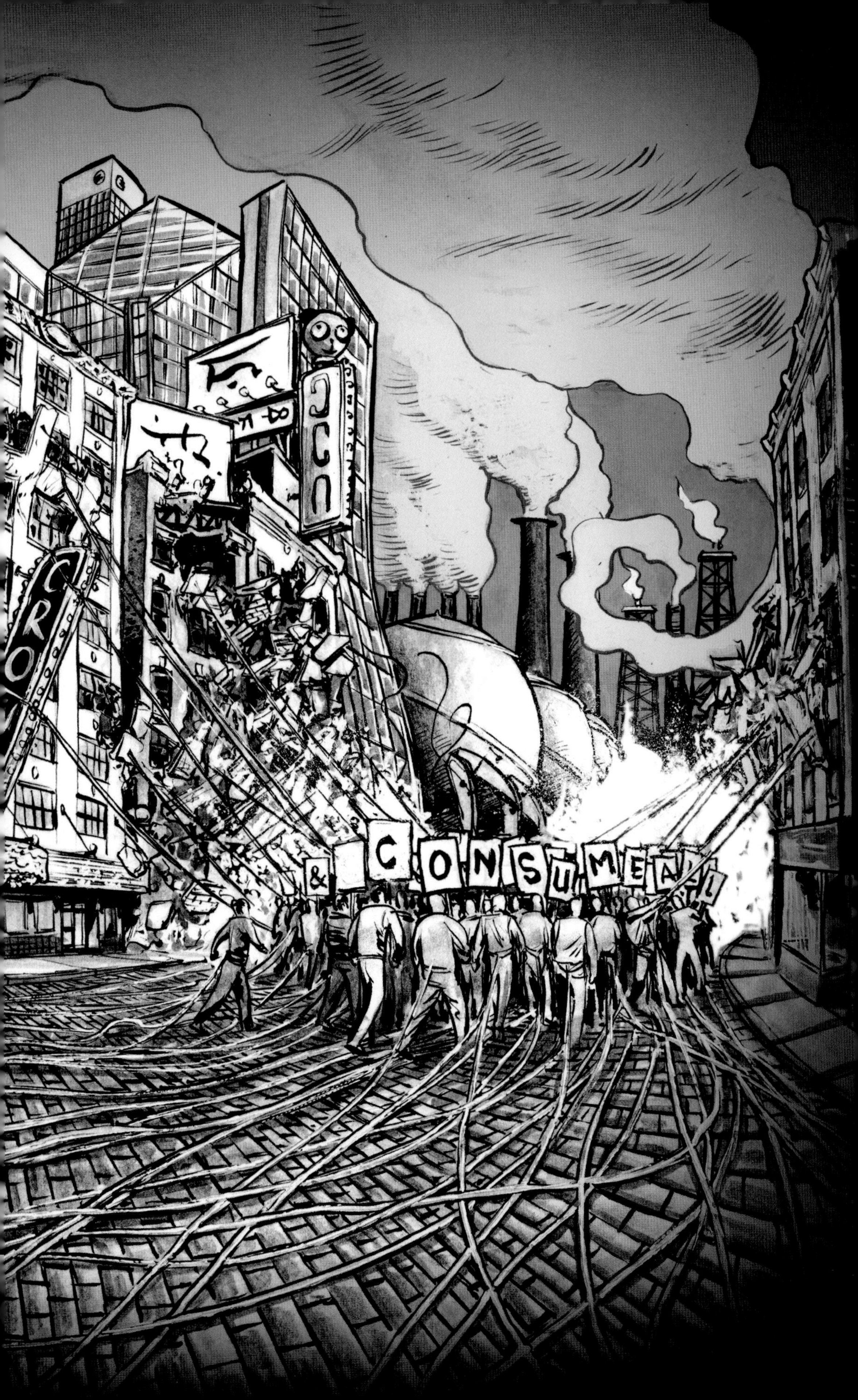
CRO
& CONSUME ALL

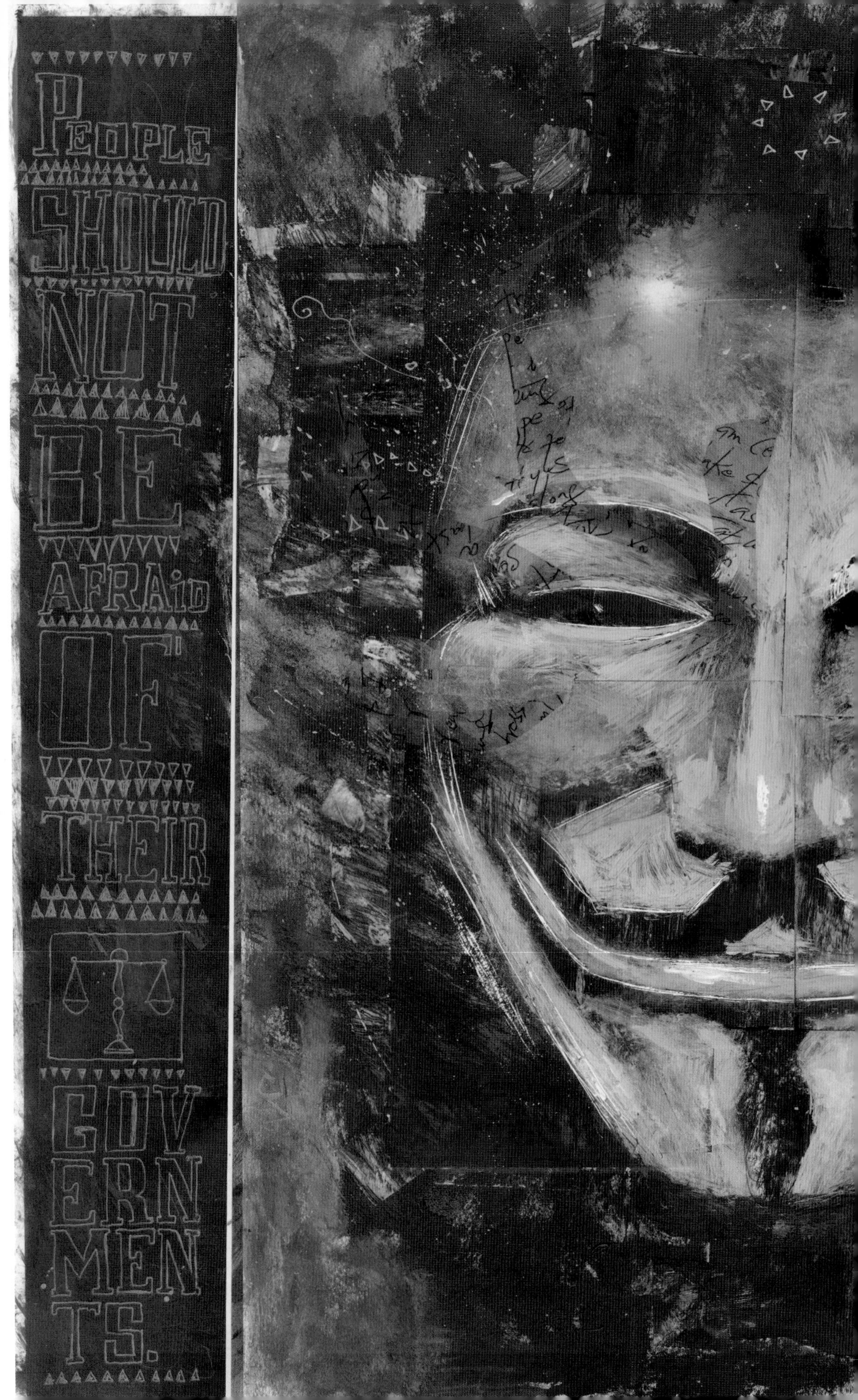
PEOPLE SHOULD NOT BE AFRAID OF THEIR GOVERNMENTS.

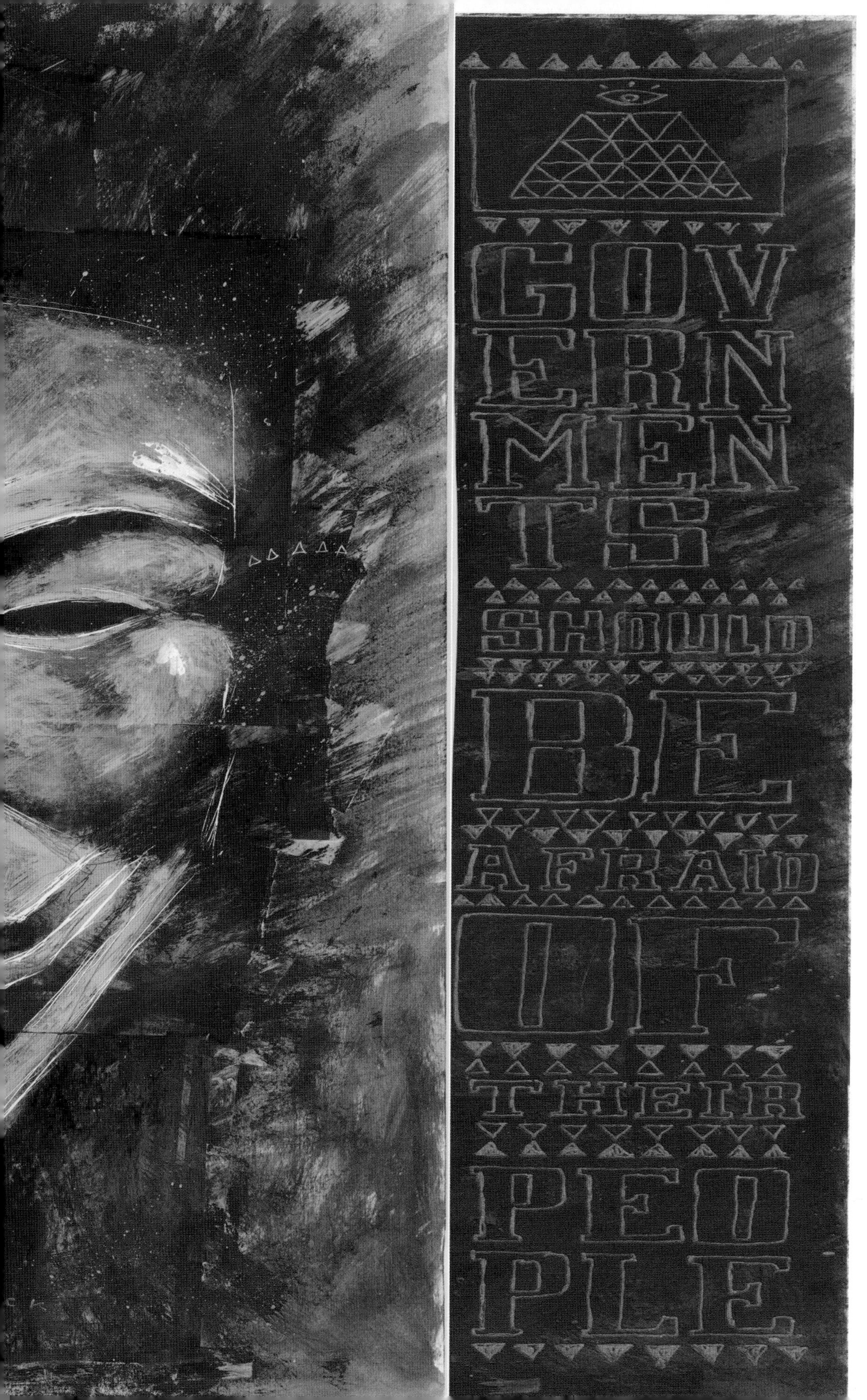
GOV
ERN
MEN
TS
SHOULD
BE
AFRAID
OF
THEIR
PEO
PLE

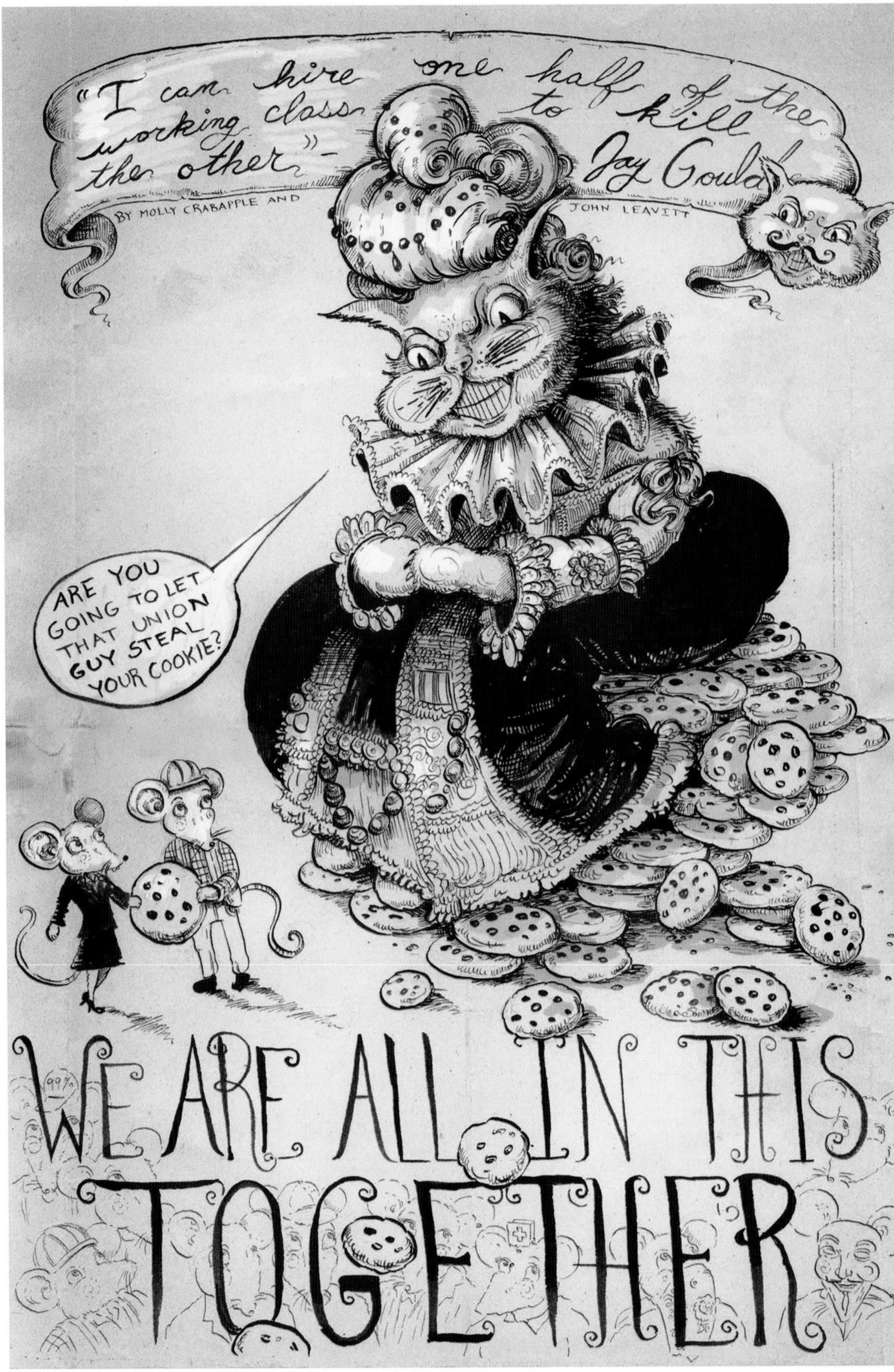
"I can hire one half of the working class to kill the other." - Jay Gould!
BY MOLLY CRABAPPLE AND JOHN LEAVITT
ARE YOU GOING TO LET THAT UNION GUY STEAL YOUR COOKIE?
99%
WE ARE ALL IN THIS TOGETHER

BUSTER BROWN AT THE BARRICADES

Foment in the Funnies & Comics as counter-culture.
by ALAN MOORE

I

The field of comics, formerly regarded as a more insidious threat to young minds and public morality than syphilis, has currently attained a level of propriety which it seems anxious to maintain. Having at last, apparently, become a critically-accepted and occasionally lucrative component of the entertainment industry, the comic-book is keen to foster its new image of social responsibility (and economic viability) with a bombardment of admiring quotes and press-release-derived puff pieces in the media. This relatively recent change in status has, it would appear, been also applied retroactively to best present a picture of the comic medium as something that has always been pro-social; that it has always been a cheery, populist expression of the status quo. In this unseemly scrabble for respectability and an historic, noble pedigree it is, for instance, fashionable to observe that comics have

their origins in the sequential strip-like hieroglyphics which record the reigns of ancient Egypt's pharaohs. What could be a better indicator of the medium's cultural worth than its ability to faithfully report the legendary acts and general fabulousness of the upper classes?

But a very different, and perhaps more vital, reading of comic-book history becomes available if we simply turn over the stone blocks on which these stylised chronicles of Egypt's kings or deities were carved. On the reverse of numerous stones that went to make the pyramids, inscribed on faces that were never meant to see the daylight, archaeologists have found what may well be the first anti-authoritarian and blasphemous satirical cartoons. These are depictions made, presumably, by bored and truculent stonemasons, of the same animal-headed gods to be found in the more conventional inscriptions, only here they're shown as sitting around playing cards like some divine Egyptian poker school, an obvious progenitor of the more recent fashion for portraying dogs involved in similar activities. It might be argued that this is the true historical precursor of the cartoon and the comic strip, the signifier of a grand tradition rooted in its healthy scepticism with regard to rulers, gods or institutions; a genuine art-form of the people, unrestricted by prevailing notions of acceptability and capable of giving voice to popular dissent, or even of becoming, in the right hands, a supremely powerful instrument for social change. It could even be said that, rather than such scurrilous and anti-social sentiments being a minor aberration in the otherwise sedate commercial history of comics, these expressions of dissatisfaction are the medium's main purpose.

In the derivation of the word 'cartoon' itself we see the art-form's insurrectionary origins: during the tumults and upheavals of a volatile seventeenth century Italy, it became both expedient and popular to scrawl satirical depictions of political opponents on the sides of cardboard packages, otherwise known as cartons. Soon, these drawings were referred to by the same name as the boxes upon which they'd been emblazoned. As a method of communicating revolutionary ideas in a few crude lampooning strokes, often to an intended audience whose reading skills were limited, the power and effectiveness of the new medium was made immediately apparent. This may also be the starting point for the receding but still-current attitude that comics and cartoons are best regarded as a province of the lower-class illiterate. However, following the realisation of the form's immense political utility, it's only with increasing difficulty that we can find a political event of any scale that has not been commemorated (and, often, most memorably commemorated) by the means of a cartoon.

"The Plumb-pudding in danger, or, State epicures taking un petit souper." Js. Gillray, inv. & fecit. 26 February 1805.

The eighteenth century, with its more readily available print media, saw the promotion of the scathing cartoon image from its lowly cardboard-box beginnings to the cheap pulp paper mass-production of the broadsheets and the illustrated chapbooks. Consequently, this same period would witness the emergence of the form's first masters, artists who could see the thrilling possibilities in this unruly and untamed new mode of cultural expression. We can see this evidenced in Gilray's often-scatological and lacerating barbed caricatures of the dementia-prone King George the Fourth, in Hogarth's stark depictions of society's deprived and shameful lower reaches and even in the

"Gin Lane" from Beer Street and Gin Lane. William Hogarth, circa 1751. Print from engraving by Samuel Davenport, circa 1806–09.

sublime illuminated texts of William Blake, in which the visionary's radical opinions...he'd stood with the firebrands of the Gordon Riots, in a red cap denoting solidarity with the French revolutionaries across the channel, watching Newgate Prison burn...were of necessity concealed beneath a cryptic code of fierce spiritual essences; invented demi-gods with grandiose and punning names that can be viewed as having much in common with the later output of the superhero industry's presiding genius, the genuinely great Jack Kirby.

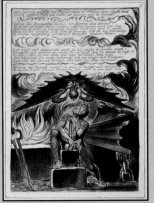

Plate 6 of "Jerusalem: The Emanation of the Giant Albion." William Blake, 1804-20.

Blake, who has been claimed as an ancestral relative by Kirby's onetime stable-mate and Submariner creator W. B. Everett, had grown up with the influence of luridly embellished chapbooks and thus seemed to find the concept of combining words and images entirely natural. In his work, despite its lack of a sequential narrative, we see perhaps an intermediary stage between the medieval monks' illuminated manuscripts and the more pyrotechnic and considerably less high-minded comic output of the present day. Lest it be thought that by including elevated figures such as William Blake amongst our list of cartoon predecessors we are seeking to uphold some sanctified and sanitised back-story for the medium, it should be stated that in the approach to the French revolution (which Blake had at first so ardently admired) the anti-monarchists were circulating scabrous and outrageous pornographic cartoon pamphlets which depicted Marie Antoinette in an incestuous relationship with her own son. The era's dissidents had evidently realised that while the cartoon alone was capable of swaying the uneducated masses, coupled with the ever-popular attraction of illicit sexual material it was to all intents and purposes invincible. This realisation would ensure that as the history of the subversive comic or cartoon continued to unfold, the challenging of censorship or socio-sexual hypocrisy was never far from the agenda.

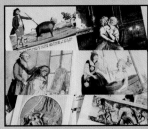

Propaganda pamphlets targeting Marie Antoinette. Circa late 1700s.

At the fractious juncture of the eighteenth and the nineteenth centuries, the western world was everywhere in turmoil. Previously unassailable religious certainties were being questioned and the era's scientific revolution had transformed the landscape from a largely rustic counterpane of fields to an expanse of sooty, flaring forges and sky-shrouding chimneystacks, Blake's 'dark Satanic mills', as the industrial revolution gathered its implacable momentum. It is possibly worth mentioning that this same period would arguably see, with Mary Shelley's *Frankenstein*, the advent of the science-fiction genre. Viewed initially in much the same demeaning light as were cartoons themselves, this fledgling literature of the imagination began life as a vehicle for voicing post-industrial fears and would eventually find a natural home for its ideas in the pulp magazines and comics of a century thereafter. With the rise of the big industries, including that of publishing, the radical dynamic of the cartoon medium was modified by increments as the attractions of a paying job and of professionally published work saw a great number of creators tailoring their output to the socially-acceptable requirements of these new employers. This is not to say that heartfelt individual political opinions were no longer expressed in a cartoon form, but simply that they were more likely to be framed within the editorial restrictions of whichever periodical was paying for their publication. Even after the arrival of satirical endeavours such as *Punch* or *Judge* during the later nineteenth century, while there were often withering and irreverent social criticisms, these were generally delivered in an almost gentlemanly manner that was careful not to cross the boundaries of taste or decency demanded by polite society. The scalding bile and no-holds-barred affront of Gilray was renounced and with it Hogarth's eye for socially-revealing squalor, not to mention the incendiary anti-materialistic visions of pugnacious and impoverished William Blake. We see here probably the first (though by no means the last) attempt to rehabilitate our gutter-generated medium and make it suitable for middle-class consumption by effectively castrating the still-infant art-form and removing all the inconvenient human socio-political or sexual urges that originally gave cartoons their relevance and potency, and which accounted for much of the medium's boundless popularity.

Weird Tales
SEPT.
25c
THE PEOPLE OF THE BLACK CIRCLE
a smashing weird novel of eery black magic
By ROBERT E. HOWARD
SEABURY QUINN
GREYE LA SPINA

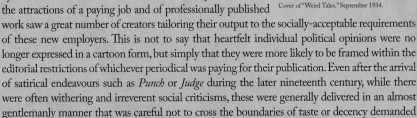

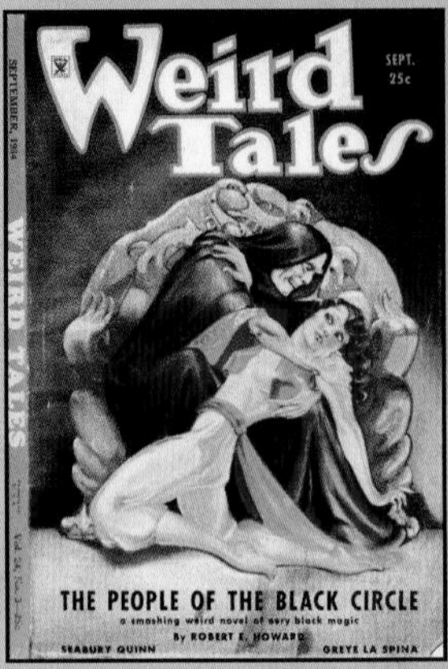

Cover of "Weird Tales." September 1934.

PUNCH
OR THE
LONDON CHARIVARI
VOLUME THE FIRST.
LONDON:
PUBLISHED AT THE OFFICE, 85, FLEET STREET.

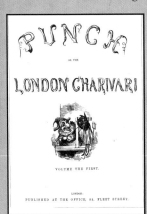

Cover of "Punch Magazine." 1841.

Clearly, despite the taming influence of the remunerative market to be found within such inoffensive and family-friendly publications, there were still creators more concerned with the expression of a personal and unrestricted statement than they were with comfortable and neutering conformity. In the gas-lighted avenues of 1890s fin-du-siècle London, the remarkable and tragically short-lived young artist Aubrey Vincent Beardsley was reducing forms and faces to their elegant and minimal essentials, with the merest notch of shadow to suggest a nose or faintly corrugated pen-stroke from which lips might be inferred. In doing so the tubercular aesthete was unwittingly establishing a great deal of the stylisation and the visual vocabulary which comic artists yet to come would utilise so liberally, while at the same time resurrecting

LYSISTRATA.

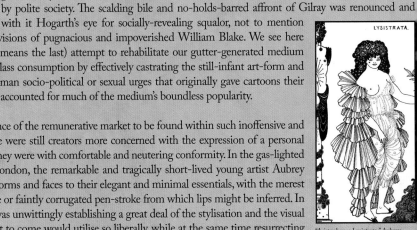

"Aristophanes Lysistrata." Aubrey Beardsley, 1896.

the disreputable ghost of cartoons past in his uproarious plates for Aristophanes' comedy *Lysistrata*, with their vaguely lesbian sex-strikers and disgruntled dwarves debilitated by the weight of their own gigantic erections. Dying of consumption at the age of twenty-six and therefore barely out of adolescence, Beardsley's urge to shock and his desire to push his work beyond the boundaries of acceptability had very possibly no more of a refined conceptual basis than that of a teenager embellishing a garage door with an improbably enormous phallus, although executed with far greater delicacy and accomplishment. This quality of adolescent brashness might also explain Beardsley's apparent moral and artistic fearlessness as a delusion of invulnerability that is most usually the province of the young and relatively inexperienced, surely the reason why our military agencies around the world seek their recruits from just this age-range.

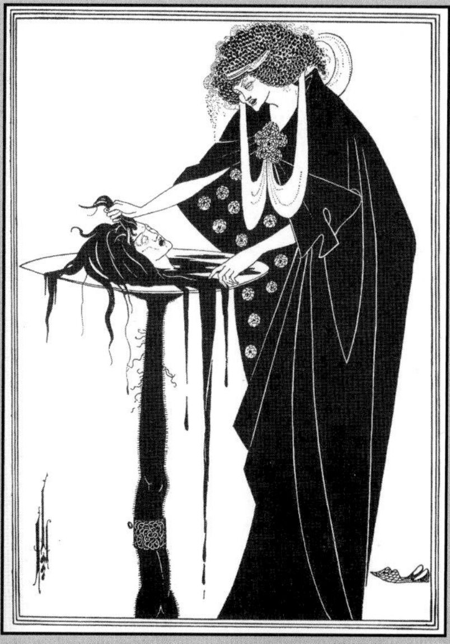
"The Dancer's Reward." Aubrey Beardsley, 1894

In the case of Aubrey Beardsley, his youthful assumption that he was impervious to the reprisals and reproaches of outraged convention proved to be misplaced. The trial of Oscar Wilde would cast a shadow of guilt by association on the whole Decadent movement in the arts, with public approbation most especially reserved for Wilde's collaborators such as the unlucky Beardsley, who had illustrated the disgraced author and dramatist's sensual and opulent Salomé. Obviously unprepared for such a punishing response...the artist's major source of funds, the stylishly progressive *Yellow Book*, was closed down after a mistaken press report that Wilde had carried the occasionally controversial journal underneath his arm while on his way to court...Beardsley's already fragile health was not improved by the emotional and psychological ordeal, and during 1898 he finally expired amid a bout of (one might think unnecessary) spiritual self-recrimination, during which he penitently begged his sister Mabel to 'burn Lysistrata and all obscene works'. His spirited and possibly naive assault upon Victorian England's sensibilities had reached a sorry and remorseful end, but in terms of his influence upon the modern comic strip, which would almost immediately follow his demise, it could be said that Beardsley's victory was already achieved, or at least that his work contributed considerably to the continuing good health of the cartoon in its unruly struggle for emancipation.

II

In the last years of the nineteenth century, the comic book and comic strip forms that we know today were forged in England and America, respectively, with the first publication of *Ally Sloper's Half-Holiday* in 1880s England, and the Hearst publishing empire's acquisition of Richard F. Outcault's *Hogan's Alley* (running in Hearst's New York Globe until 1898) featuring Alfred E. Neuman prototype *Mickey Dugan, the Yellow Kid*, in the United States. Although it might be thought that landmarks such as the first regularly-published picture-paper or the founding of America's remarkable newspaper strip tradition could be seen as indicators of the medium's enhanced respectability, this was by no means the perception at the time. In the *Half-Holiday* the lowlife antics of Dickensian inebriate *Ally Sloper* only served to provide confirmation that such vulgar content, and indeed the cartoon form itself, were only suitable for the presumably subnormal lower orders that were represented in the publication's pages.

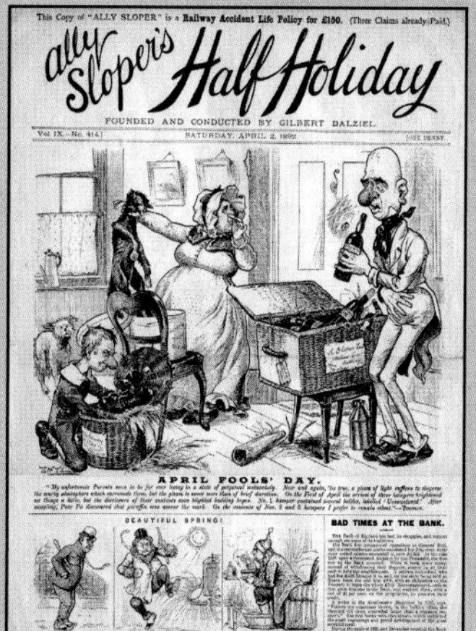
This Copy of "ALLY SLOPER" is a Railway Accident Life Policy for £150. (Three Claims already Paid.)
Ally Sloper's Half Holiday
FOUNDED AND CONDUCTED BY GILBERT DALZIEL
APRIL FOOLS' DAY.
BEAUTIFUL SPRING!
BAD TIMES AT THE BANK.
Cover of "Ally Sloper's Half Holiday." Illustration of Ally by W. Fletcher Thomas. 2 April 1892.

In America, Hearst's bald, slum-dwelling mascot would invite even more serious recriminations: prominently placed and with his nightshirt printed in the colour that most people psychologically associate with sunshine, wellbeing, and happiness, the *Yellow Kid* was seen as being a cheap and unseemly (and, more aggravatingly, wildly successful) ploy by Hearst to drag in undiscriminating readers with sensationalist gimmicks while the actual quality of his newspapers' contents headed resolutely for the gutter. As this new and worrying phenomenon became more widespread, the Kid's garment and its vivid hue were knowingly referred to in the term coined to describe such practice, 'yellow journalism.' Interestingly, in *Ally Sloper* and the denizens of *Hogan's Alley* we can see satirical depictions of the underclass, which was presumably perceived as the most likely audience for such material by both the wealthy and pragmatic publishers of the emergent cartoon medium and by the middle classes who, at least in public, would

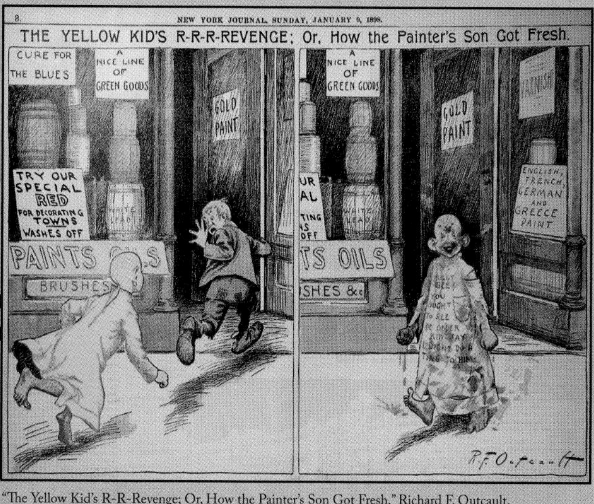
NEW YORK JOURNAL, SUNDAY, JANUARY 9, 1898.
THE YELLOW KID'S R-R-R-REVENGE; Or, How the Painter's Son Got Fresh.
CURE FOR THE BLUES
A NICE LINE OF GREEN GOODS
GOLD PAINT
TRY OUR SPECIAL RED FOR DECORATING TOWNS WASHES OFF
WHITE LEAD
PAINTS OILS
BRUSHES
A NICE LINE OF GREEN GOODS
VARNISH
GOLD PAINT
ENGLISH, FRENCH, GERMAN AND GREECE PAINT
TS OILS
SHES &c
R.F. Outcault
"The Yellow Kid's R-R-Revenge; Or, How the Painter's Son Got Fresh." Richard F. Outcault, 9 January 1898.

initially deplore the medium's existence. Though in fierce debate between themselves, both factions seemingly agreed that comics were an art-form of the ghetto, only suited to portraying ghetto life and only suitable as entertainment for the poorly educated riff-raff that inhabited such neighbourhoods.

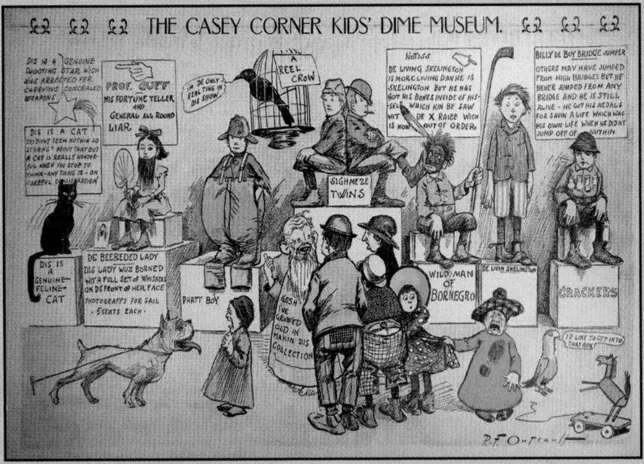
THE CASEY CORNER KIDS' DIME MUSEUM.
PROF. QUFF
HIS FORTUNE TELLER AND GENERAL ALL ROUND LIAR
A REEL CROW
I'M DE ONLY REAL TING IN DIS SHOW
DIS IS A CAT
DE BEEREDED LADY
DIS LADY WUZ BORNED WIT A FULL SET OF WHISKERS ON DE FRONT OF HER FACE
PHOTOGRAFFS FOR SAIL · 5CENTS EACH ·
DIS IS A GENUINE FELINE CAT
PHATT BOY
SIGHMEZE TWINS
NOTISS
DE LIVING SKELINGTON IS MORE LIVING DAN HE IS SKELINGTON BUT HE HAS GOT HIS BONES INSIDE OF HIS-SELF WHICH KIN BE SAW WIT DE X RAIZE WICH IS NOW OUT OF ORDER.
BILLY DE BOY BRIDGE JUMPER
OTHERS MAY HAVE JUMPED FROM HIGH BRIDGES BUT HE NEVER JUMPED FROM ANY BRIDGE AND HE IS STILL ALIVE - HE GOT HIS MEDALS FOR SAVIN A LIFE WHICH WAS HIS OWN LIFE WHEN HE DIDNT JUMP OFF OF NUTHIN
WILD MAN OF BORNEGRO
DE LIVIN SKELINGTON
CRACKERS

"The Casey Corner Kids' Dime Museum." Richard F. Outcault.

It may be worth examining this class dynamic that has evidently played so great a part in the development of comics as a medium and as an industry. The turn of the nineteenth and twentieth centuries presented an unknown and anxious landscape to the middle classes of the day who mostly felt assailed by all the changes in society occurring everywhere around them, their position and their status threatened by what must have seemed to them like a sustained erosion of the social boundaries and certainties which, previously, had defined their world. The middle class white male, a member of the demographic group exerting most control over society and therefore one of those with most to forfeit, felt especially besieged.

In both America and England, women rallied for the right to vote and challenged the long-held assumption of inviolable male superiority. Both countries were experiencing an influx of immigrants that was unprecedented, with the subsequent establishment of immigrant communities provoking the familiar fear that a prevailing culture would be swamped or lost beneath the customs, language, and behaviour of migrant populations that might one day far outgrow their status as minorities. The working classes on both sides of the Atlantic were becoming more vociferous in their demands for decent treatment at the hands of their employers, with the spectre of a striking workforce seeming much more menacing after the Bolsheviks' successful Russian revolution in the closing months of 1917. Additionally, with gay bathhouses operating in New York for some time prior to 1900, and comparable places of ill repute long since established in the streets of London, different sexualities became more visible and added to a general impression of civilisation in a state of imminent collapse. Indeed, given the prevalent belief among the middle classes that their higher status came as a result of being able to control or otherwise suppress (unlike the working class) their baser animal and sexual instincts, sexual activity of any kind was seen to be almost as great a danger to the social order as was Bolshevism. Thus beleaguered, many medical professionals saw fit to venture their opinion as to the degenerate mental or neurological conditions which they felt afflicted women, other races, homosexuals, or the biologically and intellectually degenerated poor, these proclamations were loaned weight by the fact that they had been advanced by doctors while the equally apparent fact that doctors were during that period exclusively white, male, near-uniformly heterosexual and entirely middle class was studiedly ignored. It would appear that in attempts to castigate or demonise some social element to which one feels adversity, it is as well to frame attacks as medical opinion, tactics that would come to have distressing relevance to the American comic book industry some fifty years after Hearst's *Yellow Kid* first raised the curtain on the concept of cartoon as moral panic.

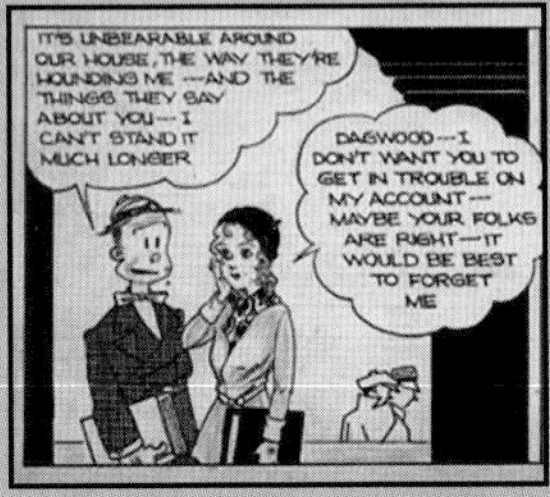
IT'S UNBEARABLE AROUND OUR HOUSE, THE WAY THEY'RE HOUNDING ME — AND THE THINGS THEY SAY ABOUT YOU — I CAN'T STAND IT MUCH LONGER
DAGWOOD — I DON'T WANT YOU TO GET IN TROUBLE ON MY ACCOUNT — MAYBE YOUR FOLKS ARE RIGHT — IT WOULD BE BEST TO FORGET ME

"Blondie Gets Married: His Master's Voice." Chic Young, 21 December 1931.

Back then, in the medium's infancy, it is apparent that the cartoon was already stigmatised by its association with the lowest strata of American or English culture. Picture-publications were regarded as the fare of the illiterate while only the more populist and less well-thought-of daily papers were prepared to dabble in the realm of editorial cartoons, and both these forms would in the coming years be made to haltingly negotiate their different routes to relatively improved levels of acceptability. The comic book would face a rougher road in this respect than the newspaper strip, being perceived in both countries as trash fit only for the cognitively-blighted offspring of the proletariat. In England, not until the advent of the beautifully produced and relatively sober *Eagle* during the 1950s would there be a children's periodical aimed consciously at youngsters of the middle class. Newspaper strips, by contrast, were intended from the outset for a largely adult readership, allowing their creators greater leeway in attempting more sophisticated narratives that would in time become beloved by poets, presidents and the less hidebound intellectuals.

Even so, perhaps it speaks to the fluidity of comics as a forum for political and social dialogues that so many of the earliest American newspaper strips appeared to use class issues as a basis for much of their humour or their drama. Harold Gray's Depression wish-fulfilment fantasy in *Little Orphan Annie*, with its lower-class protagonist adopted by a wealthy and unusually altruistic businessman, provides a perfect illustration. So, too, do the early episodes of Chic Young's *Dagwood and Blondie*, where we find that back then in the 1920s Dagwood Bumstead was a scion of the wealthy upper classes who met with the disapproval of his family over his plans to marry a lovely but uncultured flapper from the lower orders. George McManus's *Bringing up Father* describes the perhaps uniquely American trajectory of a rough-and-ready Irish immigrant succeeding in his new environment to the extent that he eventually inhabits a capacious mansion with refined Art Deco stylings. Add to this the subtly Yiddish dialogue and inflections found within George Herriman's exquisite *Krazy Kat*, or possibly the amiable lowlifes, hoboes and compulsive

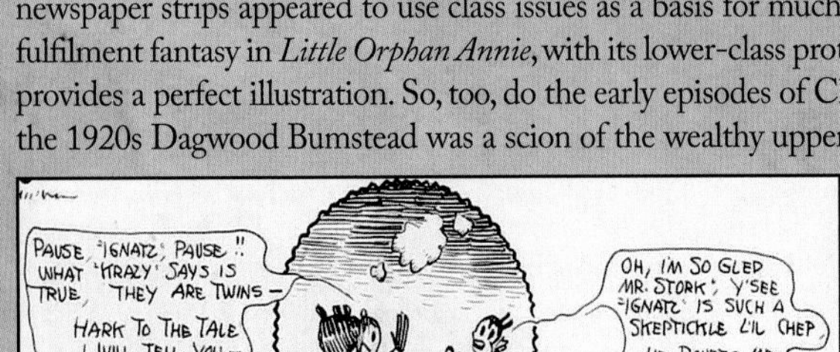
PAUSE "IGNATZ" PAUSE !! WHAT "KRAZY" SAYS IS TRUE, THEY ARE TWINS — HARK TO THE TALE I WILL TELL YOU —
OH, I'M SO GLED MR. STORK", Y'SEE "IGNATZ" IS SUCH A SKEPTICKLE L'IL CHEP HE DOUBTS ME.

"Krazy Kat." George Herriman, 4 November 1917.

gamblers to be found in the exploits of *Mutt and Jeff, Moon Mullins, Happy Hooligan* and a dozen others and we begin to see the complexity of the class discourse in these early strips. Despite the fact that in the later stages of his long career *Al Capp* became known for his pro-establishment and anti-radical opinions, at the outset, a main theme in *Li'l Abner* was the exemplary resilience, good humour, and charm of the rural poor when compared with that of the superior and sneering bastions of high society to be found in big contemporary cities. As with many of the early silent movies, the first modern comic strips addressed the difficulties of negotiating issues of both economic instability and social status that exactly mirrored the anxieties and interests of their audience. Popular culture, freed from the restrictions of respectable political debate, would rapidly become one of the only cultural spaces in which the topics and concerns that were most pertinent to ordinary life could be discussed. It's worth observing that even the classic iconography of the cartoon seemed, at least until the 1960s or the 1970s, to be entirely based upon the imagery of 1920s poverty: no skirting board without a mouse-door, no period armchair without a patch on its upholstery, no shoe-sole to be found without a hole.

The free-for-all and strikingly experimental outlook of these early comic strips, exemplified by the breathtaking visual gymnastics of Frank King's *Gasoline Alley* or visionary former architect Winsor McCay's extraordinary *Little Nemo*, was almost certainly encouraged by the sheer unprecedented novelty of the new medium. During the early decades of the twentieth century there is the sense that people barely understood what comics were, including many of the people writing and delineating them, and subsequently had not yet defined a rigid set of rules regarding what a comic could or could not be, or what a comic could or could not talk about. It's been suggested that America, by 1930, had first coalesced as a society around its burgeoning popular culture, and that in class terms, it was then that in their mutual love of the same entertainments, different social strata first commenced their 'merger to the middle.' Certainly, the rapid demographic growth-spurt of the middle classes was reflected in the gradual fine-tuning of the comic strip, removing it from its class-conscious origins and rehabilitating this disreputable medium as the reassuring mirror for a blandly standardised and rapidly expanding new suburban audience. *Dagwood and Blondie*, once a moneyed playboy and his inappropriately low-bred floozy, were presumably cut off by the aristocratic Bumsteads and reduced to the same middling existence, neither Easy Street nor Skid Row, in which an increasing number of their readership were by now semi-comfortably ensconced.

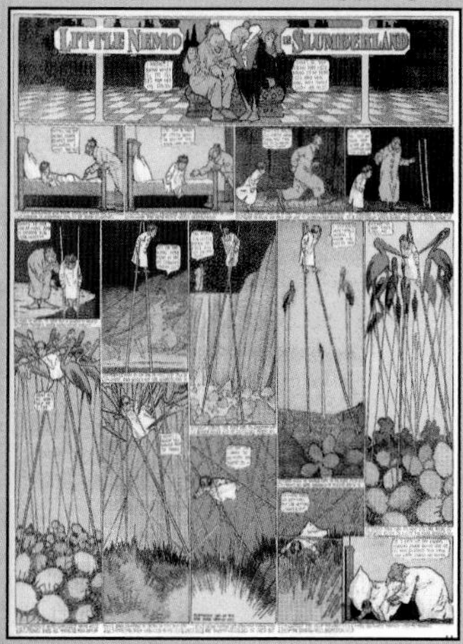
LITTLE NEMO IN SLUMBERLAND
"Little Nemo in Slumberland." Winsor McCay, 1905-1914.

While the newspaper strip, socially sanctified and mass-produced, was clearly the most visible expression of the cartoon medium during this period, it was by no means all that comic strips were doing. Co-existing with newspaper strips from sometime in the 1910s until at least the early 1960s, often sharing many of the same familiar cartoon characters, we have the scandalous and spirited American phenomenon of the now almost quaintly pornographic '*Tijuana Bibles*.' These were poorly printed eight-page pamphlets, featuring the sexually explicit escapades of various public figures, movie stars and comic strip protagonists, furtively printed and distributed throughout America's barrooms and schoolyards (presumably, the name by which these 'little dirty books' were known reflects America's then-current notion that things of a flagrant sexual nature must originate outside the nation's borders or within its immigrant communities). Though crudely drawn and written and apparently without redeeming social qualities, the Tijuana Bibles nonetheless provide an insight into the uncensored urges and ideas that bubbled underneath the family-friendly and unblemished surface of the culture. In the gleeful misappropriation of non-sexual comic strip stars such as Jiggs and Maggie, or screen icons like Mae West, we see a no-holds-barred acknowledgement of the appeal to sexuality that figures of this kind were making in a covert manner to their audiences, as with Maggie's statuesque proportions that belied her homely features. In this way, the Tijuana Bibles can be seen as puncturing the socio-sexual hypocrisy which held that sexual provocation was acceptable as long as the human activity which it was based upon was never mentioned or made otherwise explicit. (Mae West, though she, too, was no doubt forced to exercise at least some measure of restraint in the projection of her charms, would have most probably approved of the eight-pagers' riotous attacks upon convention and respectability. In 1927, her attempt to bring her passionately pro-gay and gay-acted play *The Drag to Broadway* had elicited state legislation which prohibited appearances by homosexuals or discussion of queer issues on the stage, this after West had suffered ten days jail-time for defiantly continuing performances of her preceding stage play *Sex* for six weeks after a New Jersey prosecutor ordered it be closed.)

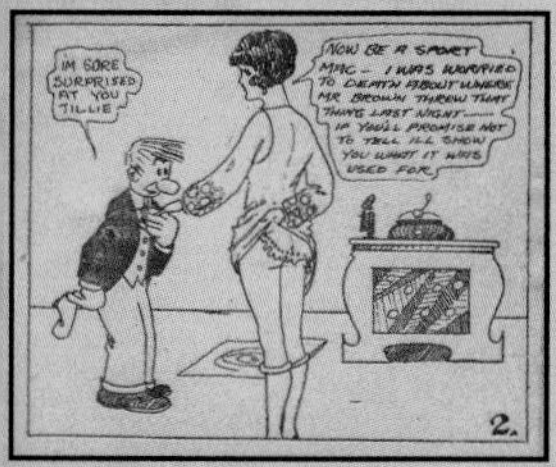
IM SORE SURPRISED AT YOU TILLIE
2.
Panel from Tijuana Bible based on 1920s comic strip character "Tillie the Toiler."

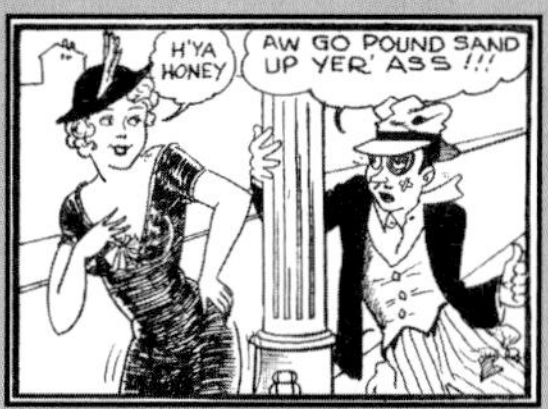
H'YA HONEY
AW GO POUND SAND UP YER' ASS !!!
Last panel of Tijuana Bible based on 1930s comic strip character "Chris Crusty."

As well as generally refuting censorship and social standards of acceptability, some of the Tijuana Bibles were perhaps a little more political in their intentions, even though such sensibilities were only expressed on the level of a titillating dirty joke. Appearances by figures from the world of politics, including one from Winston Churchill in a memorable narrative involving father-daughter incest and, inevitably, a two-headed baby, cannot but recall the similar pornographies involving Marie Antoinette immediately preceding the French Revolution. Furthermore, an interesting sub-genre of the eight-pagers was devoted to the sexual adventures of notorious criminals like Pretty-Boy Floyd or John Dillinger, a seeming indication of the sexual allure such individuals exerted (the mythology surrounding John Dillinger's penis has the posthumously-

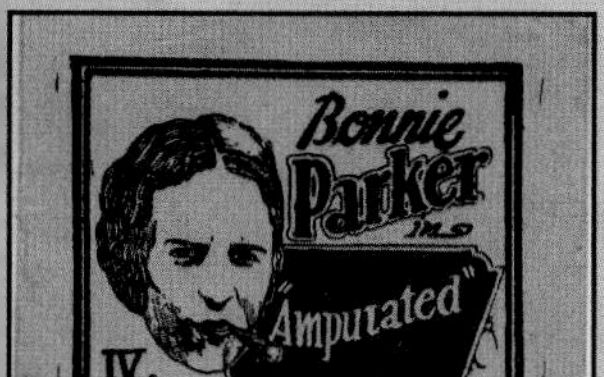
Bonnie Parker
in
"Amputated"
IV.
Cover of Tijuana Bible based on Bonnie Elizabeth Parker, of Bonnie and Clyde.

excised and predictably enormous member preserved for posterity in a locked room at the Smithsonian Institute) and also of a sneaking admiration for perceived heroic qualities in these profoundly anti-social desperadoes, similar to England's lionisation of and fascination with home-grown outlaws and terrorists like Robin Hood, Guy Fawkes, or Hereward the Wake. In some ways, by both lauding and eroticising the unpardonable outlaw, *Tijuana Bibles* would prefigure the uproarious Underground comics explosion of the later 1960s and the early 1970s.

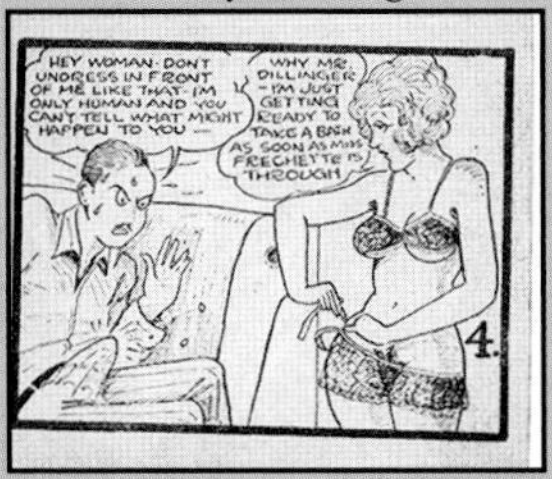
HEY WOMAN - DON'T UNDRESS IN FRONT OF ME LIKE THAT - I'M ONLY HUMAN AND YOU CAN'T TELL WHAT MIGHT HAPPEN TO YOU —
WHY MR. DILLINGER - I'M JUST GETTING READY TO TAKE A BATH AS SOON AS MISS FRECHETTE IS THROUGH
4.
Panel from Tijuana Bible based on bank robber John Dillinger.

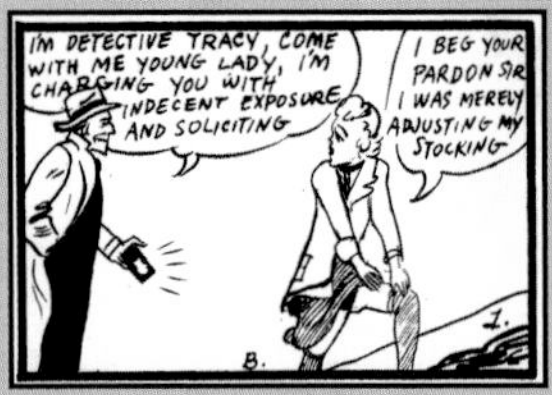
I'M DETECTIVE TRACY, COME WITH ME YOUNG LADY, I'M CHARGING YOU WITH INDECENT EXPOSURE AND SOLICITING
I BEG YOUR PARDON SIR I WAS MERELY ADJUSTING MY STOCKING
B.
J.
Last panel of Tijuana Bible based on 1930s comic strip character "Dick Tracy."

It wasn't only in the gutters of the early twentieth century that confrontational and challenging approaches to the comic strip were flourishing, but also in the more exalted pastures of what might be known (but doubtless wasn't) as high art, as evidenced by the remarkable and staggeringly influential work of graphic story pioneer Lynd Ward. Ward's wordless narratives, comprised of simultaneously stark and subtle woodcut illustrations in a smoothly flowing sequence, are astonishing in several ways. Most notably, Ward's masterful approach to visual storytelling and apparent fondness for formal experiment would prove to be the single biggest influencing factor in the subsequent medium-defining output of the marvellous Will Eisner, a devoted Ward admirer who in turn would go on to establish the vocabulary of techniques of which we can still see the remnants in contemporary mainstream comic books. Ripe for a rediscovery, Ward's narrative devices are impressively contemporary in their execution, as in *Madman's Drum* where an itinerant rural worker's actual existence is portrayed in hard and unforgiving black and white, while his own often false perceptions of events are printed in a dreamy and romantic Indian Red, allowing storytelling flourishes of breathtaking originality and startling sophistication. The insightful and often intensely moral glimpses into ordinary lives afforded by Ward's books are easily comparable to those achieved by the same period's most accomplished dramatists and authors, while the seriousness of his themes and his innovative narration surely mark his works as the first genuine examples of that much-abused and widely-touted form, the graphic novel.

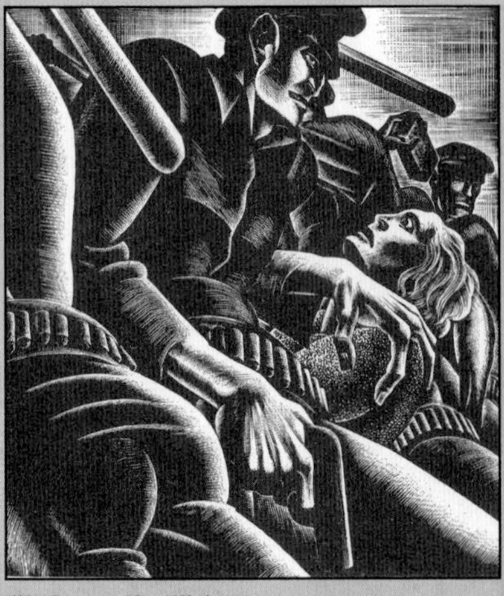
"Wild Pilgrimage." Lynd Ward, 1932.

As we slowly work our way through history towards the innovation of the modern comic-book, we are forced to acknowledge the historic circumstance and context which impinged on that development, as in the class-awareness of the earliest newspaper strips mentioned above. An event which would prove to have considerable significance for the emerging medium was the announcement in July 1919 of Prohibition's passing into law, to be enforced with the provisions granted by the Volstead Act in January, 1920. The effects of Prohibition were extensive, almost none of them intended by the moral arbiters and legislators who were the scheme's architects. Effectively criminalising a majority of law-abiding, ordinary adult Americans, while it did almost nothing to decrease the sale of alcohol, ensured instead that former model citizens would now be fraternising at speakeasies with the very undesirables that Prohibition was intended to eradicate or banish, such as homosexuals, prostitutes, and gangsters. Equally disastrous from the point of view of the authorities was Prohibition's granting of enormous wealth and influence to U.S. criminal concerns, bootlegging turning out to be the principle around which organised crime first got organised.

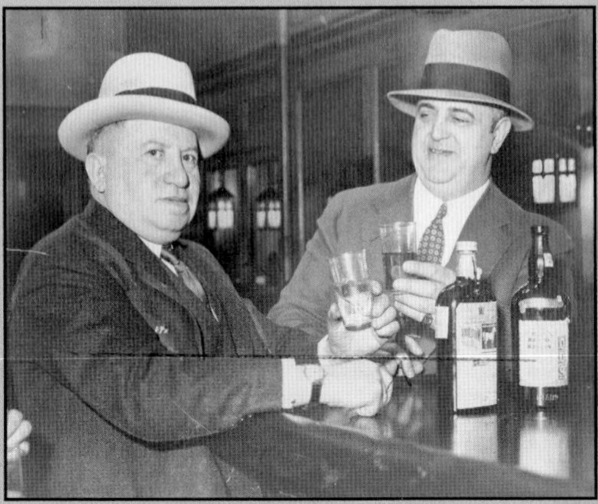
Izzy Einstein and Moe Smith, former police officers during Prohibition, sharing a toast in a New York bar. 1935.

The 1920s and the 1930s, viewed from a conventional comic-book history perspective, are perceived most often as the classic era of the great pulp magazines that would be comic-books' immediate predecessors. As to why this should be so, the interested reader is referred to Gerard Jones' *Men of Tomorrow*, a revealing factual history that documents the influence of racketeers and mobsters on the enterprise that would, with time, become the modern comics industry. Apparently, with Prohibition and the rise of bootlegging, the big-name gangsters who controlled the flow of alcohol into America were eager to develop a convenient cover-operation, a legitimate endeavour to conceal the liquor traffic from adjacent Canada, where obviously U.S. legislation could not be enforced. Fortuitously, Canada was the location of a relatively inexpensive printing industry (with many modern comics still to this day printed in Quebec), which made the fledgling market in pulp periodicals a perfect cover for the trafficking of booze: with trucks that were predominately filled with bourbon or, say, Molson's Beer, but had a big delivery of boxed magazines inside the loading doors obscuring the real contents from customs inspection, notable American entrepreneurs such as Legs Diamond, Charles Luciano and Meyer Lansky were equipped to profitably cater to the rapidly expanding market in illicit alcohol. That in so doing they were laying the foundations for the modern comic industry was almost certainly of little or no consequence to the rum-runners and black-marketeers involved, but would prove of considerable pertinence as it related to the basic character of the pulp publishing tradition which such practices were almost accidentally creating.

III

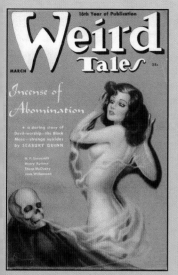

16th Year of Publication
Weird Tales
MARCH
25c
Incense of Abomination
a daring story of Devil-worship—the Black Mass—strange suicides
By SEABURY QUINN
H. P. Lovecraft
Henry Kuttner
Thorp McClusky
Jack Williamson
Cover of "Weird Tales." March 1938 (vol. 31, no. 3). Cover art by Margaret Brundage.

The pulp magazines, perceived (even by some of their most prominently featured authors such as the acutely snobbish H.P. Lovecraft) to be meant for an intended audience of nominally adult but uneducated lower class semi-illiterates, were thus permitted an unusual degree of freedom of which they took full advantage. Even relatively well-regarded and respectable pulp titles like *Weird Tales* would use the smoke-like, semi-naked female forms that were a speciality of illustrator Margaret Brundage as perennial cover-furniture to draw in the libidinous young, single men that represented a significant proportion of their readership. Meanwhile, at the marginally less-principled extremities of the pulp spectrum were the blatantly erotic so-called 'spicy' pulps such as Frank Armer's *Spicy Mystery, Spicy Detective, Spicy Western,* and *Spicy Adventure Stories*. While the actual sexual content promised by the covers of these periodicals was mostly left entirely to the reader's own vivid imagination, prompted by suggestive innuendo or increasingly strained euphemisms for unmentionable body parts, the publishers and writers clearly felt no such restraint when it came to portraying sexual sadism, brutality or torture.

With the end of Prohibition during 1933, bootlegging was quite clearly no longer an economically sustainable endeavour. Printing paper, numbering among the shortages of the Depression, was apparently still readily available to the criminal interests who had until then seen publishing as nothing more than a convenient cloak for smuggling alcohol. The prurient spicy pulps, predictably immensely popular, were seen as a potential means of partly filling the financial gap left by the inconvenient demise of the illicit liquor trade. Their profitable pages swollen by occasional moonlighting *Weird Tales* alumni such as Lovecraft confederates E. Hoffman Price and R. E. 'Conan' Howard (masquerading as 'Sam Walser'), Armer's spicy pulps successfully negotiated moral outcries and rebukes until the early 1940s, when they finally succumbed to wartime shifts of national mood and a combined assault from legislators, censorship groups, the crusading New York mayor Fiorello LaGuardia, and the Legion of Decency. For some years prior to that point, however, a decline in sales and all the added nuisance of campaigns and pressure groups had meant that publishing alternatives were being actively looked into by the business interests that had turned a handsome profit from imaginative editor Frank Armer's lurid innovation.

SPICY MYSTERY
25c
DEATH ORCHIDS
by Ellery Watson Calder
Cover of "Spicy Mystery Stories." December 1935.

FAMOUS FUNNIES
100 COMICS AND GAMES-PUZZLES-MAGIC
10 CENTS
No. 1
"Famous Funnies #1." July 1934, Eastern Color Printing. Art by Jon Mayes.

The controlling influence behind the Spicy titles was the colourful and somewhat shady printer Harry Donenfeld. Reputedly a former bootlegger and rumoured to be active in the publishing and circulating of the aforementioned *Tijuana Bibles*, it might well be thought that Donenfeld was excellently situated in a printing industry that had apparently by then become dependent on its good relations with the criminal fraternity, a necessary factor in acquiring a reliable supply of paper. During 1934 the sudden acquisition by another outfit, Eastern Color, of a significant quantity of newsprint paper, and that publisher's attendant need for product at short notice had led to the publishing of issue one of *Famous Funnies*, a makeshift repackaging of various already-popular newspaper strips. This proved to be an unexpected success on the newsstands, ably demonstrating the enormous market which existed for this novel and untested format and, almost by accident, arguably establishing America's first comic book. Pulp publishers like Harry Donenfeld, perhaps inferring from their balance sheets that the pulps' glory days were coming to an end, were quick to spot the possibilities of this new popular phenomenon. Though they did not have access to acclaimed newspaper characters like those in Famous Funnies, it was obviously possible to generate generic copies: lacking Lee Falk's *Mandrake*, one could simply substitute in-house creations like Fred Guardineer's *Zatara*. Harry Donenfeld, in partnership with former union accountant, the immensely shrewd Jack Liebowitz, seized eagerly upon the comic book as his next venture on the more disreputable lower rungs of publishing. To further these ambitions, the erstwhile alleged rum-runner and pornographer first instituted the new company that would in time be known as D.C. Comics.

STAMP DAY TODAY
Actor George Reeves as Superman in the U.S. government film "Stamp Day for Superman." 1954. Source/Author: United States Treasury Department.

Early titles from the line, such as *Detective Comics*, sold robustly with their copycat array of tough detectives, comical buffoons, and the obligatory tuxedo-clad magicians, but had yet to find the killer application that would ultimately prove to be industry's main selling point and most reliable standby. This arrived in 1938 when Jerry Siegel and Joe Shuster, teenage science fiction fans from Cleveland, first presented Harry Donenfeld's formative comic business with

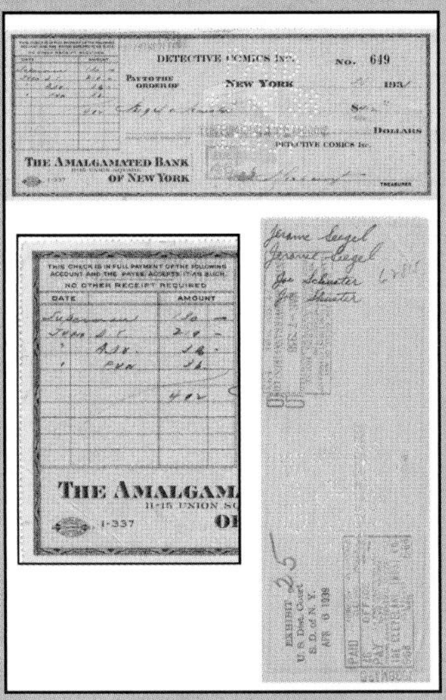
DETECTIVE COMICS INC.
NO. 649
NEW YORK
DOLLARS
THE AMALGAMATED BANK OF NEW YORK
THIS CHECK IS IN FULL PAYMENT OF THE FOLLOWING ACCOUNT AND THE PAYEE ACCEPTS IT AS SUCH.
NO OTHER RECEIPT REQUIRED
DATE
AMOUNT
THE AMALGAM
1-337

Historic March 1, 1938 Detective Comics, Inc. check for $412 payable to Superman co-creators Jerry Siegel & Joe Shuster. In addition to other services rendered, the check includes a $130 line item for ownership of Superman. As Superman rose in popularity to icon status, Siegel and Shuster's careers faltered. They embarked on a failed lawsuit to regain ownership of Superman, and in the settlement were forced not only to relinquish all rights to the character but even lost the basic right to credit themselves as Superman's creators.

the unique, vitalising character it had been looking for; a flagship concept that would both define and dominate the sprawling industry which comic books would very soon become. Debuting in the company's new title *Action Comics*, Superman turned out to be a publishing sensation. Soon, Donenfeld's company and every other trend-conscious pulp publisher were mass-producing vaguely paranormal characters in leotards, hoping to duplicate the staggering success of the original. Siegel and Shuster's pivotal creation was the cornerstone of modern mainstream comics, just as the appropriation of their character by means that some have seen as dubious would seem, unfortunately, to have laid a template for the business practices which have prevailed within the comics business ever since.

Reportedly finagled from Siegel and Shuster's unsuspecting grasp when the two young men were called up to fight in World War II, their character precipitated a tsunami of costumed or masked adventurers amidst which Superman would gradually become almost completely unremarkable. However, given the predominance that Superman and the entire genre which followed him would in the end achieve, a closer look at the initial presentation would seem to be called for. Almost certainly by instinct rather than by psycho-social analysis, two Cleveland teenagers had crafted a near-perfect and iconic fantasy which spoke to something deeply rooted in the psyche of working America: propelled to Earth (and, more specifically, America) from an exploded home-world during infancy, the character, like many of his readers or their parents, was an immigrant. Then there's the usually-unexamined matter of his humble rural upbringing, a far cry from the throng of wealthy socialites, arms manufacturers, doctors and scientists who would provide respectable and largely middle-class civilian alter-egos for the cape-clad multitude that followed hot on Superman's red-booted heels.

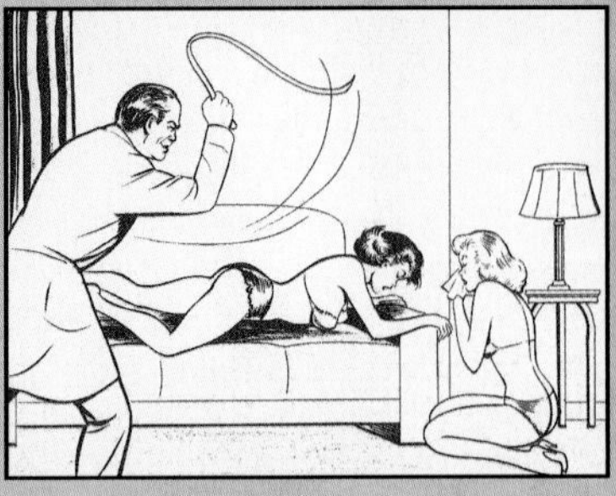

According to Craig Yoe in his book Secret Identity: The Fetish Art of Superman's Co-Creator Joe Shuster, Superman co-creator Joe Shuster anonymously illustrated likenesses of his Superman characters being beaten and tortured in the fetish comic book series "Nights of Horror" after he and co-creator Siegel lost rights to Superman and its related characters. Many believe these illustrations channel Shuster's rage at losing his creations. 1950s.

At his inception, Superman seems very much a representative of the downtrodden working classes his creators hailed from, and a wonderful embodiment of all the dreams and aspirations of the powerless. Dressed in bright primaries where most of his Depression-era readers were confined to threadbare black, or brown or grey, here was a character that in a single bound could leap above the worn-out city streets which his impoverished countrymen were forced to trudge in search of work. While the ensuing decades and expanding fortunes of America have seen Siegel and Shuster's purloined champion recast as an establishment ideal, a figure that embodies tactical superiority and thus perhaps a sense of national impunity, the archetypal superhero at his outset was a very different proposition. In his earliest adventures, with an admirably broadminded definition of what constituted criminality, a splendidly egalitarian Man of Tomorrow would rough up strike-breakers and use his super-strength to hurl unscrupulous slum landlords over the horizon. Gradually across the next few years, perhaps in keeping with the Cleveland pair's decreasing power to control their own creation, Superman would undergo a moral and political makeover to become a bastion of authority, carefully trimmed of any prickly or non-conformist attitudes.

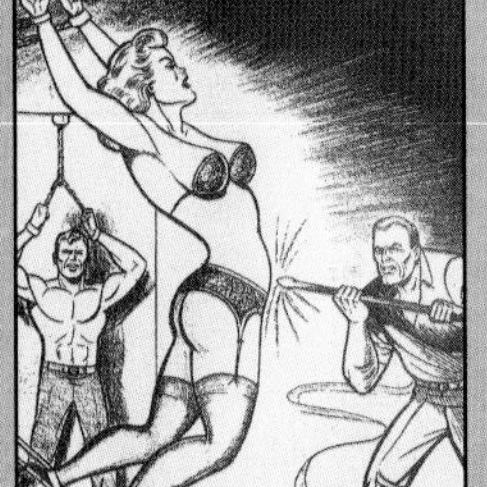

Anonymous illustration in "Nights of Horror," alleged to have been drawn by Joe Shuster after losing rights to Superman and the related characters he co-created. It's been asserted the images feature likenesses of Superman characters being beaten and tortured. 1950s.

This same trajectory is to be seen in many of America's pop-culture icons, such as the initially demonic and yet rapidly suburbanised form of Walt Disney's Mickey Mouse. If, as suggested earlier, American identity first bonded and solidified around the nation's entertainment industries, we can perhaps see why this taming process was considered necessary. Symbols which enshrined America's emergent image of itself were simply too important socially to be left in the hands of unpredictable and sometimes idealistic individuals such as their creators. Clearly, it was seen as more appropriate for these new U.S. totem entities to be in the possession and safekeeping of frequently questionable businessmen rather than that of the genuinely talented and decent human beings who'd originated them. Given that *Superman* had been rebranded as exemplifying Truth, Justice and the American Way, it seems ironic that the first two of these qualities had been so casually dispensed with, while to judge from the behaviour of the nascent comics industry it would appear that their interpretation of 'the American Way' had little to distinguish it from any other forms of spineless underhand deception, larceny or bullying.

The industry's apologists have offered various glosses for the shameful act of theft upon which the vast business that supports them seems to have been founded. One of the more despicable of these constructions has it that Siegel and Shuster should have been more shrewd in signing contracts, which appears to be a variant on the well-known American proverbial advice regarding suckers and the inadvisability of giving them an even break. More lately there have been attempts to mitigate the industry's offence with an appeal to half-baked mysticism and postmodernism, maintaining that Superman and the commercial children's comic characters which followed him are all in some sense archetypes that hover in the ether, waiting to be plucked by any lucky idiot who passes by. Ingeniously, this sidesteps the whole Siegel and Shuster problem by insisting that creators in the superhero field aren't actually creators after all, but merely the recipients of some kind of transcendent windfall fruit that should be freely shared around. Even if this were true, it's difficult to see exactly how it justifies a perhaps gangster-founded company of fruiterers (just to continue the analogy) declaring that these profitable magic apples all belong to them in perpetuity. Still, one can see why such a morally-evasive brand of metaphysics might appeal to the large corporate concerns which steer the comic industry; to those amongst the readership whose primary allegiance is to a specific superhero rather than the ordinary non-invulnerable human who originated him; and to those loyally and profitably labouring at franchises, who know they're in no danger of ever creating an original idea which would be valuable enough to steal. Alternatively, those not found in the preceding factions might question the wisdom of erecting such an important commercial and ideological endeavour on foundations so blatantly rotten and so lacking in the necessary load-bearing integrity.

By the time Superman's creators were called up to fight in Europe, waving goodbye to their homeland and reputedly to ownership of their creation, the original caped crime-fighter had spawned a host of characters in the same vein, some of them arguably as novel and as popular as their progenitor. At least a goodly number of these early super-people showed the same anti-establishment demeanour expressed by Siegel and Shuster's character during his first appearances. Carl Burgos's flammable android Human Torch was understandably seen as a hazardous and Frankenstein-like monster during his initial outings, while William (Blake) Everett's misanthropist *Submariner* quite openly wished to eradicate all non-amphibious society. The tragic Jack Cole's fascinating *Plastic Man* began life as a hardened criminal before becoming the most visually subversive and anarchic character the medium had ever known, while in Will Eisner's seminal *The Spirit* we are shown a tenderly depicted world of lowlife characters by turns endearing and despicable. Jack Kirby's kid gangs were as much a product of the slums and tenements as their creator, while even the largely Jerry Robinson and Bill Finger-created *Batman's* debut was as a gun-toting vigilante whom police did not apparently at first distinguish from his freakish, homicidal adversaries. The first superheroes obviously inhabited a more unregulated and socially-varied landscape than that of the more on-message characters who followed them after the superhero boom-time that was World War II.

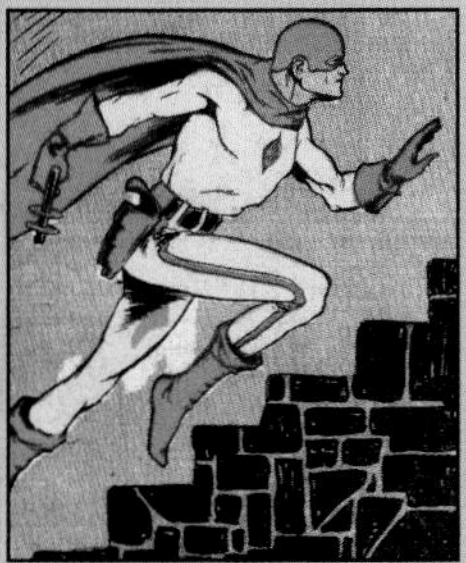

The superhero character Flame, created by Will Eisner. Image from "Wonderworld Comics #3," 1939.

In only a few years, the comic book had made itself a feature in the landscape of what would become modern America, to the extent that the young U.S. soldiers heading off to battle would proverbially boost their morale with the adventures of Captain America or Superman as detailed in the much-thumbed periodicals kept in their backpacks or their lockers. This would seem to underline an interesting difference in the way that comics were perceived in Britain and America respectively. Since Ally Sloper first embarked on his *Half-Holiday* in the late nineteenth century, Britain had seen a flourishing tradition of usually weekly picture-papers, aimed exclusively at children or at school-age youngsters. These would mostly feature juvenile comedy slapstick turns, or the invented exploits of popular entertainers from the cinema or radio. Otherwise, adventure-oriented features generally involved fictional sporting champions, investigative school-chums or square-jawed and jingoistic military heroes, all of these leavened with the same casual racism, misogyny, and anti-Semitism that were prevalent and unexamined at that time upon both sides of the Atlantic. While in England the newspaper strip was seen by then as aimed at adults (albeit adults of the lower classes), picture periodicals or comics were perceived as being meant solely for children. Thus, while British soldiers may have boosted their morale with help from Norman Petty's glamorous, wardrobe malfunction-prone heroine *Jane*, they were not famously enthused by Dudley Watkins' *Desperate Dan*. This might suggest that in America the comic was perceived as being aimed at a considerably wider age range, reaching from small children to those in their later teens or early twenties. This apparent greater ambiguity in terms of audience age could possibly account for the censorious upheavals that would so beset the U.S. comic business in the 1950s, with Bill Gaines' remarkable E.C. line clearly aimed at older readers than the ones it was accused of traumatising and corrupting, while simultaneously explaining why the U.K. made no headway into more mature comic-strip narratives until much later and why England could not have produced groundbreaking work like that accomplished by E.C. In Britain, comic books were unambiguously meant for children, and the only breakthrough in terms of sophistication would be with the 1950 advent of *The Eagle*, an informative and educational affair intended for well brought-up schoolboys of the middle classes and a far cry from E.C.'s Jack Davis-illustrated midnight baseball pitch marked out in human entrails.

It might well be said that wartime was, ironically, the super-character's true golden age. Not only did this period see a massive upsurge of invention that would put in place a number of the titles that still dominate the comic market in the present day, but the simplistic black-and-white morality of World War II would prove a perfect backdrop for the costumed hero's morally simplistic exploits. Nazi scientists and their depraved experiments provided an unending source of ready-made antagonists, while the prevailing national and international mood of moral certainty chimed nicely with the general ethos of the mask-clad mystery man. The war's end, which came with the dropping of atomic bombs upon Hiroshima and Nagasaki, would bring with it a new era of uncertainty, both for the world in general and the superhero in particular. With the abating of wartime's accompanying wave of patriotic fervour, masked adventurers seemed to increasingly lack any purpose or direction. The new genre, it appears, no longer had a mission-statement, and this seems to be reflected in the falling sales and superhero cancellations of the post-war period, with only the most popular and well-known titles lasting very far into the 1950s.

From the point of view of many superhero-prone comic enthusiasts, the 1950s seems to be regarded as almost a twilight period or at least as the tarnished last gleam of a by-then decidedly 8-carat golden age. In actual fact, the steep decline amongst the superhuman population left a food-chain gap that other genres quickly flooded in to fill, resulting in a glorious explosion of cartoon biodiversity. Now that the dependable cash-cow afforded by the superhero had proved unreliable in terms of yield, the

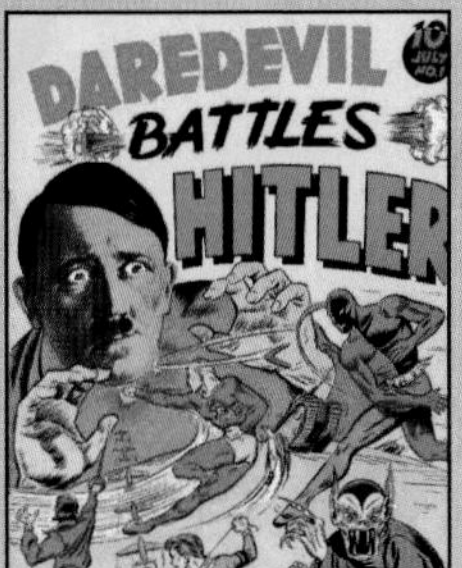
DAREDEVIL
BATTLES
HITLER

"Daredevil Battles Hitler (Daredevil #1)." July 1941, Lev Gleason Pubs.

desperate publishers were more than willing to experiment with new ideas and content in the hope of finding a remunerative replacement. Comic books would subsequently be transformed by a proliferation of war comics, western comics, romance comics, horror, crime, and science fiction comics, comics for small children, teenage humour titles, and a host of other genres that were profiting in the environmental gap left by the dieback of the supermen. Perhaps because of the (intentionally?) blurred age range which such titles were appealing to, as mentioned earlier, creators of the period appeared to feel encouraged to take chances and progress their chosen medium into unprecedented areas. Nowhere would this be more conspicuous than in the pioneering E.C. line.

The long-time comic publisher Max Gaines (who'd been involved with the newspaper-insert proto-comic books which had preceded *Famous Funnies*) had first instituted E.C. Comics as part of his sober and informative, often religious, line of publications, with the 'E' standing initially for 'Educational'. After the senior Gaines' sudden demise during a boating accident, the ownership of his conservatively-inclined company was passed on to his non-conformist, more bohemian and, one might suppose, entirely unprepared son William. William Gaines, however much he must have been surprised to find himself commanding an extensive publishing concern, would prove to be one of the most innovative and pioneering individuals in comics' history. Quickly realising that his father's staid and stuffy sensibilities were not ideally suited to the modern comic audience, Gaines junior radically overhauled the E.C. line so that the 'E' now stood for 'Entertaining'. Working on the never-failing principle of wanting to make comics he himself might like to read, he rapidly assembled the most dazzling roster of creators that the industry had ever, or in every probability, will ever see.

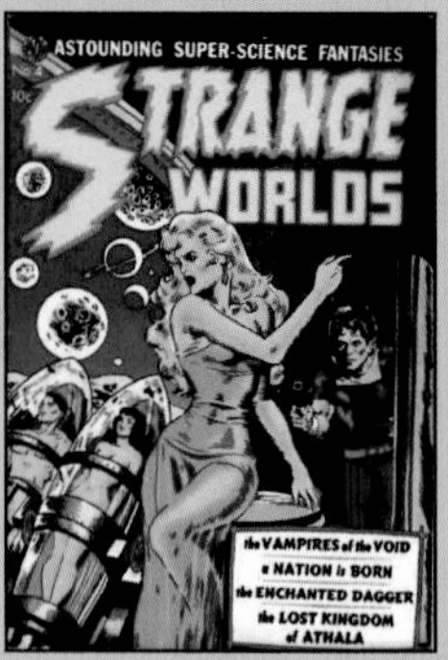
ASTOUNDING SUPER-SCIENCE FANTASIES
STRANGE WORLDS
the VAMPIRES of the VOID
a NATION is BORN
the ENCHANTED DAGGER
the LOST KINGDOM of ATHALA
Cover of "Strange World #4." January 1952, Avon Comics. Cover art by Wally Wood.

The horror, science-fiction, and suspense material that Gaines wrote alongside his major artist-writer co-conspirator Al Feldstein, beautifully delineated by the likes of Bernie Krigstein, Wally Wood, Al Williamson, Jack Davis, Johnny Craig, Graham Ingels and a host of other stellar talents, would achieve a devastating impact by addressing the post-war anxieties and fears that were then lurking unexamined just below the smooth Formica surface of a soporific Eisenhower America. A brutal small-town rapist made impervious by his position as police chief; a tyrannical slum landlord suffering the vicious, if poetic, vengeance of the harassed and abused blind tenants in his care; a former concentration camp commander incognito in America and hounded by his own unspeakably guilt-ridden past; the adaptation of Ray Bradbury's *There Will Come Soft Rains* which resurrects the famous shadows on the bank steps of Hiroshima in a post-nuclear U.S.A and thus picks at the scabs of an America still haunted by the bomb...there seemed to be no subject matter that Gaines would not turn a fiercely moral eye to. These insightful stories stood out even from the trademark E.C. tales of gleeful horror framed and reassuringly contained by the sardonic comments and distressing puns of a grotesque and leering 'horror host', and this before we spare a thought to the astounding war and humour titles which are seen by many as the best things that this best of companies ever produced.

The genuine masterworks in E.C.'s *Frontline Combat* and the medium-redefining satires to be found in *Mad* were principally creations of the unambiguously brilliant Harvey Kurtzman. His obsessively researched and detailed combat narratives such as *Corpse on the Imjin* or *The Big If* are at once the gutsiest and most realistic stories to emerge from the war comics genre, while at the same time being intense and eloquent expressions of an anti-war or pacifistic sensibility. This confrontational approach to a conformist mainstream is exemplified nowhere more elegantly than in Kurtzman's sublime *Mad*, perhaps the single greatest title that the comics business, or indeed the comics medium, has ever witnessed. Aided by most of the above list of masterful E.C. creators, plus extremely notable additions like John Severin or the exquisitely deranged Will Elder, Jewish N.Y. hipster Kurtzman would hilariously and efficiently lampoon whichever aspects of America's convulsing 1950s culture caught his eye, from politics or the absurdities of fashion to the entertainment media that were ubiquitous in that well-heeled and relatively prosperous post-war environment: the magazines, the movies, radio or television shows, and most consistently the comic books and the newspaper strips that were conspicuously an abiding interest for this hugely influential cartoon pioneer and master American satirist.

In Kurtzman's parody of George McManus's *Bringing up Father*, he ingeniously juxtaposes the McManus-aping cartoon stylings of Will Elder with the bleakly neo-realist imagery of Bernie Krigstein to show the ghastly real-life effects of Jiggs and Maggie's knockabout and humorous domestic violence. The most cutting by far of his various superhero parodies must be the Wally Wood-embellished *'Superduperman'*, in which Siegel and Shuster's character (in the previously-D.C.-employed Kurtzman's hands a sneaky and amoral thug) sees off a rival ubermensch based glaringly on Fawcett Comics' *Captain Marvel*, easily the most successful of the costumed characters to follow *Superman* and thus then in the process of a legal battle with *Superman's* publishers, who may have been seen as attempting to thin out the competition by less than legitimate means. Though sly and knowing digs like the above cannot have endeared Kurtzman to the comic book establishment, it's been suggested that the single strip that finished off the artist/writer's coruscating run on *Mad* along with E.C. comics as a whole was not attacking a much-loved newspaper strip or even aimed at the surviving superhero books, but was instead the Kurtzman-Elder lacerating of America's self-styled 'typical teenager' within the pages of their scathing satire 'Starchie'. By portraying the iconic freckle-faced exemplar of American-style adolescence as inhabiting a Blackboard Jungle world of high-school racketeering, promiscuity, and drugs, Kurtzman would seem to have incurred the wrath of influential enemies who would not have to wait long for their day of reckoning.

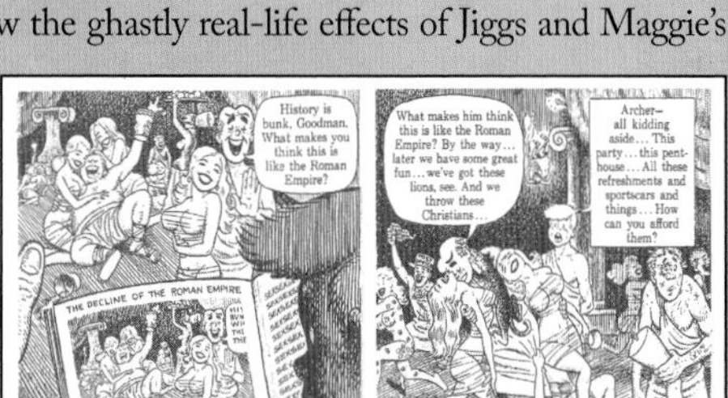
History is bunk, Goodman. What makes you think this is like the Roman Empire?
THE DECLINE OF THE ROMAN EMPIRE
RECONSTRUCTED SCENE
What makes him think this is like the Roman Empire? By the way... later we have some great fun...we've got these lions, see. And we throw these Christians...
Archer— all kidding aside... This party... this pent-house... All these refreshments and sportscars and things... How can you afford them?
Excerpt from "Goodman Goes Playboy," a Goodman Beaver story by Harvey Kurtzman and Will Elder. First published in "Help! #13." February 1962.

IV

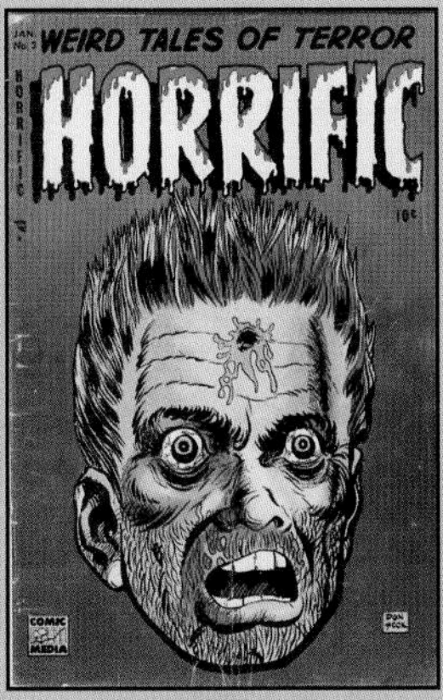
WEIRD TALES OF TERROR
HORRIFIC
Cover of "Horrific #3." Art by Don Heck.

Contrary to all televisual or cinematic retro-fittings, in America during the 1950s many days were far from happy. While the economic situation had undoubtedly improved, the prosperous new era had brought with it its own novel and unprecedented doubts and fears, most of them centred on the threat that was perceived as being posed by communism. Vice-President Richard Nixon was presenting the delusional and paranoiac fantasies of the distraught Whittaker Chambers as established proof of an insidious Red plot against America, while Senator Joseph McCarthy was successfully pursuing a campaign to drive even suspected communists from every corner of American society. The Russians had put Sputnik I in orbit, beating the United States to outer space and thus delivering a psychologically traumatic and demoralising blow to U.S. self-esteem, while all across the country sales of backyard fallout shelters were increasing as America became uneasily aware that having been the nation to commence the A-bomb's reign of terror did not mean it was itself exempt from that continual soul-destroying expectation of an imminent annihilation. Wracked with largely self-imposed hysterias and panics, U.S. culture was left flailing blindly as it searched for a convenient receptacle into which all the blame could be offloaded. Needing culprits for the fact that Soviet Russia now possessed America's 'atomic secrets' (and refusing to accept that any halfway competent atomic scientist would have worked out these 'secrets' for themselves by around lunchtime on August the seventh, 1945), Julius Rosenberg and his wife Ethel Greenglass were accused of passing on the vital information to the U.S.S.R. and were subsequently executed. Meanwhile in the social sphere, with juvenile delinquency in the ascendant on both sides of the Atlantic (possibly as a result of what the English poet and author Jeff Nuttall termed 'bomb culture,' with the hopeless nihilism of the generation born after Hiroshima made manifest in acts of violence or vandalism) there was a similar requirement for a likely scapegoat, something which was causing all this social upset and was something other than American society itself. It was at this point that the measured and authoritative diagnoses of the medical profession and its experts were once more intruded into an already volatile debate, on this occasion being the supposedly informed opinions of a criminal psychologist, one Dr. Frederic Wertham.

In the doctor's book, *Seduction of the Innocent,* as lurid and sensational in its appeal as any of the harmful and corrupting comic books which it affected to expose, we are indeed allowed a glimpse into a pathologically morbid mindset, this being that of Dr. Wertham. Richly illustrated with the most ostensibly alarming comic art available, much of it either culled from E.C. or from the crime comics published by Charles Biro, Wertham's book was excerpted in the *Ladies Home Journal* for November 1953 (which otherwise would be a month of rare and splendid vintage), prior to its full publication in the May of 1954. With rhetoric clearly designed to terrify his audience of anxious mothers, Wertham makes the somewhat confused argument that giving children comic books to read during their formative years will at best transform them into socially subnormal halfwits, utterly incapable of understanding or appreciating more sophisticated art and literature. At worst, on the other hand, the child might very well become a sexual deviant or a psychopath. As evidence of sexual perversion, Wertham cited interviews with homosexual patients who admitted fantasising about the relationship between *Batman* and his boy partner *Robin*, as if this had any bearing on the way such comics were perceived by their intended readership of children. In support of his idea that crime and horror comics could turn children into homicidal maniacs, the doctor mentioned the case histories of other patients he'd examined, like the man who had at one time enjoyed comic books and had gone on to embed several needles and sundry sharp metal things in his own groin and genitals. This does, admittedly, sound rather off-putting until one recognises from the incidental details in the case that Wertham's unnamed patient is in every likelihood the famously demented cannibal and child-murderer Albert Fish, who hardly seems to be an average comic-fan, and as a character type is unlikely to be featured in *The Big Bang Theory*, though of course one never knows. The crowning glory in *Seduction of the Innocent's* description of pernicious and corrupting comic book techniques, however, must be the obsessive reproduction of a comic panel in which a ridiculously tiny and roughly triangular random ink mark under a character's arm is enlarged until, if one should suffer from some manner of psychosis that makes everything resemble genitals, it might loosely resemble a female pudenda. Under this enlargement is the frankly paranoid announcement that there are pictures within pictures lurking in the comic book for those who are prepared to look in the right way.

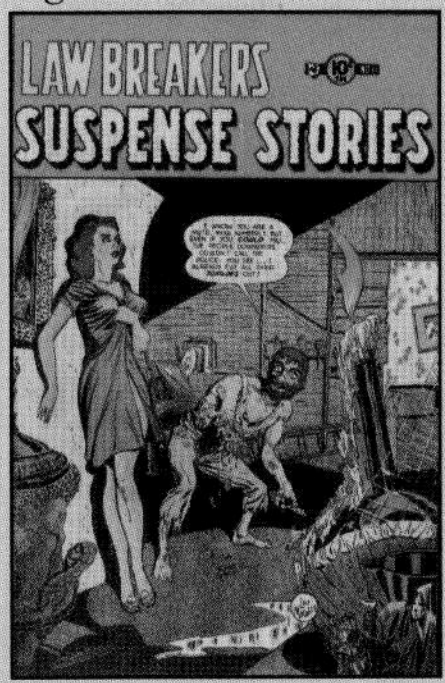
LAW BREAKERS
SUSPENSE STORIES
Cover of "Law Breakers Suspense Stories #11." Art by Lou Morales.

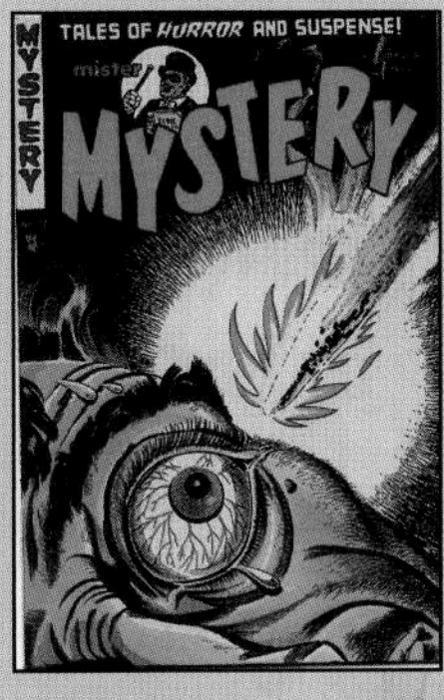
TALES OF HORROR AND SUSPENSE!
MYSTERY
Cover of "Mister Mystery #12." July 1953.

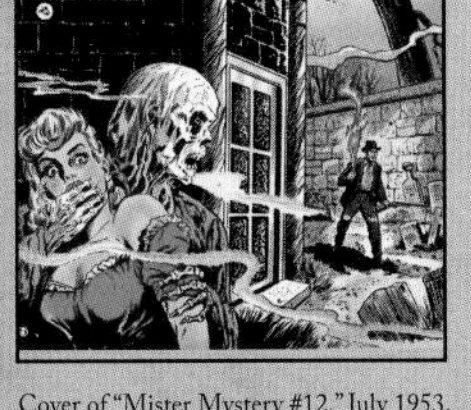
this magazine is
HAUNTED
10¢
THE BLIND, THE DOOMED, AND THE DEAD!
DOCTOR DEATH
Cover of "Mister Mystery #12." July 1953.

Seduction of the Innocent was not the only work which Wertham authored, but it seems a safe bet that in surfing on a wave of public indignation and hysteria it was the most well-known, best-selling and most lucrative. Its consequences for the comic book, however, turned out to be little short of catastrophic. After Wertham's shrill, alarmist tome, the comics business was subjected to the scrutiny of Senator Estes Kefauver at a string of hearings at which nervous comic publishers meekly rolled over and apologised for their uncouth and low-class readership's appalling tastes. The only publisher prepared to stand his ground and mount a spirited defence on the behalf of comic books, the only person who

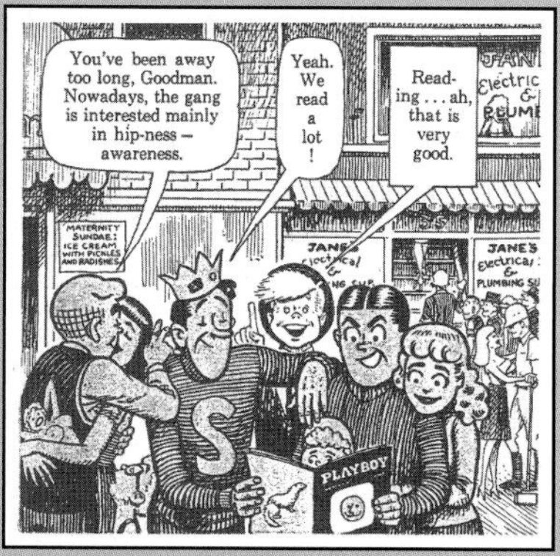
You've been away too long, Goodman. Nowadays, the gang is interested mainly in hip-ness – awareness.
Yeah. We read a lot !
Read-ing . . . ah, that is very good.
MATERNITY SUNDAE: ICE CREAM WITH PICKLES AND RADISHES
JANE'S Electrical & PLUMBING SU
PLAYBOY

Excerpt from "Goodman Goes Playboy," a Goodman Beaver story by Harvey Kurtzman and Will Elder. First published in "Help! #13." February 1962.

seemed genuinely proud of the material his company produced, was E.C.'s William Gaines. Gaines' testimony, heartfelt and intelligent, was only undermined by the unusual and disproportionate amount of time that this most controversial publisher was called upon to speak for. Gaines, during this period, was using an amphetamine-based diet pill to keep on top of all the hectic late-night deadlines for which comic publishing was justly famed. Unfortunately, due to the inordinate duration of Gaines' long interrogation, the great comics pioneer was entering the nosedive of a comedown as the questioning moved into more contentious territory. Asked to comment on an E.C. cover image which portrayed a Johnny Craig axe-murderer shuffling towards the reader with a woman's severed head held by its blonde hair in one hand, the crashing and disoriented Gaines rashly declared that he believed the cover to be an example of good taste. Asked to elucidate on what might constitute a bad-taste cover image, Gaines disastrously suggested that it would be bad taste if the maniac were holding up the severed head a little higher, so the ragged stump and dripping arteries could be seen. Quite clearly, Gaines' impromptu theory of aesthetic homicide did the already-battered image of the industry no favours whatsoever. Rather the reverse.

It may be thought that Bill Gaines' forthrightness was born of a conviction that his company had never perpetrated anything of which he ought to be ashamed. By contrast, many of the other comic imprints, with considerably greater stains upon their conscience, rapidly adopted the apologetic and placatory stance that would seem to have been the comic industry's default position from its origins with D.C. Comics toning down and anxiously policing *Superman* and *Batman* in a Lady Macbeth effort at self-cleansing to ward off the censure of the morals groups and critics. In the wake of the Kefauver hearings, a collection of the field's main business interests which included both D.C. and Archie Comics worked towards the institution of a new self-regulatory committee to control the content of all U.S. comics in an effort to forestall some outside party moving in and doing the same thing. This powerful and freshly-manufactured body would be called the Comics Code Authority.

Bolted together with almost indecent haste, the CCA was implemented in October 1954, less than six months after the May release of Dr. Wertham's book. The Comics Code itself, a long standards and practice document, is interesting mainly for the eccentricity of its demands (the living dead and treating divorce humorously are both seen as equally offensive, with this stipulation aimed presumably at titles such as Zombie Alimony Funnies, which I've just invented so please don't write in), and for the curious specificity of language in which those demands are framed. For instance, in the Code's insistence that no comic book should have the words 'Horror' or 'Terror' as a prominent part of its title, it is difficult not to suspect that this is legislation which has been designed expressly to put E.C. publications out of business. The one way in which the Code could have accomplished this more blatantly is if they'd added words like 'Vault' or 'Mad' to the above forbidden list. Given the prominence of Archie Comics in the Code's establishing and architecture, one could be forgiven for imagining that this was some form of humourless and petty payback for the jubilant irreverence of Kurtzman's '*Starchie*'. On the other hand, if we consider the enormous popularity and market share which E.C.'s line was at the time attracting, at least viewed from the perspective of embittered rival publishers, we have perhaps a more convincing reason for concerns like Archie Comics or D.C. to want Bill Gaines and his embarrassingly splendid comic books out of the picture, without need to speculate about old grudges or hurt feelings over *Superduperman*.

In an attempt to mitigate the loss of his best-selling titles, Gaines tried to establish a Code-safe alternative 'new trend' of comic books in brave and often wonderfully accomplished titles such as *Valor, Piracy*, or the ingenious and brilliantly-conceived *Psychoanalysis*.

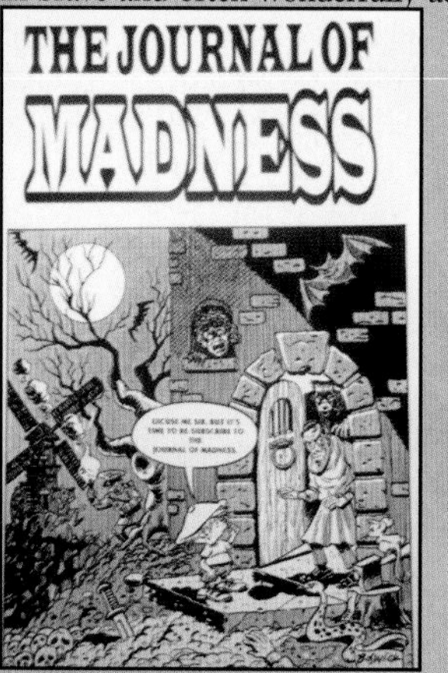
THE JOURNAL OF
MADNESS

Cover of fanzine "The Journal of Madness." Art by Boswick.

Although E.C.'s diehard aficionados would applaud the bravery of this attempt to keep providing cutting-edge comic book narrative under the new restrictions, lacking guaranteed attractions like the *Old Witch* and *Crypt-Keeper* from the horror line or the sheer chicken fat and potrzebie to be found in *Mad*, Gaines' new line foundered. *Mad* became a magazine, sidestepping the new regulations that applied only to comic books and losing most of the delinquent genius that had made it such a unique tour de force somewhere along the way. A disillusioned Kurtzman made attempts to resurrect *Mad's* socio-satirical agendas in the somehow subdued *Trump* and *Help* before accepting the Hugh Hefner shilling and agreeing to restrict himself to the initially inspired and psychedelic, but increasingly irrelevant and lifeless, *Little Annie Fanny* for the rest of his once-unsurpassable career. Into the gaping hole left by the absence of E.C. and similarly banished product like the *Biro* crime books poured a flood of relatively bland material as companies like ACG, the American Comic Group, replaced genuine horror narratives with whimsical Frank Capra-fashion supernatural comedies, and Timely/Atlas ushered in an era of non-threatening westerns, teenage humour titles, and the entertaining juvenile science-fiction monster comics such as *Journey into Mystery* or the oddly-named *Amazing Adult Fantasy*. The anodyne exploits of the annoying and almost asexual *Archie* would become the perfect symbols of the newly-neutered comic industry, while D.C. sank into a profitable torpor where Bob Hope and Dobie Gillis rubbed shoulders with Julius Schwartz's clever and inventive science fiction books or else the often-charming but predictable adventures of such proven favourites as *Wonder Woman, Superman*, and *Batman*. Anyone observing the deodorised and family-friendly comic world of the late 1950s could have justifiably concluded that the glorious subversive blip that was E.C. might as well not have happened. But, of course, it had, and E.C.'s painfully short-lived experiment would arguably have more influence upon the future of the industry and medium alike than any of the safer offerings from the publishing concerns who did so much to ensure E.C.'s downfall.

Whether consciously or not, E.C. had laid down the foundations for the revolutionary idea that comics might conceivably one day be seen as art or literature. Although this aspiration may not have been spelled out in as many words, it was so glaringly apparent from the sheer accomplishment of almost every panel that the readers could not help but feel involved in something special and unprecedented. Much as futurologist and non-musician Brian Eno once remarked that though the Velvet Underground may only have been listened to by a few hundred people all those people subsequently went on to form bands, E.C. had sown the seeds of comics yet-to-come. One of the earliest ways in which this would be manifested was in the appearance of E.C.-appreciating comic fanzines, the first time that this small press phenomenon familiar from the science fiction field would be applied to the formative comics medium. Though narrow in their focus and concerned only with eulogising and examining E.C. material (through an increasingly nostalgic retrospective lens) such publications were the cornerstone of what, within around a decade, would be known as comic fandom. The peculiar symbiotic interaction between this large body of vociferous enthusiasts and the pragmatic industry which is the object of their admiration would eventually become a dominating factor in the fortunes of the comic book, drastically altering both institutions in the process. At the time, however, a handful of self-styled E.C. fan-addicts producing amateur pamphlets and magazines devoted to the wistfully recalled body-part baseball games and maniacs dressed as Santa Claus of yore would probably be seen as proof of Dr. Wertham's warnings, had they actually been seen at all.

Despite the general atmosphere of reprimand and overall repression that had settled on the 1950s comic field, there were still isolated instances of individual magnificence that deserve mention. In Jack Kirby and Joe Simon's excellent Fighting American we have a character created during the McCarthy era as an unexceptional and straight-faced commie-baiting patriotic hero of the day, much as Simon and Kirby's earlier iconic masterstroke *Captain America* was being represented at the hands of lesser talents in that witch-hunt period. However, by the second issue it became apparent that the book's protagonist (along, we must assume, with his creators) had become aware of just how ludicrous McCarthyism was beginning to appear, as demonstrated by the introduction of ridiculous parodic Red-scare villains sporting names like *Hotsky Trotsky, Poison Ivan*, and *Rhode Island Red*. Equally worthy of attention is Dick Briefer's unique *Frankenstein*. Briefer, a proud card-carrying Red who frequently contributed his trenchant editorial cartoons to the communist Daily Worker, had been fluid and adaptable enough with the code's advent to transform his quirky, endearingly ghastly horror-comic take on Mary Shelly's monster into a delightfully absurdist and even more quirky cartoon version suitable for even the most sensitively-reared young reader. Mesmerised by the upward migration of the monster's nose (by the time that the transformation from a horror story to a comedy had been completed the retroussé organ sprouted from the creature's forehead) no-one seemed to notice that the title character was technically one of the living dead and thus, according to the Comics Code, as thoroughly unwelcome as a giggling divorcee. With the exception of ingenious evasions such as the above, though, the full stifling weight and hindrance to progress represented by the Comics Code Authority would squat unmoved, and in the main unchallenged, on the comic medium in America for the next thirty years.

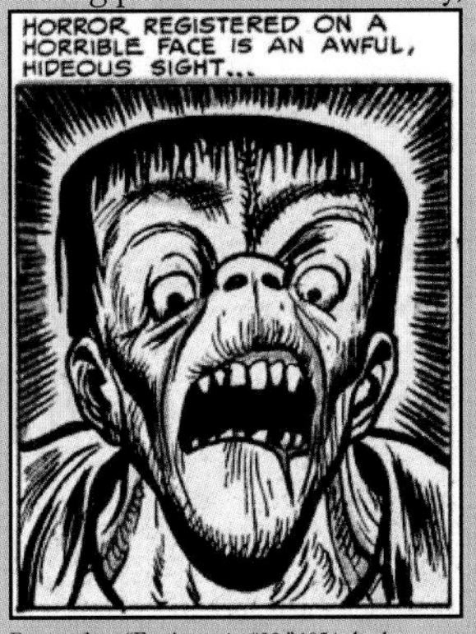
HORROR REGISTERED ON A HORRIBLE FACE IS AN AWFUL, HIDEOUS SIGHT...
Excerpt from "Frankenstein #32." 1954. Art by Dick Briefer.

Discerning readers may have noticed that the U.K. comic landscape has been scarcely mentioned since the 1880s innovation of the comic book with Ally Sloper and his scurrilous *Half-Holiday*. This certainly should not be taken as an indication that the British field was lacking in writers and artists of extraordinary talent, but rather as an acknowledgment that content, tastes, and style of presentation had remained almost unchanged in seventy or eighty years, with the exception of the previously-noted Eagle. Seen as entertainment for the very young and seemingly content to know their place, comics in Britain had avoided both the genuine progress and the moral uproar that had been experienced by their U.S. counterparts, or at least almost all of it. It's true that 1950s England saw attempts to demonise and ban the horror comic, just as happened in America, but as comic historian Martin Barker has observed this was aimed solely at American reprints or imports and, bizarrely, was an unsuccessful campaign engineered by English communists to stir up anti-U.S. sentiments. Far more significant for British comics, the late 1950s saw an influx of young and imaginative talent into the dependably staid line of children's titles from famously frugal Dundee publishing house D.C. Thompson. Gifted and enthusiastic upstarts such as the uproarious and prolific Leo Baxendale or the frenetic minimalist Davey Law, joined by the likes of the Mancunian maestro Ken Reid with his beautifully delineated mania and grotesquery, would captivate a wide swath of the nation's children with their gleeful anarchy. They'd go on to inspire a radical successive generation of British creators, but in doing so would be robbed of their most successful characters and cheated just as thoroughly and comprehensively as their U.S. contemporaries.

Back in America, the '50s hadn't breathed their last before keenly intuitive and lively former science fiction agent Julius Schwartz (who in his day had represented almost all the best-known fantasy and science-fiction authors, up to and including H.P. Lovecraft) formulated the idea that the superheroes of the 1940s, re-imagined and rebranded for the present day, might prove as popular and draw almost as big an audience as they had during their pre-television heyday. Rapidly appointing the profuse and versatile pulp author Gardner Fox along with artist Carmine Infantino to devise a streamlined and more jet-age version of D.C.'s then-discontinued character the Flash, Schwartz ushered in the all-pervasive 1960s resurrection of the costumed mystery man, redecorated with a lustrous and shiny science-fiction gloss. The success of the Flash with a new audience too young to have been previously much exposed to the concept of superheroes prompted Schwartz to use the same technique again with Bernard Baily and Martin Nodell's defunct Aladdin variant, *Green Lantern*, this time trusted to hipster and pulp science-fiction veteran John Broome as writer with the elegant and visually balletic stylings of Gil Kane providing the illustrative component. From there it was only a short step to Schwartz arriving at an updated revival of the previously surefire audience-grabbing super-combo, the *Justice Society of America*. With interiors handled by the team of Gardner Fox with artist Mike Sekowsky and attention-seizing covers from the almost archetypal pen of Murphy Anderson, Schwartz's remodelled *Justice League* was a surprise hit that sent ripples through the industry, announcing that the supermen were back.

A conversation taking place over a round of golf between somebody at D.C. and Martin Goodman, publisher of Marvel Magazines, alerted Goodman to the overnight success of Schwartz's super-team book. He instructed nephew Stan Lee, in charge of the company's own Timely/Atlas line of comic books, to come up with a group of superheroes that could duplicate and rival the D.C. best-seller. Luckily for Goodman, Lee had access to the U.S. comic industry's foremost creative dynamo, Jack Kirby. It is more than likely safe to say that Kirby, fresh from his creation of the uniformly-costumed D.C. hero team *The Challengers of the Unknown*, did more than his fair share of the creative work in coming up with *The Fantastic Four*, including a first issue cover near-identical in composition to the *Showcase* debut of the *Justice League*. Perhaps because the weather-beaten tenements and dead-end streets of Kirby's ghetto-informed sensibilities lent the new super-team an air of gritty realism that was lacking in the D.C. titles, *The Fantastic Four* proved to be a sensation, prompting Lee to set the endlessly inventive Kirby to the task of generating a whole line-up of imaginative modern superheroes like the *Hulk, Thor, Ant Man, Iron Man, the X-Men, the Avengers*, even possibly designing *Spider-Man* along the way (although Steve Ditko is undoubtedly the artist who did most to shape this character, *Spider-Man's* debut in *Amazing Adult Fantasy* depicts the hero on a Kirby cover almost certainly prepared some time before the contents of the comic, Kirby having only recently created The Fly and his arch-enemy The Spider for the Archie Comics line).

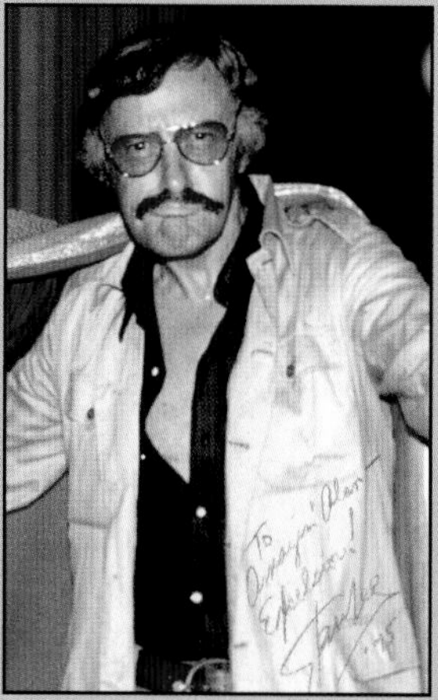

Stan Lee at 1973 San Diego Comic Con. Photo: Alan Light.

The second superhero boom was underway, and although both D.C. and their emerging major rival Marvel Comics would keep up a complement of war or western titles for a while, presumably in case the costumed-hero tide ever went out again, it quickly became evident that capes and masks were once again the industry's main selling point. Over the next few years most of the other still-surviving comic companies would put more emphasis upon their 'long underwear' titles as they tried to ride the profitable swell of the unstoppable D.C. and Marvel wave with Marvel speedily establishing itself as the most popular of the two lines, at least in part due to Stan Lee's undoubted flair for hype and salesmanship. At Archie Comics, a blatant attempt was made to mimic Marvel in the camp and often borderline-demented *Mighty Comics* which revived the 1940s Archie superheroes of their MLJ publishing imprint. Charlton Comics, perfectly exemplifying comic business standards of the period by having been conceived of when the publishers met up in jail, expanded their own range of costumed characters when they landed the talents of Steve Ditko, who had just walked out on Marvel Comics, *Dr. Strange*, and *Spider-Man* on realising that he had no ownership or share in properties that he'd invented or made popular. Even purveyors of Frank Capra whimsy such as A.C.G would introduce appropriately oddball supernatural super-types, and go so far as fitting out their most remarkable and genuinely wonderful creation, Ogden Whitney's *Herbie*, in red flannel long-johns with a plumber's suction-cup fixed to his head, as the *Fat Fury*. Superheroes had become ubiquitous, were popular on college campuses (underlining once more the unique American disparity between the age range that the comic book, ostensibly, is aimed at, and the higher age range that the business knows to be its actual readers), were discussed in newspapers and magazines, and had seen a resurgence of those formerly exclusively E.C.-based cultural phenomena, the comics fanzine and the comics fan. Flushed with enthusiasm for the re-emergent super characters, Professor Jerry Bails and his young protégé Roy Thomas published the first well-known U.S. superhero fanzine, *Alter Ego*, which, though fundamentally nostalgia-driven in its fondness for the titles of some twenty years before, would be the template around which the mass of U.S. comic fandom would eventually coalesce. The superhero, in real life as in his comic book adventures, seemed invincible.

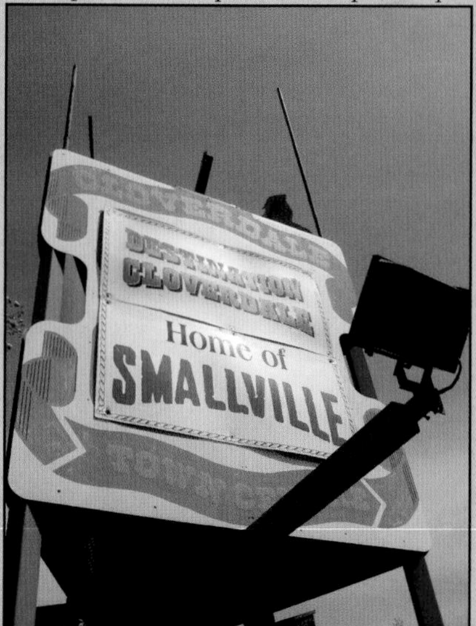
Home of
SMALLVILLE

Cloverdale welcome sign: "downtown Smallville." 2006.

Unfortunately, being seemingly reluctant or incapable of altering the seamy and disreputable practices of comics past, the publishers were raising their immaculate new edifice upon foundations that were riddled with decay. Despite the fact that the array of publishers and editors who steered the comic industry did not themselves appear to possess any noticeable talents save for cheating the more gifted out of their creations, hustling, and otherwise accumulating money; and despite the fact that lacking an exploitable parade of artists, writers, and just generally creative individuals the entire industry, the superhero, and the new house that the publisher just bought would not exist; despite these things the comics business would continue to routinely bully, cheat , abuse, and alienate the very people on whom it depended. Comic book concerns and businesses, gangster initiated, casually applied the values and techniques of their illustrious founders, treating their creators with a breathtaking contempt as if they saw the men and women who had made their fortunes as plantation slaves or some variety of fuel-rod, endlessly replaceable and therefore instantly disposable.

Regrettably, a sizeable proportion of the industry's creative individuals would seem to have internalised this image of themselves, perhaps through lack of confidence in their marketability without the proven lure of the established superhero franchises which they are working on, and have remained content in uncomplaining loyal servitude until age compromises their abilities and they're inevitably cast aside by their employers.

Amidst the vast multitude of cowed, intimated workers on the comic book assembly line, only those rare creators with a sense of their own worth have ever actively defied or walked away from their tormentors. Unsurprisingly, these turn out to be by and large the same creators who have done most to enrich the comic world. Siegel and Shuster, from a very early stage, were public in their anger over

having been deceived and cheated out of *Superman* and its related properties, though it was not until the groundswell of publicity surrounding the first Superman film in the 1970s that, largely through the tireless work of, arguably, the real *Batman* co-creator Jerry Robinson, D.C. were shamed into allowing Jerry Siegel and Joe Shuster a small pension as a thank-you for creating the whole superhero industry. That this begrudging stipend was inadequate is evidenced by the long-running lawsuit which Siegel and Shuster's families have served upon D.C., a lawsuit one suspects to be the reason why a television show that could quite reasonably be expected to be titled *Superboy* has instead aired as *Smallville*. It is safe to say that many of D.C.'s revamping efforts with the character, along with their apparently coincidental drastic overhauls of continuity, are predicated not on any true creative reasons but upon the possibility of losing ownership of certain concepts, brands or characters in an ongoing legal battle that is only now approaching its hopefully just conclusion.

Anonymous illustration in "Nights of Horror," alleged to have been drawn by Joe Shuster after losing rights to Superman and the related characters he co-created. It's been asserted the images feature likenesses of Superman characters being beaten and tortured. 1950s.

Superman's creators, obviously, aren't the only talents in the comic business to have raised objections to their treatment. In what can be seen as both an admirably heartfelt and almost poetic statement, the creator of the 1940s *Human Torch* and thus of the first Timely/Marvel superhero character, Carl Burgos, took his comic book originals out onto his front lawn and torched the lot of them. By the middle-to-late-1960s both Steve Ditko and Jack Kirby, tired of being kicked around by Marvel after all that those two legends had done to create the company, jumped ship and went instead to work at Charlton or eventually D.C., where one suspects that they fared little better. In Jack Kirby's case, as with Siegel and Shuster, Kirby's family are engaged in an ongoing legal contretemps with Marvel Comics over ownership of all the characters that Kirby undeniably created. Given that no-one at Marvel Comics wants to contemplate what all its movie franchises would look like with the Kirby characters removed, it may well be imagined that the full might of their law department has been marshalled to prevent this nightmarish scenario from occurring.

V

It was also in the middle-to-late 1960s that the coterie of science fiction writers and pulp novelists who had between them either

formulated or developed most of D.C.'s superhero line, such as John Broome and Gardner Fox, decided that they really ought to have at least a pension or a medical insurance plan in place if they were going to carry on providing D.C. with its lifeblood. Being reasonable modern working men (and this is an important point: these men weren't comic fans but were instead hard-working pulp professionals who happened to be making a significant percentage of their income from their comic work), they took their concerns to the management and sensibly suggested that they form a union to represent them in legitimate, grown-up negotiations, at which point they were informed by management that they were fired, and that replacement writers would be found to fill the titles on which they were working. With characteristic canniness, the company recruited these replacements from the all-too-eager ranks of U.S. comic fandom, bringing in a generation of fan writers who were only too pleased to be working with the costumed heroes that they'd been fixated on since they were children, and apparently were not concerned that in accomplishing their adolescent dreams they'd helped to put the far superior talents who'd created the beloved emblems of their endlessly extended childhoods out of work. Nor, for the

"Bucket o Soldiers." Photo by Maclapessoa, 2012. (Creative Commons CC0 1.0 Universal Public Domain Dedication.) (CC) (0)

most part, were they likely to risk their nostalgic opportunity to rummage in 'the toy-box', as the major companies' repertoire of misappropriated super-characters is sometimes known by the enthusiastic fans-turned-pro who now account for a majority of the professionals employed within the industry, by raising any of the questions or complaints that led to the dismissal of their luckless predecessors. In this shift from working writers to promoted fans we can see the beginnings of a process whereby the creative duties on a title will most likely be assumed by someone who's a devoted admirer of some previous creator's run upon the book in question, and will fill his or her tenure on the title with fan-pleasing references rather than originating the fresh concepts that all comics need if they are to survive. As a result, with some few decades of fans referencing fans who in their turn were referencing fans, we have a program of inbreeding which almost surpasses that of European monarchy, assuring that the product will be subject to genetic weaknesses, will speed up the decline and ultimate extinction of whichever line it happens to be part of, and will be inordinately stupid. If the *Tijuana Bibles* are to be believed, it may well also have two heads.

Of course, by the mid-1960s there were changes happening in the vastly wider world beyond the insular and narrow confines of the comics business. By this time Jeff Nuttall's 'bomb culture' delinquents of the 1950s had transformed to beatniks and then once again into the hippies who would characterise 1960s counter-culture. As the term implies, this counter-culture was comprised of an alternative approach to cultural artefacts and media, demanding different clothing, different movies, different music, different publications, different lifestyles and, inevitably, different comic books. Underground comix, while emerging mostly from the underground newspapers of the period such as *The San Francisco Oracle* or from the flurry of underground comic publishers arising in response to Robert Crumb's seminal *Zap*, had their undoubted point of common origin in William Gaines' much-missed E.C. line. In fact, hardly had the blood and feathers settled from the Comics Code disaster, with the folding of E.C. and transformation of Kurtzman's *Mad* comic book into a code-avoiding magazine in the mid-50s, than underground comics were initially established. The intelligent and principled Paul Krassner, whose *The Realist* is perhaps the first underground publication of this era, was employed at that time on *Mad* magazine and used Bill Gaines' facilities to publish the first issues of his radical, satirical, and scathing journal. Krassner also used at least one of Gaines' major artists when he famously persuaded the immortal and authority-averse delineator Wally Wood to craft an illustration that depicted all the leading Disney characters engaged in flagrant copulation, this event known as the Disneyland Memorial Orgy. In this single image we see many of the tropes that would be featured in the underground cartoons of roughly ten years later, notably the highly sexualised interpretation of deliberately asexual commercial characters. What's most remarkable about Krassner and Wood's triumphant resurrection of the Tijuana spirit is that Disney, perhaps taken by surprise and unsure how to prosecute without ensuring vast publicity for the offending picture, didn't sue. When Dan O'Neill's *Air Pirates* tried a variation on the same theme getting on a decade later, the response would be more resolute and punitive, Disney's attorneys being perhaps more prepared by this time.

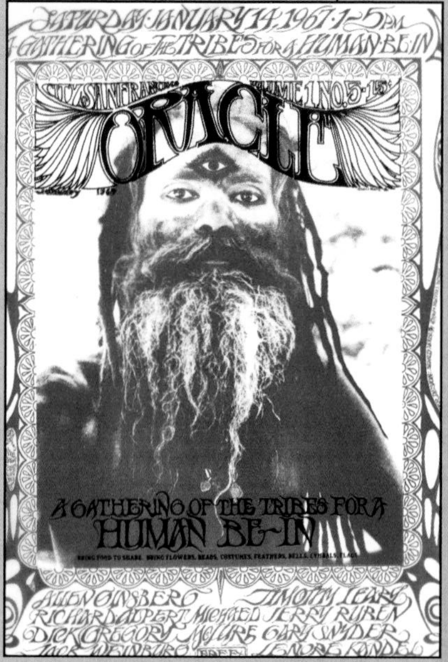
SATURDAY·JANUARY 14·1967·1–5PM
A GATHERING OF THE TRIBES FOR A HUMAN·BE·IN
ORACLE
A GATHERING OF THE TRIBES FOR A
HUMAN BE-IN
ALLEN GINSBERG
TIMOTHY LEARY
RICHARD ALPERT
JERRY RUBIN
DICK GREGORY
GARY SNYDER

Cover of "San Francisco Oracle," Vol. 1 No. 5, January 1967. Author: Estate of Allen Cohen and Regent Press, publishers of the San Francisco Oracle Facsimile Edition (Digital Version) available at www.regentpress.net. (GNU Free Documentation License. Creative Commons Attribution-Share Alike 3.0 Unported license.)

With the inception of a comics underground to follow early pioneers like *Gothic Blimp Works*, *Yellow Dog* and Crumb's movement-defining *Zap*, the anti-social urge towards explicit violence, sexuality and criticism of the status quo that had been brutally repressed since William Gaines' unfortunate speed-comedown during the Kefauver hearings would surge to the surface in a form that was explosive, shocking, and deliberately confrontational. Although the movement's leading lights were technically spectacular and produced many memorable works, it could be argued that their main commitment was to simple fun and hedonism, and that the main targets for subversion (leaving to one side the readily-caricatured Dick Nixon) were the prissy and sedate traditions of the medium itself, and the sheer sexless dopiness of mainstream culture's institutions and beloved icons. While one might experience a brief iconoclastic frisson from a beautifully-produced Victor Moscoso image showing Planter's Mr. Peanut in receipt of oral stimulation, or the excellent Kim Deitch's reinvention of the Michelin tyre mascot as his lusty and priapic *Uncle Ed*, more weighty issues such as race, class, or misogyny were in the main left unexamined, as was any serious investigation of potentially viable political alternatives. There were exceptions like Jay Kinney's *Anarchy* or many of the interesting female voices raised within the pages of *Wet Satin* or the later *Wimmen's Comix*, and one would not wish to casually dismiss the visionary spectacles of Robert Williams or Dave Sheridan, but it is difficult not to observe the absence of a coherent political, moral, or ultimately even aesthetic sensibility at work within the undergrounds. The movement's one sustained and major work of genius, in the marvellous Justin Green's *Binky Brown Meets the Holy Virgin Mary*, is today all but forgotten, with only the memory of all the blowjobs, drugs, and youthful sense of hedonist entitlement left to commemorate the undergrounds' occasionally glorious contributions to the medium.

The rapidly expanded or at least hallucinating consciousness that typified the 1960s would affect the comic book by other means than those exemplified within the mostly-San Francisco generated undergrounds. Shrewd mainstream comic artists such as Jim Steranko, perhaps realising that the greatest innovators in the medium had simply introduced ideas to the blinkered and self-regarding field that were already being utilised to great effect in other areas of culture, started borrowing effects from counter-culture standbys such as Op Art, psychedelic poster art, or the Surrealists. More flexible old masters like Jack Kirby were allowing ideas from the underground and flights of cosmic introspection to intrude upon their mainstream comic narratives, and at the margins of the industry the disaffected E.C. luminary Wally Wood was publishing his inspirational, courageous, and experimental *Witzend*, showcasing the Code-transgressing comics work of dissident mainstream contemporaries like Reed Crandall, Jim Steranko or Steve Ditko alongside new talents that were springing up at comics' underground extremities such as Vaughn Bodé, Wood's assistant Roger Brand, and then-unknown Art Spiegelman. Even the mostly-retrospective U.S. comic fanzine field had been affected in the form of the Bill Spicer/Richard Kyle exemplary progressive publication, *Graphic Story Magazine*, where the most trenchantly insightful and incisive writings ever on the form were interwoven with examples, from Vaughn Bodé or perhaps the fiercely individual and overlooked George Metzger, of what Kyle and Spicer presciently termed 'the graphic story'. Add to this the mind and eyeball-bending comics underground and all the cultural, political, and social uproar of the period and it is relatively easy to appreciate why these were such exciting, pyrotechnic and important times for the evolving and mutating comics medium.

Almost unnoticeable in its day although it would eventually be of some significance, England in 1968 would see the advent of its own comic book fan scene when the seventeen year-old science fiction fan and English comic industry professional Steve Moore, along with comic fan Phil Clarke and the proprietor of the U.K's (if not the world's) first comics and science fiction shop, Derek 'Bram' Stokes, convened the country's first comic conventions, approximately at the time when the first comic fanzines (Moore's *Ka-Pow* in England and the Anthony Roche-produced *Heroes Unlimited* in Ireland) were beginning to establish an initially minuscule readership of previously isolated comic fans. Those first U.K. conventions, almost unimaginable from today's perspective of hybridised mind-control experiments and trade fairs where the captive target audience is paying to be advertised to and where comics are the last thing anybody cares about, were attended by a tiny, almost wholly teenage membership of perhaps fifty to a hundred comic book enthusiasts. Such negligible numbers, from an industry perspective, meant that none of the big companies could bother to be represented and that consequently the convention could remain a place of meeting and discussion rather than a sweaty, predatory consumer cattle-market that exists as no more than an opportunity for pushing product to a largely undiscriminating audience.

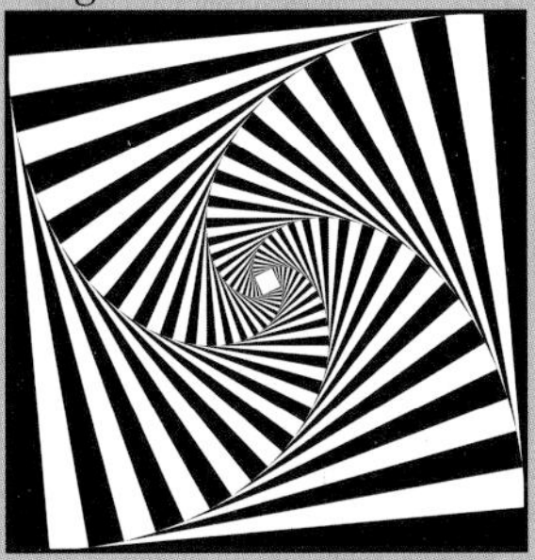

An "Op art"-looking, spiraling, four-sided tunnel generated by an extremely simple iterative mathematical transformation: Draw a square, then inside that square draw a smaller centered square in negative color rotated by 5°, and with sides 92.30623% the length of the sides of the enclosing square. (Released into public domain by author March 2012.)

Most significant of the considerable differences between the start-conditions that existed for American and English comic fandom at their outset is most probably the dates of their inauguration. U.S. fandom, launched at the beginning of the 1960s, was as we have previously noted in the main a retrospective and nostalgic enterprise that set out to enshrine the relatively crude creations of the 1940s as an unsurpassable and perfect comics 'Golden Age'. Fandom in England, on the other hand, was forged amidst the fireworks and upheaval of the middle 1960s psychedelic era and would have, in consequence, a more progressive, radical and forward-looking character, at least in those most crucial and most influential early stages. A surprising number of the talents that would go on to affect the comic industry in England and the wider world were to be found amongst the tiny crowd at those first few conventions, or amongst the roster of contributors to the U.K.'s own underground paper and comix scene which back then was so closely intertwined with fan activity, the offices of British underground tabloid the *International Times (IT)* being next door to Bram Stokes' prototype comic and science-fantasy emporium, *Dark They Were* and *Golden Eyed*.

The 1970s, though starting optimistically with 1960s afterglow material like Kirby's cosmic *New Gods* epic for D.C. (for many years an unacknowledged influence on George Lucas's Star Wars) or the various remaining titles from the underground, would rapidly deteriorate into one of the least-inspired and most drearily moribund decades in comics history, at least as far as mainstream comics in America would be concerned. Though early efforts to establish no-returns trade through the comic shop network that was by then slowly emerging (what would be known as the 'Direct Sales Market') seemed at first to promise more fan-oriented and intelligent material, these hopes would be short-lived as opportunist traders undercut attempts to find an audience for more ambitious projects like Kirby's *New Gods* or similar experimental and fan-oriented D.C. offerings like Steve Ditko's idiosyncratic and adventurous post-Marvel work or Howard Post's inventive Neolithic saga *Anthro*, causing these intriguing titles to meet early cancellation before their potential could be fairly tested.

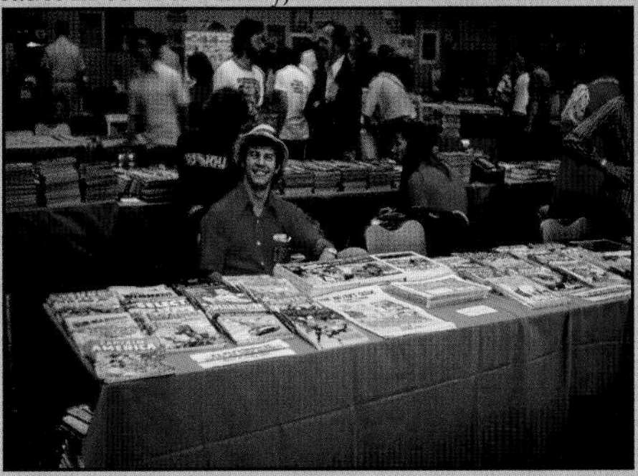

Murray Bishoff at the DynaPubs table at the 1976 San Diego Comic Book Convention, now known as Comic Con International. Photo by Alan Light. (Creative Commons Attribution 2.0 Generic license, 2006.)

Gradually becoming disillusioned in an industry where they were never likely to be compensated equitably for their labours, many of the comic landscape's most important and most influential talents were to either drift out of the business in disgust or else be marginalised by the major comic companies who were sure, in their complacency, that there'd be plenty more prolific and exploitable creators where the last batch came from. Sadly, this proved not to be the case, as the last batch had come from an America with different expectations, different values, and a different attitude to craftsmanship; in short, from an America that nobody had seen in some considerable time. With these more capable and venerable artisans either estranged from the comic business or so sick and tired of its shenanigans that they were no longer prepared to give it their best efforts, and with the new fandom-reared creators proving seemingly incapable of generating any truly new ideas, the comic business seemed to enter into a potentially fatal tailspin. While it's true that there were a few titles in this period that stood head and shoulders above the material surrounding them, given that this material was mostly dross, it meant that any flicker of success was merely relative and that there was still nothing happening that might conceivably revitalise the industry.

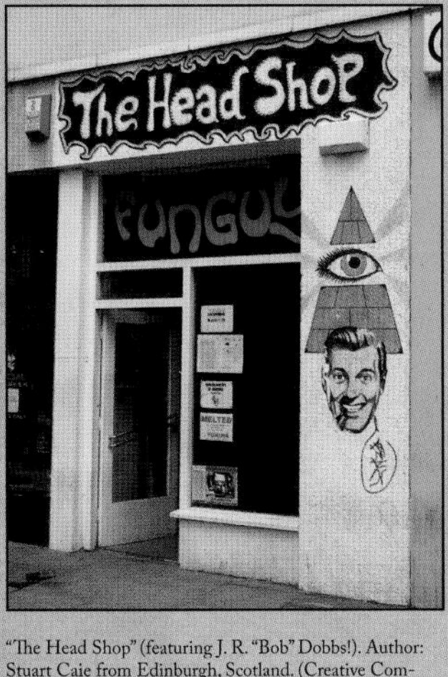
The Head ShoP

"The Head Shop" (featuring J. R. "Bob" Dobbs!). Author: Stuart Caie from Edinburgh, Scotland. (Creative Commons Attribution 2.0 Generic license, 26 July 2008, 11:25.)

Making things worse, in the mid-1970s new laws were passed prohibiting the sale of drug paraphernalia, closing down the hippy 'head shops' that had prospered since the 1960s and coincidentally thus removing pretty much the only outlet for underground comix in America. With the exception of established institutions such as Zap, most of the undergrounds would simply disappear, practically overnight. Their last hurrah, Bill Griffiths and Art Spiegelman's astonishing *Arcade*, served almost as a summary of what the comic underground accomplished, along with a transcending of the genre's self-imposed sex-and-dope limitations that would take underground comics into territory that was genuinely avant-garde, paving the way for later milestones like Spiegelman's *Raw* or Robert Crumb's eclectic *Weirdo*. As one-time *Weirdo* editor the estimable Peter Bagge has pointed out, there were still a few excellent post-underground comics emerging even in the later reaches of that torpid decade, like the sterling *Let Me Out of Here*, although as this last title seems to indicate, the 1970s in comics weren't the most well-decorated or inspiring place to be.

In England, though, the 1970s would have a slightly different cast to them. The country's infrastructure, social, moral and political, appeared to be collapsing, breaking down as if preparing for the decade's end when Margaret Thatcher would arrive to finish off the demolition. In amidst the unemployment, dust, and rubble of the era were the seeds of what would blossom into the Punk movement, a prolonged barely-coherent howl of righteous anger at the blighted circumstances that incompetent economists and politicians had left Britain to endure. In the predictable and largely-unchanged world of British comics, this new mood would manifest around the middle of the decade in the newly-minted controversial boys' adventure weeklies from IPC Publishing, *Battle and Action*. Attracting the incensed attentions of the country's decency campaigners, these two titles had resulted from the steady changes that had taken place within the British industry over the past few decades. A new generation of artists and writers had grown up, exposed to influences from the wealth of vibrant culture that had burst forth with the end of World War II, and they were beginning to make an impression. Seemingly spearheaded by enthusiastic, capable young writers such as the sardonic and satirical John Wagner or the energetic and politically aware Pat Mills, *Battle and Action* played upon the adolescent love of combined gore and humour much as William Gaines had done in the U.S. some twenty years before and, like E.C., sometimes attempted to work serious material in amongst the blood and entrails. Special mention must be made of artist Joe Colquhoun and writer Pat Mills' *Charley's War in Battle*, a intense and visceral anti-war strip that in terms of writing, art, and it's immaculately-researched evocation of the First World War is equal to the best of Kurtzman's *Frontline Combat* masterpieces.

With both Battle and especially the gleeful carnage to be found in Action threatened by offended Christian moralists, it was decided to launch a third title that would have the same approach and energy as its two predecessors but would this time cater to the growing science-fiction audience. In 1976, the year of the Sex Pistols, IPC would launch their radical new title *2000AD* and set in motion a productive vector of fresh creativity destined to have a major influence on comics both in Britain and America. Once more with Pat Mills and John Wagner manning the creative helm, ably abetted by some of the now-grown attendees of those first few British conventions such as Steve Moore or the dementedly inventive Kevin O'Neill, *2000AD* would attract a novel strain of young and wilfully progressive artists who had grown up with the influence of home-grown talents such as Leo Baxendale or Ken Reid, but had also managed to absorb the lessons of the then-still-recent undergrounds and, most importantly, the past two decades of American comic material brought over to this country principally as ballast in the holds of cargo ships. Knowledgeable and dedicated comic-strip enthusiasts, they had assimilated everything from *Alley Sloper* through to *Zap*, taking in nearly eighty years of the best U.S. newspaper creations, the E.C. line, Harvey Kurtzman and Will Eisner, undergrounds, English and European comics, Marvel and D.C. and every other comics pinnacle of note along the way. Craftsmen like the impeccable Brian Bolland or the brilliantly expressive and Jack Davis-influenced Mick McMahon would take *2000AD* as an opportunity to put the skills they'd learned and the array of influences they'd absorbed into spectacular and stunningly effective practice.

In John Wagner's wacky *Robo-Hunter* or totalitarian parody *Judge Dredd*, as in the Pat Mills/Kevin O'Neill-crafted *Ro-Busters* or *Nemesis*, there was the sense of something new and thrilling in the English comics weekly, and despite the doldrums that the U.S. comics scene appeared to be enmired in, there was a pervasive atmosphere of possibility suffusing the long-dormant British market for the first time since the Baxendale-and-Reid-fuelled glory day of almost twenty years before. The British wing of Marvel Comics, perhaps feeling that they ought to up their game faced with the competition from *2000AD*, responded with a revamp of their *Captain Britain* character and the generally progressive work on their *Dr. Who Weekly/Monthly* title. Taking full advantage of this surge of energy, the independent comic publication *Warrior* debuted in 1980, with a critical reaction which suggested that the rapidly-evolving British comic scene had taken its next major step.

Meanwhile, the U.S. comics business was still going through what must have been a worrying, if gradual, decline. The major companies had dismissed or alienated almost all of comics' most productive and innovative idea-mongers, seemingly still working on the flawed assumption that creative talents were completely interchangeable, that Kirbys, Woods and Ditkos grew on trees and that the fandom-reared replacements who'd been parachuted in during the 1960s would prove capable of generating new and viable ideas of their own, rather than simply revelling in an arrested adolescence with the characters they'd loved when they were children. None of these assumptions turned out to be accurate, and sales continued to decline: back in the 1950s, even averagely-selling comic books like the Charles Biro-published *Daredevil* were selling a few million copies every month, whereas by the late 1970s the unrelated Marvel title *Daredevil* was rumoured to be selling less than twenty thousand by the time the title was entrusted to a young and keen Frank Miller. The keen sense of desperation in the U.S. industry during this time can perhaps best be judged by the extremely desperate measures that the business was employing as it laboured to revive its flagging fortunes.

Crucially, the art in mainstream U.S. titles was beginning to appear lacklustre and

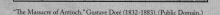

"The Massacre of Antioch." Gustave Doré (1832-1883). (Public Domain.)

homogenous, hardly surprisingly when major publishers (and by this juncture of the 1970s that would be just D.C. and Marvel, all their smaller rivals that once lent the field diversity by then defunct) were actively encouraging their artists to adopt a bland and uniform 'house style'. Perhaps belatedly considering that this deficiency might have something to do with the deteriorating sales, the people governing the industry began to look for more exciting talents elsewhere. A prevailing problem with the newer breed of U.S. artist was that they had become used to working only on, let's say, the pencils for a comic book, safe in the knowledge that deficiencies of style and dull arrangements could be livened up or fixed by the book's colourist or by its inker. Consequently, skills such as lending one's illustrations weight or texture by the application of sheer hard-won craft were swiftly disappearing, at least in America. The Philippines, however, had its own tradition of black-and-white comics where the lack of colour left a lazy artist's basic flaws humiliatingly exposed. As a result, the Filipino artists had devised a rigorous aesthetic of lavish embellishment with a dramatic use of blacks and an accomplished fluency with rarely-used and time consuming techniques such as hatching, beautifully applied to the point where it most resembled the engraved plates of a nineteenth century master such as Gustav Doré. Shamefully, rather than treat this largely-undeserved influx of captivating and industrious talents (such as Rudy Nebres, Alfredo Alcala and the thrillingly experimental Alex Niño) as the industry's potential saviours, editors and publishers were unable to help themselves in doggedly repeating all of the abusive and mean-spirited mistakes which had for so long ensured that the comics business was a byword for the second-rate and juvenile. Rather than pay these stunning artists fairly for producing work which was so glaringly superior to anything to which the mostly flaccid and complacent U.S. talent might aspire, it was apparently decided in an unconcerned and casual act of racism that these rescuers of U.S. comics should instead be paid greatly reduced amounts, far short of those remunerations paid to U.S. artists, with these slyly trimmed-down sums known, charmingly, as 'Filipino Rates'. One can only assume it felt wrong paying Filipinos on a higher tariff than the help.

No doubt encouraged by this partially successful plundering of other lands' creative wealth, the flourishing new comic scene in Britain would be next to attract the attentions of America's product-and-money scenting talent scouts. The hypnotically-rendered iconography of Brian Bolland would be snapped up to provide the art for a twelve-issue D.C. 'maxi-series' and then, more realistically, a line of powerful and enthralling covers. The more standard U.S.-influenced work of Dave Gibbons quickly followed, but it was perhaps the subsequent decision to experiment with the import of British writers that would most impact the future of the U.S. comic industry. Although America could still claim some accomplished and imaginative comic-scribes, most notably the irreplaceable and peerless Archie Goodwin, many of the U.S. field's more radical and interesting younger writers like the late Steve Gerber or the stylish and intelligent Steve Englehart seemed to be hemmed in and frustrated at each turn by the reactionary comic culture which surrounded them, preventing rather than encouraging their growth and their development as artists. The incoming British talent, on the other hand, arriving from a background where experiment and innovation had been met with healthy sales, were possibly allowed more leeway. When the minor risk of placing English writers on those titles that were on the verge of cancellation anyway paid off with similarly-boosted readerships and some small measure of acclaim both within and, increasingly, outside the narrow confines of the industry, experiment and narratives aimed at an older reader seemed to be an economically rewarding strategy. As a result the newer writers were, if not always supported in their wilder flights of creativity, at least not actively prevented from embarking on them in the first place, letting their abilities evolve and expand into new ground at a sometimes dizzying rate. In 1984, after a reign of thirty years, the Comics Code was finally discarded, broken by its own inflexibility and inability to cope with the demands to which the new wave of creators, justified by unassailably increasing sales, were suddenly subjecting it (towards the end of its incumbency, the Code decreed that anything drawn by the artist and bon vivant Mr. Kev O'Neill could not be published with the Code's approval). The removal of this longstanding impediment to creativity allowed new freedoms in the industry, not always wisely exercised but all contributing to the new air of possibility with which the field seemed suddenly imbued.

This sudden input of adrenaline in mainstream U.S. comics seemed to coincide with an exciting burst of fresh activity beyond the limits of the superhero industry. The 1970s attempts at the establishment of a new comics business model in the form of the direct sale market were now able to be implemented, with a throng of comic shops across both Britain and America that catered to an older and hopefully more discriminating audience providing an enthusiastic market for a wider range of genres, formats, and ideas. This meant that an enormous plethora of what were termed alternative or independent comics publishers sprang into being, greatly energising and enriching the enlivened medium. It also meant that the more flexible survivors of the comix underground could once again distribute their matured and finely-honed new work to an excited audience, as with Art Spiegelman and Francoise Mouly's *Raw* or Robert Crumb, Aline Kominsky and Pete Bagge's extraordinary *Weirdo*. With what seemed a sudden avalanche of fascinating titles and original new talent, ranging from Crumb's many career-best pieces in *Weirdo* or Mark Beyer's paranoiac world of people flattened into patterns as displayed in *Raw*, through the exhilarating and diverse delights of the Hernandez brothers' inspired *Love & Rockets*, Chester Brown's hilariously distressing *Ed the Happy Clown* and Michael Gilbert's retro-romp in *Mr. Monster*, to the often pyrotechnic offerings from the reinvigorated mainstream, 1980s comics were transformed, seemingly overnight, into a thrilling and productive place to be. In Britain, although the migration of important talent to America would see the start of a decline in mainstream comic publications such as *2000AD*, there were still healthy signs of life from veteran independent comic publishers like Knockabout, effervescent fresh approaches to the medium by artist/writers like Phil Elliott and Eddie Campbell in the pages of *Escape*, and the inception of the splendidly irreverent and modern-culture-focussed *Viz* would introduce a comic book phenomenon which, thirty years on, has become a more important and more venerable British institution than the D.C. Thompson comics that it started out by satirising. Crucially, the wider world beyond the medium appeared for once to actually be taking notice of these sudden shifts and changes in the once-despised and lowly comic strip, and it was difficult to come across a newspaper or magazine that didn't have an article entitled (usually) "Bam! Sock! Crash! Pow! Comics aren't just for kids anymore!"

Unfortunately, in their use of onomatopoeic sound effects taken straight from the *Batman* television show, such pieces tended to unwittingly point out the flaw in their own premise: a majority of readers, many of the general public and a large percentage of the people working in the industry were happier with comics that were just for kids. These weren't, it should be stressed, the nine-to-thirteen year old readers that most comic heroes were originated solely to appeal to, and who, finding nothing to appeal to them inside the violent, sexually prurient, and unpleasantly adolescent comics of the period, had since moved on to other entertainments such as movies or computer games. Specifically, the 'kids' referred to were by now increasingly the early middle-aged habituated comic readers of the 1960s, '70s and '80s, many of whom were devoted to the exploits of some favourite character for reasons that were more based on nostalgia than on any real continuing enjoyment of the book in question. Readers of this kind were happy to pay lip service to the idea of comic book maturity or 'graphic novels' or the other trappings that the industry was rapidly developing, as long as this meant that they could continue reading *Spider-Man*, *Green Lantern* or some other title that they loved when they were twelve without appearing to be socially subnormal. Other than the small handful of comic strip works from the period that could conceivably be thought of as equivalent to actual novels, the new notion that the comic book had finally grown up was largely a convenient way for comics to continue turning out the same material they always had but under the pretence that this was both sophisticated and mature material intended for a semi-intellectual adult readership. The publishers rushed to collate the rambling individual issues of their superhero titles into 'graphic novels', meaning that the too-few genuinely worthy books were quickly lost beneath an avalanche of puerile rubbish that would kill the fledgling market before it had had a chance to properly establish itself in the very different ground of mainstream culture.

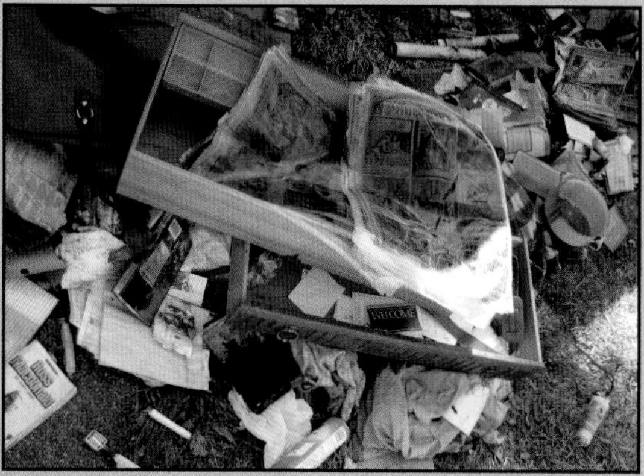

1940s Prince Valiant Sunday comics in pile of debris outside flood damaged home of a collector (New Orleans after Hurricane Katrina). Author: Infrogmation of New Orleans. (GNU Free Documentation License, Version 1.2 or any later version published by the Free Software Foundation. Creative Commons Attribution-Share Alike 2.5 Generic, 2.0 Generic and 1.0 Generic license.)

Similarly, U.S. comic publishers seemed utterly incapable of operating differently from the parade of larcenous Little League mobsters who'd preceded them. They treated the new talent with just the same sugar-coated and duplicitous contempt with which they'd treated everyone since Jerry Siegel and Joe Shuster first walked through their doors. Unable to learn any lessons from the past and intellectually too nondescript to craft a viable future, once again the massively over-promoted office boys who in the main controlled the comics business managed to completely alienate the crucial talent upon which their new, unearned respectability depended. In belated realisation of their error they made an attempt to duplicate the missing talent's basic style and superficial qualities in what was sold as cutting-edge material but which, with the exception of a very few original and capable creators like Neil Gaiman, Warren Ellis or Garth Ennis, failed to generate the same transformative excitement or attract the same attention from the world beyond the comics industry. Even these few genuine comic talents would, with time, move either into other media altogether or at least relocate to an area of the comics landscape that was as far distant from the mainstream companies as possible.

VI

One of the most significant comic related incidents to happen in the 1980s must surely be the historic corporate merger between D.C.'s parent company, Warner Brothers, and the hefty media concern sprung up around Time magazine. This merger, the most sizeable and most unprecedented of its day, is arguably the building block upon which modern corporate America, and by extension the whole modern and contentious corporate world, was founded. It is interesting to note that, according to Gerard Jones' D.C.-approved and vetted book Men of Tomorrow, the midwife and architect of this colossal and game-changing merger was none other than Jack Liebowitz, the former left-wing legal and financial mastermind who'd travelled to the dark side as the main accomplice of the putatively racketeer-connected Harry Donenfeld; the man who had assisted Donenfeld in parting two naive young Cleveland teenagers out of their ownership of Superman and thus established the corrupt foundations of the entire costumed hero industry. As if in honour of the glamorous and allegedly gangster-connected world of comics past, the deal that sealed the merger was allegedly conducted old-school style at Frank Sinatra's mother's house. Such are the origins of the enormous corporate institutions who have done so much to make our world the place it is today, and who've provided a convincing demonstration of what the amoral, treacherous, and catastrophically incompetent behaviour that has left the mainstream comics industry an impotent and lifeless husk would look like if it were applied throughout our wider business world and our financial institutions.

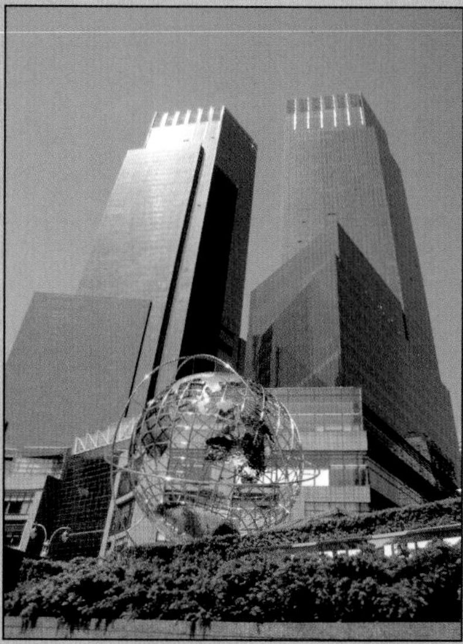

The Time Warner Center as viewed from Central Park West. The globe from the Trump International Hotel and Tower can also be seen. Author: OptimumPx. (Released into public domain by author May 2010.)

Times rolled onward, inexorably, and dragged the frantically protesting and reluctant comic business with them. Even though the industry had fumbled and mismanaged the great opportunities of the mid-1980s, something had still altered in the public's overall perception of the comic book. The English-speaking world at large was now at least prepared to accept that the comic form could sometimes be regarded, with legitimacy, as a worthy vehicle for art or literature. As more and more inspired creators pitched their works at this developing new audience, the canon of accomplished graphic narratives would gradually accumulate until a body of mature material existed that could at last justify the misplaced 'comics have grown up' hype of some ten or fifteen years before. This change, though, would be slow and gruelling, with the mainstream superhero manufacturers continuing to dominate at least the conventional comic market through the 1990s, a decade which would commence with the inauguration of the Image Comics line. Image, a collection of high-profile young fan-favourites who'd worked on some best-selling superhero characters for Marvel Comics, would establish their own independent company with a great fanfare of publicity and quickly reach a peak of popularity that seriously dented the two major companies' dominance in terms of sales. Regrettably, whatever revolutionary expectations people may have harboured for these rebel superhero artists were short-lived as Image went on, in the main, to offer only virtual duplications of the titles that had made their reputations in the mainstream industry. Sometimes, in the hands of comic artists who mistakenly seemed to believe that they were also writers, or who did not have sufficient powers of discrimination to know what adequate comic writing was, these duplications could seem even more inane, insipid, and derivative than the crowd-pleasing sludge which was their inspiration. Although Image Comics has since managed to transform itself into a more progressive and creator-friendly company, the damage that it wrought within the comics industry was not confined to the aesthetic backward-step it represented.

The preposterously inflated sales of those first Image titles would be comics' entry into the unhinged and harebrained realm which unrestrained capitalism had become since the removal of the Berlin Wall in 1989, a symbolic event which in the west was seen as the demise of communism, capitalism's only rival, and therefore as an excuse to throw a celebration party of unbridled excess, utter disconnection from reality, and rapidly disintegrating ethics which went on for nearly twenty years until its sorry and wholly predictable conclusion during 2008, with the whole world now sitting round the party table, pale with dread, and wondering how they can avoid paying the bill. A foretaste of this all-consuming madness was provided by the early 1990s comic boom, where the reported great success of a few Image titles prompted a new and presumably self-taught, inexpert breed of comic speculator, who would seem not to have heard of the relationship between supply and customer demand, buying two hundred copies of a comic with a print run of perhaps a million in the ludicrous belief that there would ever be enough demand for these widely-distributed and unexceptional scraps of ephemera to somehow massively appreciate in value and so put the speculator's unborn kids through college. In the hazardously swelling bubble of that era's comic business and its subsequent inevitable bursting, our contemporary fiscal meltdown can be seen in action-packed full-colour microcosm. Companies came into being with whole lines of ill-considered titles that existed for no other reason than to surf the wave of money. Desperate gimmickry prevailed in limited-edition special-cover efforts to distinguish one book from the next, there being nothing in the content, style or presentation of the work with which to otherwise make such distinctions. 'Crossover events', transparent ploys to make a loyal and trusting readership buy every title in the line for fear of missing some important part of a ridiculously sprawling and incomprehensible non-story, would become the major companies' sole strategy for selling their directionless, lacklustre wares. The one objective of the comics industry, it seemed, was to strip-mine the pockets of its trusting and semi-addicted customers as ruthlessly and as effectively as possible, with no thought for the crash and ruin that were certain to occur as a result of these rapacious, predatory tactics.

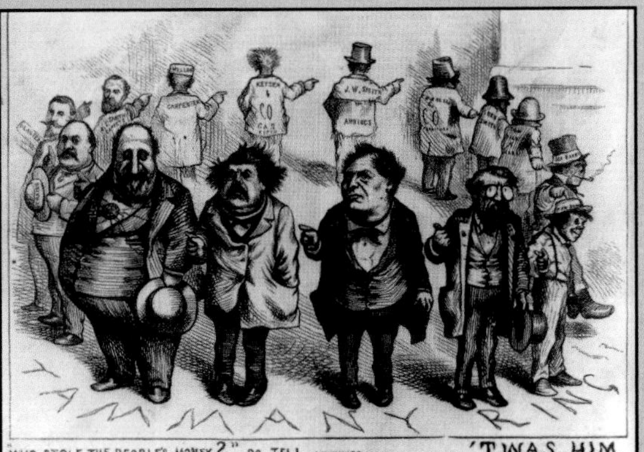
TAMMANY RING
WHO STOLE THE PEOPLE'S MONEY? — DO TELL. NY.TIMES.
'TWAS HIM.

"Who Stole The People's Money?" Thomas Nast. 1871. Nast's political cartoons helped push Boss Tweed out of NYC public office and into jail when a Spanish customs official apprehended Tweed after recognizing him from one of Nast's political cartoons. (Public Domain)

Fortunately, working doggedly throughout this feeding-frenzy were that small but vitally important handful of creators who'd emerged from one or other of the medium's many energetic areas or eras, comic artisans of genuine ability with individual voices and entirely personal agendas who were patiently creating the significant, enduring works that would make comics the legitimate artistic form that it deserved to be, regardless of the sound and fury of the mainstream's inarticulate and steroid-boosted superhero circus. The proficient and inventive storyteller Howard Cruse used comics to examine gay identity in his magnificent *Stuck Rubber Baby*, while Kim Deitch (one of the only underground practitioners to properly explore the possibilities of an extended narrative) unfurled his unique and eccentric vision in works such as *Boulevard of Broken Dreams*. Cleveland columnist and writer Harvey Pekar, one of the most lyric and essential talents to emerge out of the medium, who'd almost single-handedly created the increasingly important autobiographical or real-life observation comic genre in his 1980s classic *American Splendor*, was expanding into longer works and turning his keen eye towards more challenging material. Peter Bagge, Dan Clowes, Chris Ware, the charmingly delirious Dame Darcy, the intrepid and commendable Joe Sacco, and the always-fascinating Chester Brown, along with an encouraging variety of other unique and committed talents, were establishing the solid bedrock of the medium's reputation.

By the decade's end, despite the panics, *South Sea Bubbles* and convulsions of the mainstream industry, the comics medium had become accepted as a valid part of modern culture, with the fact that many major comics works were now available in ordinary bookshops, further weakening the grip of the traditional comic-book publishers upon the rapidly evolving market. The diversity of comic strip material now able to attract a healthy audience would prompt a wider range of new creators with new concepts to approach the field, ensuring that the comics medium was now perceived as being capable of dealing with matters of history, philosophy, gender and sexuality, biography and, obviously, politics. Since the late 1980s, isolated inroads had been made into the comic book as a mode of political expression, with the intrepid Joyce Brabner organising the pro-soldier, anti-war collection of true narratives, *Real War Stories*, and the startling C.I.A. exposé, *Brought to Light*. A decade later, with Joe Sacco's Palestine and Seth Tobocman's cutting and informed *World War Three Illustrated* featuring the angry and incisive spray-paint work of the inspiring Peter Kuper, political discourse would become a major item on the ever-growing comic book agenda. The medium was finally developing into the smart, sophisticated, and diversely useful instrument that it was always meant to be.

Not that this would be altogether evident from an inspection of the comics mainstream as it teetered on the brink of the new century. With sales declining as even the audience of hardcore superhero fans towards whom the whole industry was geared became dissatisfied with the half-hearted product being offered, both the major players of the comics business were becoming more and more dependent on the motion picture industry to grant them an extended lease of life. Perhaps as evidence that comics hadn't truly grown up in the 1980s but instead had just met retro-adolescent mainstream 'kidult' culture coming in the opposite direction, the success of superhero franchises combined with modern CGI techniques proved to be unexpectedly enormous. D.C. and a reinvigorated *Batman* franchise met with some considerable success, attributable partly to the death of a lead actor and the surrounding publicity, but Marvel Comics clearly led the superhero movie field with a spectacular array of characters, mostly created (but emphatically not owned) by truly gifted and original comic book legends like Jack Kirby or Steve Ditko. Even with these various

box office hits under their belts, however, neither company was able to translate successful movies into increased comic sales, or at least not to a point where these might make a difference to the mainstream industry's pointed decline. It gradually became apparent that the only purpose of the major companies was not as publishers of well-made and original comic material, but as providers of potential franchises for a film industry as bankrupt in creative terms and desperate for ideas as was the comics field itself. Worse, most of those participating seem convinced that superhero movies, clearly no more than a long-lived fad, would remain popular and viable forever, in defiance of the changing tides of popularity and fashion every other genre is subjected to. The only solid basis for the superhero publishing and movie industries can be new and imaginative stories well-told, something neither business would appear to presently have the capacity to generate. It's telling that the vast majority of superhero properties to reach the big screen are derived from titles that are forty, fifty, sixty, seventy years old. One might suppose that if the companies' more recent offerings had actually possessed any originality or energy that they'd have been made into movies too but, sadly, it appears not to be so.

THE "BRAINS"

THAT ACHIEVED THE TAMMANY VICTORY AT THE ROCHESTER DEMOCRATIC CONVENTION.

"The Brains," Thomas Nast. Harper's Weekly p. 992, October 12, 1871. (Public Domain.)

Where, then, does that leave comics as we launch into the second decade of this new and unpredictable twenty-first century? In terms of the prevailing superhero monoculture, it would appear that this is in a perilous condition. Constantly beset by lawsuits from key industry creators or their families, which, should the lawyer-strong but morally completely indefensible comic-book companies lose would instantly deprive the business of most of the major properties to be found in its 'toy-box'; wholly propped up by their franchised characters and nervously aware that they no longer possess the creative capability to come up with new properties once audiences inevitably tire of their last-century creations; it would seem that the most likely future role for the big comic businesses is as vestigial publicity and merchandising operations for their parent companies. When the movie business loses interest in adapting comic-books and graphic novels, it may well be that the major mainstream comic concerns will be relegated to producing in-house comic adaptations of the latest Warner Brothers or Walt Disney blockbuster. It will most probably occur a little sooner for the flagging D.C. than for Marvel, but this fate may well have overtaken both the former superhero giants in the next few years.

As for the medium itself, it's arguably never been in a more enviable or empowered position. The sheer hard work and furious inventiveness of comics' best creators has paid off in a newfound respect for comics and a growing audience of intelligent, discriminating adults. In the realm of the newspaper strip, after a lengthy period in which practically the only constant and reliable political material was to be found within Walt Kelly's sublime *Pogo*, we now have impeccable political cartoonists of the calibre of the great Garry Trudeau or the U.K.'s own majestic, *Beano*-influenced Steve Bell as modern heirs to Gilray. With the mainstream industry and all its Comic Codes and clueless editorial interference now increasingly irrelevant, the sole restrictions on what comics can or cannot be are those of the creator's own imagination. The investigations undertaken by the U.S. military with Will Eisner as its technical consultant demonstrated that the comic form is easily the most engaging and effective method of communicating vital information in a way that the recipient will retain and understand. It is a personal suspicion that this may be the result of bringing the brain's visual and verbal functions into play at once, as comics demand by their very nature, but whatever the true reason for this capability, the supreme usefulness of comics as an instrument for the dissemination and increased retention of ideas is both immediate and obvious. Unlike more high-tech and therefore more costly media, the opportunity to work in comics is available to anyone with access to a pencil and a piece of paper. An accessible and truly democratic medium, despite all the dazzling and sophisticated narrative techniques that have been demonstrated by the field's most talented creators over the last century or more, there yet remains the sense that comics are an art-form in its infancy with most of its great breakthroughs and its most enduring masterpieces yet to be accomplished. Given that the comic strip is, in the right hands, capable of almost anything attainable by other media and considerably more besides, it surely must present an irresistible array of possibilities to the adventurous young would-be artist or communicator. Furthermore, with women now comprising an increasingly important slice of both the comics audience and the roster of significant comics creators, from the revelatory Alison Bechdel to the intimate and captivating Lynda Barry, the gender restrictions which applied within a comic business governed by white males whose attitudes were badly out of date even in the last century are lifted, and the huge power of the medium is now accessible by anyone, of any race or gender, any sexuality, any political or spiritual persuasion.

It's fortuitous that comic narrative should have evolved into the vital, multi-purpose tool that is its current status, just in time for the worldwide collapse of ideologies, economies, and cultures that we're witnessing at present, probably from in between the parted fingers clapped over our eyes. It might be argued that never before has our incendiary gutter medium been so necessary, an exquisitely developed instrument allowing each of us a voluble and individual voice in these noise-saturated, anti-individual times, just lying there in plain view waiting for someone to pick it up and use it properly. The comic medium can do almost anything. It can make fun of poker-faced Egyptian gods. It can unsettle, maybe even ultimately topple any tyrant, with British wartime cartoonist David Low reputedly one of the men that Adolf Hitler feared the most. It can inform with a clear, memorable voice in times when information is restricted or else made inaudible beneath society's relentless buzz. It can even provide a wonderful adventure playground perfect for developing a healthy child's imagination, although it hasn't really carried out that function noticeably over the last forty years.

The present generation, those who mostly (although by no means exclusively) make up a large part of the modern protest movements, are the first who've grown up since the comic book upheavals of the 1980s and therefore the first who've grown up in a world where comics were a natural and accepted feature of the cultural landscape. This is perhaps evidenced by their gleeful appropriation of comic book iconography and highly-visible cartoon theatrics. It would seem that there has never been a generation for whom comics as a tool or an effective weapon are more eminently suited, nor a time of social crisis better able to lend comics a true sense of urgency and purpose. Times like these are arguably exactly those which comics were created to engage with.

So, by all means, occupy the world of comics. Occupy the doorsteps and the lobbies of the industry if you've a mind to...certainly the comic industry is as deserving of such treatment as is any other greedy and unscrupulous business concern...although it might be thought that mainstream comics are best left to manage their own imminent destruction, this being the one task which they've demonstrated a real aptitude for over the last seven decades. A more positive and useful protest might be to support the families of the true titans of the medium, the cheated giants like Jerry Siegel or Joe Shuster or Jack Kirby or the scores of others that have never received fair remuneration or redress, in their courageous efforts to confront these massive corporate entities with their immense resources and battalions of lawyers. Rather than disrupt these massive companies in the transaction of their already-disrupted businesses, more could perhaps be done to call them to account for seventy or eighty years of vile and reprehensible behaviour. If nothing else, you may be certain this would occupy the industry's attention, and perhaps help people for whom help's long overdue.

An even more effective long-term strategy would surely be to occupy the medium itself. The many glories of comic strips past have never been so instantly accessible to the would-be comic creator, giving him or her the means to steep themselves, to educate themselves, in an astonishing array of concepts and techniques, from *Little Nemo* through to *Jimmy Corrigan*. Thus armed, with nothing more than a blank page and some variety of drawing implement, dissenting voices can refine and broadcast their ideas more widely and compellingly, while at the same time possibly making their protest into an enduring work of art that can enrich the medium and the broader culture in which it exists. Today's technology has made self-publishing more easily achievable, and in addition there are an increasing range of small and honourable publishers with a more flexible approach to new material, allowing access to new formats and fresh concepts which perhaps have a potential to transform the medium.

In these times of transition that the comics medium and the world at large are making an attempt to navigate, it would seem that the future is entirely up for grabs to an extent that has not previously been apparent. If you care about what you are saying, if you seek a more effective way of saying it, then pick up that brush, pencil, pen, that mouse or even that discarded cardboard box out in the alleyway and pour your heart, your mind, your self into as many little panels as it takes to make your statement. You may find it opens up modes of expression and dissent that you have previously not considered or imagined.

You may even find you've got yourself an occupation.

Alan Moore
Northampton,
May-June 2012.

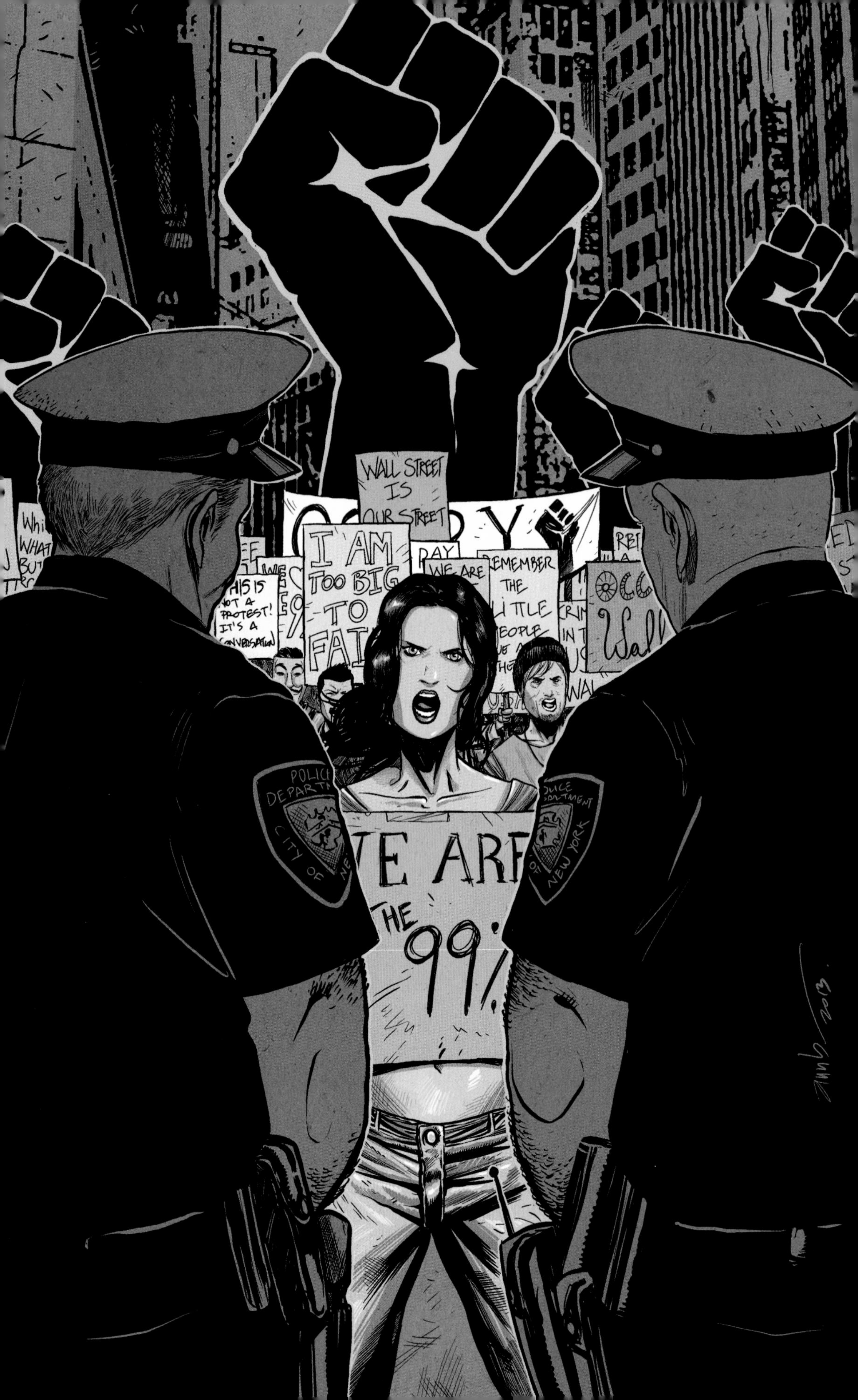

WALL STREET IS OUR STREET
I AM TOO BIG TO FAI
HIS IS NOT A PROTEST! IT'S A ONVERSATION
WE ARE
EMEMBER THE ITTLE EOPLE
POLICE DEPARTMENT CITY OF NE
POLICE DEPARTMENT OF NEW YORK
E ARE THE 99%

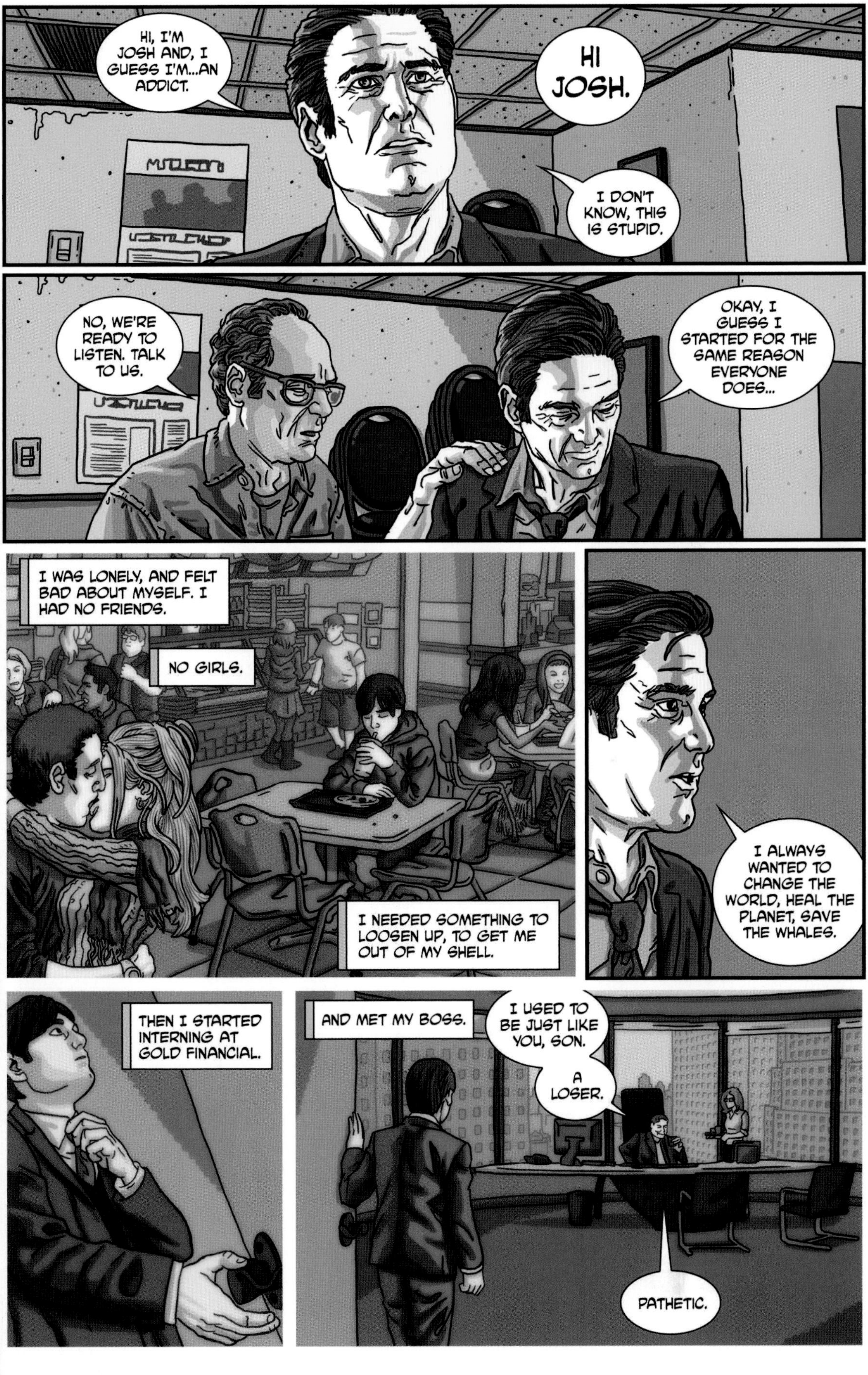
HI, I'M JOSH AND, I GUESS I'M...AN ADDICT.
HI JOSH.
I DON'T KNOW, THIS IS STUPID.
NO, WE'RE READY TO LISTEN. TALK TO US.
OKAY, I GUESS I STARTED FOR THE SAME REASON EVERYONE DOES...
I WAS LONELY, AND FELT BAD ABOUT MYSELF. I HAD NO FRIENDS.
NO GIRLS.
I NEEDED SOMETHING TO LOOSEN UP, TO GET ME OUT OF MY SHELL.
I ALWAYS WANTED TO CHANGE THE WORLD, HEAL THE PLANET, SAVE THE WHALES.
THEN I STARTED INTERNING AT GOLD FINANCIAL.
AND MET MY BOSS.
I USED TO BE JUST LIKE YOU, SON.
A LOSER.
PATHETIC.

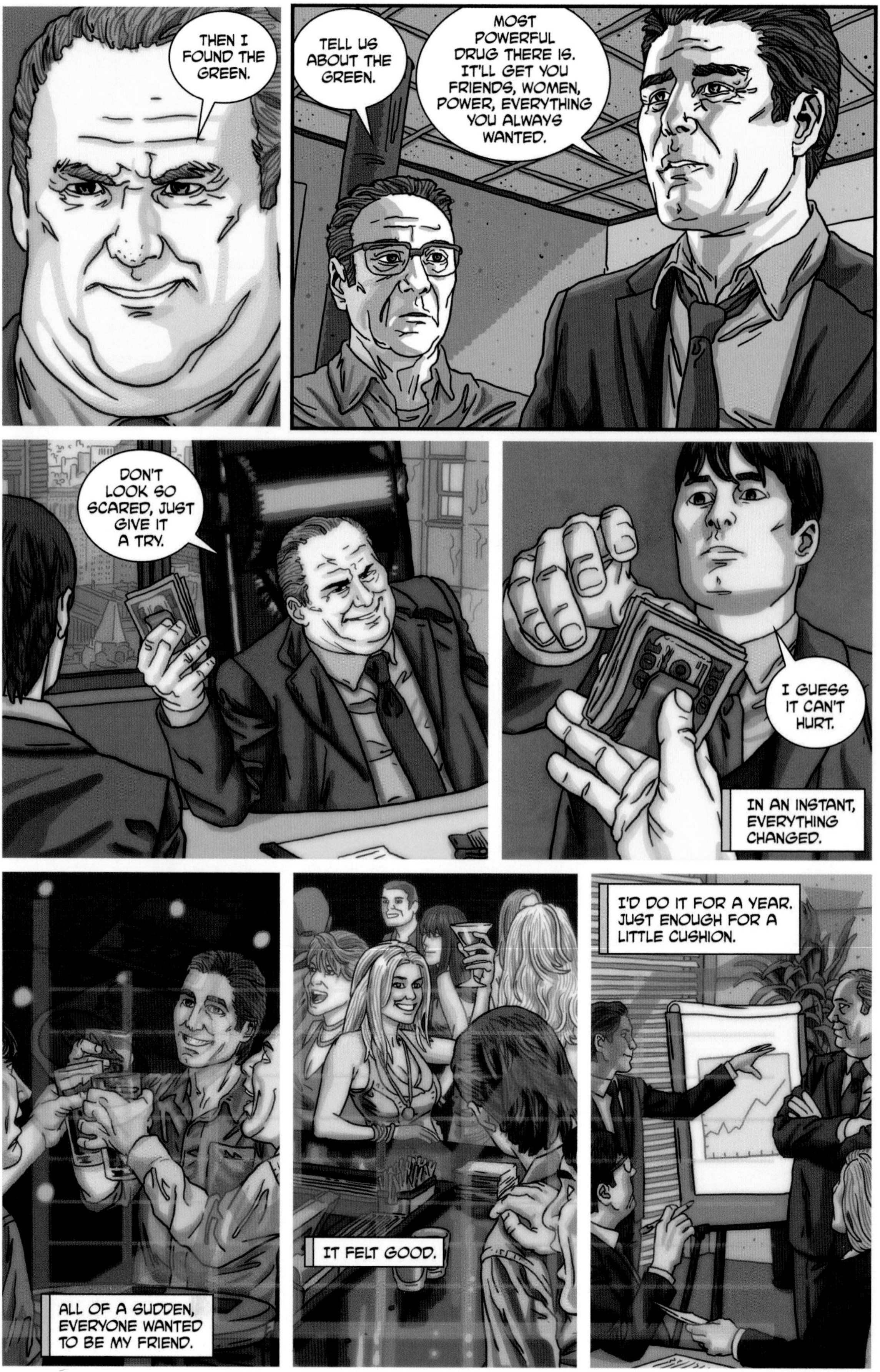
THEN I FOUND THE GREEN.
TELL US ABOUT THE GREEN.
MOST POWERFUL DRUG THERE IS. IT'LL GET YOU FRIENDS, WOMEN, POWER, EVERYTHING YOU ALWAYS WANTED.
DON'T LOOK SO SCARED, JUST GIVE IT A TRY.
I GUESS IT CAN'T HURT.
IN AN INSTANT, EVERYTHING CHANGED.
ALL OF A SUDDEN, EVERYONE WANTED TO BE MY FRIEND.
IT FELT GOOD.
I'D DO IT FOR A YEAR. JUST ENOUGH FOR A LITTLE CUSHION.

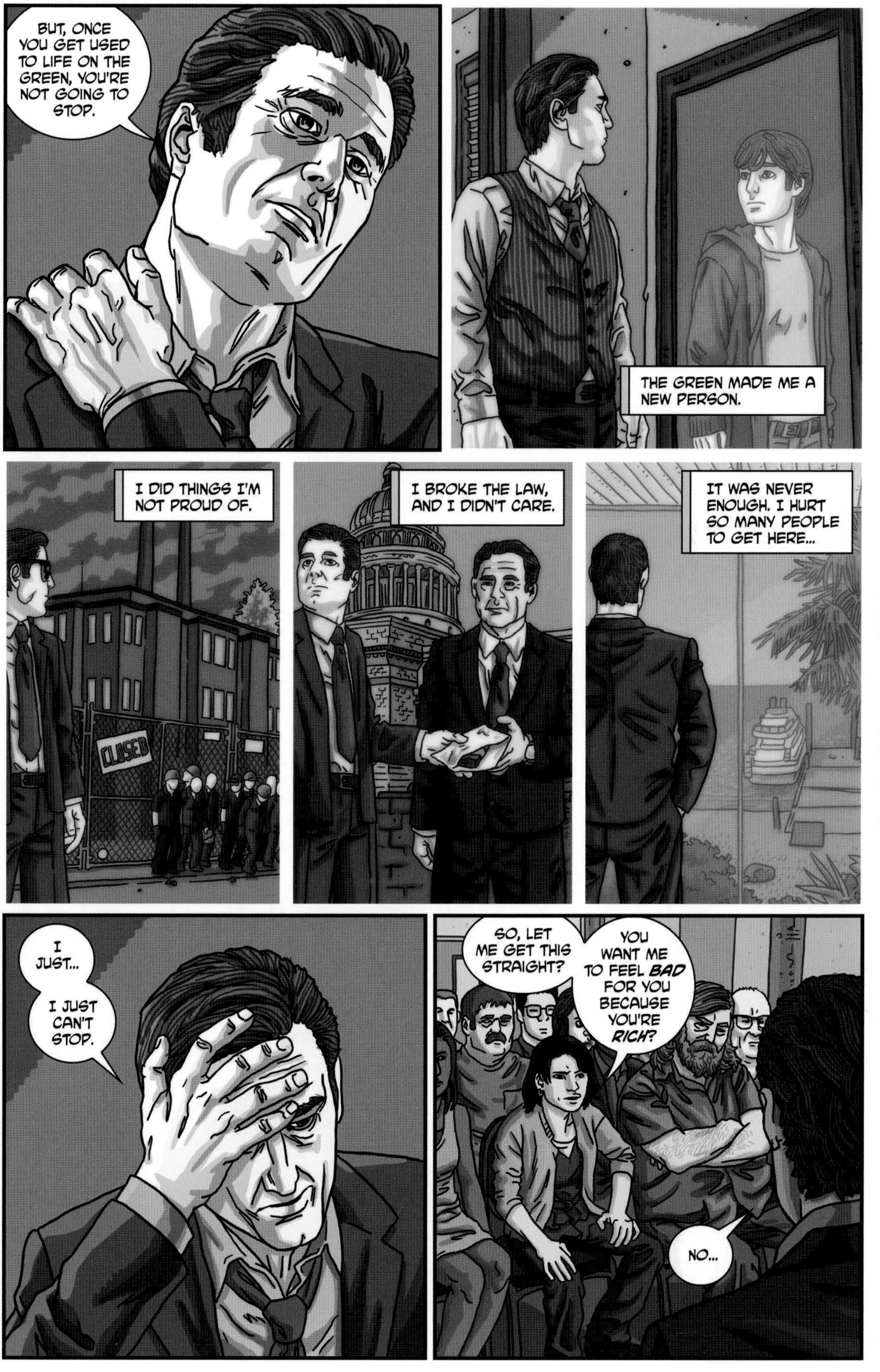
BUT, ONCE YOU GET USED TO LIFE ON THE GREEN, YOU'RE NOT GOING TO STOP.
THE GREEN MADE ME A NEW PERSON.
I DID THINGS I'M NOT PROUD OF.
CLOSED
I BROKE THE LAW, AND I DIDN'T CARE.
IT WAS NEVER ENOUGH. I HURT SO MANY PEOPLE TO GET HERE...
I JUST...
I JUST CAN'T STOP.
SO, LET ME GET THIS STRAIGHT?
YOU WANT ME TO FEEL *BAD* FOR YOU BECAUSE YOU'RE *RICH*?
NO...

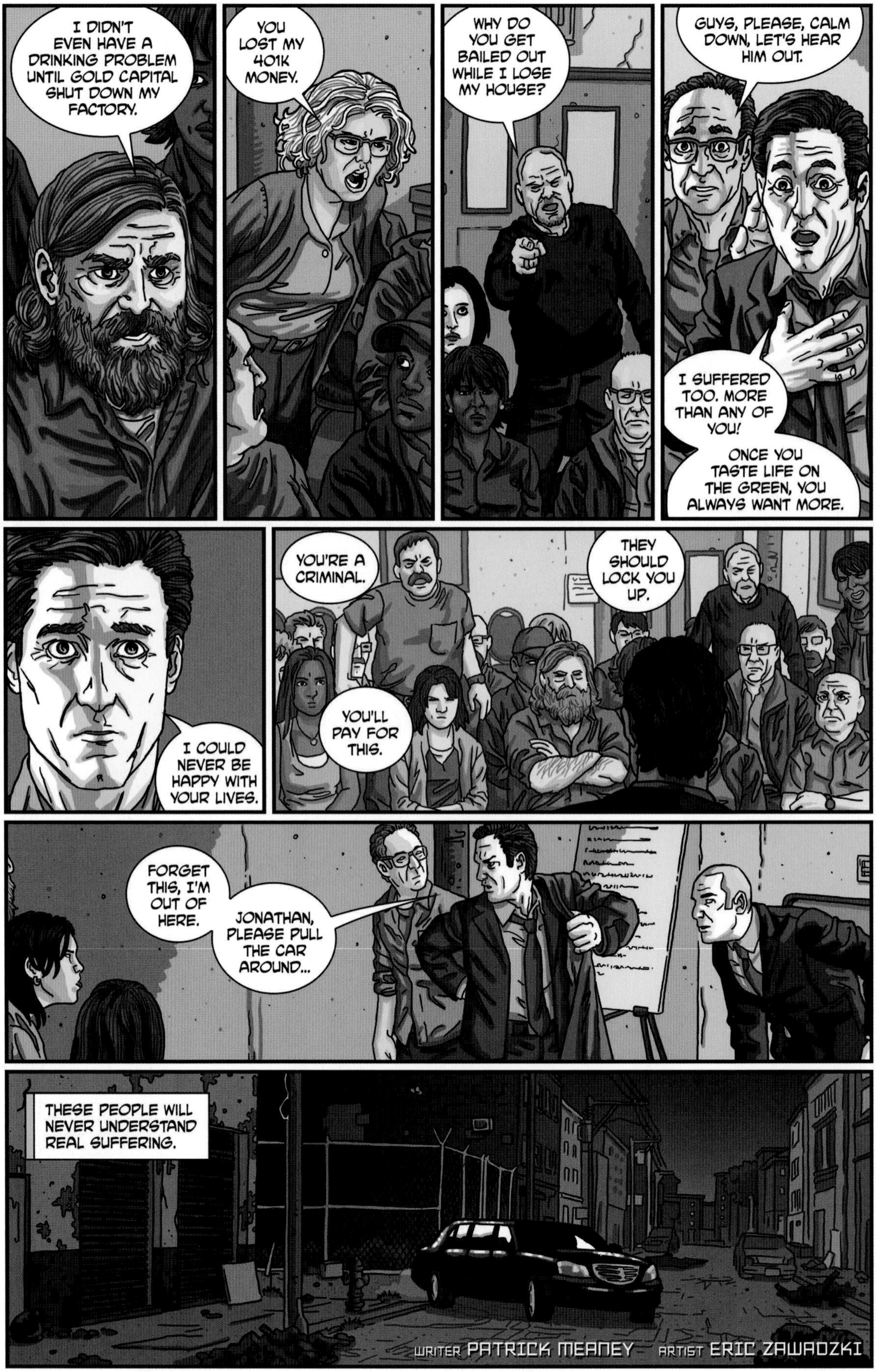

I DIDN'T EVEN HAVE A DRINKING PROBLEM UNTIL GOLD CAPITAL SHUT DOWN MY FACTORY.
YOU LOST MY 401K MONEY.
WHY DO YOU GET BAILED OUT WHILE I LOSE MY HOUSE?
GUYS, PLEASE, CALM DOWN, LET'S HEAR HIM OUT.
I SUFFERED TOO. MORE THAN ANY OF YOU!
ONCE YOU TASTE LIFE ON THE GREEN, YOU ALWAYS WANT MORE.
I COULD NEVER BE HAPPY WITH YOUR LIVES.
YOU'RE A CRIMINAL.
THEY SHOULD LOCK YOU UP.
YOU'LL PAY FOR THIS.
FORGET THIS, I'M OUT OF HERE.
JONATHAN, PLEASE PULL THE CAR AROUND...
THESE PEOPLE WILL NEVER UNDERSTAND REAL SUFFERING.
WRITER PATRICK MEANEY ARTIST ERIC ZAWADZKI

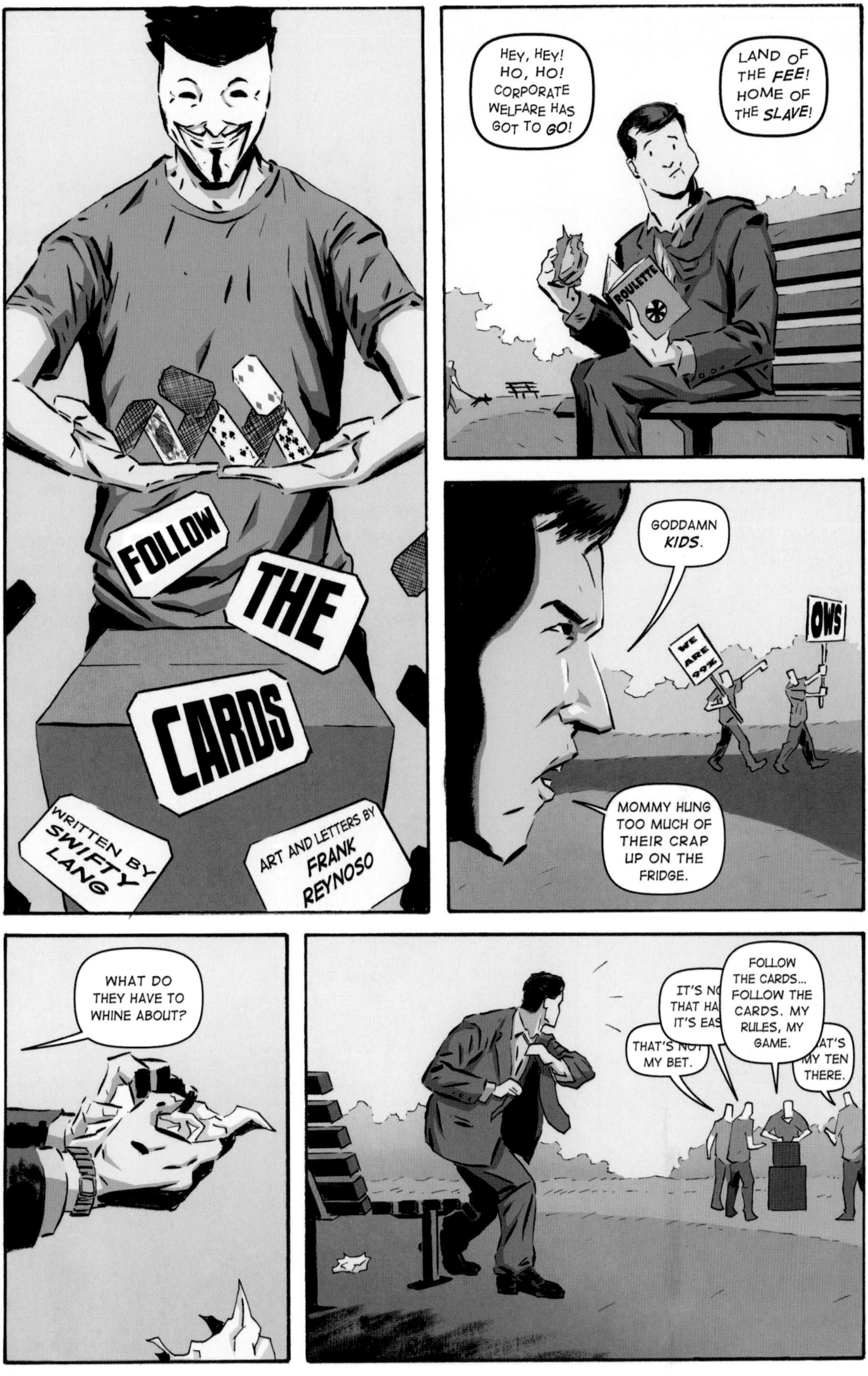
FOLLOW
THE
CARDS
WRITTEN BY SWIFTY LANG
ART AND LETTERS BY FRANK REYNOSO
HEY, HEY! HO, HO! CORPORATE WELFARE HAS GOT TO GO!
LAND OF THE FEE! HOME OF THE SLAVE!
ROULETTE
GODDAMN KIDS.
WE ARE 99%
OWS
MOMMY HUNG TOO MUCH OF THEIR CRAP UP ON THE FRIDGE.
WHAT DO THEY HAVE TO WHINE ABOUT?
THAT'S NOT MY BET.
FOLLOW THE CARDS... FOLLOW THE CARDS. MY RULES, MY GAME.
MY TEN THERE.

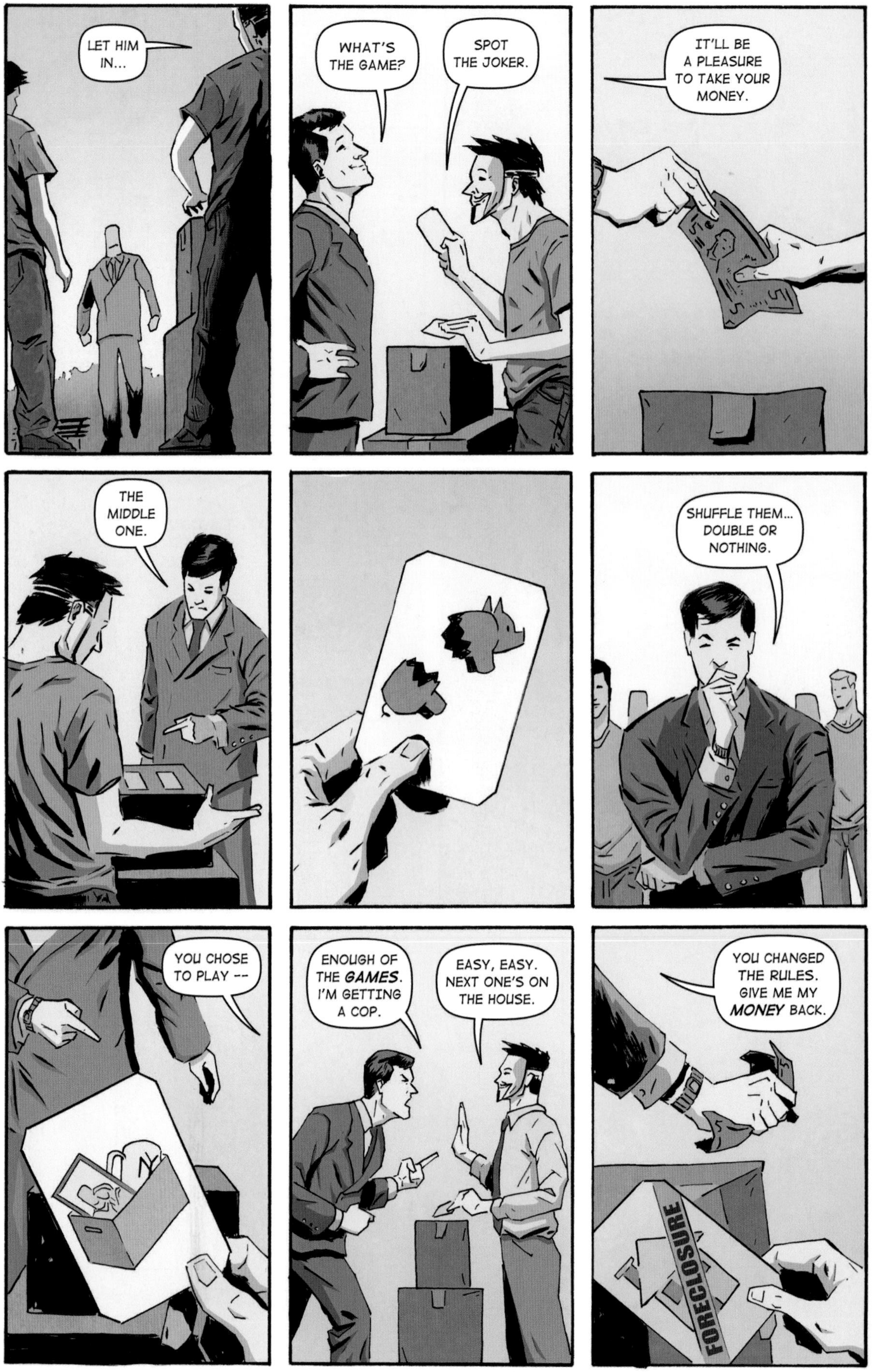
LET HIM IN...
WHAT'S THE GAME?
SPOT THE JOKER.
IT'LL BE A PLEASURE TO TAKE YOUR MONEY.
THE MIDDLE ONE.
SHUFFLE THEM... DOUBLE OR NOTHING.
YOU CHOSE TO PLAY --
ENOUGH OF THE GAMES. I'M GETTING A COP.
EASY, EASY. NEXT ONE'S ON THE HOUSE.
YOU CHANGED THE RULES. GIVE ME MY MONEY BACK.
FORECLOSURE

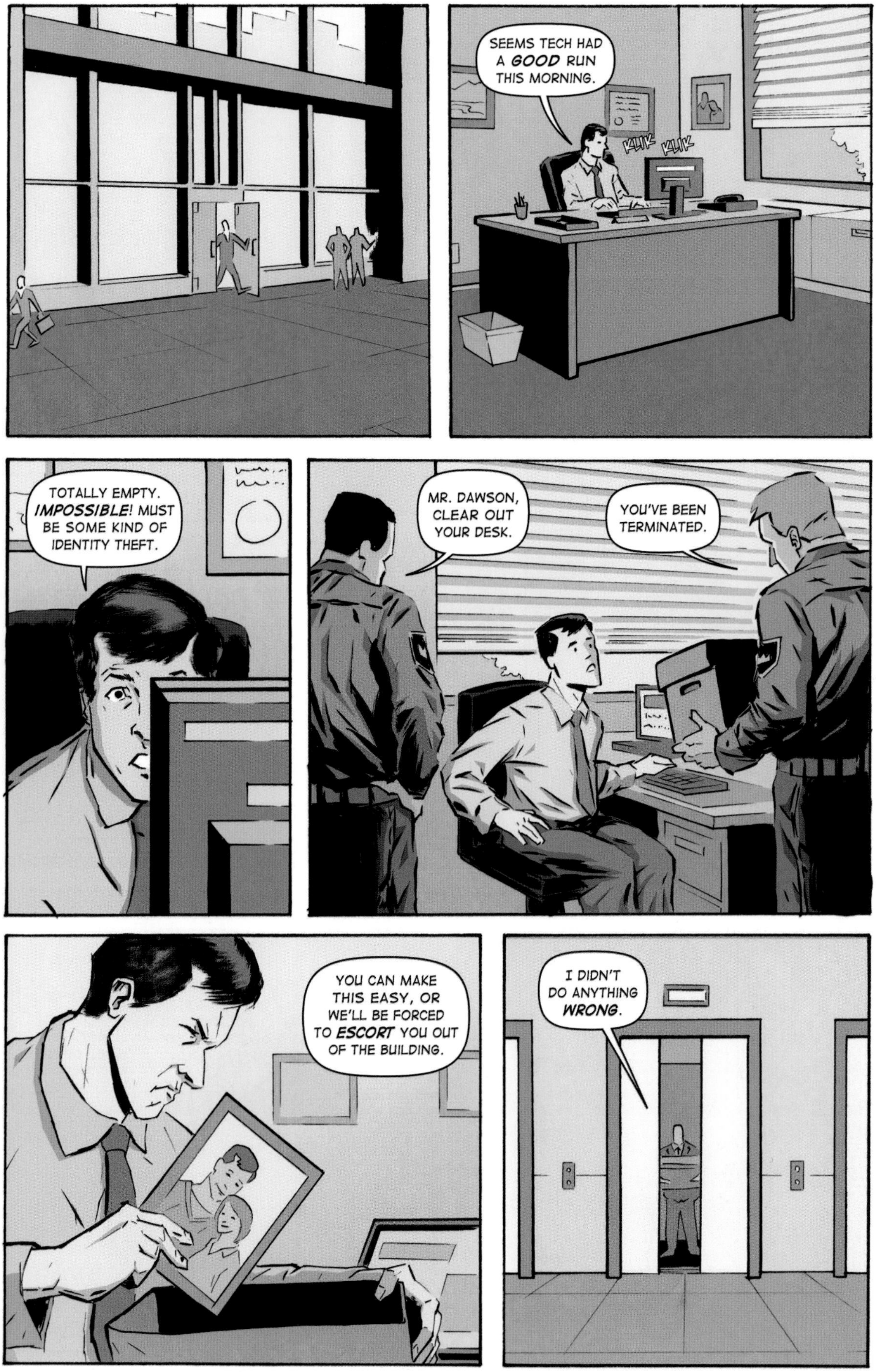
SEEMS TECH HAD A GOOD RUN THIS MORNING.
KLIK KLIK
TOTALLY EMPTY. IMPOSSIBLE! MUST BE SOME KIND OF IDENTITY THEFT.
MR. DAWSON, CLEAR OUT YOUR DESK.
YOU'VE BEEN TERMINATED.
YOU CAN MAKE THIS EASY, OR WE'LL BE FORCED TO ESCORT YOU OUT OF THE BUILDING.
I DIDN'T DO ANYTHING WRONG.

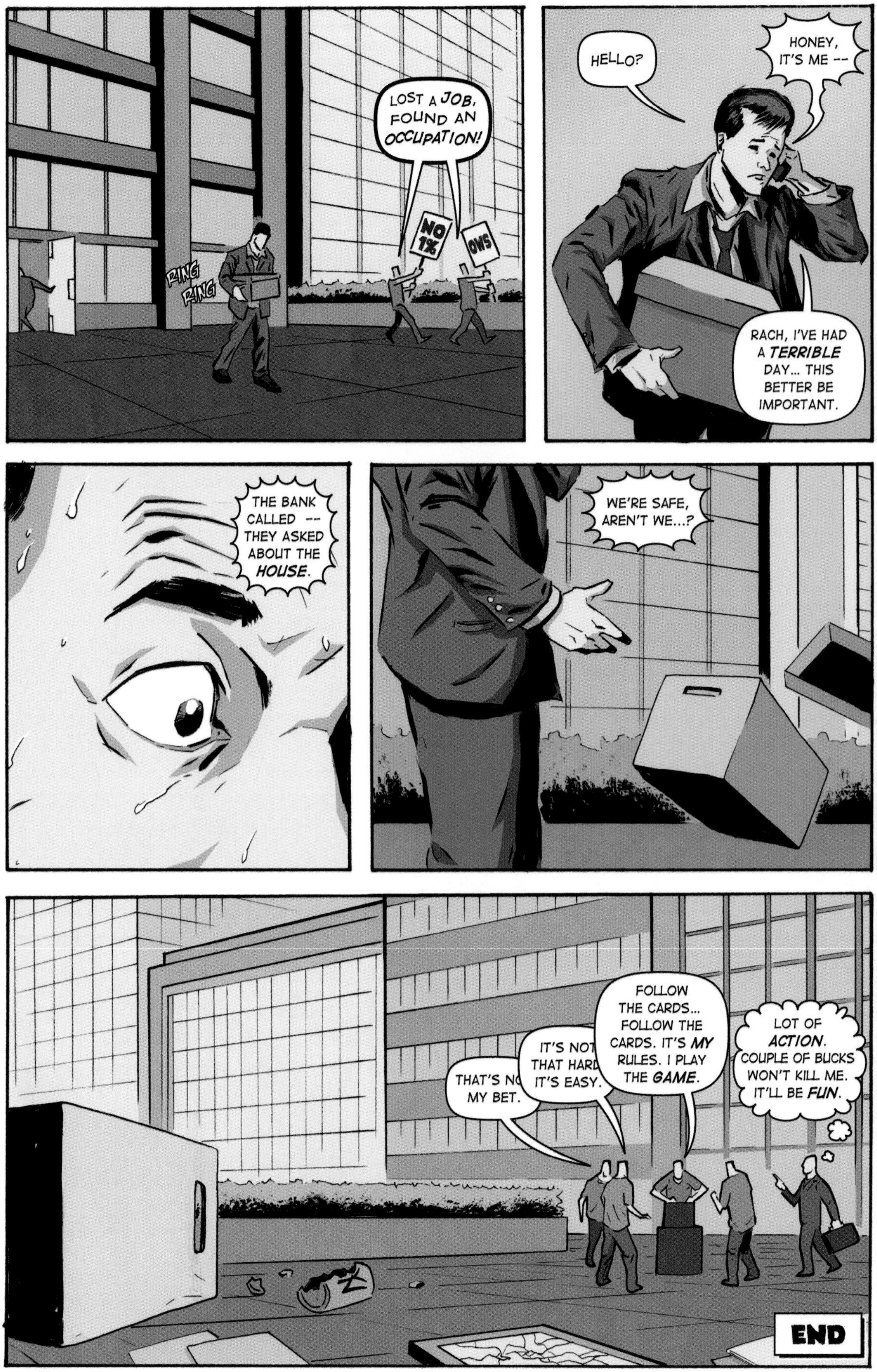
RING
RING
LOST A JOB, FOUND AN OCCUPATION!
NO 1%
OWS
HELLO?
HONEY, IT'S ME --
RACH, I'VE HAD A TERRIBLE DAY... THIS BETTER BE IMPORTANT.
THE BANK CALLED -- THEY ASKED ABOUT THE HOUSE.
WE'RE SAFE, AREN'T WE...?
THAT'S NO
MY BET.
IT'S NOT
THAT HARD
IT'S EASY.
FOLLOW THE CARDS... FOLLOW THE CARDS. IT'S MY RULES. I PLAY THE GAME.
LOT OF ACTION. COUPLE OF BUCKS WON'T KILL ME. IT'LL BE FUN.
END

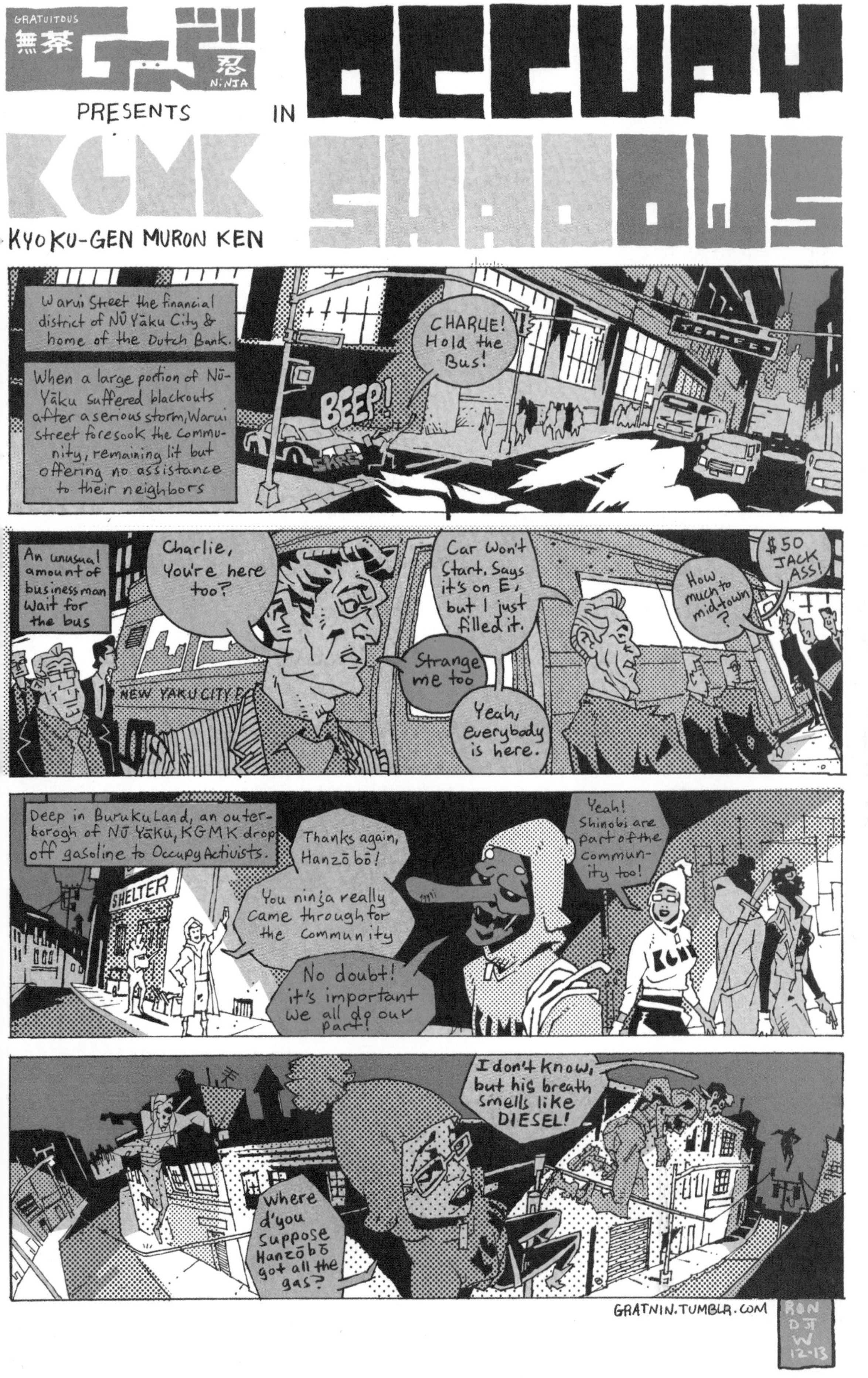
GRATUITOUS 無茶 ゲーデジ 忍 NINJA
PRESENTS
KGMK
KYOKU-GEN MURON KEN
IN
OCCUPY
SHADOWS
Warui Street the financial district of Nū Yāku City & home of the Dutch Bank.
When a large portion of Nū-Yāku suffered blackouts after a serious storm, Warui street foresook the community, remaining lit but offering no assistance to their neighbors
CHARLIE! Hold the Bus!
BEEP!
An unusual amount of businessman wait for the bus
Charlie, You're here too?
Car Won't Start. Says it's on E, but I just filled it.
Strange me too
Yeah, everybody is here.
How much to midtown?
$50 JACK ASS!
NEW YAKU CITY
Deep in BurukuLand, an outer-borogh of Nū Yāku, KGMK drop off gasoline to Occupy Actiuists.
SHELTER
Thanks again, Hanzō bō!
You ninja really came through for the community
No doubt! it's important we all do our part!
Yeah! Shinobi are part of the commun-ity too!
I don't know, but his breath smells like DIESEL!
Where d'you suppose Hanzōbō got all the gas?
GRATNIN.TUMBLR.COM
RON DJ W 12-13

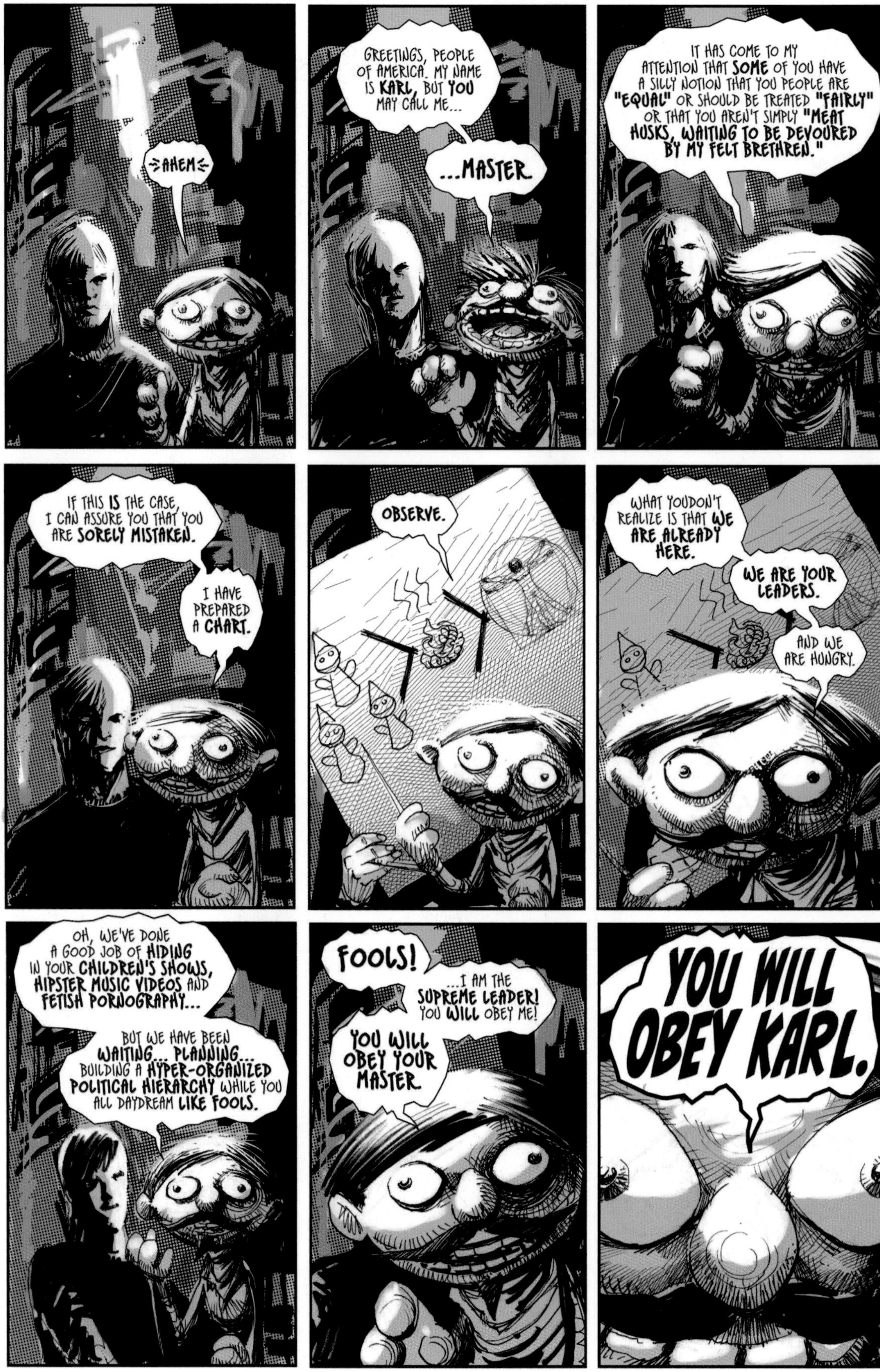
AHEM
GREETINGS, PEOPLE OF AMERICA. MY NAME IS KARL, BUT YOU MAY CALL ME...
...MASTER.
IT HAS COME TO MY ATTENTION THAT SOME OF YOU HAVE A SILLY NOTION THAT YOU PEOPLE ARE "EQUAL" OR SHOULD BE TREATED "FAIRLY" OR THAT YOU AREN'T SIMPLY "MEAT HUSKS, WAITING TO BE DEVOURED BY MY FELT BRETHREN."
IF THIS IS THE CASE, I CAN ASSURE YOU THAT YOU ARE SORELY MISTAKEN.
I HAVE PREPARED A CHART.
OBSERVE.
WHAT YOUDON'T REALIZE IS THAT WE ARE ALREADY HERE.
WE ARE YOUR LEADERS.
AND WE ARE HUNGRY.
OH, WE'VE DONE A GOOD JOB OF HIDING IN YOUR CHILDREN'S SHOWS, HIPSTER MUSIC VIDEOS AND FETISH PORNOGRAPHY...
BUT WE HAVE BEEN WAITING... PLANNING... BUILDING A HYPER-ORGANIZED POLITICAL HIERARCHY WHILE YOU ALL DAYDREAM LIKE FOOLS.
FOOLS!
...I AM THE SUPREME LEADER! YOU WILL OBEY ME!
YOU WILL OBEY YOUR MASTER.
YOU WILL OBEY KARL.

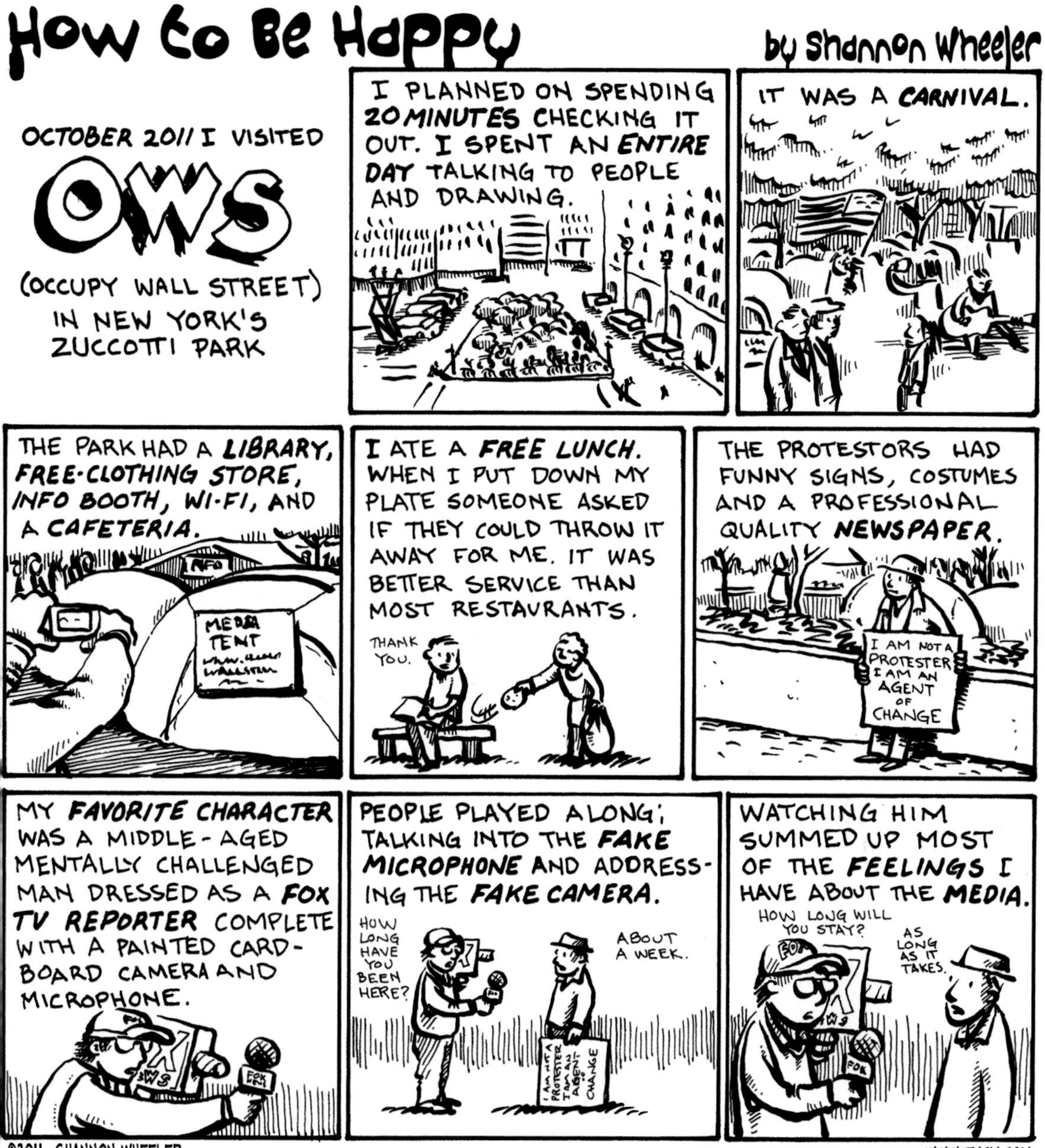

How to Be Happy
by Shannon Wheeler
OCTOBER 2011 I VISITED
OWS
(OCCUPY WALL STREET)
IN NEW YORK'S
ZUCCOTTI PARK
I PLANNED ON SPENDING 20 MINUTES CHECKING IT OUT. I SPENT AN ENTIRE DAY TALKING TO PEOPLE AND DRAWING.
IT WAS A CARNIVAL.
THE PARK HAD A LIBRARY, FREE-CLOTHING STORE, INFO BOOTH, WI-FI, AND A CAFETERIA.
INFO
MEDIA TENT
I ATE A FREE LUNCH. WHEN I PUT DOWN MY PLATE SOMEONE ASKED IF THEY COULD THROW IT AWAY FOR ME. IT WAS BETTER SERVICE THAN MOST RESTAURANTS.
THANK YOU.
THE PROTESTORS HAD FUNNY SIGNS, COSTUMES AND A PROFESSIONAL QUALITY NEWSPAPER.
I AM NOT A PROTESTER I AM AN AGENT OF CHANGE
MY FAVORITE CHARACTER WAS A MIDDLE-AGED MENTALLY CHALLENGED MAN DRESSED AS A FOX TV REPORTER COMPLETE WITH A PAINTED CARDBOARD CAMERA AND MICROPHONE.
PEOPLE PLAYED ALONG; TALKING INTO THE FAKE MICROPHONE AND ADDRESSING THE FAKE CAMERA.
HOW LONG HAVE YOU BEEN HERE?
ABOUT A WEEK.
WATCHING HIM SUMMED UP MOST OF THE FEELINGS I HAVE ABOUT THE MEDIA.
HOW LONG WILL YOU STAY?
AS LONG AS IT TAKES.

 WWW.TMCM.COM

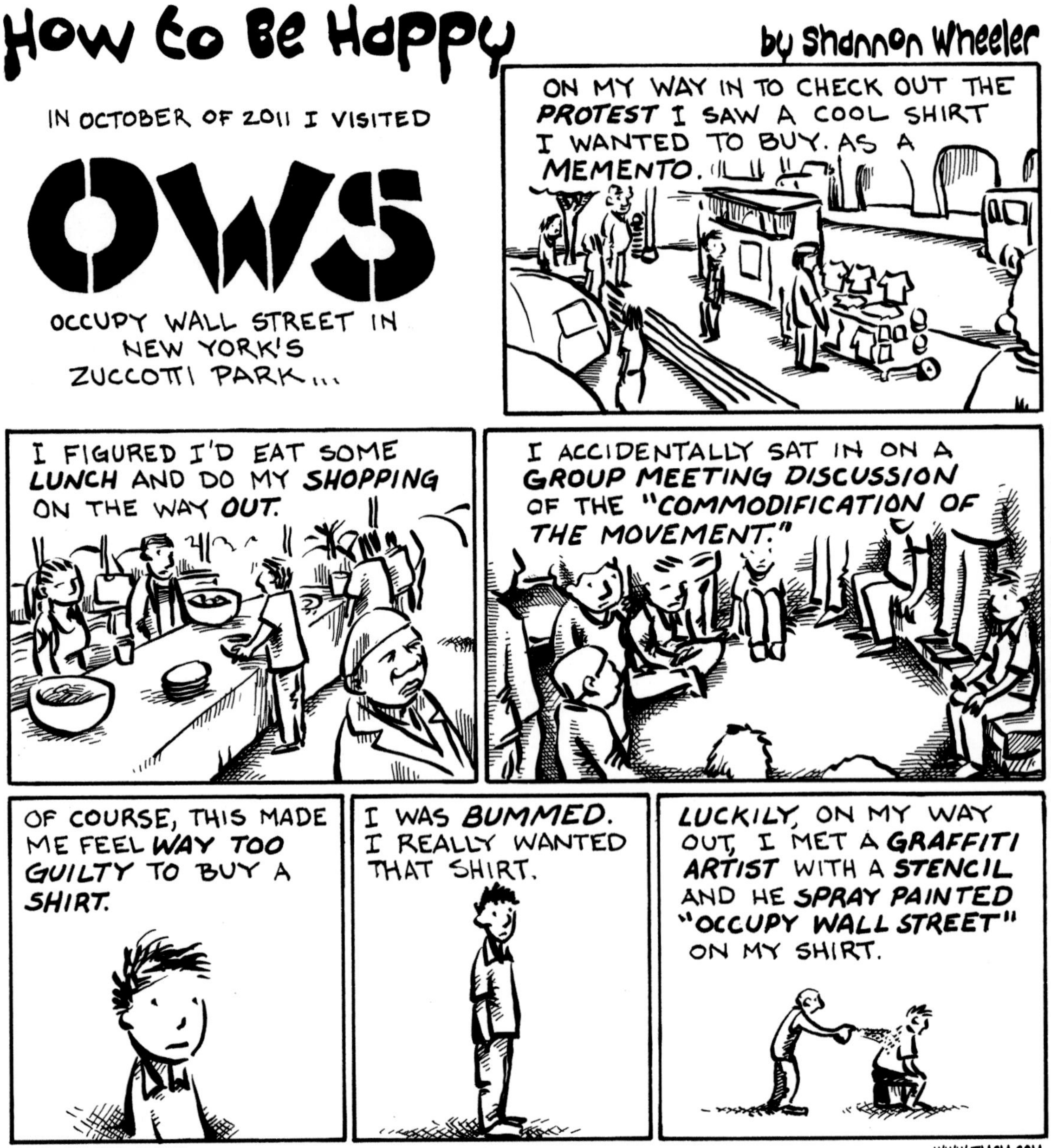
How to Be Happy
by Shannon Wheeler
IN OCTOBER OF 2011 I VISITED
OWS
OCCUPY WALL STREET IN NEW YORK'S ZUCCOTTI PARK...
ON MY WAY IN TO CHECK OUT THE PROTEST I SAW A COOL SHIRT I WANTED TO BUY. AS A MEMENTO.
I FIGURED I'D EAT SOME LUNCH AND DO MY SHOPPING ON THE WAY OUT.
I ACCIDENTALLY SAT IN ON A GROUP MEETING DISCUSSION OF THE "COMMODIFICATION OF THE MOVEMENT."
OF COURSE, THIS MADE ME FEEL WAY TOO GUILTY TO BUY A SHIRT.
I WAS BUMMED. I REALLY WANTED THAT SHIRT.
LUCKILY, ON MY WAY OUT, I MET A GRAFFITI ARTIST WITH A STENCIL AND HE SPRAY PAINTED "OCCUPY WALL STREET" ON MY SHIRT.

WWW.TMCM.COM

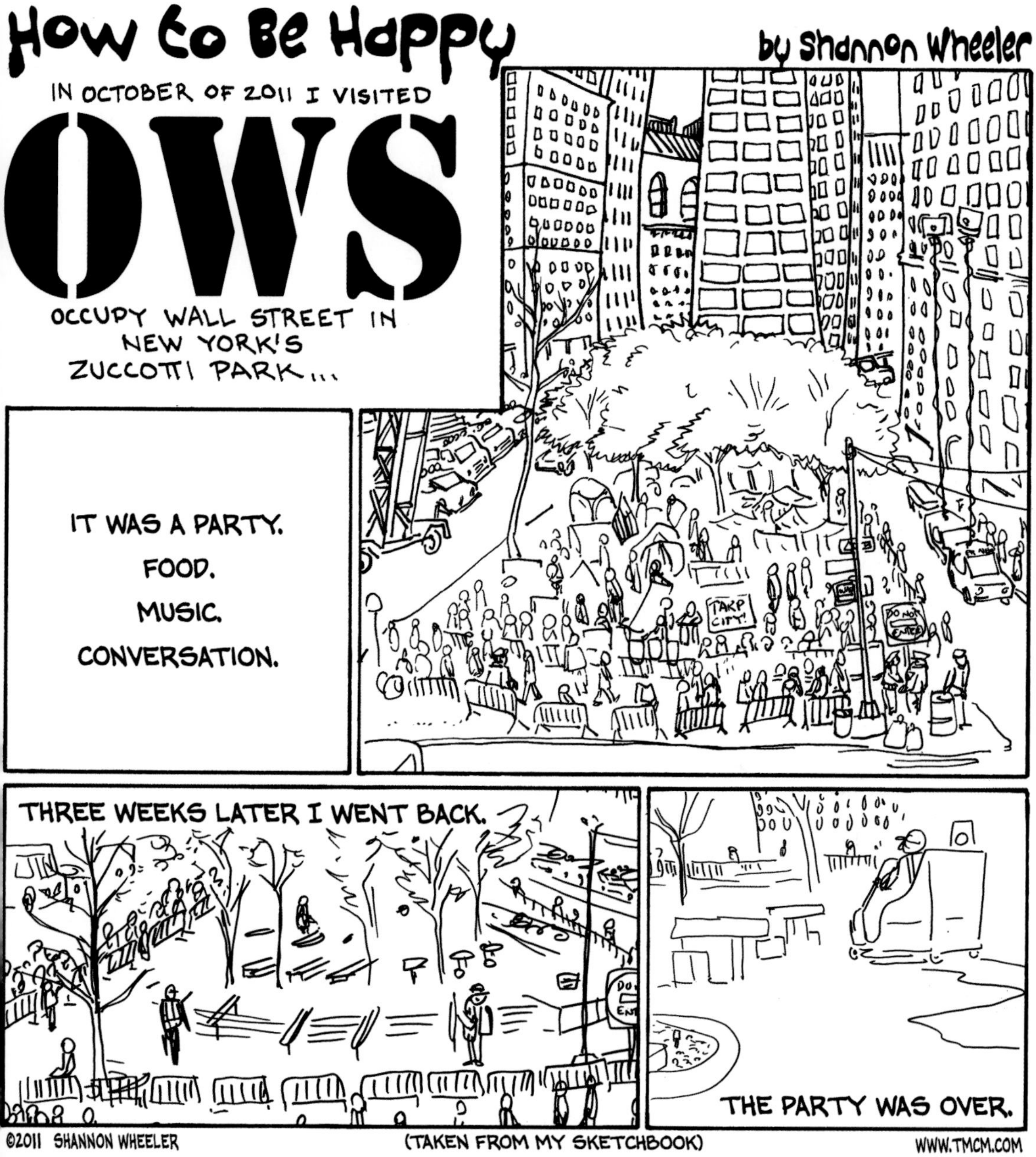

How to Be Happy
by Shannon Wheeler
IN OCTOBER OF 2011 I VISITED
OWS
OCCUPY WALL STREET IN NEW YORK'S ZUCCOTTI PARK...
IT WAS A PARTY.
FOOD.
MUSIC.
CONVERSATION.
TARP CITY!
DO NOT ENTER
THREE WEEKS LATER I WENT BACK.
THE PARTY WAS OVER.
©2011 SHANNON WHEELER
(TAKEN FROM MY SKETCHBOOK)
WWW.TMCM.COM

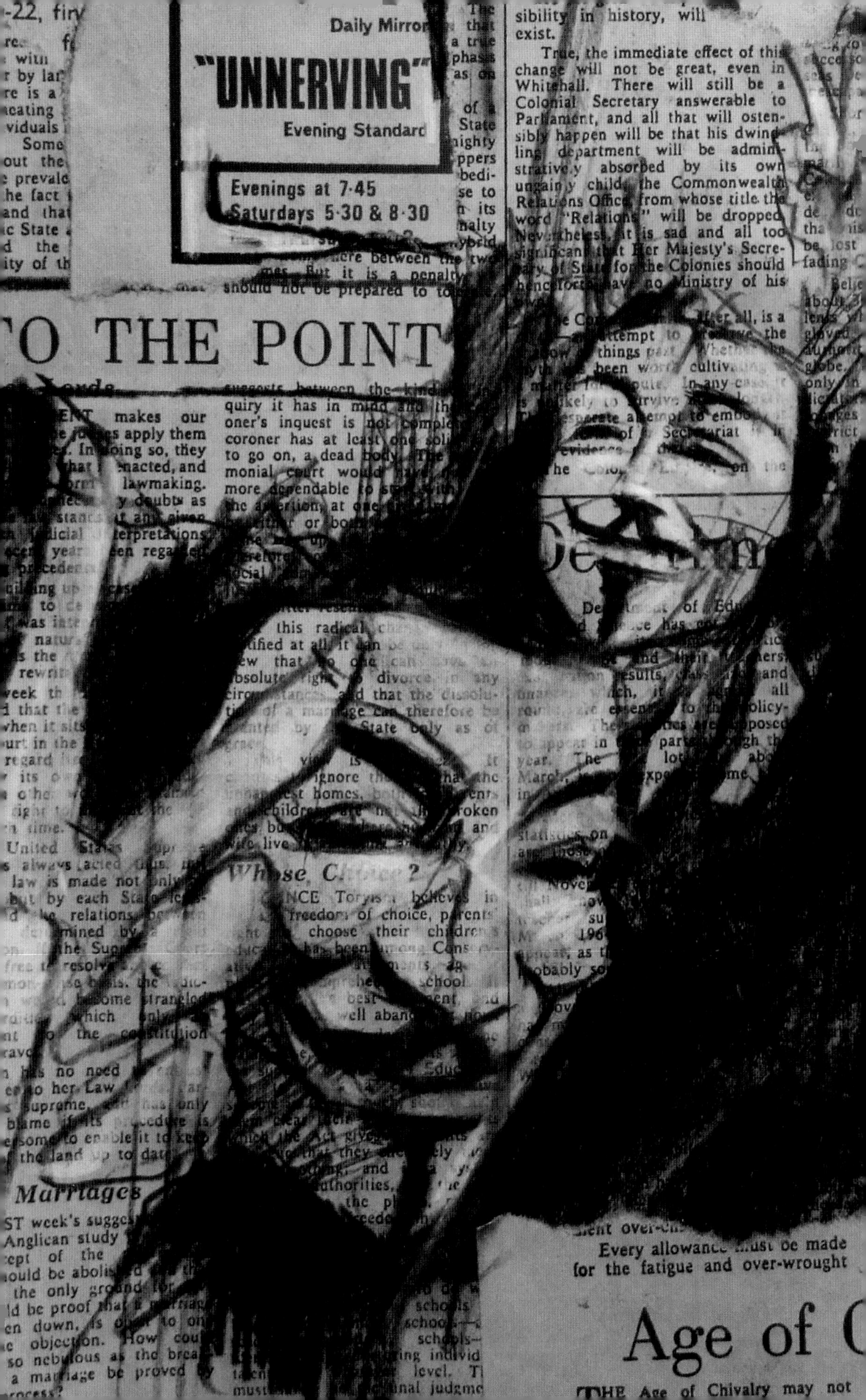
Daily Mirror
"UNNERVING"
Evening Standard
Evenings at 7·45
Saturdays 5·30 & 8·30
O THE POINT
True, the immediate effect of this change will not be great, even in Whitehall. There will still be a Colonial Secretary answerable to Parliament, and all that will ostensibly happen will be that his dwindling department will be administratively absorbed by its own
Marriages
Every allowance must be made for the fatigue and over-wrought
Age of C
THE Age of Chivalry may not

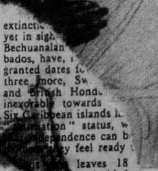

so emo...al
...rbara Castle and
...e Ministry of Over...
...nt, it represents an
...ish responsibility.

...ntimental cant, the
...orous step-sister of
...ice has existed pri-
...British interests. The
...on the contrary, has
...e the interests of
...c. It is regrettable
...inction should now
...ambivalence of...
...wealth...

...nor... ...eir equiva-
...ed and w...
...e Que...
...nt places round...
...ve power...the...old
...other...
...my m...per...
...others...rified
...sioners. But b...ween
...esponsible for eight
...and it...no help...
...they...ill Britain.

extinct...
yet in sigh...
Bechuanalan...
...bados, have, ...
granted dates f...
three more, Sw...
and British Hond...
inexorably towards
Six Caribbean islands h...
...ation" status, w...
...ependence can b...
...y feel ready...
leaves 18
whose...undecided.
...pose inte...
...their future
...of the
O...at is to b...
the...wer...s of em-
...cattered islands and dep...
...to...ull or too
stand...ne thing...

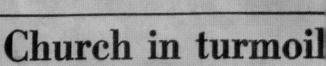

Church in turmoil

...ght
...ch,
...nd
...be
...nt

...rns...

...d to do...
...departme... ...repa...
county hall I was told
...the forms make for a lo...
...but we need the informa-
...ourselves and we really can't
...how they can be simplified. Up
...per cent. of the forms returned
...s contain evident errors."

...inexcusable, though, is statistical
...rmation which is needlessly con-
...g, like the figures for school
...costs given occasionally in
...e in reply to Parliamentary
...Since the department
...to make up its mind
...where...cost limits"
...benefit of
...rch...permitted
...cost...rainage,
...ands...
...ngre...
...clud...
...cost...
...site).
...bench...to
...inqui...publ...
...swim...

...ky section...
...tered" on...
...ise, is no...
...cil si...es a...
...th, I...
...overn...
...but often...
...id...
...a foot-
...take...

...eating

...e of affairs is a symptom...

want Franco to give up his "right
of patronage," as the Vatican
Council suggested. This right
enables the Government to sub-
mit the names of six candidates
for episcopal office to the Vatican,
which cuts the list to three and
returns it to the Government for
the final choice.

In February this year Franco,
ignoring the Vatican's suggestion,
appointed a Castilian as auxiliary
bishop with the right of success-
...to the See of Barcelona. The
...talans were furious that a
...lan had not been chosen.

March, in Barcelona, friars
...d 400 students, including
...to hold, in their mona-
..."free assembly" which
...previously banned at
...ty, and they housed
...wo days until the
...forced entry.

...demonstration in
...0 priests protest-
...alleged brutal
...police of one
...t. This clerical
...broken up by
...d their trun-
...rchy did not
...om pulpits
...de it clear
...ice action.
...ted to
...fer to
...They
...t by
...olic
...pa-
...te.
...aga
...s,
...ir

Left and Right, for
churches in moments of

One of the Vatican de...
that on religious liberty, i...
given a very lukewarm rec...
even by the progressive e...
in the Church. Franco m...
a march here by issuing a...
law.

Foreign correspondents
summoned the other day...
Foreign Ministry and told
draft law had been prepar...
main features would be te...
denominational schools an...
religious discrimination.

The Ministry of...
promptly warned editors th...
must not publish this sta...
by the Foreign Office. "...
is controlled by Opus Dei...
Spanish journalist hissed...
"But the Foreign Office is...

Opus Dei, founded in...
became the first lay ins...
in Spain to receive pap...
proval. It is today the...
powerful religious organisa...
the country, and has men i...
of the key posts.

Some of its member...
priests, though they dre...
laymen and engage in la...
fessions. It has several...
of membership, with the...
that Spaniards call it the...
Masonry." Several Mini...
the Government belong to...

It is detested by the...
whom it has outplayed a...
own game, and by the mor...
tional Catholic Action. It...
to have great power in ...
and banking. Though ...
in secrecy, it is thought...
Monarchist.

Like all the political part...
all Spanish organisation...
Church is divided into...
and groups. But in the b...
it will always obey Rom...
...the Pope is not to its...

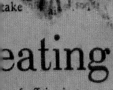

2m

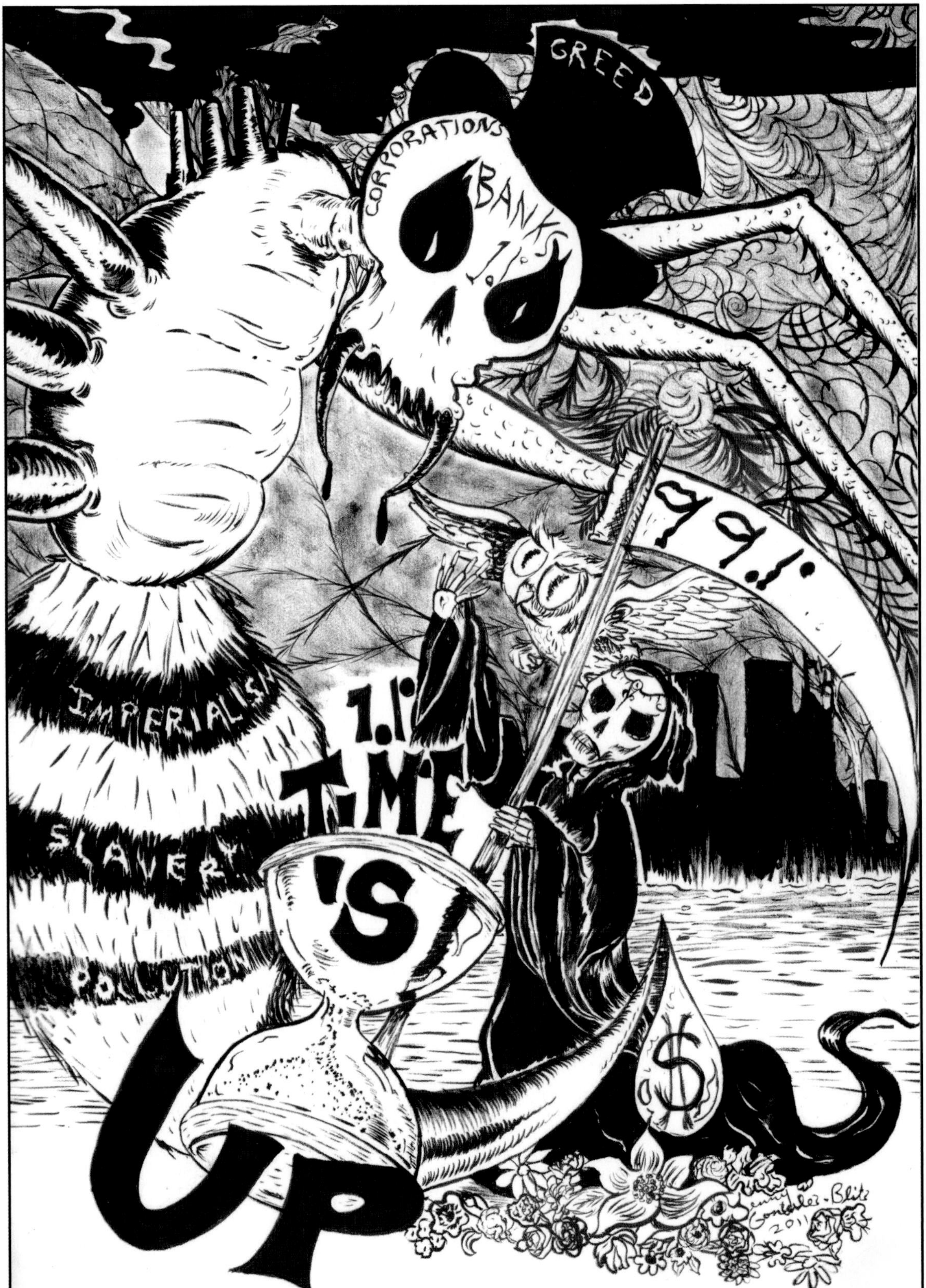
GREED
CORPORATIONS
BANKS
1%
99%
IMPERIALIS
SLAVERY
POLLUTION
1%
TIME'S
UP
$
Gonzalez-Blitz 2011

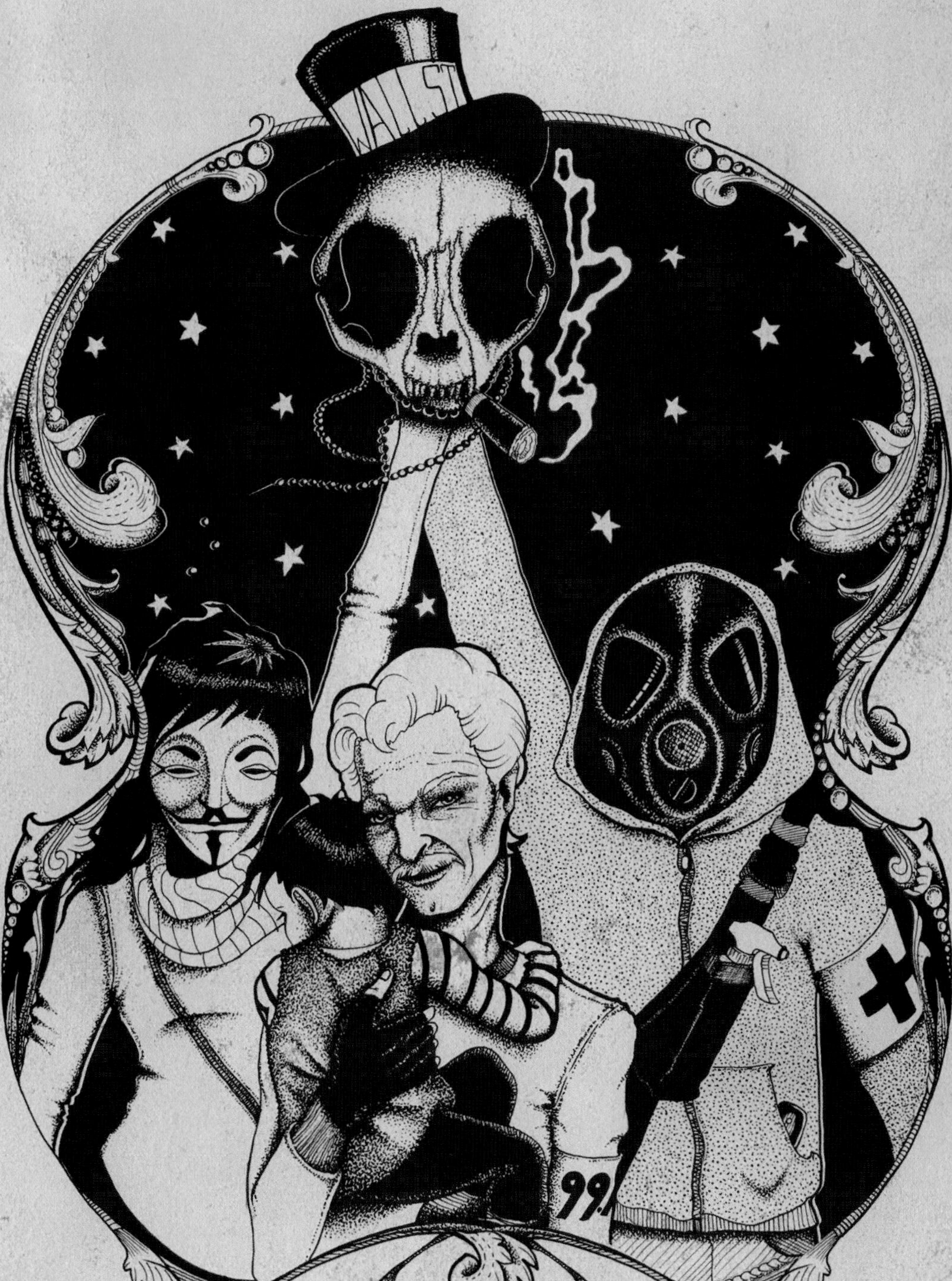
99.

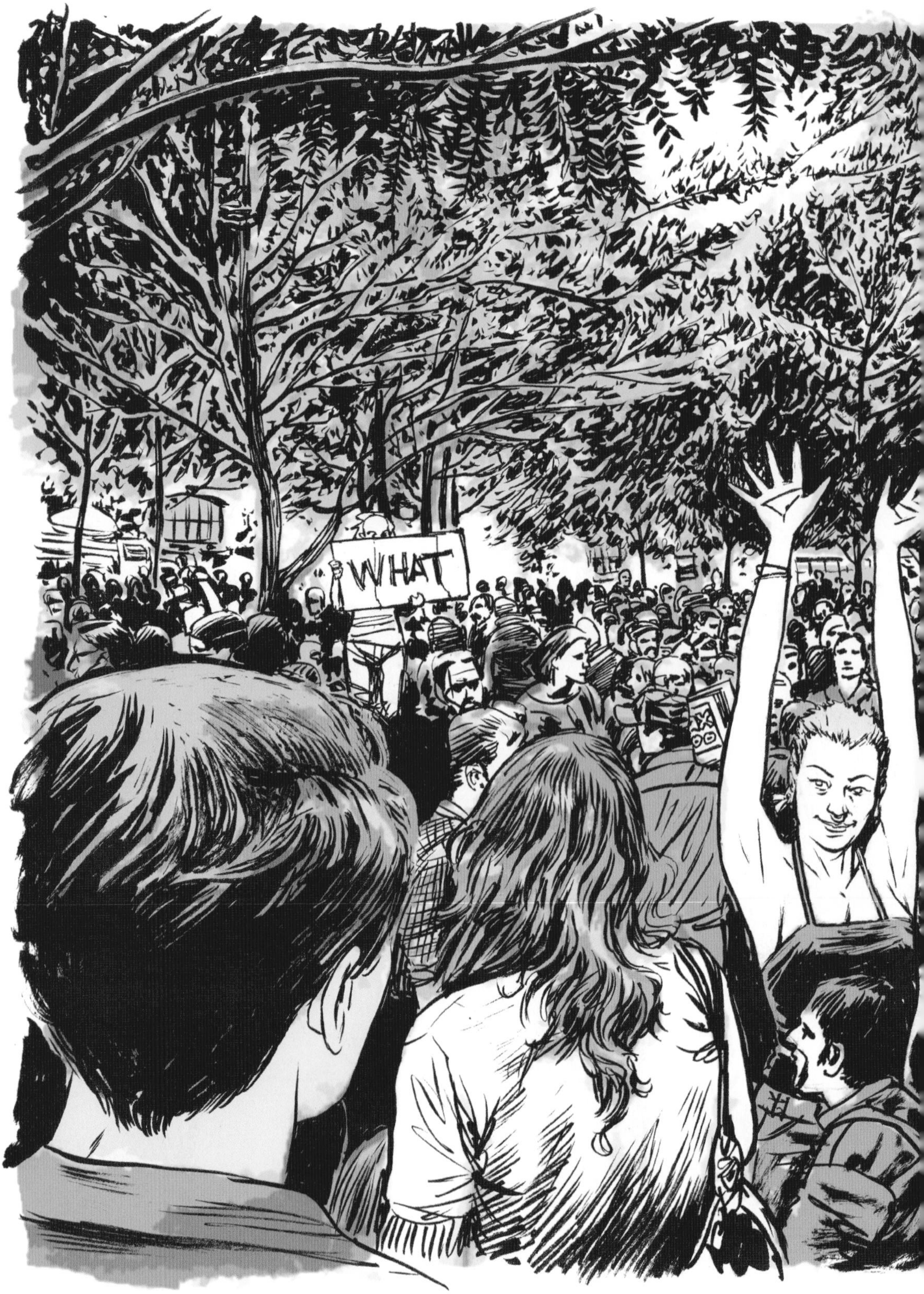
WHAT

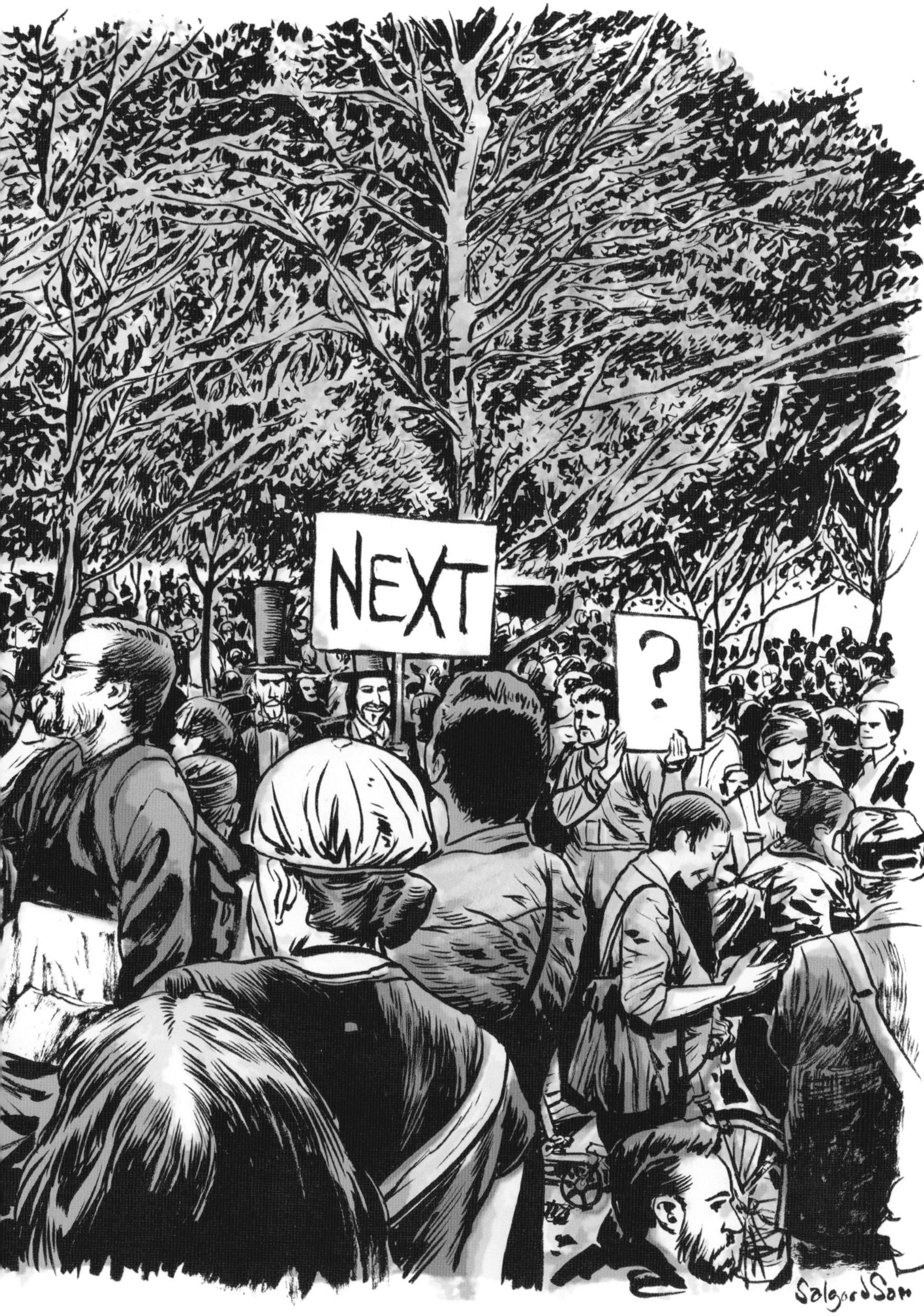
NEXT
?
SalgoodSam

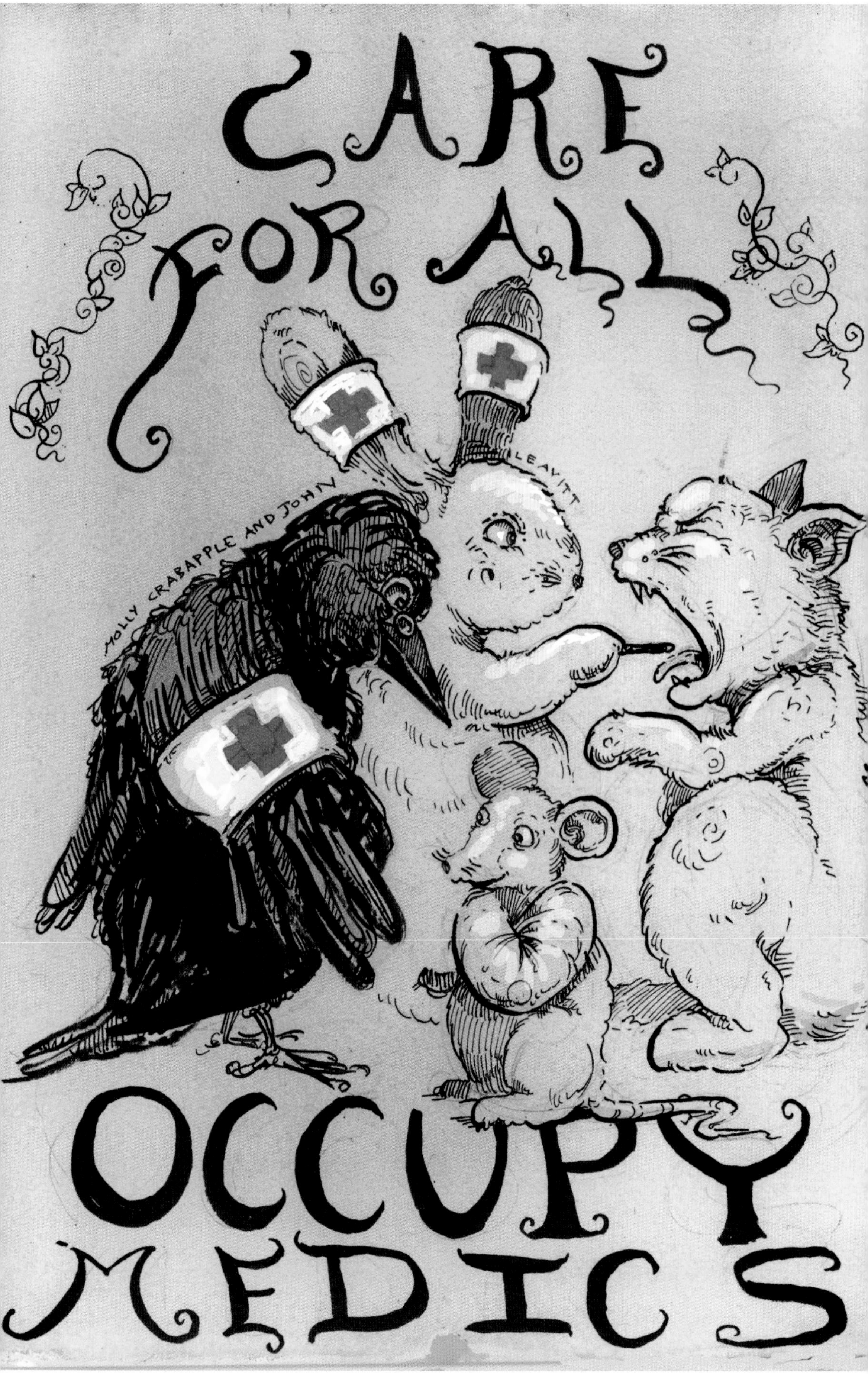
CARE FOR ALL
MOLLY CRABAPPLE AND JOHN LEAVITT
OCCUPY MEDICS

PAY ATTENTION! BE ASTONISHED! ACT!

WRITTEN BY BILL AYERS   IMAGES FOUND ON FLICKR.COM, ILLUSTRATED BY RYAN ALEXANDER-TANNER

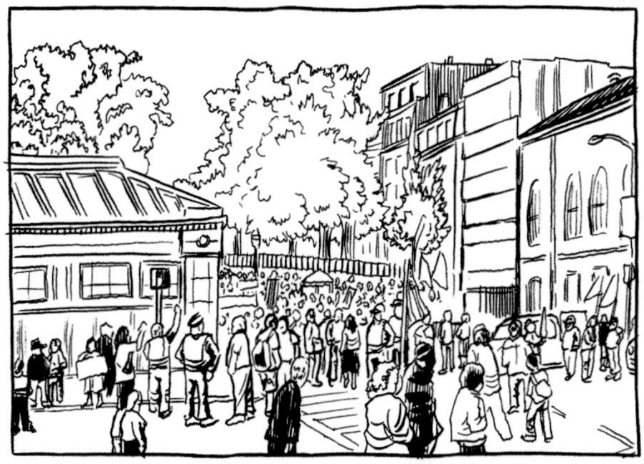

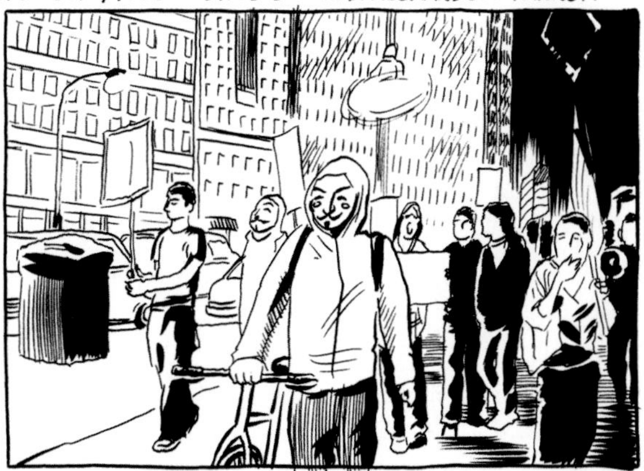

AN INVITATION TO CREATE SUDDENLY APPEARS, INCUBATED IN THE MINDS OF MILLIONS AND IN THE COLLECTIVE CONSCIOUSNESS FOR YEARS, AN EXPLOSION OF HOPE AND A HOWL OF INDIGNATION. WE ARE NOT ALONE! EVERY INJURY IGNORED, EVERY GRIEVANCE ARROGANTLY DISMISSED, EVERY DEMAND DENIED FOR THE GATHERING BUT INVISIBLE STORM.

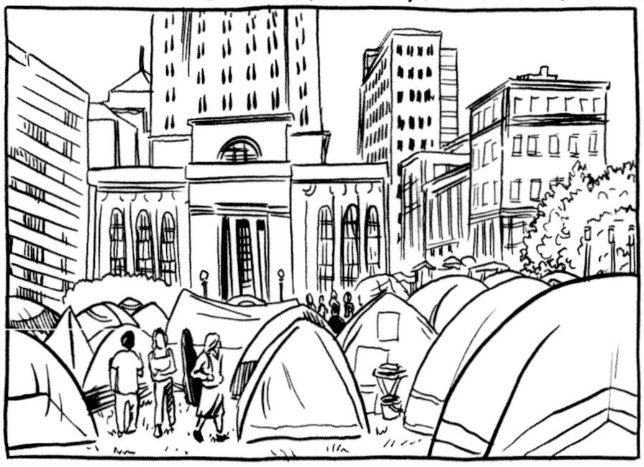

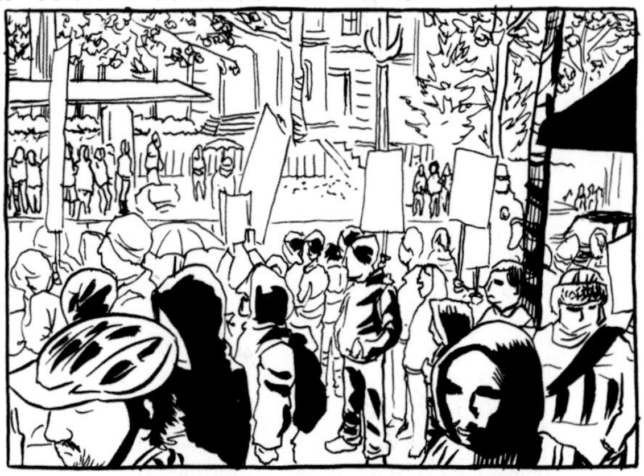

OCCUPY IN THE AIR. PRODUCTION AND REPRODUCTION, DEVELOPMENT AND GENESIS, MORE PROVOCATION THAN PROGRAM, MORE OPENING THAN POINT OF ARRIVAL: OCCUPY THE BOARDS OF EDUCATION! OCCUPY THE PRISONS! OCCUPY CHRISTMAS! OCCUPY THE HOOD! OCCUPY YOUR IMAGINATION! OCCUPY THE FUTURE! OCCUPY THE METAPHOR! *WHICH SIDE ARE YOU ON?* WE RAISE A BANNER OF REFUSAL.

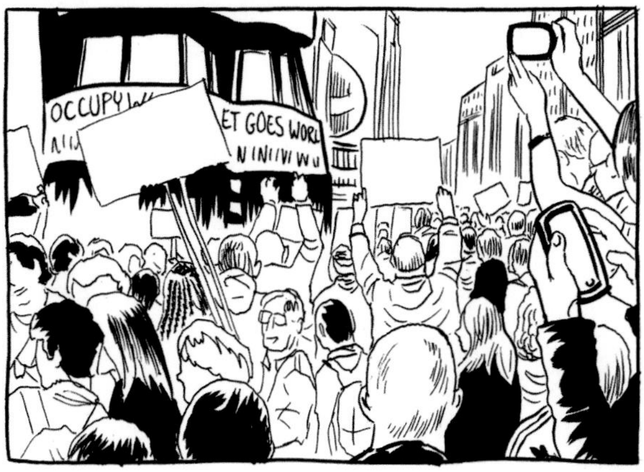
OCCUPY

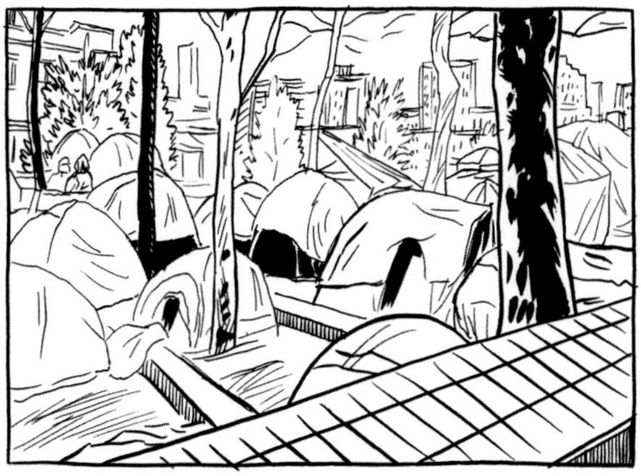

THE IDEA MADE MANIFEST THROUGH ACTION: WE POUR INTO THE PUBLIC SQUARE AND THE ACTION ENLARGES INTO A MOVEMENT; THE MOVEMENT IS DOCUMENTED WITH PHOTOS AND VIDEOS AND SOCIAL MEDIA AS IT CATCHES THE WIND AND GOES VIRAL. WILDLY DIFFERENT AESTHETICS AND CHARACTERS, BUT HERE WE ARE TOGETHER: JOIN US! WE ARE THE 99%!

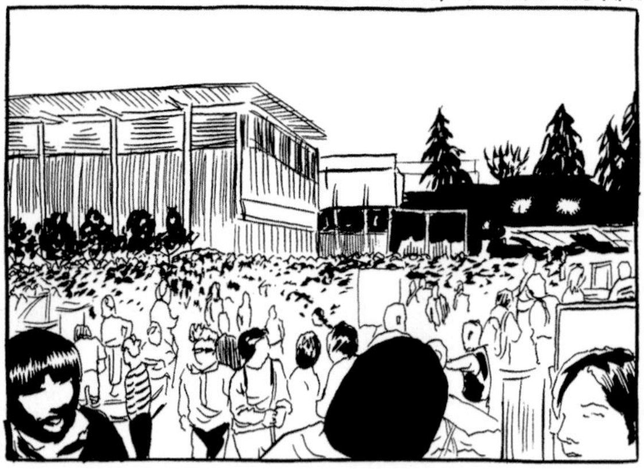

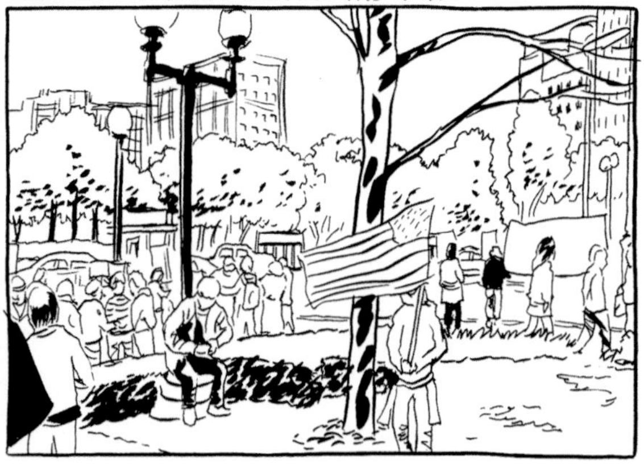

THE VIRUS ENTERS THE IMAGINARY AND THE IMAGES ARE RE-WORKED AS ART AND GRAFFITI, MUSIC AND COMICS. THE IDEAS BECOME A TORNADO – CATCHING AND ABSORBING, SUSTAINING AND CIRCULATING. WHERE DO WE GO FROM HERE – CHAOS OR COMMUNITY? WE DIVE INTO THE WRECKAGE, SWIMMING HARD TOWARD A DISTANT AND INDISTINCT SHORE. LOOK FOR US IN THE WHIRLWIND.

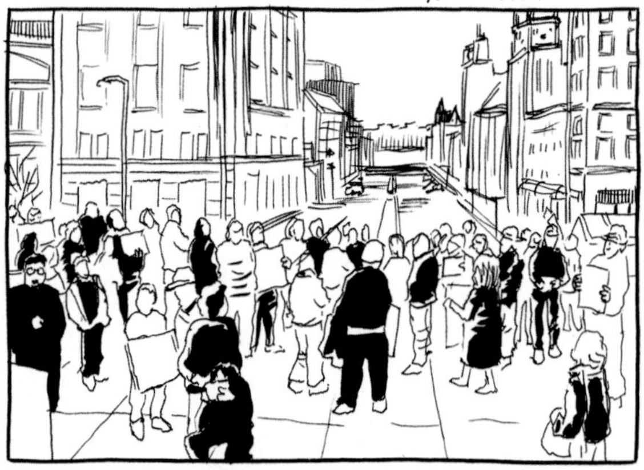

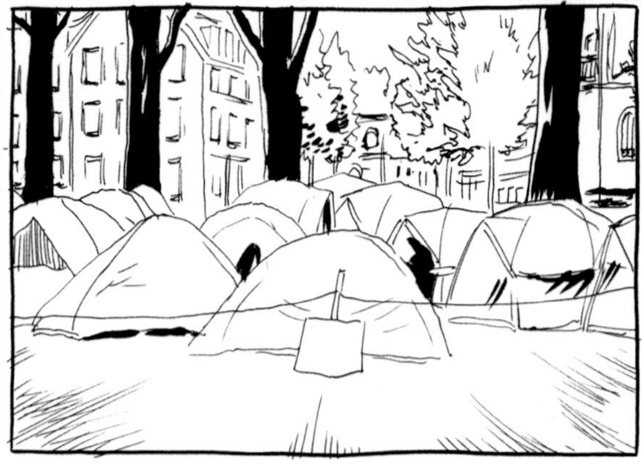

OCCUPY TRANSFORMS, SPREADS, RE-INSCRIBES ITS DAZZLING DNA EVERYWHERE, THE HEART OF A HEARTLESS WORLD AND THE SOUL OF A SOULLESS CONDITION. A CRY OF ANGUISH AND A CALL FOR JUSTICE – THE CIRCULAR DREAM MACHINE. A MOVEMENT-IN-THE-MAKING, OCCUPY WAS *IMPOSSIBLE BEFORE IT OCCURRED*, AND *INEVITABLE* THE DAY IT TOUCHED DOWN. WE CAN'T WILL A MOVEMENT INTO BEING, BUT NEITHER CAN WE SIT IDLY BY, WAITING.

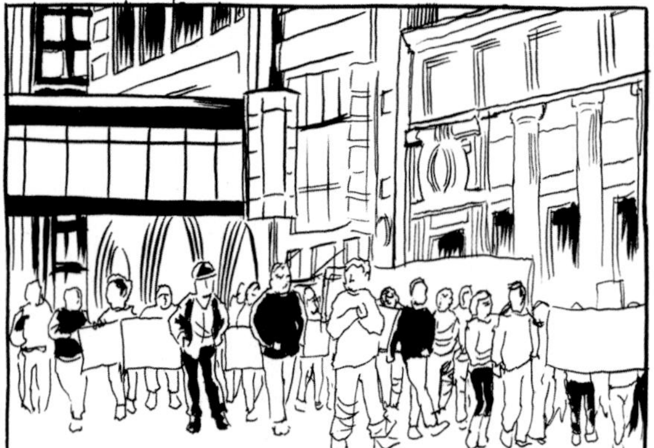

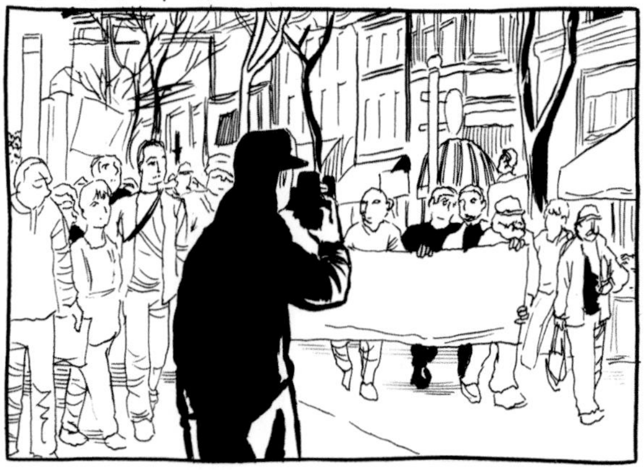

ANOTHER WORLD IS POSSIBLE – ANOTHER WORLD IS NECESSARY. THE TOOLS ARE EVERYWHERE – HUMOR AND ART, PROTEST AND SPECTACLE, THE QUIET INTERVENTION AND THE URGENT THRUST — AND THE DEMAND OF ACTIVISM IS THE SAME: DON'T LET YOUR LIFE MAKE A MOCKERY OF YOUR VALUES! OCCUPY!

OCCUPY

WALL ST.

Divining Perry's Meaning On Galileo Remark

After Deb

By NATE SILVER

How did each candidate
Wednesday night's Republica
debate do to improve his or he
chances of winning the nomin

Newt Gingrich, for one, got
some good one-liners
seemed more poised than he
in past debate. But in delibe
ate
himself other candidate
he give Republica
to pick him
needs to do, sinc
standing at about 3 perce
the polls.

And then there was Gov. Ri
Perry of Texas, who had a ver
good opening sequence, surpri
ing his main opponent, Mitt Ron
ney, by going on the offense an
challenging Mr. Romney's job cr
tion as the governor of Ma
sachuse, comparing a re
pleasing to
who unfavorably
matic former gover
S. Dukakis.

Mr. got we
the night along. Some of
der moment — like his inv
tion of Galileo belief in respon
to a question about clima
change — may make for
funny segment on the Da
Show, be forgotte
What noteworthy w
Mr. response to a que
tion on Social Security, whe
he down on points
book and
terized him as a
scheme

This remark is not likely
exceptionally well even with
publicans, conservative
they may be. A CNN
lished last month
cent of Republica
major chan
and Medic

Republica
will turn out in the primari
who tend to be more conser
tive than Republicans as a who
— the numbers are closer
even, or a little bit in Mr. Perry
favor. But one could argue th
Mr. Perry's remarks were neve
eless unwise.

The reason is that this will pla
into concerns about his appeal
general election voters. (Wi
good reason: some 62 percent
independents, and 69 percent
rates, are opposed
ges on the scale that M
Perry has advocated, accordin

Come

One aims at th
G.O.P. base, o
broader elect

...change science was "not
...d." And he got one of the
...st cheers of the night from
...rowd by vowing that killers
...as would "face the ultimate
...e."

...roughout, the governor's
...was not apologetic or defen-
...He seemed to care little
...t how he might be perceived
...oderate Republicans or in-
...dents, even suggesting at
...oint that Mr. Obama might
... "object liar."

...Romney took a different
...oach altogether, highlighting
...es that he suggested would
...Republicans the chance to
...Mr. Obama and offering a
...down brand of conserva-
...that could be found accept-
...by the widest possible audi-

...rejected Mr. Perry's char-
...zation of Social Security,
...g that the program needed
...fixed, not dismantled. And
...emed eager to present a
...unified Republican front in
...attle against Mr. Obama,
...g. "We have some differ-
...etween us, but we agree
...than president has to go."
...l, Mr. Romney, a former
...rnor of Massachusetts, did

then, hey, I'm for the
Mr. Romney said in a
answer to the questio
er he is a member of th
servative political mo

Mr. Perry, by contra
built a career in Texas
thing that will...In tw

A challenge... ...Wednesday's deb
...ove past... ...governor of a lib...

...not back away... ...in some of his
...more conservative... ...talk, in-
...cluding his vow to...
...utive order to end the...
...ot of Mr. Obama's h...

"The strategies on...
Wedne...day...ight will...
part by ne...ney, an...hereby
history.

Mr. Romney...

...h...past as the g...
...ad state and th...
...ections he to...
...as a candidate...
...izing t...
...the ide...or...

...Massachusetts
...ven m...st...it
specifics of...ir acc...
...ents.

...For the...x...bet...a
the...publican conte
shape up...s...ngam
...n...or Re...Mic...
...hey seek...can...
...sen...e Mr...ana
...occupy...c...hi...
...their wa...as Re
a Mas...s one.

...partisan Shift Towar... ...s Program

...anxious mood,
...ggesting no
...dden movements.

...states — they referre...
...changing...cial Secur...

Now they have...
presi...tial...anda...
is taking on...ci...
so-called th...ra...
politics — with bu...

The collapse...
...gotiations be...
and Mr. Boe...
...tative trade-o...
from entit...
new reven...es, l...
parties co...nced...
...ant debt-reduction...
...kely...fore the 2012...
Unle...Republicans accept...
er ta...es on the wealthy, and t...
...sw...r they will not, Democrat...
w...not support reductions in fu-
...e entitlement benefits.

Yet both parties are feeling the
pressure to act sooner. That reflects not only the seriousness of
the nation's looming debt crisis
as baby boomers age, but also the
possibility later this year that just
as in this summer's fight over
raising the debt limit, the finan-

...plurality of Republicans.
...one-third of Republicans
...hey would be more likely to
...for someone who espoused
...g Social Security.
...til Mr. Perry's recent entry
...the Republican contest, the
...te over reining in the pro-
...d growth of the entitlement
...rams focused on the health
...rams, Medicare and Medic...
...Their projected costs, given
...ging of the population and
...rising medical expenses, are
...ter and growing faster...
...e for Social Security.
...hile House Republican...
...ed in April of the...
...eir budget — it would turn
...care into a voucher program
...rivate insurance and Medic-

...be...h...dy-
...Washing...n plan
...mapped out by the new
...b...k...reduction...and
...stacked by C...t...
...he...ar
...uild-
...2010, c...Dem...
...mproved a...llion
...vings from Medicare
...new...
...t-
...ar's
...onset
...mittee's
...cathing
...ng has
...a...

Ab...t...meeting of the
House-S...ate committee on def-
icit reduction, which is to make
recommendations by Nov. 23 for
a quick up-or-down vote in Congress, several Republicans said
that entitlements were the main
cause of annual deficits and
should be the panel's focus.

"In order to succeed, I kno

about the business o
reforming social saf
grams that are not
many beneficiaries,
broke at the same
Representative Jeb
Republican of Texa
chairman of the
which is evenly divi
Republicans and Dem

James E. Clyburn o
olina, a House Demo
on the panel, said tha
"smart and compassi
et cuts" and "ending
venturism," but tha
must not shred Soc
Medicare and Medica

Separately, the se
crat on the House
Means Committee,
Levin of Michigan,
memo listing two de
that could squeeze
$500 billion out of Me
next 10 years. Aides
said that he was no
the ideas but helping

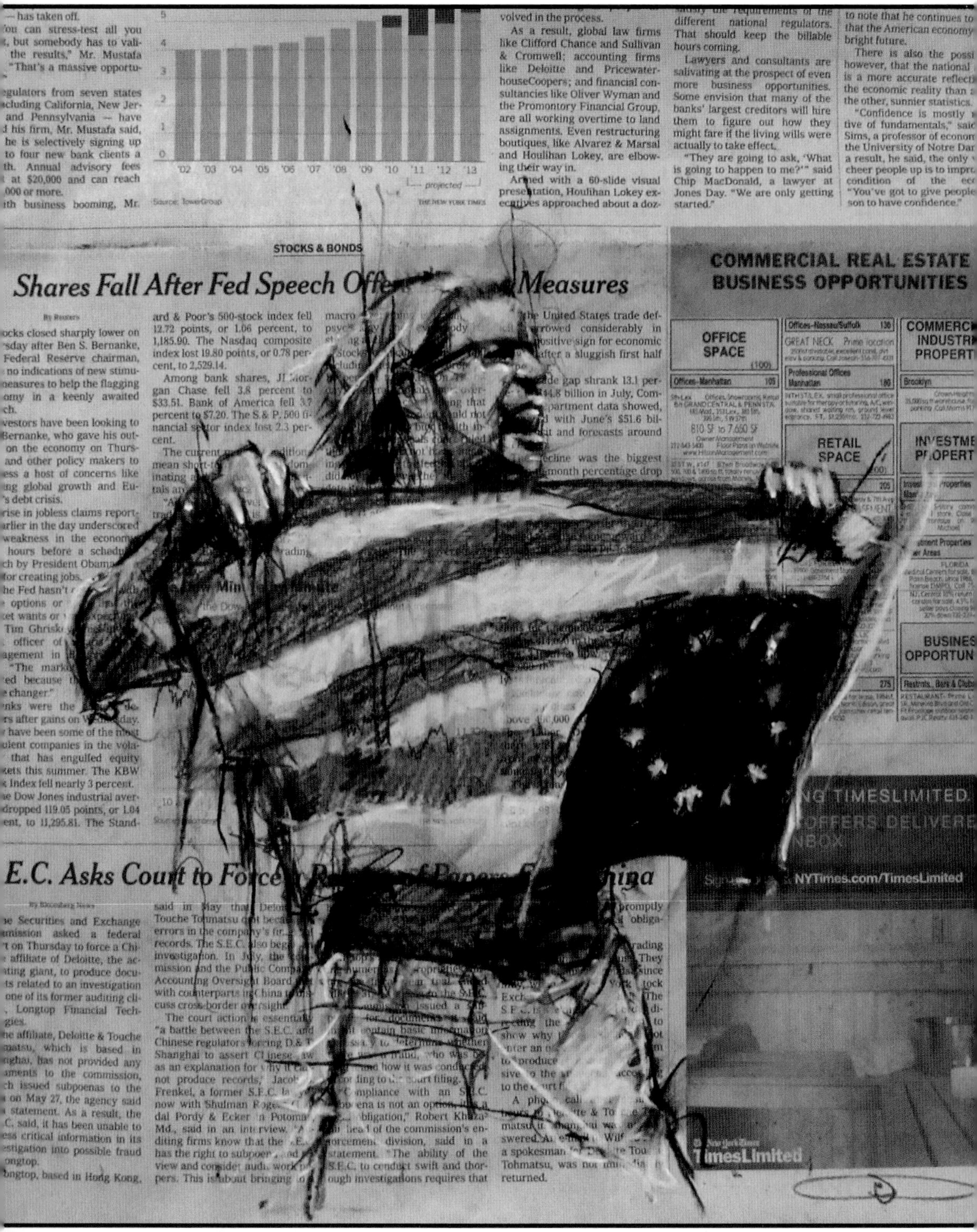
STOCKS & BONDS
Shares Fall After Fed Speech
Measures
COMMERCIAL REAL ESTATE
BUSINESS OPPORTUNITIES
OFFICE SPACE
RETAIL SPACE
NYTimes.com/TimesLimited

Casino Nation

Deck of Playing Cards

Featuring the hard players, grift-jammers & bubble builders who failed upward on the backs of the American people & redistributed our national wealth to themselves.

text: Joshua Dysart & Kelly Bruce art: Allen Gladfelter bibliography at OccupyComics.com

You Don't Know Jack!

Angelo Mozilo = Jack of Diamonds

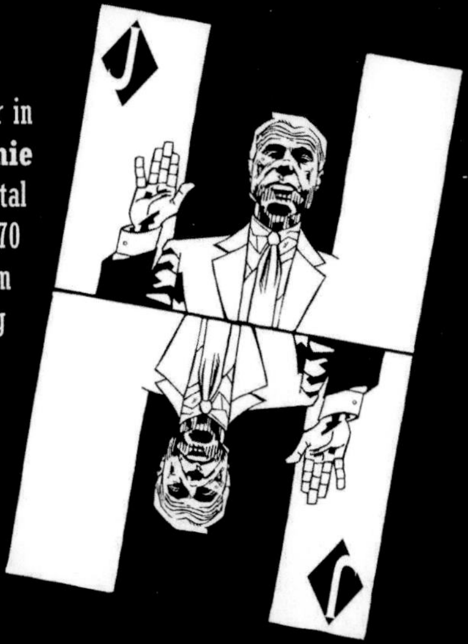

Founder/CEO of **Countrywide Financial**, the nation's largest mortgage lender in 2008. He demanded in 2004 that **Fannie Mae** buy his risky loans. When **Fannie** refused he threatened to terminate their partnership, which could have been fatal to **Fannie Mae**. From 2005 - 2008, **Fannie Mae,** under threat, bought $270 billion in risky loans. ***Mozilo*** created a "Friends of Angelo" VIP loan program through which several lawmakers & politicians, including the Senate Banking Committee Chairman & Senate Budget Committee Chairman, received favorable mortgage financing. In 2010, ***Mozilo*** reached a settlement with the Securities & Exchange Commission over securities fraud & insider trading charges & was ordered to pay a small fraction of the amount he made. *Mozilo* earned ***$400 million*** in 2007.

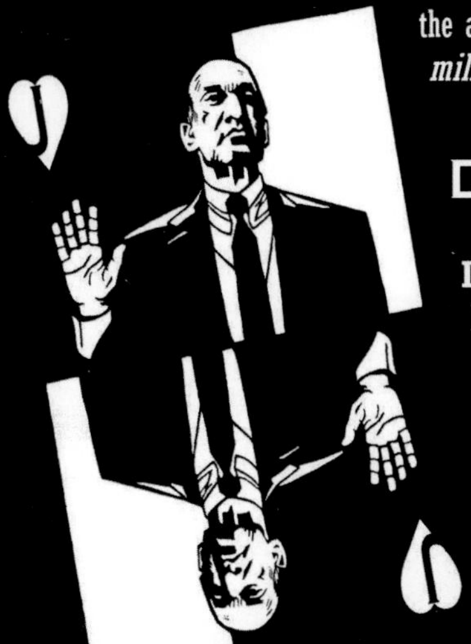

Dick Fuld=Jack of Hearts

Lehman Brothers' CEO whose arrogance crashed the massive institution. By March of 2008, a bailout of **Bear Stearns**, which had not been approved by Congress & was handled almost exclusively by the New York Fed, had occurred. *Fuld* assumed that **Lehman**, a larger institution, would be bailed out as well. So he simply kept playing his risky game until he reached maximum failure, when he would then take hypothetical American tax dollars rather than an actual rescue offer made by *Warren Buffet.* During that time, **Lehman** under *Fuld* sold $4 billion in bad assets, spreading the disaster like a virus. When the time came for him to ask for a government handout, the Fed refused. Condé Nast Portfolio ranked *Fuld* the #1 "Worst American CEO of All Time," calling him "belligerent & unrepentant." *Fuld* made ***$34 million*** in 2007 &, before **Lehman** filed for bankruptcy, he sold off his stock for another ***half billion.***

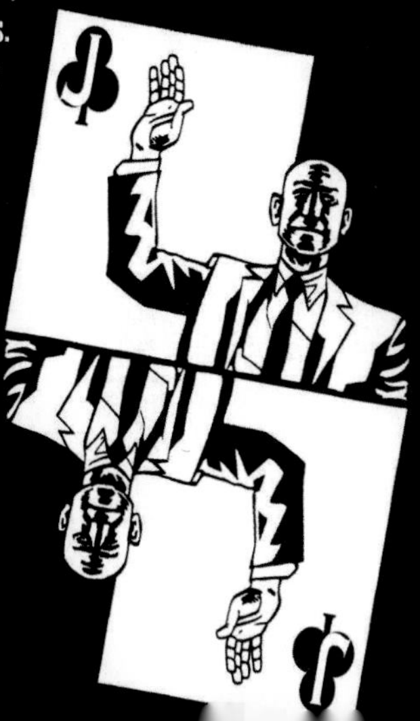

Lloyd Blankfein=Jack of Clubs

CEO/Chairman of **Goldman Sachs** since 2006. **Goldman** was sued in 2010 by the SEC for the fraudulent selling of a synthetic CDO tied to sub-prime mortgages, a product which **Goldman** created. Under *Blankfein's* watch, **Goldman** has been accused of helping Greece mask the size of its debts. He has admitted that **Goldman** did things that were "clearly wrong" & says he "regretted" contributing to the

financial crisis. **Goldman** was the company from which *Obama* raised the most money during his 2008 campaign & *Blankfein* has visited the White House 10 times. In 2007 *Blankfein* made *$70 million*.

JOSEPH CASSANO = JACK OF SPADES

Officer at **AIG** who came from Junk Bonds, dubbed "Patient Zero of the global economic meltdown" & "The Man Who Crashed the World." *Cassano* sold hundreds of billions of Credit Default Swaps (CDS). A CDS is when a buyer makes a series of payments to the seller of a loan & in exchange receives a payoff if the loan defaults. But *Cassano* never had to put up any actual money as collateral due to deregulation of CDS (more on that later). When the 2008 financial crisis began, investment banks demanded the money for their collapsing derivatives **AIG** couldn't deliver. Taxpayers then had to bail out AIG. To date we have given the company *$173 billion*. *Cassano* continued to make *$1 million* a month from **AIG** until his forced retirement in October of 2008. The year that his mistakes help directly crash the economy, *Cassano* made *$315 million*.

GOD SAVE (US FROM) THE QUEEN

ROBERT RUBIN = QUEEN OF DIAMONDS

Secretary of Treasury under *Clinton* & later the Director/Senior Counselor/temporary Chairman of **Citigroup** where he profited greatly from advice he gave *Clinton*. *Rubin* is an Investment Banking lifer (spent 26 years at **Goldman Sachs**) & was strongly opposed to oversight of credit derivatives. In 1995, he testified that Congress should repeal Glass-Steagall. This was an ongoing crusade for *Rubin*, & he's one of the greatest driving factors in the 90's deregulation frenzy. **Citibank**, the company that would later reward *Rubin* with extraordinary funds, was also involved in the crusade to such an extent that when *Clinton*, partly under advice from *Rubin*, stopped regulating derivatives & pressed for a more "21st Century" economy, it was mockingly called the "Citigroup Authorization Act." Once described as "joined at the hip with *Greenspan*," it seems *Rubin* has changed his tune on deregulation. In 2009, he told Newsweek "the market-based model must be combined with strong & effective government, nationally & transnationally, to deal with critical challenges that markets won't adequately address." *Rubin* has been touted as a possible appointee to a cabinet post for *President Obama*. He resigned from **Citigroup** in 2009. He received more than *$126 million* in cash & stocks during his time there.

PHIL GRAMM = QUEEN OF HEARTS

First a Democratic Congressman, then a Republican Congressman, then a Republican Senator, *Gramm* spearheaded the 1999 repeal of the Glass-Steagall Act that *Rubin* championed. In fact, *Gramm* is so responsible for the repea

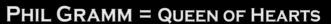

that was significantly to blame for the 2007 sub-prime mortgage crisis & 2008 global economic crisis that the repeal itself bares his name: the Gramm-Leach-Bliley Act. *Gramm's* support was later critical in keeping derivatives transactions, including credit default swaps, free from regulation. In 2000, he was one of the key sponsors of a bill called the Commodity Futures Modernization Act (CFMA) that was introduced on the last day before Christmas recess It was never debated in the House or Senate & was attached as a rider to an 11,000-page budget bill signed by *Clinton.* The CFMA is famous for creating the Enron Loophole. Surprise! *Gramm's* wife was on the **Enron** board at the time. It is no exaggeration to say that no single elected official bears more blame for the collapse of the market than *Gramm.* As a public servant he pursued a personal wealth agenda rather than protecting the American People *Paul Krugman* has called *Gramm* the #2 person responsible for the economic crisis behind *Greenspan.* In 2008 *Gramm* denied the nation was in a recession & stated, "We have sort of become a nation of whiners… America in decline." From 1993-2001 **Enron** alone paid *Gramm* between $915,000 & $1.85 million.

LAWRENCE SUMMERS = QUEEN OF CLUBS

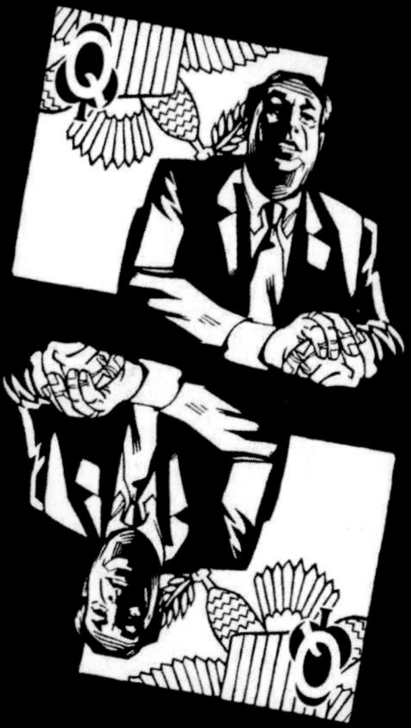

Q
Q

Protégé of *Robert Rubin,* Secretary of the Treasury from 1999 to 2001 under *Clinton*, Director of the White House United States National Economic Council for *Obama* & President of Harvard University until he was forced to resign, Summers is a major deregulation evangelist & anti-environmentalist. When Glass-Steagall was repealed, *Summers*, then Secretary of the Treasury, said, "Today Congress voted to update the rules that have governed financial services since the Great Depression & replace them with a system for the 21st century." During the California energy crisis of 2000, *Summers* teamed with *Alan Greenspan* & **Enron** executive *Kenneth Lay* to lecture California Governor *Gray Davis*, explaining that the cause was overregulation by the government. In January 2009, as the *Obama* Administration tried to pass an economic stimulus spending bill, *Summers* advised *Obama* that less of the stimulus should be spent on infrastructure & more should be focused on tax cuts instead. In 2008, *Summers* was accepting perks from **Citigroup**, including free rides on its corporate jet. Around this time, *Summers* called *Senator Chris Dodd* asking him to remove caps on executive pay at firms that had received stimulus money, including Citigroup. He earned ***$5 million*** from the hedge fund **D.E. Shaw** & collected ***$2.7 million*** in speaking fees from Wall Street firms that received government bailout money (which saved them from massive losses they incurred while exploiting loopholes & deregulations Summers championed).

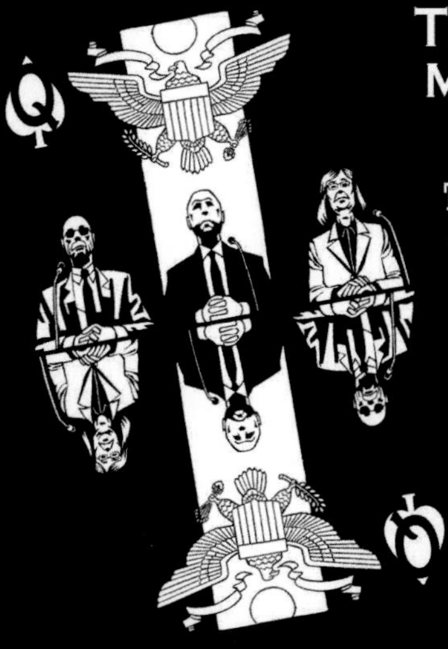

Q
Q

THE BIG 3 RATING AGENCIES: MOODY'S, STANDARD & POOR'S, FITCH = QUEEN OF SPADES

The rating agencies receive fees from investment banks and securities firms to analyze and rate the risk of investment in other companies, bonds and even other countries. But a system that was designed to provide investors with an objective analysis was useless and even harmful during the run-up to the subprime mortgage crisis. Many large institutions such as trusts and pension funds can only invest in top-rated securities, making the market dependent on the rating agencies. As the market in mortgaged-based securities boomed, rating agencies focused on earning fees for themselves rather than performing rigorous analysis. As early as 2004, S&P employees warned of pressures to increase favorable ratings for clients rather than risk losing business fees. One analyst stated, "It could be structured by cows and we would rate it." A

Senate report found that 90% of securities rated as triple-A in 2006 & 2007 were later downgraded to junk, defaulted or withdrawn from the market. A key element in the breakdown of the ratings systems is lack of regulation — little government supervision was in place to police the rating agencies, which often failed to follow their own procedures & guidelines. Legislation enacted in 2010 gives the SEC greater oversight of the rating agencies.

IN THE KINGDOM OF THE BLIND

BEN BERNANKE = KING OF DIAMONDS

Chairman of the Federal Reserve after *Greenspan* in 2006, confirmed to a 2nd term by *Obama* in 2010. The Bernanke Doctrine first postulated that "we are in a new era, where modern macroeconomic policy has decreased the volatility of the business cycle." That was the beginning of a pattern of inaccurate forecasts of coming economic problems & a profound misunderstanding of economic policy in general. As housing prices spiked, *Bernanke* argued those prices would never drop in a meaningful way. In October 2007, when signs of trouble began to appear, *Bernanke* stated, "It is not the responsibility of the Federal Reserve to protect lenders & investors from the consequences of their financial decisions." Less than a year later, the Fed began doing exactly that; in 2008, under his leadership, the Fed began pumping what would become a total of $7.7 trillion, approximately 20 times the amount of TARP, into the U.S. economy, greatly expanding the Fed's power with little congressional oversight or public transparency. Details of the full Fed Bailout under his reign have only recently been made public after the Fed was sued under the Freedom of Information Act. The Fed is mandated with supervising banks, but poor oversight allowed predatory lending practices to feed the housing bubble. The Fed's gargantuan infusions of cash & long-term ultra-low interest rates have served to support the economy over the past 3 years, but they have put the nation at great risk of future inflation & compromised the ability of the general public's savings to grow. What is a safety raft today will no doubt sink under the weight of inflation tomorrow.

HENRY PAULSON = KING OF HEARTS

The Secretary of the Treasury, appointed under *George W. Bush*, from 2006-2009 & former CEO of **Goldman Sachs,** where he headed the effort to convince the SEC to waive rules on how much money was needed in reserves & promised to "self-regulate." *Paulson* then pursued high profits at high risks using American mortgages as the base for the securities & derivatives boom. In mid 2007, as Secretary of Treasury, he called the American Economy "healthy." In 2008, this experiment in "self-regulation" ended in spectacular failure as all of the big investment firms vastly overextended their economic bets compared to their money in reserve. Of the big 5, **Bear Stearns** & **Merrill Lynch** were sold in fire sales, **Goldman Sachs** & **Morgan Stanley** converted from investment banks to commercial banks so as to access more government bailout $ & **Lehman Brothers** went bankrupt, resulting in a global financial panic. Once the crisis became undeniable, *Paulson* repeatedly underestimated its scope. He called the mortgage crisis "contained" before the failure of **Lehman Brothers** cascaded through the entire economy, threatening firms soon deemed "too big to fail," including **AIG** & **Citigroup**. As Secretary of the Treasury, *Paulson's* initial request to Congress for

$100 billion in TARP funds consisted of a brief, legendarily arrogant 3-page document that included the provision that "decisions by the Secretary [Paulson]... may not be reviewed by any court of law or administrative agency." Congress later passed a different version of TARP after receiving more information & adding additional guidelines. *Paulson* has been accused of shifting priorities for bailout money away from firms that may support lending to Main St. & towards banks' bottom lines. For instance, one bank received $7 billion in bailout funds while spending $5.8 billion to buy another bank, all further illuminating the separation between the Wall St. Economy & the real economy.

TIMOTHY GEITHNER = KING OF CLUBS

The Bailout King" has been the Secretary of the Treasury under *Obama* since *Paulson* stepped down & was head of the New York branch of the Fed Reserve before that. As head of the NY Fed, he lobbied to decrease the amount of money investment banks were required to keep in reserve. He relied on close relationships with Wall Street insiders to assess — therefore misread — economic trends. He shares Wall St.'s deregulatory philosophy, limiting his ability to provide true oversight. While at the NY Fed, *Geithner* took a leading role in the *$29 billion* bailout of **Bear Stearns**, the *$182 billion* bailout of **AIG** & the *$45 billion* bailout of **Citigroup**. During crisis meetings regarding the **AIG** bailout, *Geithner* included **Goldman Sachs** executives in the negotiations, although **Goldman** had no legal standing to be present & the firm was owed billions by **AIG,** raising conflict of interest questions. *Geithner* later said he had suggested **Goldman** get involved because "time was running out." Begging the question, what does "time running out" have to do with **Goldman** being present at another institution's bailout meetings? As Treasury Secretary, *Geithner's* department worked with the Federal Reserve to buy toxic mortgage-based assets & helped spend *billions* to prop up the banking sector. He has stated that the U.S. needs to spend less on health care & retirement benefits to pay for the damage his own philosophies have wrought. In 2006, he was audited by the IRS & found to owe more than *$40,000* in back taxes.

ALAN GREENSPAN = KING OF SPADES

Chairman of the Federal Reserve of the United States, appointed by *Reagan* in '87 & retiring in 2006. He served the 2nd longest term in the Fed's history. *Greenspan* is a follower of the anti-government economic philosophies of Ayn Rand. As such, his role as a flawed ideologue is deeply embedded in the DNA of the current financial crisis. In his first year at the Fed, he struggled with & successfully managed the '87 market crash. The market came to believe, & rightly so, that *Greenspan* would perform crisis intervention when needed, making risk-taking much less risky. The irony was that *Greenspan* was an anti-regulator who turned the Fed into an unprecedented intervention machine. He had, within months of taking over at the Fed, become a walking contradiction. He focused on the stock market instead of the actual economy, reversing course from his predecessor *Paul Volcker*. If you think the stock market & the actual economy are the same, think again. From 2001-2008, as the stock market ascended on a credit & housing boom & brokers netted sometimes hundreds of millions, the actual American dollar lost 40% of its purchasing power. Then, in 2002, Wall St. changed the very definition of what it meant to borrow & lend to expand their speculation market. Where once the ability to repay a debt was the primary factor in the borrowing/lending cycle, the lending of money began to be based on the lender's ability to sell the debt instead of the borrower's ability to pay the debt back. Suddenly a flood of low-interest mortgages hit the market, fueled by *Greenspan*'s decision to keep interest rates at historic lows. Japan & China & other countries were buying American mortgage from American investment banks to speculate against. Foreign buyers & institutional investors were scooping up American mortgages & mortgage-based securities without regard to the likelihood of any mortgage being repaid. Multiple people, including those inside the Fed, tried to warn *Greenspan* that this was a fatally bad idea. *Greenspan* had been using the Fed in ways its charter never allowed. The real job of the Fed is to supervise credit & lending. Instead of heeding multiple warnings, *Greenspan* called the new lending practices "innovative." What followed was a credit & housing bubble, & then a bust which prompted the largest market crash in human history. Since 2006, 306 US lending institutions have failed & 2 million US homes have been foreclosed. Yet the great interventionist *Greenspan* was fiercely opposed to regulating these new forms of investments. In 2008, in response to the rapidly expanding crises, *Greenspan* finally came to his senses, "Those of us who have looked to the self-interest of lending institutions to protect shareholders' equity, myself included, are in a state of shocked disbelief."

AN ACE IN THE HOLE

ARACK OBAMA = ACE OF CLUBS

44th & current President of the United States, serving from '09 to present. He campaigned on a platform of change. *Obama,* however, has done nothing but support economic status quo. He has filled key government positions from the same group of financial insiders & deregulators that crashed the economy in the first place, making *Timothy Geithner* Treasury Sec. & *Lawrence Summers* Dir. of the White House Economic Council. He reconfirmed *Bush's* hire *Ben Bernanke* as Dir. of the Federal Reserve, despite the fact that under *Bernanke* the Fed has provided approximately *$7.7 trillion* in bailout funds, 20 times the amount of the approved TARP, & greatly expanded the Fed's power while lessening congressional oversight & transparency. According to the Washington Examiner, *Obama* raised more campaign funds from **Goldman Sachs** than from any other single company in 2008. Stimulus plans under *Obama* have prevented the crisis from worsening & *Obama* has advocated for the extension of unemployment benefits & relief from payroll taxes that help Main Street Americans in this recession, however, for the most part it's still business as usual in America. Few of the predatory lenders or securities firms who pushed toxic assets knowing they were worthless have been investigated or charged for any crime. So we are forced to assume one of two things: either *Obama* did not have the financial understanding to properly vet his economics team when he took office or he was just as interested in reaping the benefits of big Wall St. money as any other card in our nefarious deck. You be the judge.

GEORGE W. BUSH = ACE OF DIAMONDS

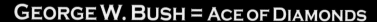

The 43rd Pres. of the U.S., serving from '01 – '09. Under *Bush*, the U.S. national debt doubled from *$5.6 trillion* to *$11.3 trillion* largely as a result of tax cuts coupled with increased spending on two wars. *Bush* pushed for increasing home ownership while also promoting deregulation, setting the stage for predatory lending & the high-risk financial betting that led to the sub-prime mortgage crisis. Ultimately, housing prices skyrocketed under *Bush* while incomes for most Americans remained flat, resulting in many people either being priced out of the housing market or buying in with high-risk mortgages. Like those before him, *Bush* continued to support *Fed Chairman Greenspan* who preached free-market ideology while continuing to intervene by lowering rates & inflating the money supply, fueling bubble after bubble. Ultra-low interest rates for unprecedented long periods of time under *Bush's* watch encouraged reckless lending & discouraged saving. The sub-prime mortgage crisis exploded onto Wall St. in the fall of 2008, with **Lehman Brothers** going bankrupt, which threatened to cause a domino effect that could have brought down the insurance giant **AIG** as well as other banks & investment firms such as **Citigroup** & **Merrill Lynch**, freezing credit worldwide. In the midst of unprecedented financial disaster, *Bush* failed to provide leadership to the nation, Congress or his own financial administrators. *Fed Chair Bernanke* & *Treasury Sec. Paulson,* both anti-regulators, stepped into the leadership vacuum with *Paulson* presenting the first draft request for TARP bailout funds to Congress. After Congress approved $700 billion in TARP funds, *Bush* noted, "It wasn't that hard for me, just so you know. I made the decision to use your money to prevent the collapse from happening."

BILL CLINTON = ACE OF HEARTS

The 42nd President of the United States, serving from '93 – '01, he assisted in aggressive deregulation of the financial markets. *Clinton* signed the Gramm-Leach-Bliley Act in '99, which repealed parts of the landmark, Depression-era Glass-Steagall Act, allowing for the consolidation of commercial banks, investment banks, securities firms & insurance companies and discarding the conflict of interest prohibitions between commercial banks & securities firms. There is a direct line from Gramm-Leach-Bliley to the "too big to fail" firms of our era, including **Citigroup** & **AIG,** both of which received huge government bailouts during the current recession. *Clinton* also signed the Commodity Futures Modernization Act in 2000, mandating that newer financial products such as credit default swaps & mortgage-based securities NOT be regulated by state & federal agencies. These types of securities have been referred to as "financial weapons of mass destruction" & their explosion was a huge factor in the '08 financial crisis & current recession. *Clinton* later admitted that not regulating derivatives was a mistake, though he continued to support *Greenspan* as Fed Reserve chair, even as the Fed's low interest rates fed the high-tech bubble & bust of the late '90's. *Clinton* hired Wall St. insiders for key posts such as **Goldman Sachs** alum *Robert Rubin* as Secretary of the Treasury. *Clinton* is, more than any other US president, responsible for the crisis we are in today.

RONALD REAGAN = ACE OF SPADES

The 40th President of the U.S, serving from '81 – '89 & the intellectual father of deregulation philosophy. He advocated for a smaller role of government in business, championing the unfettered capitalism of "free" deregulated markets. He hired *Greenspan* to head the Fed in '87, replacing *Paul Volcker. Greenspan* believed free markets regulate themselves without intervention, then he proceeded with unprecedented intervention. *Volcker,* on the other hand, understood the importance of market regulation & steered the U.S. economy out of the stagflation of the '70's. Under *Reagan,* the '82 Garn-St. Germain Depository Institution Act deregulated commercial banks & Savings & Loans, allowing S&Ls to make high-risk loans to developers. When these banks overextended themselves & faced bankruptcy due to bad bets in the late '80s/early '90s many were deemed "too big to fail" – sound familiar? Eventually 747 S&Ls were bailed out with *$87.9 billion* in US taxpayer money, all under *Greenspan*, who was the natural extension of *Reagan's* deeply flawed anti-regulation stance.

THE JOKE'S ON YOU!

Though the Joker may seem like the least serious card, it was originally introduced in the standard deck to be used as the highest trump. The Joker is unpredictable & can turn the tables of a game at a moment's notice.

THE AMERICAN PEOPLE

JOKER
JOKER

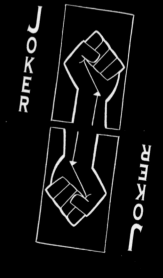

The joke is most certainly on us. How is there not more outrage? How is it that so many people continue to vote against their own interests by supporting deregulating politicians & "free" markets long after the seemingly ceaseless bubble/crash cycle has driven us to compromise our national financial security? In reality, the US's "free" markets are greatly compromised by invisible forces put into play by corrupt, negligent & complacent politicians, lobbyists, Wall St. insiders & government administrators who have forgotten what fair play actually is. Our "free" market serves to redistribute our wealth to the 1%. The American Dream has become less & less accessible to the average American as wealth, resources & a voice in government are increasingly concentrated in the hands of the very, very few. The average American's share of the pie has shrunk over the past 2 decades, but we've all been too busy trying to keep from being hungry to be angry. Meanwhile those who wrecked the economy have been rewarded. Incentive packages & bonuses were once defined as perks for a job well done. Instead these people did the worst job of management possible, then received historically large bonuses & incentives. It is the way of things that those in power will use the means of power to stay in power. And it is a tactic as old as civilization to deny true education & real information to the masses while providing complete distraction & disinformation. This is the physics of power, & the sooner the American People wipe the pie they've been sold from their face the sooner we can work towards establishing a more just & equitable system.

THE OCCUPY MOVEMENT

JOKER
JOKER

Is OWS the revolution we've been waiting for? How is it that the outrage that HAS been expressed through the movement has been marginalized by the media & cast as a fringe youth "phase" instead of a populist uprising? Critics say we should be marching in front of Washington instead of Wall St., & while we should & are marching in Washington & at all Halls of Political Power across the country, the truth is Wall St. is the greatest hall of political power there is. Wall St. funds & crafts economic policy, not the other way around. Critics say the protesters want to be driving Cadillacs, that they are freeloaders looking for a handout. In fact they are students who were told if they went to college they could buy into the American dream to the tune of tens of thousands in debt, but found a nation stripped of jobs because **Wall St. wrecked the economy**. They are young couples who were the victims of predatory mortgage & credit scams, foreclosed on after **Wall St. wrecked the economy**. They are the millions & millions whose savings are sitting stagnant in the bank, earning nothing, because Bernanke continues to keep interest rates at or near 0% so the big investment banks can pay back their loans because **Wall St. wrecked the economy.** They are the war vets who came back to discover they were fighting overseas to protect 1% of the population while police were using crowd control tactics on Americans that the vets themselves, the best trained in the world, found abhorrent. The critics say the protesters have no demands, yet it is not the protesters' job to make policy - that's what we elect politicians for. Angry Americans are an engine of commentary. They are a symptom of broken policies. It is for the elected to look at the protesters & not demonize, not trivialize, not move to "restore order," but to address what enrages the protesters in the first place. To look the protesters in the eye & say, "We hear you, we understand." We are louder than their sound-bite media that's owned by those who profit from keeping us stupid. WE are the Joker in THEIR deck & if we stick to the game, if we stand in the cold & rain & sun, day & night, & continue to evolve as a constructive movement, then our voice will, unquestionably, change the card game forever

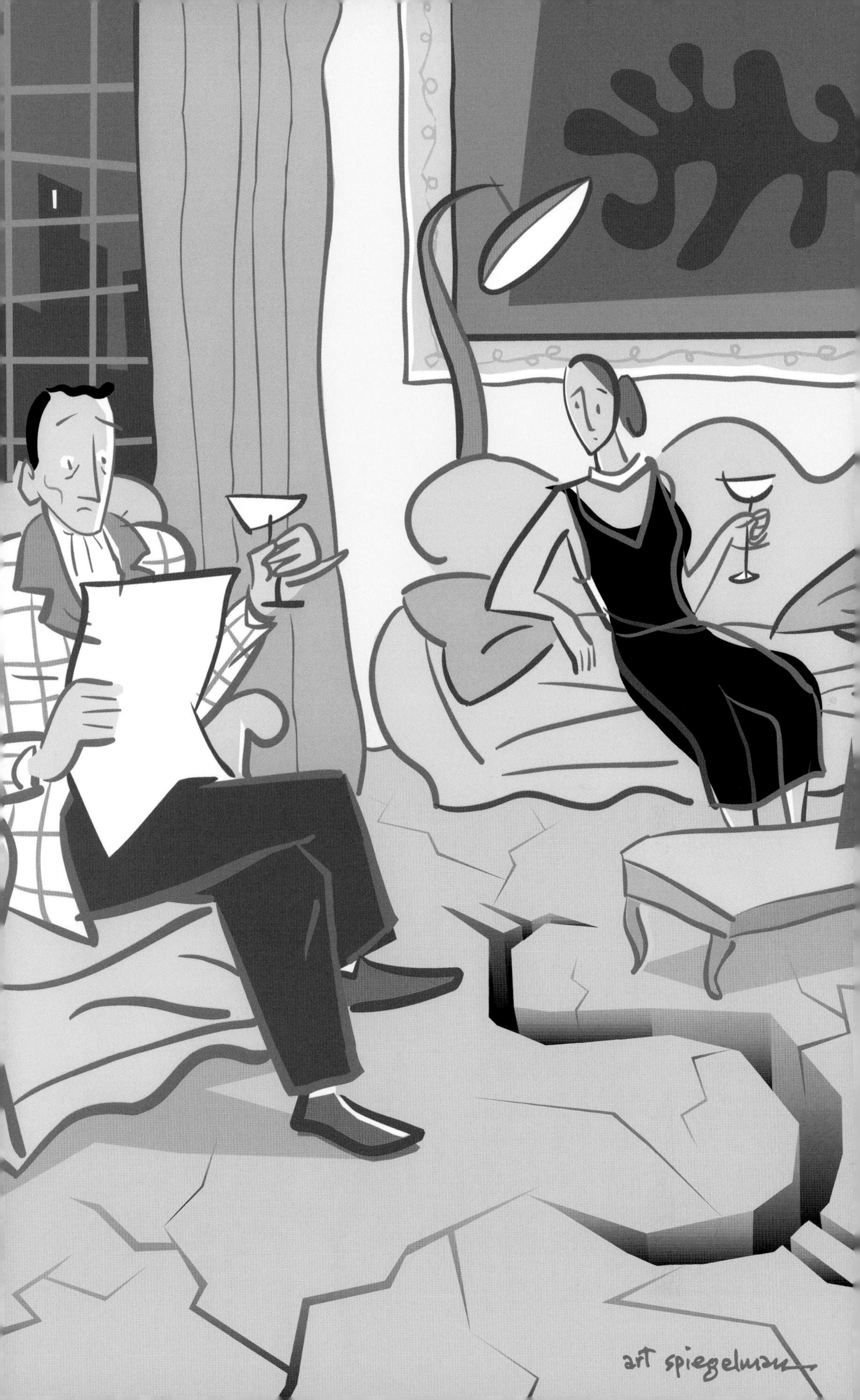
art spiegelman

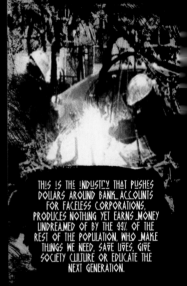

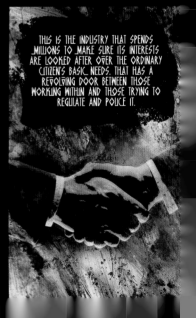

THESE ARE THE PEOPLE WHO CONTROL YOU.

10 1010101010
101110001101011 011010
001101010 01101011
1011 010101001

THESE ARE THE PEOPLE WHO USE COMPLEX ALGORITHMS TO SIMULATE HUMAN INTERACTION, GREED AND ASSUME THEY KNOW HOW YOU THINK.

THIS IS THE INDUSTRY THAT MANAGES AND MOVES FINANCES FOR GIGANTIC PENSION FUNDS, HEDGE FUNDS AND INVESTMENT FIRMS LARGER THAN MANY COUNTRY'S ECONOMIES, AT THE PRESS OF A BUTTON.

THESE ARE THE PEOPLE WHO WATCH THE NEWS AND SHIFT BILLIONS OF DOLLARS IN PANIC BECAUSE A SPARROW FARTED IN INDIA.

THESE ARE THE PEOPLE WHO SPECULATE IN "THE FUTURE," AND TRADE IN THE VERY PRICE OF THE HOUSE YOU THOUGHT YOU OWNED, WINNING IF YOU LOSE.

THIS IS THE INDUSTRY THAT PUSHES DOLLARS AROUND BANK ACCOUNTS FOR FACELESS CORPORATIONS, PRODUCES NOTHING YET EARNS MONEY UNDREAMED OF BY THE 99% OF THE REST OF THE POPULATION, WHO MAKE THINGS WE NEED, SAVE LIVES, GIVE SOCIETY CULTURE OR EDUCATE THE NEXT GENERATION.

THESE ARE THE TOP PEOPLE IN AN INDUSTRY THAT BUILDS NOTHING BUT DEBT AND RISK, LONG AGO EXCHANGING THE REAL WORLD NOTION OF CAPITAL WITH "FINANCIAL LEVERAGE" AND TREAT WORLD ECONOMIES LIKE CASINO CHIPS, THAT CALL THEIR OWN CUSTOMERS "MUPPETS."

THESE ARE THE PEOPLE WHO RUN BANKS THAT CAN'T MAKE A PROFIT WHEN GIVEN FREE MONEY WHILE CHARGING YOU INTEREST.

THIS IS THE INDUSTRY THAT SPENDS MILLIONS TO MAKE SURE ITS INTERESTS ARE LOOKED AFTER OVER THE ORDINARY CITIZEN'S BASIC NEEDS, THAT HAS A REVOLVING DOOR BETWEEN THOSE WORKING WITHIN AND THOSE TRYING TO REGULATE AND POLICE IT.

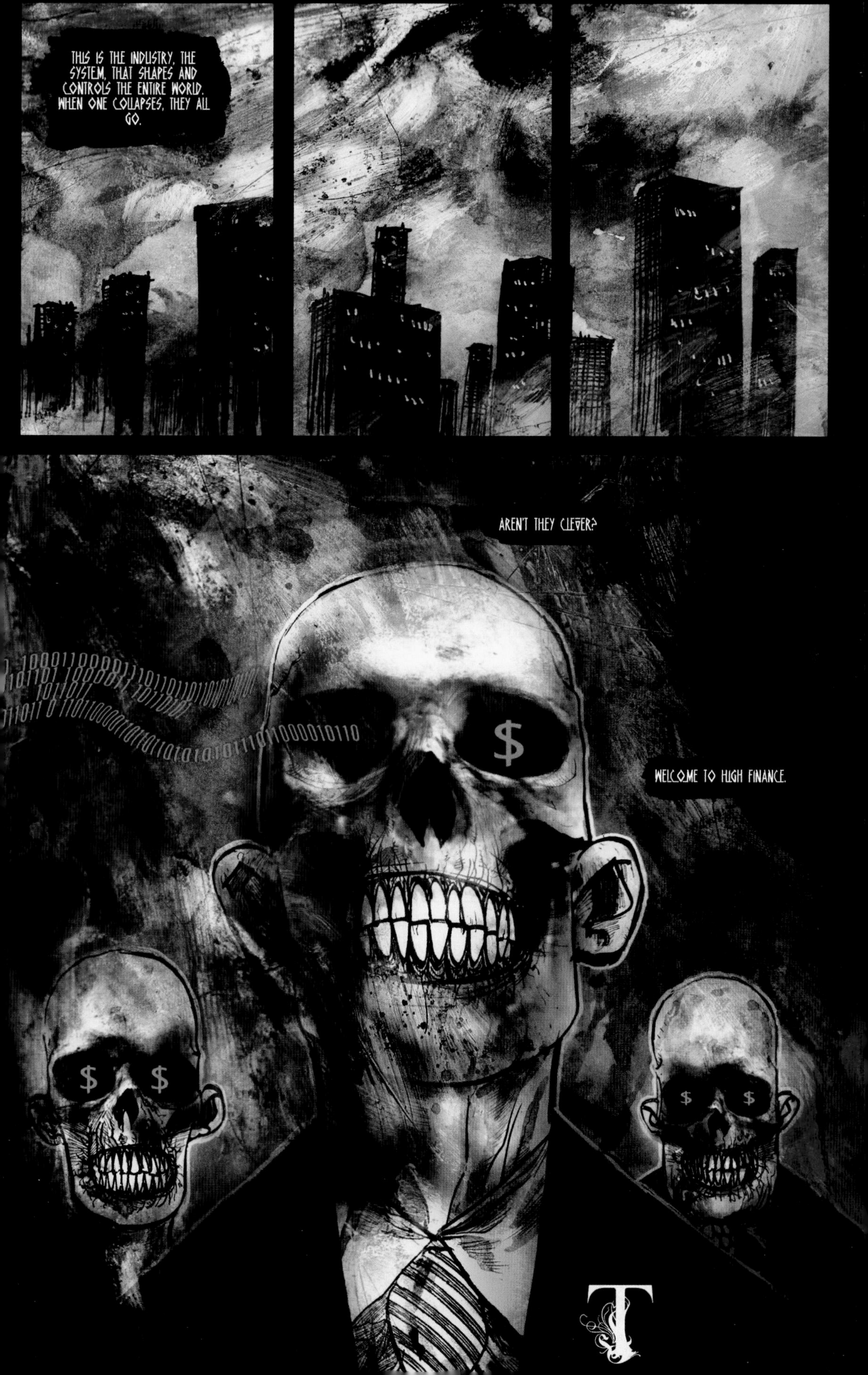
THIS IS THE INDUSTRY, THE SYSTEM, THAT SHAPES AND CONTROLS THE ENTIRE WORLD. WHEN ONE COLLAPSES, THEY ALL GO.
AREN'T THEY CLEVER?
WELCOME TO HIGH FINANCE.

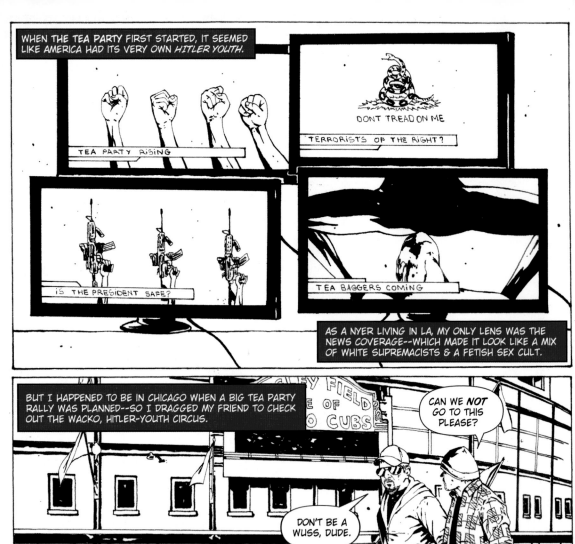

WHEN THE TEA PARTY FIRST STARTED, IT SEEMED LIKE AMERICA HAD ITS VERY OWN *HITLER YOUTH.*

TEA PARTY RISING

DONT TREAD ON ME

TERRORISTS OF THE RIGHT?

IS THE PRESIDENT SAFE?

TEA BAGGERS COMING

AS A NYER LIVING IN LA, MY ONLY LENS WAS THE NEWS COVERAGE--WHICH MADE IT LOOK LIKE A MIX OF WHITE SUPREMACISTS & A FETISH SEX CULT.

BUT I HAPPENED TO BE IN CHICAGO WHEN A BIG TEA PARTY RALLY WAS PLANNED--SO I DRAGGED MY FRIEND TO CHECK OUT THE WACKO, HITLER-YOUTH CIRCUS.

CAN WE *NOT* GO TO THIS PLEASE?

DON'T BE A WUSS, DUDE.

ON THE WAY THERE, WE STOPPED AT A FAIR TRADE, SHADE GROWN, ORGANIC COFFEE SHOP WHERE EACH BEAN IS GENTLY CARESSED BY A CARING BARISTA.

WHY ARE YOU JACKASSES GOING TO A TEA PARTY RALLY?! THEY'RE LIKE THE KLAN!

THAT'S WHAT I SAID! THE NEWS IS CALLING THEM CRAZY EXTREMISTS WHO WANT TO KILL OBAMA!

WELL, TO BE FAIR, THE NEWS CALLED *YOU* A *DOMESTIC TERRORIST* FOR PROTESTING A FUR FARM.

THAT WAS DIFFERENT.

YOU PROTESTED A FUR FARM?

WHEN WE GOT TO THE RALLY, IT WAS REALLY JUST A BUNCH OF RETIREES PISSED OFF ABOUT BANK BAILOUTS & UNNECESSARY WARS. THE HYSTERIA WAS A BIT OVERBLOWN.

End The Federal Reserve

NO MORE BAILOUTS

NO WARS WITH MY TAX

IT WAS POPULISM THAT THE NEWS FALSELY BRANDED AS DANGEROUS EXTREMISM. (LEGITIMATELY DANGEROUS EXTREMISTS *THE KOCH BROTHERS* WOULD LATER ADOPT THE NAME FOR THEIR HARD RIGHT BLOC.)

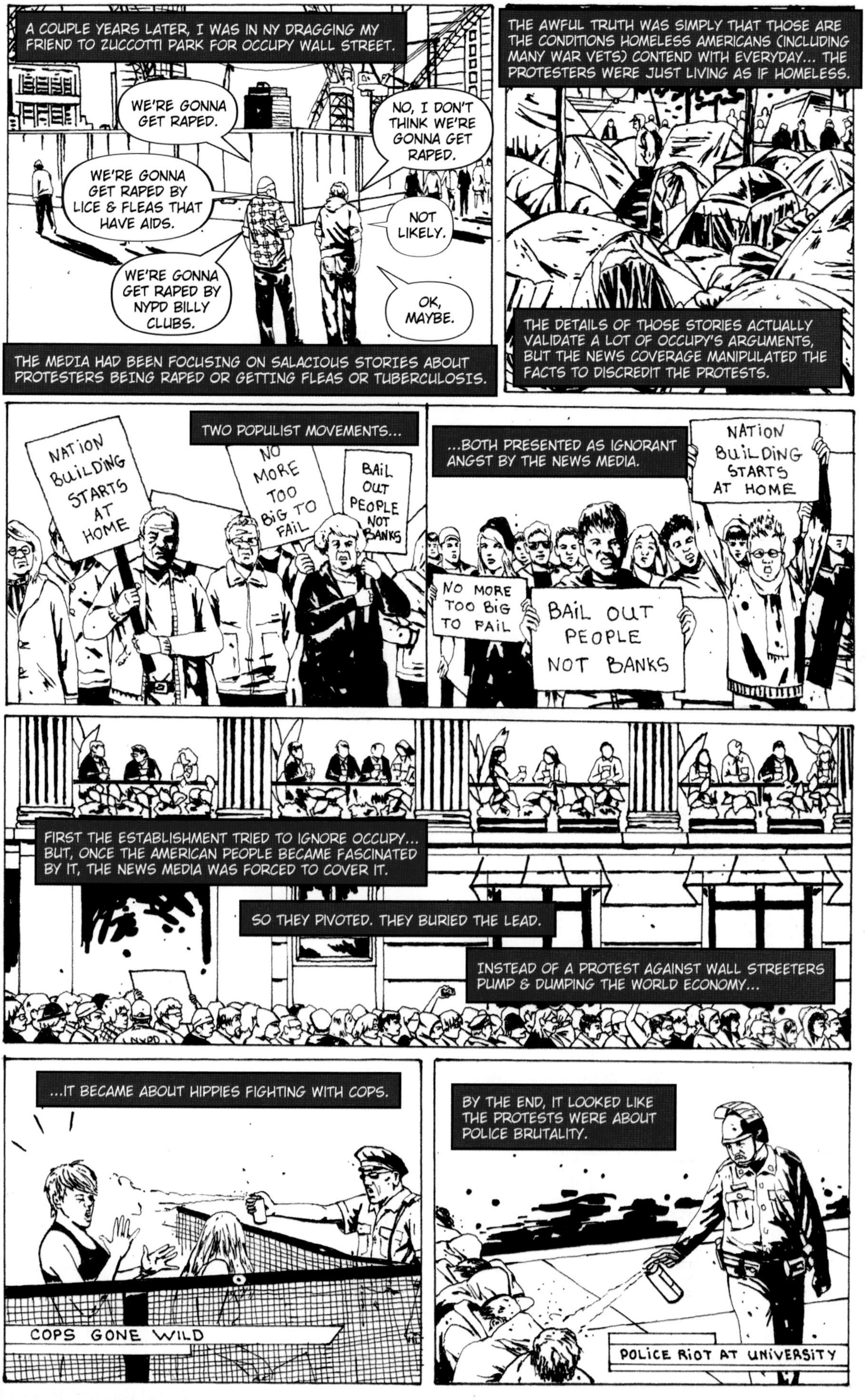

A COUPLE YEARS LATER, I WAS IN NY DRAGGING MY FRIEND TO ZUCCOTTI PARK FOR OCCUPY WALL STREET.
WE'RE GONNA GET RAPED.
NO, I DON'T THINK WE'RE GONNA GET RAPED.
WE'RE GONNA GET RAPED BY LICE & FLEAS THAT HAVE AIDS.
NOT LIKELY.
WE'RE GONNA GET RAPED BY NYPD BILLY CLUBS.
OK, MAYBE.
THE MEDIA HAD BEEN FOCUSING ON SALACIOUS STORIES ABOUT PROTESTERS BEING RAPED OR GETTING FLEAS OR TUBERCULOSIS.
THE AWFUL TRUTH WAS SIMPLY THAT THOSE ARE THE CONDITIONS HOMELESS AMERICANS (INCLUDING MANY WAR VETS) CONTEND WITH EVERYDAY... THE PROTESTERS WERE JUST LIVING AS IF HOMELESS.
THE DETAILS OF THOSE STORIES ACTUALLY VALIDATE A LOT OF OCCUPY'S ARGUMENTS, BUT THE NEWS COVERAGE MANIPULATED THE FACTS TO DISCREDIT THE PROTESTS.
TWO POPULIST MOVEMENTS...
NATION BUILDING STARTS AT HOME
NO MORE TOO BIG TO FAIL
BAIL OUT PEOPLE NOT BANKS
...BOTH PRESENTED AS IGNORANT ANGST BY THE NEWS MEDIA.
NATION BUILDING STARTS AT HOME
NO MORE TOO BIG TO FAIL
BAIL OUT PEOPLE NOT BANKS
FIRST THE ESTABLISHMENT TRIED TO IGNORE OCCUPY... BUT, ONCE THE AMERICAN PEOPLE BECAME FASCINATED BY IT, THE NEWS MEDIA WAS FORCED TO COVER IT.
SO THEY PIVOTED. THEY BURIED THE LEAD.
INSTEAD OF A PROTEST AGAINST WALL STREETERS PUMP & DUMPING THE WORLD ECONOMY...
NYPD
...IT BECAME ABOUT HIPPIES FIGHTING WITH COPS.
COPS GONE WILD
BY THE END, IT LOOKED LIKE THE PROTESTS WERE ABOUT POLICE BRUTALITY.
POLICE RIOT AT UNIVERSITY

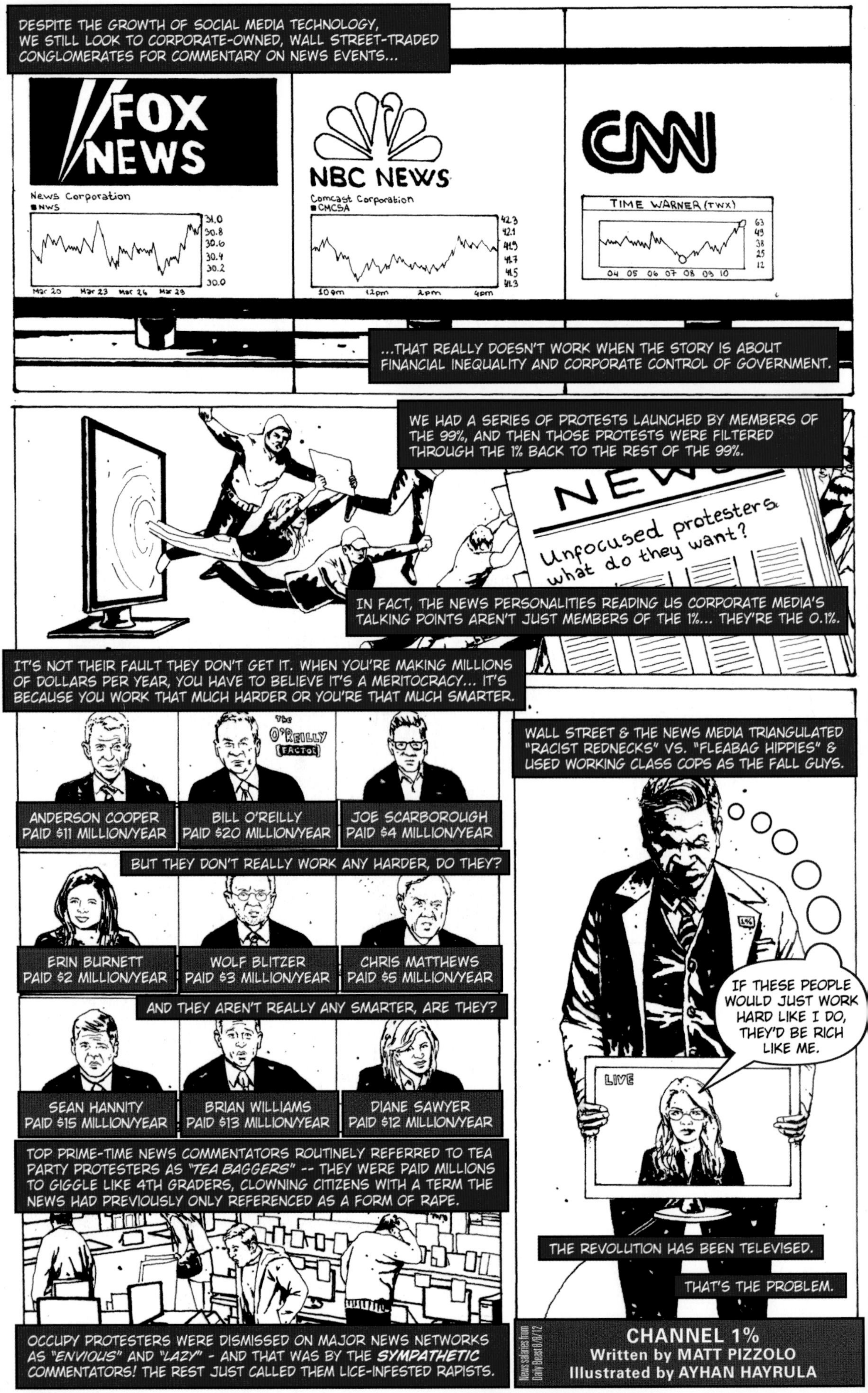
DESPITE THE GROWTH OF SOCIAL MEDIA TECHNOLOGY, WE STILL LOOK TO CORPORATE-OWNED, WALL STREET-TRADED CONGLOMERATES FOR COMMENTARY ON NEWS EVENTS...
FOX NEWS
News Corporation
NWS
31.0
30.8
30.6
30.4
30.2
30.0
Mar 20
Mar 23
Mar 26
Mar 29
NBC NEWS
Comcast Corporation
CMCSA
42.3
42.1
41.9
41.7
41.5
41.3
10am
12pm
2pm
4pm
CNN
TIME WARNER (TWX)
63
49
38
25
12
04
05
06
07
08
09
10
...THAT REALLY DOESN'T WORK WHEN THE STORY IS ABOUT FINANCIAL INEQUALITY AND CORPORATE CONTROL OF GOVERNMENT.
WE HAD A SERIES OF PROTESTS LAUNCHED BY MEMBERS OF THE 99%, AND THEN THOSE PROTESTS WERE FILTERED THROUGH THE 1% BACK TO THE REST OF THE 99%.
NEWS
Unfocused protesters what do they want?
IN FACT, THE NEWS PERSONALITIES READING US CORPORATE MEDIA'S TALKING POINTS AREN'T JUST MEMBERS OF THE 1%... THEY'RE THE 0.1%.
IT'S NOT THEIR FAULT THEY DON'T GET IT. WHEN YOU'RE MAKING MILLIONS OF DOLLARS PER YEAR, YOU HAVE TO BELIEVE IT'S A MERITOCRACY... IT'S BECAUSE YOU WORK THAT MUCH HARDER OR YOU'RE THAT MUCH SMARTER.
ANDERSON COOPER PAID $11 MILLION/YEAR
The O'REILLY FACTOR
BILL O'REILLY PAID $20 MILLION/YEAR
JOE SCARBOROUGH PAID $4 MILLION/YEAR
BUT THEY DON'T REALLY WORK ANY HARDER, DO THEY?
ERIN BURNETT PAID $2 MILLION/YEAR
WOLF BLITZER PAID $3 MILLION/YEAR
CHRIS MATTHEWS PAID $5 MILLION/YEAR
AND THEY AREN'T REALLY ANY SMARTER, ARE THEY?
SEAN HANNITY PAID $15 MILLION/YEAR
BRIAN WILLIAMS PAID $13 MILLION/YEAR
DIANE SAWYER PAID $12 MILLION/YEAR
TOP PRIME-TIME NEWS COMMENTATORS ROUTINELY REFERRED TO TEA PARTY PROTESTERS AS "TEA BAGGERS" -- THEY WERE PAID MILLIONS TO GIGGLE LIKE 4TH GRADERS, CLOWNING CITIZENS WITH A TERM THE NEWS HAD PREVIOUSLY ONLY REFERENCED AS A FORM OF RAPE.
OCCUPY PROTESTERS WERE DISMISSED ON MAJOR NEWS NETWORKS AS "ENVIOUS" AND "LAZY" - AND THAT WAS BY THE SYMPATHETIC COMMENTATORS! THE REST JUST CALLED THEM LICE-INFESTED RAPISTS.
WALL STREET & THE NEWS MEDIA TRIANGULATED "RACIST REDNECKS" VS. "FLEABAG HIPPIES" & USED WORKING CLASS COPS AS THE FALL GUYS.
1%
IF THESE PEOPLE WOULD JUST WORK HARD LIKE I DO, THEY'D BE RICH LIKE ME.
LIVE
THE REVOLUTION HAS BEEN TELEVISED.
THAT'S THE PROBLEM.
News salaries from Daily Beast 8/8/12
CHANNEL 1%
Written by MATT PIZZOLO
Illustrated by AYHAN HAYRULA

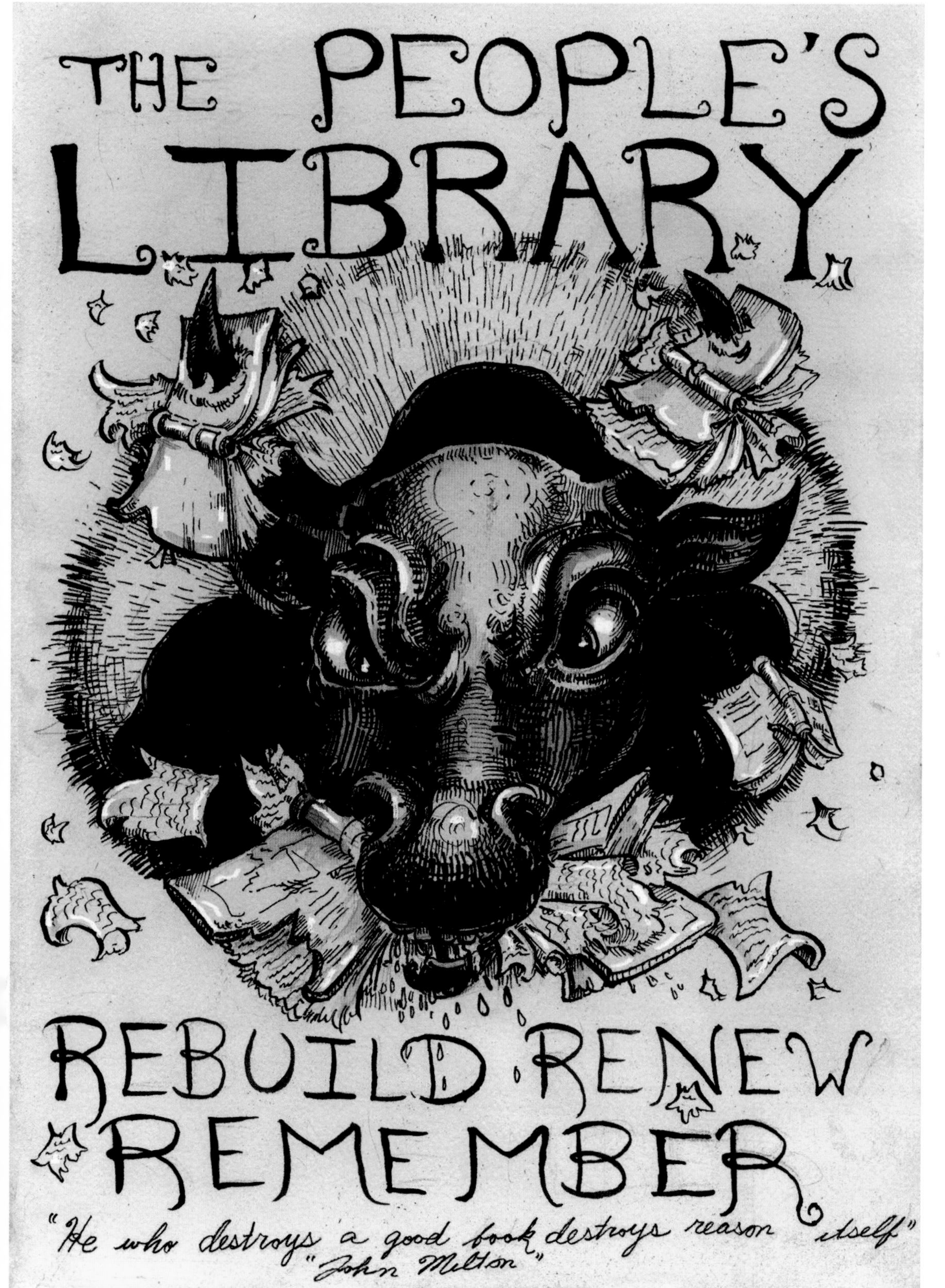
THE PEOPLE'S LIBRARY
REBUILD RENEW REMEMBER
"He who destroys a good book destroys reason itself"
"John Milton"

> POSTSCRIPT

Occupy isn't something that happened.

Occupy is part of what is happening.

"The TAZ [Temporary Autonomous Zone] is like an uprising
which does not engage directly with the State, a guerrilla
operation which liberates an area (of land, of time, of
imagination) and then dissolves itself to reform elsewhere/
elsewhen, *before* the State can crush it. Because the State is
concerned primarily with Simulation rather than substance,
the TAZ can 'occupy' these areas clandestinely and carry on
its festal purposes for quite a while in relative peace…
As soon as the TAZ is named (represented, mediated), it must
vanish, it *will* vanish, leaving behind it an empty husk,
only to spring up again somewhere else, once again invisible
because undefinable in terms of Spectacle. The TAZ is thus a
perfect tactic for an era in which the State is omnipresent
and all-powerful and yet simultaneously riddled with cracks
and vacancies."

> - Hakim Bey. T.A.Z.: The Temporary Autonomous Zone,
> Ontological Anarchy, Poetic Terrorism. 1985, 1991.

Before we completed the Kickstarter for Occupy Comics,
Zuccotti Park was cleared. We picked up the 'husk' it
left behind and drew pictures on it, wrote stories on it,
celebrated it.

When we finished the first issue in May 2012, I ended my
postscript with "What's next?" But I now realize Occupy isn't
a series of individual events, it's part of a march across
land, time, and imagination.

This is a time capsule, but it's not about nostalgia… it's
simply a step toward where we go next.

This book is a question, not an answer.

It is a direct question. To you.

Where next?

Onward,
Matt Pizzolo
February 2014